PLAYING AD LIB

PLAYING AD LIB

IMPROVISATORY MUSIC IN AUSTRALIA 1836–1970

JOHN WHITEOAK

Currency Press
Sydney

First published in 1999 by
Currency Press Limited
PO Box 2287
Strawberry Hills, NSW, 2012, Australia
website: www.currency.com.au
email: currency@magna.com.au

National Library of Australia - CIP Data

Whiteoak, John.
Playing ad lib : improvisatory music in Australia 1836-1970.

Bibliography.
Includes index.
ISBN 0 86819 543 X.

1. Music - Australia - History and criticism. 2. Improvisation (Music) - History and criticism. I. Title.

781.360994

Book design by Jürgen Lawrenz
Production by the Master Typographer

Cover design by David Johnston, Graphicflow
Cover illustrations: Graphic score: Robert Rooney, 'Second Landscape', courtesy of the artist. Ethopian Serenaders, 1846, from the *Illustrated London News*. State Library of Victoria.

Printed by Australian Print Group, Maryborough, Victoria.

Contents

vii Acknowledgements
ix Notes on Musical Examples

xi Introduction
1 Chapter 1: The Approved Genres before Jazz
27 Chapter 2: The Anonymous Genres
83 Chapter 3: Early Blackface Minstrelsy
111 Chapter 4: Ragtime and Ragging in Australia
168 Chapter 5: Jazzing
231 Chapter 6: Towards Experimentalism
265 Chapter 7: Beyond Jazz Improvisation

313 APPENDIX: Concert Programs:
The Society for the Private Performance of New Music

315 Notes
332 Select Bibliography
334 Discography
338 Index

Acknowledgements

This book is very substantially the result of the generous support of many people. This support came in many forms over a long period and the following acknowledgments fall far short of indicating its scale or the unstinting way it was given. Sadly, a number of those who contributed to the book have not lived to see it published.

Four individuals, each in their own way, strongly influenced the direction of the book. Keith Humble, and the context for musical exploration and learning he created at La Trobe University, opened the way to many of the perspectives presented here. Jeff Pressing revealed many facets of improvisatory music and, through the example of his own approach to research, taught me just how much commitment is needed to make any sort contribution to knowledge about music. Bruce Johnson's boundless exploration of ways to understand the social significance of the improvisatory process has been an ongoing inspiration, while ethnomusicolgist Aline Scott-Maxwell taught me to resist the conditioning that accumulates with Western musicological training. Each provided sustained practical support over a long period and ongoing belief in the value of the work being undertaken.

This book could never have been written without access to a very wide range of printed and recorded source material not available through library channels. Here I am especially indebted to Tony Baldwin, Val Banks, Simon Banks, Roger Beilby (Mostly Jazz), Helen Benny (Well Read Bookshop), Charlie Blott, Peter Burgis, Lyn Challen, Ernst Grossmann, Keith and Jill Humble, Herb Jennings, Russell Jones, Bruce Johnson, Mark St Leon, Chris Long, Barry McKimm, Peter Milley, Jack Mitchell, Robert Rooney, Ken Snell, Arthur Stirling and Mike Sutcliffe.

Many others besides those already mentioned provided access to invaluable documents, recordings, or information via interviews, correspondence or conversations. These include Shirley Andrews, Robyn Annear, Les Barnes, Graeme Bell, Andrew Bisset, Allan Blott, Ken Brentnall, Alan Brinkman, Brian Brown, Wesley Brown, Errol Buddle, June Carey, Viv Carter, Bruce Clarke, Syd Clayton, Bob Clemens, Bob (King of Bop) Crawford, George Dobson, George Dreyfus, Edwin Duff, Barry Duggan, Peter Ellis, Donald Erb, Denis Farrington, Jean-Charles François, Brian Fraser, Doug Gamley, Helen Gifford, George Golla, Tony Gould, Philip Hayward, Ian Hellings, Herb Jennings, Frank Johnson, Ray Jones, Mervyn King, John Leslie, Chris Lesser, Bobby Limb, Rainer Linz, Graham Lyall, Don McFarlane, Mickey Maher, Monty Maizels, Bill Miller, Graham Morgan, Valantyne Napier, Carmen Naylor, Wally Norman, Eddie Oxley, Geoff Orr, Tom Ovenden, Colin Pike, Joan Pollock, Graham Pont, Barry Quinn, Adrian Rawlins, Don (Splinter) Reeves, Don Reid, Ron Richards, Les Robertson, Esther Rofe, Ron Rosenberg, John Sangster, Gunther Schuller, Ron Shand, Mervyn Simpson, Stewart Speer, Orme Stewart, Bradley Thomas, Fred Thomas, Alan Turnbull, Yvonne Turner, Frank Walsh, Pat Ward, Felix Werder, Joe Washington, Lawrence Whiffin, Ken White, Bill Witnish, Arthur Withers, Bruce Worley, Harold Wray, and Barclay Wright (Mastertouch Piano Roll Company).

Amongst those who greatly contributed in other ways were Samantha Hanna, who conducted interviews and undertook extensive library searches, Kathy Whiteoak, who gave immeasurable support over a long period including library research and word processing, Ralph Whiteoak, who checked and redrafted all musical transcriptions, and Doug Scott-Maxwell who set the more complex examples. Rainer Linz, Jenny Nation, and Helen Neville all read and offered advice on early drafts, while Helen O'Shea did a masterly job in cutting the manuscript for submission to the publisher. I am also very appreciative of Harriet Parsons' patience, dedication and advice as editor, and of Richard Vella's and Katharine Brisbane's encouragement and faith in *Playing Ad Lib.*

I must also acknowledge the invaluable help received from the purchasing, Audio Visual Services, Reference, and Interlibrary Loans staff of the Borchardt Library, La Trobe University. These include John Horacek, Lea Beranek, Margo Heslop, and in particular Julie Marshall, who went to great pains to extract obscure but essential materials from overseas libraries. I am similarly grateful for the long term support of past and present staff of La Trobe University Department of Music, and especially administrative staff, Rosemary Bellair and Marilyn Richmond. I also received invaluable assistance from the National Film and Sound Archive, the manuscript section of the National Library, the Mitchell Library and the La Trobe Library collection of the State Library of Victoria.

Lastly, I would like to acknowledge the institutions and individuals who provided or gave permission for the use of graphic or photographic images and music scores reproduced in this book. Besides the institutions which are acknowledged elsewhere, I would especially like to thank Val Banks, Brian Brown, Rev. Dr Keith Cole, Terry Counihan, Ian Hellings, Jill Humble, Dr John Floyd, Barry Mc Kimm, Robert Rooney, Ken Snell, Arthur Stirling, Mike Sutcliffe, Bradley Thomas, and Pat Ward. Other items have been reproduced from my personal research collection, which includes the extensive Arthur Stirling Collection and several other discrete collections of archival books, periodicals, instructors, sheet music, photographs, scrapbooks, and programs relating to the history of music in Australia.

Transcriptions

The musical transcriptions from recordings presented in this book are intended to be self explanatory and the only non-orthodox symbol used is the upward or downward curved or shaped line, depicting a pitch glide, or significant fluctuation of pitch. It should be noted that only some of the transcriptions have a symbol (placed after the tempo marking) showing that straight quavers are to be read as a crotchet and a quaver played within the duration of two quavers. All other transcriptions are to read as notated. For the recorded source of each transcription see Discography.

Notes on Musical Examples

Many of the musical examples in this book have come from private collections, including the author's own collection but the following details may help the reader to locate them where copies are also held in public collections. Acknowledgements for musical examples reproduced from public collections are also given here.

CHAPTER 1: 1.1 Carl Czerny, *A Systematic Introduction to Improvisation on the Pianoforte* (Systematische Anleitung zum Fantasieren auf dem Pianoforte) Op. 200, trans. & ed. Alice Mitchell, New York: Longman, 1983, pp. 108-9; 1.2 3rd ed., London: Chappell Music, undated, p.24; 1.3 Some of the variations from this 'school' appear in the extremely rare *Bulch's Cornettist*, Melbourne: T.E. Bulch (before 1920); 1.4 Sydney: Kern & Mader (before 1862; courtesy of Mitchell Library, State Library of NSW); 1.5 Emily S. Patton, *Harmony Simplified for Popular Use: an Original Method of Applying the First Principles of Harmony to the Object of Accompanying the Voice on the Pianoforte*, Melbourne, Allan & Co., and Novello, London Ewer & Co, c.1877, p. 75; 1.6 Novello's Music Primers and Educational Series, no. 33, London: Novello, undated (1890s), p.56; 1.7 London: Oxford University Press, 1927, p.86; 1.8 Melbourne: H.A. Evans & Son, c. 1940 (courtesy of Dr. John Floyd); 1.9 2nd ed., c. 1930 (courtesy of Rev. Dr Keith Cole).

CHAPTER 2: 2.1 Play and music published Melbourne: Nicholson & Ascherberg (courtesy of Mitchell Library, State Library of NSW); 2.2 *Francis & Day's 2nd Two Step*

Album, USA: Francis, Day and Hunter, c.1903; 2.4 Cleveland: Sam Fox Publishing Co.; 2.5 Melbourne: E. Lyons.

CHAPTER 3: 3.1. Boston: Oliver Ditson, 1858, p. 29; 3.2 Chicago: Sol Bloom, 1897 (courtesy of the New York Public Library); 3.3 *Briggs Banjo Instructor*, New York, Oliver Ditson, 1855, facsimile edition, Virginia: Tuckahoe Music, 1992 (PO Box 146 Bremo Bluff, VA 23022, USA. Tel: 1 (804) 842 3573). 3.4 Boston: Oliver Ditson, 1858, facsimile edition of *Phil Rice's Correct Method*, Virginia: Tuckahoe Music, 1993 (see above for details); 3.5 Sydney: Albert & Son, p. 29.

CHAPTER 4: 4.2a & 4.2b New York: Winn's School of Popular Music, 1913, pp. 12, 18; 4.3a & 4.3b From the music album *Scott Joplin*, Melbourne: Allan's Music, undated, pp. 22, 8 respectively. The two lower staves are from 'Maple Leaf Rag'; 4.4 & 4.5 New York: Witmark & Sons, 1896; 4.6 Victor 17885, 1915; 4.7 Sydney: Joe Slater (courtesy of Mitchell Library, State Library of NSW). In *The Tivoli Album* no. 14 (1901) 'The Cake Walk Dance' reappears as 'McAdoo's Popular Cake Walk (Rag Time)'; 4.8a New York: George Spalding; 4.9 Geelong: Bulch & Co., c. 1903; 4.10 *Albert's American Annual*, no. 1, 1904, p.40; 4.11a *Tivoli Album* no. 23, 1904 (courtesy of Mitchell Library, State Library of NSW); 4.11b *Allan's First Coon Album*, 1904, p.5; 4.12a Sydney: *Albert's American Annual* no. 4 , 1907, p. 9; 4.12b *Allan's First Coon Album*, 1904, p. 13; 4.13 *Joe Slater's Tivoli Album* no. 19, 1902 (courtesy of Mitchell Library, State Library of NSW); 4.14c Sydney: Albert & Son, c.1912; 4.15 Sydney: W. Deane & Son, 1916; 4.16a Melbourne: J. Harris & Co.; 4.16b Melbourne: J. Harris & Co.; 4.17 Melbourne: Reginald Stoneham Music Publishing Co., c. 1921; 4.19 New York: Winn's School of Popular Music, 1923. 4.20a Sydney: Albert & Son; 4.20b This track is from a compilation of original ragtime recordings, *Ragtime Entertainment*, Folkways RF22; 4.23 Chicago: W.C. Polla. (Score from the Alhambra Cinema orchestra library.)

CHAPTER 5: 5.1 Melbourne: Allan & Co., c. 1920 (from Allietti's dance band library); 5.2a & 5.2b *Schirmer's Dance Music For Orchestra* series, New York: G. Schirmer (from the Alhambra Cinema orchestra library, Melbourne); 5.3a Rev. and trans. Gustav Saenger, New York: Carl Fischer, 1905, p. 190; 5.3b Arranged by Maurice Guttridge, 1922, composed by Jack Marley and Harry Grunden, Melbourne: Collins; 5.4 Melbourne: Allan & Co., undated (new arrangement: New York: Yellen & Hornstein, 1938); 5.5a Allan & Co., c. 1920; 5.5b S. Harris, c. 1919; 5.5c Reginald Stoneham, Melbourne: Loebel & Co., c. 1920; 5.7a 'Bees' Knees' is the first item on *The One Step Dance Roll Medley*, Mastertouch numerical listing no. 645, one of several rolls sent to me courtesy of Barclay Wright of Mastertouch. It is not dated, but it could not have been cut before 1922, the copyright date of the sheet music version of 'Bees' Knees', which became available in Australia between 1922 and 1923; 5.7b Melbourne: Allan & Co. (Original copyright: New York: Leo Feist, 1922); 5.8a *Melody*, March 1918, p.20. The composer is cited as 'the Great Howard'; 5.9 Sydney: Chappell & Co., c. 1921; 5.10a & 5.10b New York: Jack Mills, 1923, pp. 11, 26; 5.11 Melbourne: Collins; 5.15 Sydney, Albert & Son, undated (first published New York: Bibo, Bloeden & Lang, 1928), pp. 66-7.

CHAPTER 6: 6.2 & 6.3 courtesy of the Grainger Museum; 6.9 New York: Leo Feist, 1930.

Introduction

> . . . if there again should dawn an age in which the bulk of civilised men and women will come to . . . again possess sufficient mental leisure in their lives to enable them to devote themselves to artistic pleasures on so large a scale as do members of uncivilized communities. Then the spectacle of one composer producing music for thousands of musical drones (totally uncreative themselves, and hence comparatively out of touch with the whole phenomenon of artistic creation) will no longer seem normal or desirable, and then the present gulf between the mentality of composers and performers will be bridged.
>
> 'The Impress of Personality in Unwritten Music' Percy Aldridge Grainger, 1915[1]

The life and music of Percy Grainger provide the ideal metaphor for the subject of this book. PLAYING AD LIB is the expression of my fascination with what Grainger terms the 'unwritten music' of Australia's past. By this I mean the 'folk musics', popular musics and art musics that drew vitality and character from musical alteration, embellishment and creation in performance. It is also an exploration of musical freedom in Australian music-making as opposed to that which was the product of musical replication or fidelity to the score. As such, it hints at how improvisatory musics functioned as a complex field of negotiation for what became socially and artistically permissible in Australian music between 1836 and 1970. The breadth of Grainger's interests also parallels the range of musical types discussed in this book. He was intrigued by improvisation within extremely narrow stylistic boundaries (such as he observed in folk musics), yet he was among the earliest pioneers of experimental improvisatory music and spent much of his life in search of what he called his 'free music', that is, music free of conventional boundaries.

In this book, the term 'improvisatory' embraces a wide range of practices: from the significant liberties taken in performance (even in the interpretation of a conventional score) through to the most spontaneous or indeterminate forms of music-making imaginable, such as the spontaneous musical interpretation of an abstract painting. This liberal definition of the term improvisatory is justified by the very incapacity of conventional notation to predetermine much beyond the fixed pitches of the stave and the approximate dynamics and rhythmic placement of sounds. A score cannot direct how these sounds will interact within a performance venue soundscape, or how they are perceived. Yet these factors can contribute greatly to the meanings encoded in improvisatory musical performance.

The American ethnomusicologist Charles Keil has drawn attention to the expressive power of the microstructural elements of performance with his important and much debated theory of participatory discrepancies. Participatory discrepancies are not the musical composition or its basic syntax but the surface transformation, embellishment or rearrangement that is, to use Grainger's term, 'the impress' of the musical personalities who alone or collectively participate in the music-making process. Keil further suggests that 'musical syntax may just be the macroprocess and macrotexture or, when written down, a petrified skeleton on which to hang the flesh and blood of actual music-making'.[2]

It has long been argued that a continuum of practice exists between composing and improvising. In his 1974 article, 'Thoughts on Improvisation: A Comparative Approach', another major American figure in ethnomusicology, Bruno Nettl, asks whether it would be better to speak of 'rapid and slow composition rather than of composition juxtaposed to improvisation'.[3] Once the definition of composing is extended beyond the fully notated work (which applies to most contemporary popular music) there is no doubt whatsoever that such a continuum exists.

Keil's notion of participatory discrepancies therefore cannot embrace the breadth of discussion presented in PLAYING AD LIB, which covers a very wide variety of genres and musical practices within genres, including improvisatory process as composing. Even the action of freezing musical spontaneity into notation (as in the writing of fantasias, ragtime or jazz), or the creation of graphic notation or other forms of instructions for improvising musicians, is considered an important aspect of improvisatory music-making in the Australian context.

From such an inclusive approach, a map of improvisatory music-making in Australia becomes an extremely dense and complex patterning of musical action unfolding over more than two hundred years of white colonisation and extending back very much further into the 'silence' of pre-colonial Aboriginal cultural history. However, as the first attempt to view Australian cultural history in this way, PLAYING AD LIB is necessarily much more limited in scope, with most emphasis placed upon the role of African-American inflected musics, particularly Australian jazz.

A comprehensive study of improvisatory musics in Australia would have to examine the transplanted non Anglo-Celtic musical traditions; the music of indigenous Australians; gum leaf, mouth organ and Hawaiian steel guitar music; country music yodellers and so on. All manner of amateur, professional or traditional music-making in which some form of improvisatory flexibility was permitted or required would have to be examined. Appropriate taxonomy would also have to be developed to unravel this vast web of largely undocumented practice. It is hoped, however, that this book offers a method of inquiry which will contribute towards a broader, genuinely inclusive history.

While the spirit of Grainger and the spectre of his melancholy Grainger Museum strongly influenced the writing of this book, the town of his birth, Melbourne, was favoured as the main locus of the study for historical reasons. The beginnings of Melbourne conveniently correspond to a flowering of colonial musical life and the first relatively substantial reports of colonial music-making. The chronological scope, 1836 to 1970, represents a journey of musical exploration culminating in the 1960s, the decade that brought to Melbourne (and elsewhere) an orgiastic, but unsustainable, expansion of musical and social freedoms.

PLAYING AD LIB points to the special character of Melbourne's musical past but it also serves as a benchmark for improvisatory music in Australia. It is constructed within the constraints inevitably associated with writing about musical sounds, actions and thoughts that, being for the most part unrecorded, existed only for the moment of their production. Yet the transitory nature of improvisatory performance is all the more reason to recognise that any study of Australian music that focuses only upon the composer or the score and fails to consider music as process, as cultural, social and political action, as a vehicle for artistic expression or exploration, tells only a small part of the story.

Decontextualisation

Many of the activities discussed in PLAYING AD LIB represent examples of transplanted musical culture. White Australian musical development has taken place largely in isolation from direct interaction with the mainstream of European, American and African-American creative thought and activity. Consider, for example, the difficulties faced by early Australian jazz musicians attempting to learn what is basically an aural tradition of improvisation in total isolation from live contact with African-American musical culture. Even the increasing availability of imported sound recordings in the 1930s could not provide an adequate substitute; instead, Australian musicians were confronted with bewilderingly out-of-sync waves of decontextualised musical influence.

Individuals in a decontextualised environment are only partly informed. All performance is an act of communication that is transmitted on many different levels and received through several sensory channels. The consequences for isolated musicians attempting to adopt a performance culture by observing visiting performers or studying notations, recordings or instruction manuals were the loss of certain vital information and the mutation of what remained. This mutation could take the form of blurring, grey-out (watering-down) and especially simplification of distinctive performance characteristics.

A significant outcome of decontextualisation is what I have termed 'imitation-ecstatic' performance practice. This is a mode of performance which seeks to present an imitation or representation of qualities that are associated with authentically ecstatic performance, such as immediacy, excitation and spontaneity. The term imitation-ecstatic is used in particular to describe attempts by white performers to create representations of perceived qualities of African-American performance. It should be remembered however that artificial representation of the immediacy and excitement of 'natural', even abandoned, performance is a traditional aspect of theatrical stage craft, including musical stage acts.

Decontextualisation partly explains why Australians chose the approaches to improvisatory practice they did and why Australian jazz on record often sounds markedly different to African-American and even white American jazz. It would be a mistake, however, to assume that Australians always failed to grasp certain principles. In the early jazz era, for instance, the discrepancy between Australian and African-American improvisatory practice was often a case of Australian reference to alternative rather than incorrect models.

Tyranny of distance – especially before Australian urbanisation – has led Australians in all fields of endeavour to work intuitively (explore, experiment, synthesise, improvise) towards solutions to problems. More importantly, isolation from reliable models sometimes provided conditions which allowed a musician to synthesise according to his or her own rules. Examples of uniquely innovative musical experimentation are rare, but local musicians working without suitable models or with decontextualised models (such as recordings) have sometimes produced strange and interesting experimental syntheses based on whatever models were on hand. Various examples of this phenomenon are discussed.

Experimentalism

The notion of 'improvisatory experimentalism' is by far the most difficult and elusive concept presented in PLAYING AD LIB, particularly given the level of disagreement surrounding the term experimental music. For the purposes of PLAYING AD LIB, however, the term experimental is presented as synonymous with exploratory, except where it refers to some aspect of the so-called experimental music movement. An experimental or exploratory approach to music-making is therefore one that involves the process of trying things beyond the familiar. It is important to note that this approach to music-making is generally (but imprecisely) attributed to the more progressive or avant-garde of particular social groupings. The notion of 'progressive tendencies' in improvisatory music becomes the central narrative of the final chapters.

Many of the progressive figures discussed in the final chapters were engaged in what can be described as 'problem-finding' experimentation: musical exploration as a highly valued process in itself. This type of experimentalism is often associated with a particular type of modernist ethos referred to just after the 1960s in Malcolm Bradbury's convenient, if outdated, definition of modernism in art:

> [modernism in art is] experimental, formally complex, elliptical, contains elements of decreation as well as creation, and tends to associate notions of the artist's freedom from realism, materialism, traditional genre, and form, with notions of apocalypse and disaster. Its social context is characteristically avant-garde or bohemian; hence specialised. Its notion of the artist is of a futurist, not the conserver of culture but its onward creator; its notion of the audience is that it is foolish if potentially redeemable.[4]

It must be stressed, however, that exploratory/experimental approaches to improvisatory music have never been the exclusive domain of a self-aware, musical avant-garde. Australian musicians working in the commercial sphere have always engaged in forms of 'problem-solving' experimentation. This has often been the function of having to improvise musical products for particular applications, such as the need for a novelty sound effect, texture or mood.

While these musicians may not have engaged with modernism in the way described by Bradbury, they were engaged with modernity as a specific attitude toward the present or the 'now'. For example, much of the performance of popular music discussed in PLAYING AD LIB was associated with the requirement that it be 'modern-sounding', up-to-date or in vogue. Before the 1960s Australians who performed or identified with this music were often labelled modernists or progressives. Furthermore, it was (and still is) incumbent upon leading commercial musicians to stay ahead of their particular field in knowledge, practice and even creativity: to engage in 'modern practice' and be a type of avant-garde, whether they care for this notion or not. Yet beyond these truisms the period under discussion did see many Australians consciously concern themselves with seeking the new and engaging with the now with an intensity that would seem strangely outmoded today.

Approved and Anonymous Genres

Early colonial reviews of public performances usually refer to improvisatory music-making in a matter-of-fact way, but such references are less common in the late nineteenth-century. This was in line with a general shift of attitude in Western art music away from the whole notion of improvisatory music. Nevertheless one, albeit nebulous, grouping of musical activities continued to play an important role in carrying elements of improvisatory music-making up to and in some cases beyond the beginnings of an Australian tradition of improvised jazz.

It is useful, therefore, to imagine pre-jazz music-making as represented by two increasingly divergent streams: one in which improvisatory music-making was diminishing and the other in which it continued to evolve. I have defined these two streams according to the socio-cultural status of the activities they embrace and have labelled them respectively Approved and Anonymous. These categories help to illustrate how improvisatory music-making in Australia has been shaped by the social contexts of specific performance environments and also by broader social factors.

The Approved category of music-making embraces activities such as professional concert-hall and salon recitals, opera, organised amateur musical activities such as choirs and brass bands, and the systematised teaching or learning of performance practice. In other words, this category embraces those types of musical activity which provided participants with some form of social or cultural dividend – what sociologist Pierre Bourdieu terms 'cultural capital'. Approved musical activities are also those which were considered to reinforce social cohesion. Together, they represent one aspect of what was described in the nineteenth century as 'rational recreation'. Calls for rational recreation are frequently found in the colonial literature. In many cases these are simply pleas to support activities which stood in contrast to drinking, gambling, fighting and other socially erosive activities. In describing the period 1850-1880 in Britain, Richard Middleton states:

> The striking feature is the extent of congruence across a range of different musical practices, resulting in a not exactly homogeneous musical field but one clearly dominated by bourgeois synthesis.[5]

The drive for rational recreation was also a prominent characteristic of Melbourne and provincial musical life over the same period and, similarly, fostered systematisation, congruency and rigid orthodoxy – an ethos that was oppositional to improvisatory freedom.

By contrast, Anonymous musical activities were associated with less socially approved, or more 'irrational', forms of entertainment such as street or hotel entertainment, circus, variety or blackface minstrel shows, silent cinema, public dancing and so forth. Much of this music-making falls into the category of utilitarian accompaniment practice, which further underlines its lower socio-cultural status. The term Anonymous reflects the fact that these musical activities were largely ignored by the musical literature of the period and even in reviews of the entertainments with which they were associated. All the Anonymous activities fall into one or another category of what is described today as popular entertainment. Most of them constitute either theatrical entertainments music, which includes musical accompaniment and musical acts, or musical accompaniment for dancing. In addition, they are all associated with playing for money.

It is important to note that there is not a correspondingly rigid division among the musicians who performed these various genres. Even up until the 1920s, professional orchestral musicians in Melbourne commonly moved between the two 'categories' as their musical status or employment opportunities fluctuated. It is also obvious that not all Anonymous genre performers were literally anonymous and the fame of early Australian circus bandmaster Henry Von Der Mehden serves to illustrate this. However, even the numerous and detailed reviews of Fitzgerald's circus reveal very little indeed about the music-making of Von Der Mehden and his band.

However, it is significant that each of the Anonymous genres represented a specific type of performance situation and environment with its own musical conventions and requirements. These special conventions and requirements were informed by fickle and fluctuating lowbrow taste, whereas the Approved genres were, for the most part, tied to orthodox musical convention, conservatism and tradition.

The two streams of musical activity are interconnected through the improvisatory techniques of the Approved stream, such as embellishment and variation technique, which had practical application in the Anonymous genres. In other words, the European conservatorium tradition that underpinned the Approved genres provided a pool of technical knowledge, literature and notated musical models that could be drawn upon by improvising musicians working in the Anonymous genres (which, by the 1920s, included Australian jazz).

The pre-jazz Anonymous genres included improvisatory musics played in a manner which related to the later jazz performance tradition in Australia. Some were performed in relatively informal contexts of the type most conducive to playful musical interaction, embellishment and extroversion. They also often included unorthodox performance practices, whereas the Approved genres were associated with orthodox, standardised, systematised and congruous musical practice. The general level of indeterminacy associated with less formal types of public entertainment (e.g. circus ring action) often translated into heightened improvisatory skills among the musicians and a style of accompaniment with jazz performance-like elasticity. Open-ended musical forms that allowed for the spontaneous interpolation or removal of segments were often used. Furthermore, in contexts in which the same pieces were constantly repeated, musical detail could be added layer by layer through a combination of intuitive group interaction and leader direction – a process suggestive of the 'head arrangement' of jazz.

The performance environments of the Anonymous genres also fostered a non-linear approach to exploring individual musical abilities, in contrast to the strict linearity of conservatorium-tradition learning. The requirements and contingencies of Anonymous genre performance situations often called for personal inventiveness. These situations could demand a sound or a technique that may have already been invented by countless others in similar situations. In other words, the Anonymous genres fostered what could be described as problem-solving experimentation. The requirements, the contingencies and the relatively informal and indeterminate nature of music-making in the Anonymous genres also provided conditions for the preservation of an aural tradition: Anonymous genre musicians often had to be able to 'fake' (play without a score).

There were other similarities between the performance environments of pre-jazz Anonymous musical genres and jazz. The sound environment resulting from the ebb and flow of interaction between jazz performers and their audience or dancing public (coupled with other indeterminate sounds associated with jazz venues) is an accepted component of how live jazz should sound. In theatrical entertainment music, the ebb and flow of sonic interaction between musical accompaniment and spectator is largely channelled through the stage, ring or screen action. Nevertheless, this interaction provides a sense of immediacy and excitement similar to jazz performance. In circus music, in particular, the dramatic juxtaposition of music, silence and background noise is one of the ingredients that gives it its unique and exciting sound.

Anonymous genre performance contexts also required showy, sharply defined music, characterised by a certain sense of abandonment, hustle and exaggeration – a type of music that could cut through underlying noise and demand attention. In other words, legitimate musicians working in the Anonymous genres had to be able spontaneously to modify their normal mode of tone production and articulation to get the appropriate showy or 'circusy' sound. Colonial (and later) Australians noted certain qualities of boastfulness, exaggeration and propulsive energy in Americans themselves and the popular culture they brought to Australia. When translated into musical performance or composition (e.g. American show music) these qualities already featured something of what Australians later found appealing about white ragtime and, later still, white jazz.

Accompaniment to theatrical entertainment genres such as variety, burlesque and pantomime provided musicians with considerable latitude to transgress legitimate practice in a creative way. Through ragtime and jazz, however, such musical iconoclasm became a normal and widely distributed element of popular music. It thus created a broader base for the acceptance of a spontaneous or seemingly spontaneous, exploration of extended musical possibilities.

Improvisatory Music as Gesture

While improvisation is influenced by social context, it is also social gesture. Like any form of behaviour, the meanings encoded in improvisatory behaviour differ according to time, place and social context. For example, the trombone 'turkey gobble' (a novelty effect created with a hand-held mute) spontaneously performed at a 1920s Northcote Town Hall orchestral or brass band concert would undoubtedly have been interpreted as a gesture of rebellion against the prevailing order and taste. Yet the same effect would have evoked approving chuckles from the same social group had the occasion been the Town Hall dance. Introduced into early 1960s modern jazz performance at the same venue, the turkey gobble would have been considered insultingly outmoded, whereas a late 1960s 'new music' audience might have applauded it as a gesture of radical experimentalism and political, social and cultural freedom.

It is apparent, therefore, that whereas colonial improvisatory practice increasingly signified deviance, irreverence and iconoclasm in 'serious' music-making, in other musics it was often applauded as clever, humorous or quaintly grotesque. Yet even in the Anonymous genres this tolerance was not diachronically or synchronically consistent: what was tolerated in early melodrama music or blackface minstrel music was later considered less tolerable. The level of musical clowning associated with early Australian variety-act jazz was not acceptable in palais jazz of the same period.

By the late 1930s, however, the improvisatory practices that had become associated with jazz began to signify something new. The local palais musician who could stand up and 'take a chorus' became a hero: someone to be admired and noisily applauded in almost the same way that improvising virtuosi like Miska Hauser had been feted in mid-nineteenth-century Melbourne. The improvised jazz solo now signified individuality and originality.

At the same time, collectively-improvised jazz style was beginning to signify both aesthetic and political radicalism and a recognition (and probably some misunderstanding) of the intensity of expression associated with authentic African-American jazz performance. By the late 1940s, association with the new style of jazz improvisation, bebop, briefly signified a level of aesthetic radicalism for young 'modernists' who assembled under the banner of the Modern Music Society. In art music, members of a small subculture of student musicians (and a few others such as Felix Werder) were signalling their impatience with the deeply ingrained conservatism of the Melbourne musical establishment through their personal explorations of relatively radical ways of organising sound. Only those associated with jazz, however, seem to have signalled this impatience through improvisatory music.

After the mid-1950s, rock 'n' roll music permanently superseded jazz improvisation as a musical signifier of social and musical radicalism in popular culture. Jazz improvisation briefly represented aesthetic radicalism in the late 1950s through the ecstatic 'hard bop' style and, later, the 'free' or experimental jazz of the early 1960s. In Melbourne jazz, however, the most radical gesture came from three musicians, Barry McKimm, Robert Rooney and Syd Clayton, who were in the process of making a complete transition from jazz to experimental art music.

For Keith Humble, an influential figure of the avant-garde in Melbourne in the late 1960s, the aesthetic and social radicalism signified through the improvisatory organisation of sound was sometimes more important than the musical product itself. That Melbourne was entering an age in which social change was 'as easy as growing your hair' and nowism and happenings were the order of the day undoubtedly contributed to a widespread misunderstanding of the serious intent behind his approach.

Coda

Although the last part of PLAYING AD LIB discusses improvisatory practice in the context of progressive or avant-garde tendencies, in jazz alone there are many valid positions that can be taken in relation to the notion of the avant-garde. The jazz saxophonist Barry Duggan claims that in the 1960s he and various colleagues collectively discovered 'the roots of something fundamental' about jazz improvisation which the famous bebop pioneer, Charlie Parker, had discovered many years earlier. He referred to a basic sincerity or intensity of approach to playing jazz, which he believed made the notion of the avant-garde irrelevant. He contended that those who chose to work in this 'mode' have continued to mature and develop as improvising musicians, whereas those who became trapped by the desire for instant improvisatory freedom in the 1960s soon tired of what they were doing and often just dropped out of jazz. [6]

The Melbourne artist, electronic music experimentalist and self-ascribed iconoclast, David Tolley, presents a contrasting view – one that, incidentally, corresponds exactly with the experience of McKimm, Rooney and Clayton:

> Well, leaving jazz and bass playing was being released from bondage, you know. The constraints of bass playing are so severe . . . they're so defined, so rigid. And so are the preconceptions about jazz improvisation in this country . . . [an] almost total reluctance to accept anything out on a limb.[7]

The repetition of patterning inherent in jazz style undoubtedly imposes the type of creative restriction to which Tolley refers. On the other hand, the ingenious recycling of deeply internalised patterning can be one of the most aesthetically satisfying aspects of listening to African-American influenced music.

All the idiosyncratic figures discussed in the last two chapters, 'Towards Experimentalism' (-1940) and 'Beyond Jazz Improvisation' (-1970) were, in their own way and to varying degrees, unwittingly involved in an historical process: the ongoing search for new ways to liberate sound from the shackles of traditional notation. By the end of the period discussed, however, a level of musical freedom approaching Grainger's late nineteenth century reveries of 'free music' had already been achieved, in a sense making the modernist ethic and whatever else had been driving this process appear redundant. For the first time in Melbourne's cultural history spontaneous experimentalism in an array of socio-cultural activities had clearly become an end in itself.

Yet it is ironic that many of the events leading up to this situation became insignificant in comparison to the influence of youth counterculture music, which by 1967 had given rise to experimental pop. This aspect of the new musical 'freedom' was something of an illusion. As this music was stylistically shackled to a persistent rhythmic ostinato and, more often than not, projected Western notions of love, it could not be free quite in the way that Grainger had envisaged. This type of freedom in Australian popular music had to await the advent of digital sound sampling technology.

By the end of the 1960s some jazz musicians were becoming aware that improvisatory practice in jazz was burdened with distinctive musical characteristics which could not be shed without the loss of the tradition itself. In art music circles it was becoming clear to some that improvisatory practice as 'art in sound' was ideally an open dialogue between structure and freedom – and that freedom often brought with it unwanted blemishes and incoherence. The 1960s also revealed something that may still prove to be the most significant aspect of improvisatory musical practice: its potential as musical Esperanto or, perhaps, pidgin, enabling expressive cross-generational, cross-gender, cross-cultural, cross-aesthetic, creative, harmless, educational and joyful human play.

1 The Approved Genres before Jazz

The period from white colonisation to the turn of the twentieth century in Australia spans almost the entire transition in Western art music, from the profound improvisatory freedoms of the baroque style to the minute interpretative licence permitted to early twentieth-century instrumentalists and vocalists. In 1835, the year John Pascoe Fawkner's party established itself on the banks of the Yarra, London concert halls still echoed periodically with wild applause for the improvised variations of the 'master' performers, such as J.B. Cramer. Colonial literature leaves no doubt that some aspects of this albeit declining tradition of improvisatory practice were imported into the colony, along with British melodrama and other familiar facets of cultural life. It refers to, for example, the activities of touring and resident improvising instrumentalists such as the violinists Vincent Wallace, Miska Hauser, Jenny Claus and Eduard Reményi and the pianists Edward Boulanger, Dom Rosendo Salvador, Arabella Goddard and Henri Ketten, not to mention improvising vocalists, church organists and other instrumentalists. An 1841 Melbourne concert program notes with striking casualness that 'Mr [Isaac] Nathan will preside at the pianoforte, and will in the course of the evening give extemporaneous performances on that instrument'.[1] Yet by the end of the century such activities were coming to represent a cultural aberration.

It is impossible to know what degree of spontaneity was involved in colonial performance, even where terms such as 'extemporise', 'improvise' or 'fantasia' are used in programs or reviews. Many of the performers were also composers and it was obviously safer to present 'extemporisations' which were partly, if not fully, prepared. Furthermore, the widening availability of published fantasias by Czerny, De Beriot and others only discouraged mediocre performers from demonstrating their own creativity in extempore public performance. Yet even this notion of performing fantasias, which were anything from partly prepared to fully notated and published, is a useful reminder of the continuum of practice between improvisation and composition. It also illustrates that something akin to 'imitation-ecstatic' improvisatory practice was an established element of nineteenth-century concert hall performance.

The establishment of early Melbourne was contemporaneous with the first significant period of Australian concert hall music development. The year 1836 also witnessed the arrival of the Wallace and Deane families and the French couple, Mme and Mons. Gautrot, in Sydney. In 1840 the Gautrots became seminal figures in the beginnings of Melbourne's concert performance tradition.

Improvisation on a Theme

Vincent Wallace, 'the Australian Paganini', only remained in Australia for two years, but throughout that period he was associated with concerts which included various forms of improvisatory performance. For example, at his second concert in Sydney:

> Mr Wallace was presented with various pieces of music, which he played extemporaneously [on the piano], introducing occasionally some brilliant variations, which excited much general astonishment. He ended that performance with 'Currency Lasses' (as composed by our talented towns lady, Mrs. John Paul Senior) adding to it some extemporaneous variations; many ladies and gentlemen were to be seen with scraps of music in their hands ready to present them, but being so well satisfied, no doubt did not wish to trouble him.[2]

Wallace may have been further encouraged to improvise by the colonial custom of noisily applauding each variation in a manner suggestive of present-day jazz performances. A later review notes, for example, that 'Wallace performed various evolutions on the violin, every occasional close of which was rewarded with rapturous applause'.[3]

While many accomplished artists besides Wallace played variations on the Australian concert platform without apparent preparation these were mostly, and as we shall see significantly, the simplest form of improvisation: a set of variations on a single theme.

The forms of improvisatory practice which were heard and took hold here were significantly determined by factors unique to the colonial context. For example, the level of cultural sophistication required for a proper appreciation of high art music was not present in the colony until after the 1850s gold-rush period. The predominant taste was for unambiguous, familiar, entertaining music and preferably that which also had bonds to the predominant cultural group, the British. Virtuosic solo improvisation was acceptable and even applauded, as long as it was woven around familiar musical landmarks; but the coarse informality of the early concert environment discouraged artists from presenting more sophisticated forms.

Colonial taste for simple variations is indicated, for example, in a comment recorded in the *Sydney Herald* of 1836, that 'The real beauties of [Wallace's music] . . . could only be relished by an accomplished taste; a simple air with extemporaneous variations would have a much greater impression on our audiences'.[4] From the time of the first concerts, colonial critics began to express suspicion of 'foreign' (alien sounding) or overly 'scientific' (complex) music. One such critic noted in the same year, for example, that:

> People affecting the reputation of 'cognoscenti' pretend most to admire sometimes what they least understand. We must acknowledge ourselves so far un-Italianised as to prefer English, Scotch, or Irish melody in songs.[5]

It is therefore not surprising that many of the references to improvising performers in colonial Australia mention variations based upon 'simple airs'. Miska Hauser often featured 'Rule Britannia' with 'Beethoven-style variations' or 'Irish folk songs with variations'.[6]

The Process of Creating Simple Variations

Colonial isolation from the culture of live performance in Europe was less of a handicap to learning about improvisation than might be imagined. Nineteenth-century treatises on improvisation suggest an approach in which students were expected to internalise written models of improvisation. Treatises on piano technique, such as Muzio Clementi's popular *Introduction to the Art of Playing on the Piano Forte* (1801), often contain both the basic building blocks for simple variations, such as broken chord patterns in every key, and actual models for variation technique. Carl Czerny writes in his *Fantasy Playing* (1836) that 'Mainly those themes are suitable for variations that have lovely melody, few modulations, two evenly proportioned sections, and a distinctive rhythmic profile'.[7]

As changes in style were slow in the nineteenth century by comparison with the twentieth, local musicians only had to internalise a relatively small range of familiar models to be able to create variations that were stylistically acceptable. They also had the opportunity to refine the improvisatory application of these models over several decades of a career. Compare this situation with that of the later Australian jazz musicians, who had to deal with continuous style change and attempt to internalise the ambiguous style elements of African-American music.

One of the most fundamental characteristics of pre-jazz variation technique is the 'filling-out' of the implied basic harmonic framework while retaining the melodic profile (see Musical Ex. 1.1). For a single-line instrument, the process of varying a theme (beyond a rudimentary paraphrase of the melodic line) therefore requires a knowledge or sense of harmony sufficient to determine the basic harmonic structure of the piece (unless this chordal information can be read directly from the score). This level of ability was common last century.

At a primary level of variation the implied harmonic framework and melodic profile are decorated by dividing the basic pulse with chordal, passing and neighbour tones (tones above and below the melody note) and repeated notes. This process, called division, was also a normal aspect of improvised accompaniment of the period. The basic framework can then be further decorated by various ornaments and effects, as discussed below. In *Violin Technique and Performance Practice in the Late Eighteenth and Early Nineteenth Centuries*, Robin Stowell also points out that even 'changes of articulation, phrasing and bowing should not be underestimated in the process of melodic variation'.[8]

Musical Ex. 1.1. Model and variations 1-3 showing simple variation technique. From Carl Czerny, *Fantasy Playing*, (1836).

Figure 1.1. 'A Concert on a New Rush or Gold Digging in Australia' from *Sketches of Australian Life and Scenery Complete in Twelve Plates* by S.T. Gill (La Trobe Rare Books Collection, La Trobe Library).

It therefore becomes credible that even modestly equipped colonial musicians could have emulated local masters such as Wallace by creating simple variations on an air without apparent preparation. On the evidence of nineteenth-century formal concert programs and reviews, this would have occurred mostly in the form of encores, such as those habitually presented by virtuosi in the sometimes extremely boisterous and informal contexts of colonial Australian performance. An 1850s Melbourne reviewer noted, for example, the 'whistling, cat calling, cooeeing, and other eccentric local ways of demanding an encore'.[9] A Sydney reviewer noted in 1863 that after the pianist Edward Boulanger was 'enthusiastically encored . . . some astounding original variations on "Semiramide" [were] substituted'.[10] The average colonial instrumentalist was more likely to publicly demonstrate his or her ability to extemporise variations in relatively informal performance environments, such as goldfields concerts, musical variety acts, dance venues, or parlour entertainment.

Pot-Pourri

> Mr Peck gives each evening a solo on the violin. On the occasion of our visit he performed, on the first and fourth string alone, a new piece, arranged by himself from various well-known airs.[11]

The subject of this description may be the 'pot-pourri', a common device for adding variety to a musical program. In this form, popular tunes of the day were woven together or else introduced into a more sophisticated musical context. For example, in his *Fantasia di Bravura* (dedicated to Paganini) Wallace introduced simple ballads such as 'Tis the Last Rose of Summer' into a demonstration of technical gymnastics representing Paganini's virtuosic style. One colonial critic noted that the 'ability of the execution of some of the most difficult passages, as also to the swiftness with which he introduces many extemporaneous introductions is beyond description'.[12] At later concerts in Melbourne, critics noted, for example, that 'a very brilliant pianoforte solo was performed by [Henry] Hemy, introducing favourite Italian airs', and that 'Mons. Herwyn's concluding fantasia on one string, introducing three national airs, was by no means the least deserving of praise'.[13]

The virtuoso violinist Miska Hauser was noted for his spectacular ability to spin out a program with the spontaneous juxtaposition or merging of popular tunes with his own compositions. He even inadvertently describes this process in a letter describing his experiences in Australia:

> I forget exactly which bloody affray it was that had occurred between America[n] and English gold-diggers, but as I was playing the last bit of my 'Little Bird', the devil, either in my preoccupation or because of a long habit, plagued me into working in *Yankee Doodle*. This hated ditty aroused John Bull in a flash and stirred him up . . . and so [I] bent my bow against the Yankees and substituted a well-known satirical tune. God knows what fortunate chance brought this tune back to my memory.[14]

Carl Czerny's treatise, *Fantasy Playing,* also offers insight into the nature of pot-pourri. The following excerpt could easily describe the usual situation of the mid-1800s colonial artist:

> in dealing with a largely heterogeneous public, surely the majority by far will be entertained only by pleasant, familiar tunes and will be sustained in spirit by piquant and glittering performances. Under these circumstances, the true potpourri, namely an ingenious and interesting combination of such themes that are already favourites of the public, is indeed in place.[15]

Given the absence of informed musical criticism and the extremely informal context of many early colonial concerts, I suspect that bored or indifferent colonial performers were often able to get away with casting almost anything that came to mind into the fantasia or pot-pourri form. This hypothesis is supported by the disdain expressed, many times, in Hauser's letters:

> Whenever I started off on some other piece [other than his standard specialities], noisy shouts of disapproval arose and often turned to hisses. And that was at Ballarat . . . I make no secret of the fact that public performance in these countries has become an indifferent profanation devoid of charm.[16]

The Instrumental Prelude

The 'short prelude' or 'flourish', as it was sometimes called, was more common to colonial Australia than the longer and more elaborate 'fantasy prelude'. Czerny describes this as:

> quite short, as though through only a few chords, runs, passagework and transitional materials, one were trying out the instrument, warming up the fingers, or arousing the attention of the listeners. These must conclude with the complete chord of the principal key of the work to be performed.[17]

The short prelude was also an improvisatory introduction to a composition and many early nineteenth-century piano tutors provide simple prelude models in each key to be played as a preliminary to the exercises themselves. Nineteenth-century pianists were therefore always able to fall back on these memorised prelude models when required to improvise an introduction (see Musical Ex. 1.2).

Further insight into preludes is provided by Emily Patton's *Harmony Simplified for Popular Use: An Original Method of Applying the First Principles of Harmony to the Object of Accompanying the Voice on the Pianoforte* (Melbourne, 1880), possibly the first colonial publication to deal specifically with improvisation. Patton writes:

> A Symphony may always be made from the first four or eight bars of the air, by putting a similar beat of bass to it as would be suitable for the accompaniment, the beat of the Symphony Bass being always supposed to *suggest* the form of accompaniment that is to follow. If no Symphony be played, a short Prelude sounds richer and freer than mere chords to introduce a song, or to insert between the verses to give the singer a short rest.[18]

It is interesting that a clear distinction is made between the terms 'symphony' and 'prelude'. Symphony seems, in this context, to refer to an introduction constructed from the melodic material of the work, while prelude refers to a formulaic introduction 'from which transpositions can be made into all the other major or minor keys, as occasion

Musical Ex. 1.2. Prelude from J.B. Cramer, *Instructions for the Piano-Forte.*

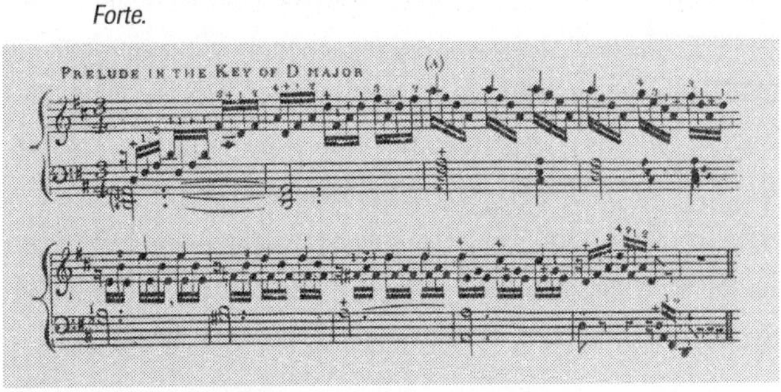

PRELUDE IN THE KEY OF D MAJOR

requires . . . [T]he same Arpeggio runs can be adapted to any other beat of time'.[19]

The short prelude survived in Australia into the twentieth century principally because of the importance of its function in improvisatory keyboard accompaniment for popular music. Even by the time of Patton's treatise this practice had probably more or less vanished from the concert platform, just as responsibility for musical detail had transferred from the performer to the composer in a more general sense. Yet, as late as 1914, a short article appeared in the *Musical Australian* denouncing local accompanists who persisted in improvising a 'postlude' after the final cadence of vocal items.[20]

Ornamentation

Robert Donington comments in *The Interpretation of Early Music* that:

> Free ornamentation began to lose its status as a primary element of interpretation during the second half of the eighteenth century. Its decline was one symptom of a profoundly changing attitude, of which another symptom was the decline of the more or less improvised accompaniment on a figured bass.[21]

The Melbourne author of an article entitled 'The Use of Musical Signs' claimed in 1889 that 'Signs as distinct from notes indicating the method of musical performance, were until within the last 30 years in general use'.[22] This would suggest that before 1860 local musicians were expected to spontaneously interpolate musical segments (e.g. a particular ornament) selected from a memorised 'library' of patterns just on the basis of symbols, not notation. It therefore follows that observations made before 1860, such as 'after a racking andante he broke into a chaotic jumble of spurious trills and cadenzas' often do refer to improvisatory ornamentation.[23] Furthermore, it means that local musicians who learnt their craft before the 1860s carried their library of ornaments, and the ability to apply them spontaneously, well into the latter part of the century.

The practice of improvising instrumental cadenzas over a dominant at the break between sections or before a final coda also continued well into the nineteenth century, although principally among notable European composer-performers such as Liszt and Chopin. Composers continued to indicate whether an improvised cadenza was optional or obligatory at these strategic points and some treatises, such as Czerny's Op. 200, still provided instructions and models for them. An example of a 'cadenza ad libitum' indicated only by the foregoing instruction and a pause sign can be found in Miska Hauser's 'Second Impromptu', published in *The Australian Album*, Sydney, 1857.

Where an optional or obligatory cadenza is written into a score the performer can choose either to play what is written, score in modifications (simplifying or elaborating, according to ability), pre-compose an alternative cadenza, substitute a cadenza memorised from another source, spontaneously modify (for example, by simplifying) a written cadenza, or improvise an entirely new one according to well-established conventions.

There were many accomplished colonial instrumentalists, particularly composer-performers, with the ability to elaborate cadential points. A Melbourne review from 1889 mentions that Mat Klein performed 'an elaborate cadenza displaying his accustomed artistic style' but there is no certainty that this was in fact improvised embellishment.[24] There is no doubt, however, that by this time musicians were increasingly reluctant to improvise cadenzas in formal contexts. The closing sentence of a humorous paraphrase by Berlioz of Hamlet's soliloquy, 'To be or not to be', published that year in the same Melbourne music periodical sums up the attitude that had begun to prevail:

> A masterpiece is entrusted to you, you pervert it, mutilate it, change its character, dress it out with wretched ornaments, make insolent cuts in it, introduce grotesque passages, laughable arpeggios, facetious trills; you insult the master, people of taste, art, and common sense.[25]

It should be observed, however, that where Emily Patton mentions (in *Harmony Simplified for Popular Use)* the insertion of a prelude between verses 'to give the singer a short rest', she is referring to the practice of filling-in cadences, sustained notes or

Musical Ex. 1.3. A typical cadenza for cornet from 'Bulch's Virtuoso Cornet School', an unpublished manuscript collection of theme and variation works for cornet by T.E. Bulch. These are undated, but as Bulch was born in 1860 they probably reflect late nineteenth-century practice.

pauses. This practice, which became known as the improvised 'fill' or 'break', later became significant in relation to African-American influenced popular music.

Vocal Elaboration

> As soon as my piece is finish[ed] I retreat to a corner and . . . listen to the screaming shakes, belaboured roulades and cooing arias with the quiet resignation of a German.
>
> Miska Hauser's impressions of a Melbourne concert in 1855.[26]

Colonial arrivals brought with them, if nothing else, a voice and the recollection of a few simple tunes reminiscent of home. Various accounts suggest that lonely colonial men were satiated by the female voice in a way that is difficult to understand today. Singing, particularly by women, was therefore a major shaping force behind the forms of improvisatory practice that became established here; and transplanted vocal traditions brought with them remnants of a passing tradition of improvisatory vocal embellishment.

References to vocal elaboration in colonial literature are relatively frequent, although they were often generated by colonial concern over the degree of ornamentation and whether it lay within the bounds of good taste (see Musical Ex. 1.4). Several years before Hauser's first Melbourne season, a local critic noted benevolently of Mrs Testar that:

> in passing from the glee to the aria, from the aria to the ballad, each was sung with purity and good sense; the playful ornament of the one giving way in the second, to the high embellishment of the Italian school; and contrasting beautifully with the artless simplicity of the Scottish ballad.[27]

Similarly, a Sydney review noted of Mrs Waller that she 'has a clear and sweet voice and in certain snatches of song she produces great effects by what we term the beauty of her melodious cadenzas which rise and fall, and die off'.[28]

Harold Love points to the improvisatory nature of early colonial opera in *The Golden Age of Australian Opera*, both in terms of its production and the performance behaviour of some of its divas. He notes that staging was highly experimental, appro-

Musical Ex. 1.4. Optional vocal elaboration from Isaac Nathan's arrangement of *'Lunghi dal Caro Bene'*.

priate scores and instrumentalists were often unavailable and, as vocal parts had to be memorised, all too frequently inadequate rehearsal left the ultimate performance even more indeterminate.[29] He also mentions, for example, Rosalie Durand's efforts to 'improve on Mozart, by introducing several appoggiaturas in airs whose simplicity form[ed] perhaps their greatest charm', and Ida Vitali, who was censured for 'endeavour[ing] to cover natural incapacity by a great deal of illegitimate vocal embellishment'.[30] In 'Vocal Ornamentation in Verdi: the Phonographic Evidence', Will Crutchfield's notated transcriptions of early opera recordings demonstrate that Nellie Melba carried the practice of strophic embellishment into the early twentieth century.[31]

Australian opera retained a degree of improvisational freedom throughout the latter half of the nineteenth century (much less so after the introduction of comic opera in the 1870s), but it should be noted that it was one of the least decontextualised of all nineteenth-century Australian musical activities. Opera represented the relatively direct and unadulterated transplantation of internationalised culture on a massive scale. It became more or less part of an international world of opera and, as I discuss in Chapter Three, operatic vocal embellishment even found its way into the blackface minstrel show format.

Improvisatory Piano Accompaniment

A colonial preoccupation with the acquisition of material wealth, comfort and security notwithstanding, by the 1860s, versions of the institutions of European high art music were becoming firmly established in Australia. Nevertheless, the Australian population at large still maintained its taste for simple melodic line and texture – the type of music that could be played, or sung and accompanied by even the modestly accomplished. Despite the increasing availability and promotion of sophisticated musical arrangements, the continuing popularity of widely accessible music played a role in preserving some aspects of the art of 'impromptu accompaniment' in Australia.[32]

Thorough Bass Accompaniment

The art of improvised accompaniment reached its peak in the baroque period as 'thorough bass'. In the thorough bass (or basso continuo) system, improvised accompaniment was constructed above a written bass line supplied with special chord symbols (figuring). This system saved the time of writing out a piece in full and enabled textural density to be varied to suit the particular instrument (e.g. organ or harpsichord), ensemble or acoustic environment.[33] It also enabled works to be presented with the 'fresh and flexible feeling of an improvisation'.[34]

Although improvisatory accompaniment in nineteenth-century Australia was undoubtedly a continuation of the same tradition, its function and realisation were somewhat different. Thorough bass could simply refer to practical harmony. A clue to the meaning of 'thorough bass accompaniment' in early colonial Australia however, is suggested in a series of lectures on the 'Theory and Practice of Music' given by Isaac Nathan in 1844. Vocal accompaniment is not the main subject of the published lectures. Nevertheless, they do provide information on how to play simple song accompaniments based, not on a bass line with figures, but on the harmonic implications of an upper voice – a simple 'melody or song'.[35] Such a system allowed the colonial musician to accompany a song or dance tune by ear, or from a single written line of music and, importantly, accompaniment could be provided in any key to suit the range of the vocalist.

Patton's Accompaniment System

Harmony Simplified for Popular Use is directed towards young amateurs who wished 'to form correct accompaniments or Basses to popular airs . . . [or] change the key at pleasure'.[36] It may well represent a modest watershed in colonial thinking regarding improvisatory accompaniment. In more than 180 pages of detailed explanation and musical examples, Patton analyses various melodic types and provides simple models for their accompaniment transposed to every key. Modulation models are also provided and there are sections on 'How to Sing an Extempore Second to a Melody'; 'On Original Musical Composition' (composing waltzes, polkas, mazurkas, ballads etc.); 'Useful Hints For Extempore Accompaniments'; how to adapt the system for guitar accompaniment; and, as discussed above, 'Symphonies and Preludes'.

Patton's models also provide some precise detail about how simple improvisatory accompaniment, as well as more professional elaboration, may have sounded around this time (see Musical Ex. 1.5). The fact that these models resemble the simple accompaniment textures in extant scores and harmony tutors which were available in Australia in the late nineteenth century suggests that written accompaniment and improvised accompaniment style were much the same except that improvisatory accompaniment was – because of human limitations – simpler and less exacting in harmonisation and voice leading. Patton's basic formula for elaborating the harmonic framework is again based on division. As she puts it, 'Accompaniments are produced by dividing the Chord into single or double notes . . . Thus, twenty-seven different accompaniments in all the various times can be formed by simply dividing the fundamental chords in various ways'.[37]

Musical Ex. 1.5. Various accompaniment models from Patton's *Harmony Simplified for Popular Use*.

Her treatise may well be, as she claims, a highly original colonial document. Music is not presented simply as a process of interpreting and technically realising notation, but as structured sound. She includes, for example, a short section on 'Connecting Lines of Sounds in Chords' and states that her 'method is to teach the *rules of sound* as applied to melody first'.[38] She uses a set of simple sketches (a 'landscape') to present the concept of various stages of elaboration from 'The Melody' to 'Elaborated

Accompaniment' (see Figure 1.2). Later, in 'On Elaborating Accompaniments to Airs by the Employment of More Extended Rules', she employs the analogy of the different levels of structure in language.[39] A colour-coded block system is used to indicate the relative status of vertical harmonies (tonic, dominant, etc.) and modulations, regardless of transposition.

In addition to this emphasis on structure (and as a corollary, structural hearing), Patton is concerned with other unnotated aspects of music. For example, she includes a section on the correct method of accenting syncopated figures. In her conclusion she writes, 'this work was undertaken mainly with an honest desire to supply to every-day pianoforte playing and singing, that vitality without which it is at best but a musical corpse decked out with flowers'. This concern is similar to the one mentioned by Donington in relation to baroque musicians.

> What a treasure of original native talent for musical composition may have been hitherto lost merely for a little lack of knowledge of its principles.
>
> [J.B.] Logier, cited on the cover of *Harmony Simplified for Popular Use*

Patton's approach is also concerned with encouraging local compositional talent; but, interestingly, she is careful not to draw a line between composition and improvisatory practice. In the 1960s, Melbourne musicians would again be influenced by the notion that 'improvising' and 'composing' were not necessarily two separate creative activities.

Emily Patton's method underlines the importance of women in the early history of improvisation in Australia and, in particular, the association between women and pianos. Many writers have commented on the importance of the piano in colonial Australia, both as a source of cultural capital and as a major form of entertainment. They often cite Oscar Comettant's (unsubstantiated) claim that 700,000 pianos had been shipped to Australia by 1888 and point to the convention that 'the daughter of the household' was expected to learn, entertain and accompany upon this instrument, either at home or in small social gatherings.[40] In *Town Life in Australia* (1883) the journalist Richard Twopeny claims that 'Almost every working-man had his girls taught to strum the piano', at the same time implying that a lot of this piano playing was of a very mediocre standard.[41] This may well be true; yet among the half a million or so colonial women required to accompany on the piano by the 1880s it is likely that there were a considerable number, particularly among the many who had been taught personally by Patton, who could improvise an accompaniment with a skill and ease that would astonish the average formally-trained pianist today.

FRONTISPIECE

EXPLANATION OF THE ABOVE SKETCHES, AS APPLIED TO THE OBJECT OF THIS WORK.

FIG. 1.—In this sketch a simple hut is shown, without any surrounding objects, which exactly resembles a MELODY without either BASS OR ACCOMPANIMENT.

FIG. 2.—Next, the hut is given, with smoke issuing from the chimney, a few additions of foreground, and a cluster of bushes behind it; all of which, acting upon the hut itself, give it prominence and perspective. This exactly expresses the action of a correct BASS OR ACCOMPANIMENT upon a MELODY.

FIG. 3.—Here the hut with the same accessories as in Fig. 2, is placed by a few bold strokes of the pencil, upon the summit of a hill, showing the effect of the MAJOR MODE OF ACCOMPANIMENT upon a MELODY, which *elevates* it into greater prominence.

FIG. 4.—By a few strokes of an exactly opposite character the hut is now found to be in a valley, a mountain rising behind it. This typifies the effect of the MINOR MODE OF ACCOMPANIMENT on a MELODY, which has a tendency to *depress* it.

FIG. 5.—Lastly, the hut is shown with all its accessories of smoke, bushes, and foreground, hill and valley, and the sketch is further elaborated, at the pleasure and taste of the artist, by the addition of a distant landscape and of some figures in the foreground, resembling a MELODY treated with both MAJOR AND MINOR ACCOMPANIMENT, and further embellished by a judicious knowledge and employment of the laws of HARMONY.

Thus, the child is content with the simple hut, and so is the street boy when he whistles a popular air.

The majority of people, from want of knowledge of its principles, are satisfied to be pleased by music without understanding it, but the true artist, whether he be painter or musician, is unsatisfied unless he avail himself of all the resources that the rules of his art place at his disposal.

To place, therefore, the Fundamental Rules of Music within reach of all, in the simplest and most attractive manner possible, has been the author's aim throughout this book, in order that everyone may be enabled to regard MELODY from an artistic point of view, which they may rest assured will, by enlarging their appreciation of it, greatly enhance their enjoyment of music generally.

Figure 1.2. Frontispiece of Emily Patton's *Harmony Simplified for Popular Use,* illustrating the construction of a musical accompaniment. Courtesy of Arthur Withers.

Vamping

Patton does not use the word 'vamping', a common term for improvised accompaniment, in her treatise, possibly because it was associated with working class music-making. Yet by the 1890s a number of Melbourne musicians were offering vamping lessons and several of them had produced their own 'methods'. Among these are *De Lacy's Book on Vamping for the Piano* (c.1890 or earlier), *Mrs Russell's Vamping Method* (c.1890 or earlier), and *W.M. Perrier's Harmonizer or, Instructions in the Art Of Vamping or, Extemporizing on the Piano or Organ* (1890). Other methods published in Melbourne were *Smith's Method* (undated), *Dinsdale's Vamping Card* (early 1900s) and *Reeve's Vamping Tutor* (undated).[42] Many others were produced interstate or imported into Australia through local music houses.

Relatively speaking, the most sophisticated of these methods is Perrier's *Art of Vamping*, which comprises twenty-nine pages of text covering modulation, transposition and 'Accompanying Entirely By Ear'. Separate charts provide chord patterns (with inversions) transposed into every key, with accompaniment textures (similar to Patton's) to be memorised for subsequent improvisatory interpolation. Perrier stipulates that the patterns must be 'mechanically learnt and ready, so to speak, at the fingers' ends; as in starting an air or song, the attention needs to be given entirely to the *arranging* of the changes in use'.[43] Once learnt, they 'are not necessarily to be played to songs in the order given for practising them, but must be used according as the ear directs, to suit the harmony of the air to be accompanied'.[44] In his introduction Perrier brushes aside the contention that vamping is an art confined to those who have 'an intuitive knowledge of it' and makes a radical proposal that would remain unorthodox until the emergence of the Australian collectively improvised jazz tradition: that 'it may be taken for an axiom that if you have sufficient ear to hear that you are playing discord [sic], then you have quite enough to guide you, with trial and perseverance, to obtaining a correct harmony'.[45]

Other systems likewise comprise simple instructions and accompaniment patterns in every key, to be memorised and interpolated by ear on the basis of a written-out melody line. Although these tutors are based upon the same central principles as Patton's *Harmony Simplified for Popular Use* (such as the interpolation of internalised patterns) they are far less sophisticated and comprehensive. Nor do they offer the type of cultural dividend associated with orthodox musical training (see Figure 1.3). In fact, Perrier apologetically explains that vamping should be 'considered apart, as catering for a long felt want of a certain portion of the public, who, for various reasons cannot enter into the study of music'.[46]

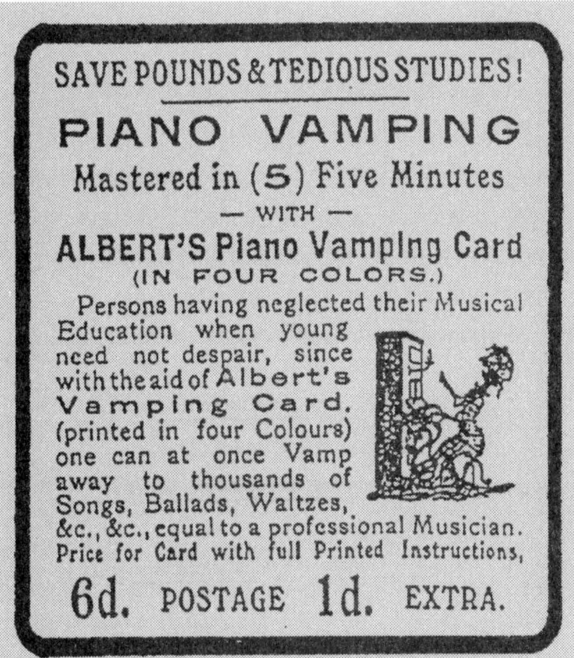

Figure 1.3. Advertisement for *Albert's Vamping Card* from *Albert's American Annual*, no. 5, Sydney: Albert & Son, 1908. Note the unorthodox and almost ecstatically abandoned approach to piano playing depicted in this illustration; it could just as easily be a 1920s illustration of a jazz pianist.

Other Accompaniment Systems and Related Literature

Vamping systems such as Perrier's offered a simple systematic approach to providing basic accompaniment in any key and thus, in theory, were an invaluable tool to both amateur and professional musicians. These systems were, however, too simplistic to have any serious application for the accomplished musician. Professional or highly-trained amateur accompanists were more or less expected to be able to transpose complex keyboard arrangements with ease and their rigorous formal training and study of practical harmony provided the basic knowledge and technique for this – especially in the case of organists. Given that such players had sufficient natural ability to internalise the basic melodic, harmonic and rhythmic models encountered in their years of practice and performance, they were already equipped with a library of memorised models and the technical ability to reproduce these in any key without preparation.

For musicians of this proficiency there were much more appropriate methods available directly from local music houses such as Allan's. Important among these are Frank J. Sawyer's *Extemporisation* (1890s; intended for organists), the influence of which is acknowledged in the section on improvisation in W.H. Webbe's *The Pianist's ABC Primer and Guide* (© 1900), which was also available here (see Musical Ex. 1.6).[47]

There were also various works available which dealt specifically with accompaniment practice. Edwin Evans' *How to Accompany at the Piano* (1917) is particularly comprehensive. It systematically presents an array of stock accompaniment types which the student is asked to transpose into every key at the piano.[48] A major section of Evans' book is devoted to 'practical harmony for accompaniment', including (like most methods of this type) transposition and modulation (see Figure 1.4).

By the time that Evans' book was published improvisatory practice was declining in

Musical Ex. 1.6. First page of a chapter on the use of hymn tunes in extemporisation, from Frank J. Sawyer, *Extemporization.*

56

CHAPTER IX.

ON THE USE OF THE HYMN-TUNE IN EXTEMPORIZATION.

1. The organist is so frequently obliged to make use of a hymn-tune in his extemporization, that it will, perhaps, be best to devote a separate chapter to the various ways in which this may arise. The ability to treat skilfully the melody of a hymn-tune will frequently enable him to produce suitable voluntaries for special festivals or other occasions, whereby he can maintain the prevailing idea of the day.

ON EXTEMPORIZING AFTER THE CONCLUSION OF A HYMN.

2. This, the only piece of *compulsory* extemporization during Divine Service, is at once one of the least artistic, as it is one of the most awkward, occasions in which the organist's power is called into play Since the period during which he will have to extemporize is to him unknown, no definite movement form can be adopted. Yet this by no means implies that the so often heard "mooning" from chord to chord is necessary.

Supposing the hymn to have been, "O God, our help in ages past," and the tune the well-known "St. Ann's"—

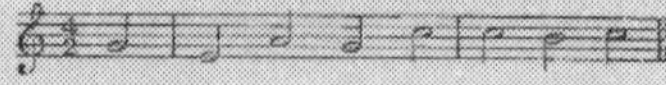

SHORT METHODS.

PLAN 1.—After the "amen" make a short modulation to the dominant key of G, and, modifying the melody of the tune, extemporize a sixteen-bar theme, beginning thus:—

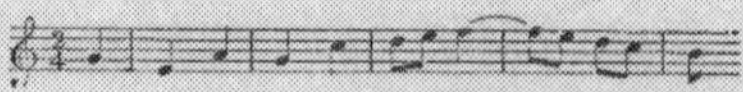

Should this prove nearly sufficient, a coda of four or eight bars, with a rallentando, will bring your improvisation to a graceful termination.

PLAN 2.—After the "amen" proceed as before, by a short modulation to the key of the dominant, and then play over the first line of the tune (reharmonizing it if possible). At the end of this line extemporize four bars, over some easy figure, leading to the second line, which can also have fresh harmonies. Again play four extemporaneous bars between lines two and three, and after playing the third line, again between lines three and four. After line four a short coda may conclude the whole.

PLAN 3.—Proceed as before to the key of the dominant, place the melody of the hymn-tune as a tenor solo for the left hand on diapasons or swell reed, and accompany with the right hand, arranging the parts, and, where possible, putting fresh harmony. Add a short coda. (See Smart's Choral, Variation 2).

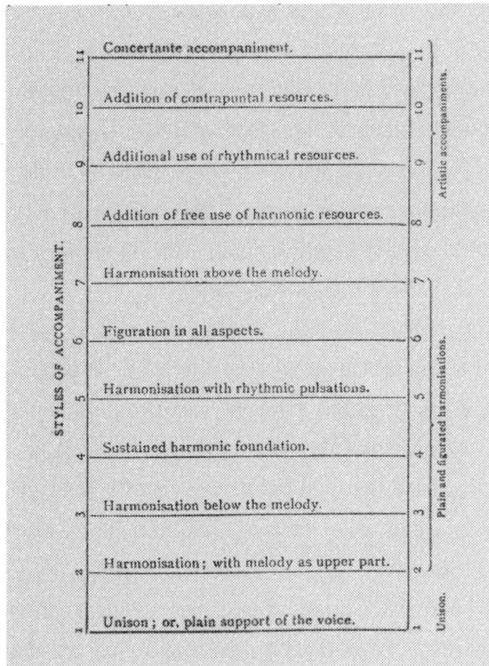

Figure 1.4. A tabulation illustrating the comprehensive nature of Edwin Evans' *How to Accompany at the Piano*, p. 16.

formal concert performance; but an otherwise proficient accompanist who took the trouble to study the information and models provided in Evans' method was, theoretically, well-equipped for providing improvisatory accompaniment in the Anonymous genres such as silent cinema. Yet, as I illustrate in later chapters, the style of the accompaniment textures provided in this method were no longer adequate for the popular music of the day.

Church Organ and Gospel Piano Music

Church organ music is an Approved genre which has supported improvisatory practice throughout the period discussed and up to the present day. This tradition is a particularly notable aspect of Melbourne's music history.

Church Organ Music

One reason for the survival of improvisatory practice in the church organ tradition is its usefulness as a flexible musical bridge to fill in the variable time spans between sections of a service, thereby preserving the devotional mood from prelude to postlude. A passing comment in the memoirs of Melbourne pianist and former church organist, Claude Kingston, that he 'improvised a few bars on the organ while waiting for the girl to appear so that [he] could strike up the Bridal March'[49] provides a down-to-earth example of this practice in the early 1900s.

The highest level of improvisatory practice inherited by colonial Australia from the British cathedral organ tradition was the improvisation of extensive preludes, postludes and even multi-sectional works. An anecdote about the notable colonial musician Charles Horsley who worked as a church organist in the 1860s relates that his extemporisation of a concluding voluntary at St Peter's Church, Melbourne, was so extended that Canon Hadfield had to send the verger to stop him.[50]

More common forms of improvisatory practice were the development or elaboration of a hymn just concluded (modulated to the dominant key), spontaneous reharmonisation of hymn accompaniments and, in some church traditions, the harmonisation of plainsong (Musical Ex. 1.7). This last became the focus of controversy in Australia in 1904 with one Catholic church leader declaring that singers would be able to cope with the change 'When Cockatoo and wattle-bird take to living in water; [and] when schnapper and barracuda make nests in trees'.[51]

In any case, the church organ, and the romantic organ in particular, is itself a natural vehicle for exploratory improvisatory practice. Beyond what is notated on a score, and beyond even the improvisatory melodic, harmonic or rhythmic modification of what is notated, the organist – unlike the pianist – has a palette of almost infinite timbral variety for personal expression – or, more properly, divine inspiration.

One important example of the transplantation of the cathedral music tradition can be found in the distinctive and influential work of Dr. A. E. Floyd who, from 1915, was for several decades resident organist and choirmaster at St Paul's Cathedral, Melbourne. Floyd's improvisatory preludes and vocal accompaniments were a special feature of St Paul's musical programs and transcriptions of some his preludes were

Musical Ex. 1.7. From J. H. Arnold, *Plainsong Accompaniment.*

published (Musical Ex. 1.8). His restrained contrapuntal style of extemporisation can be traced back directly through his early Cambridge 'masters' to Samuel Sebastian Wesley. Floyd's student, Norman Kaye, recalls from his own training in this tradition the expectation that students would learn by osmosis, through watching, listening and assisting the master.[52]

In describing Floyd's accompaniment practice Robert Boughen refers to his use of elaboration to generate ecstatic excitement. This is an aspect of church organ playing that is quite similar in function to the use of improvisatory embellishment in some genres of African-American music such as gospel. More importantly, it is similar to what I describe in Chapter Five as 'jazzing up', the white imitation of African-American embellishment practice. Boughen states, for example, that Floyd:

> used to crash out the beginning in unison notes . . . in the accustomed style and *off* would go the choir – and Floyd['s] harmonies were something that invigorated and enlivened the whole process of worship.[53]

Kaye also claims that Floyd 'could lift them out of their brains! He would do it with a grin on his face [and] say: "listen to this, I'll kick them along"'.[54] Many other organists consulted mentioned intensifying the effect of the final chorus of a hymn through elaboration of harmony, rhythm or simply by increasing the volume.

Innovative Early Australian Gospel-Piano Style

One interesting 'intensification' practice relates to a kind of gospel-piano accompaniment style developed around the turn of the century by Robert Harkness, a musician known by many as the Bendigo Hymnwriter because of the many (over 2,000) hymns that he wrote. A 1940s American publication, *Music in Evangelism,* describes Harkness as 'one of the greatest gospel pianists of the present generation', perhaps an exaggerated claim in the light of the African-American gospel-piano tradition.[55] The Reverend Dr Keith Cole, author of *Robert Harkness: the Bendigo Hymnwriter* (1988), writes that:

> Ira D. Sankey and those associated with him had developed the gospel song with a direct message set to simple tunes. Robert [Harkness] was the one who developed the revolutionary new style of *accompaniment,* which has been used by pianists in evangelistic gatherings ever since, and with which his name is usually associated.[56]

Harkness innovated his style of sacred accompaniment while reluctantly acting as piano accompanist for the 1902 Bendigo visit of the touring evangelists, Dr R. Torrey and Charles Alexander:

> [My annoyance] prompted me to attempt a more elaborate improvisation than originally planned. When the chorus was taken up by the audience, I introduced a full octave

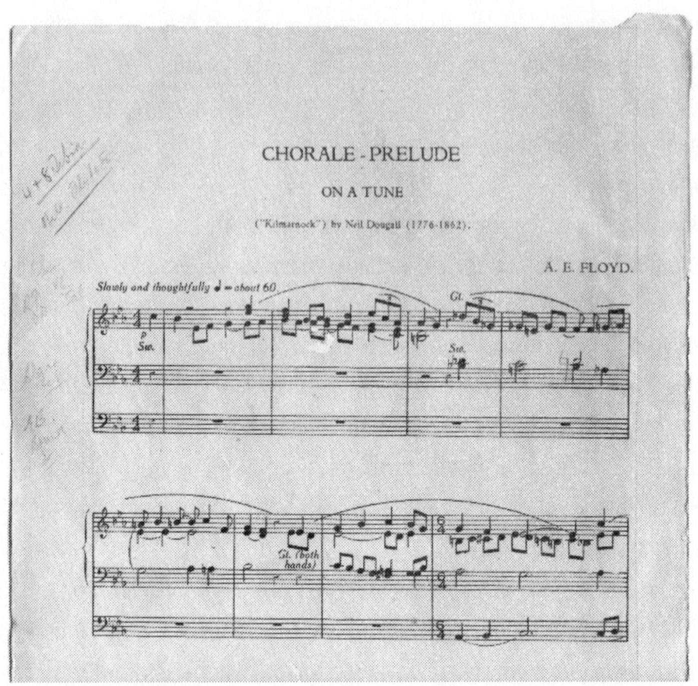

Musical Ex. 1.8. Bars 1-8 and the final section of 'Chorale-Prelude on the tune "Kilmarnock"' by A.E. Floyd.

> accompaniment quite distinct from the melody . . . Instead of annoying the song-leader, his interest was so aroused as to lead to an ultimate round-the-world association of many years.[57]

This style subsequently became a special feature of Alexander's world-touring mass-meeting campaigns for more than a decade. In America, Harkness formalised it in his *Beginner's Hymn Playing Course*, *Evangelistic Hymn Playing* and the relatively advanced (80 lesson) *The Art of Sacred Accompaniment*, which includes sections on rhythm, preludes, interludes, improvisation, memory training and chimes (a special piano effect).[58] As demonstrated in Musical Example 1.9, the basis of his approach was to analyse harmonically, memorise and therefore internalise each hymn and continuously extend his technique and knowledge of practical harmony. Through these means he could vary the embellishment of a hymn in fresh and innovative ways every time he performed it.[59] His approach was described in 1904:

> He plays entirely from memory, requiring no book, and no sooner is the hymn announced than he strikes the opening chords, adding harmonies and cadences to the simple melody, which transforms it into a swelling tide of music.[60]

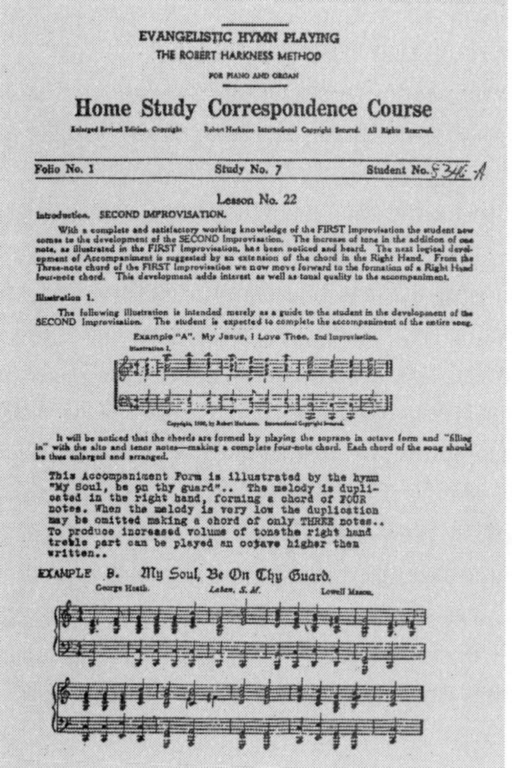

EVANGELISTIC HYMN PLAYING
THE ROBERT HARKNESS METHOD
FOR PIANO AND ORGAN

Home Study Correspondence Course

Enlarged Revised Edition. Copyright Robert Harkness International Copyright Secured. All Rights Reserved.

Folio No. 1 | Study No. 7 | Student No. 5346-A

Lesson No. 22

Introduction. SECOND IMPROVISATION.

With a complete and satisfactory working knowledge of the FIRST Improvisation the student now comes to the development of the SECOND Improvisation. The increase of tone in the addition of one note, as illustrated in the FIRST Improvisation, has been noticed and heard. The next logical development of Accompaniment is suggested by an extension of the chord in the Right Hand. From the Three-note chord of the FIRST Improvisation we now move forward to the formation of a Right Hand four-note chord. This development adds interest as well as tonal quality to the accompaniment.

Illustration 1.

The following illustration is intended merely as a guide to the student in the development of the SECOND Improvisation. The student is expected to complete the accompaniment of the entire song.

Example "A". My Jesus, I Love Thee. 2nd Improvisation.

Illustration 1.

It will be noticed that the chords are formed by playing the soprano in octave form and "filling in" with the alto and tenor notes—making a complete four-note chord. Each chord of the song should be thus enlarged and arranged.

This Accompaniment Form is illustrated by the hymn "My Soul, be on thy guard".. The melody is duplicated in the right hand, forming a chord of FOUR notes. When the melody is very low the duplication may be omitted making a chord of only THREE notes.. To produce increased volume of tonethe right hand treble part can be played an octave higher then written..

EXAMPLE B. My Soul, Be On Thy Guard.

George Heath. *Laban, S. M.* Lowell Mason.

Musical Ex. 1.9. From Robert Harkness, *Evangelistic Hymn Playing*,

It is ironic that after personally developing an approach to musical performance which involved authentically spontaneous harmonic and rhythmic elaboration to generate ecstatic excitement, Harkness later became an outspoken critic of jazz, publicly declaring it 'musical chaos'.[61] Nevertheless, his work is an important example of how the artistic isolation of Australian musicians sometimes fostered significant synthesis of styles or innovation. His story is also a reminder that much of the performance of sacred music in pre-jazz Victoria and other parts of Australia took place outside the church buildings of the principal denominations. Home worship to the accompaniment of reed organ or piano was widespread.

The Decline of Improvisatory Practice in the Approved Genres

Between the late 1830s and the early twentieth century, a distinct shift in Australian perceptions of improvisation took place. Whereas in 1836 improvisatory practice was commonplace and an accepted facet of musical life, by 1918, the time of the first Australian so-called jazz band, it was considered at best a curiosity of musical history and at worst an inferior practice unworthy of serious consideration. In 'Musical Progress' (1916) the Sydney Conservatorium teacher, Cyril Monk, states that 'any good teacher' would be shocked at the type of improvisatory practice (e.g. fantasias and pot-pourris on popular themes) that was acceptable in the early 1800s.[62]

Frequently colonial criticism dismisses improvisatory embellishment as 'meretricious' and endorses music from which it was absent as 'chaste', 'classic', 'tasteful' or 'correct'. This points to an aesthetic which remained influential in Australia well into the twentieth century, one oppositional to the sonic chaos, distortion and incongruity that were perceived by many to be inherent in uncontrolled improvisatory freedom.[63]

It is difficult to determine exactly when the study of harmony ceased to have direct practical application to such things as improvisatory accompaniment and became instead a theoretical appendage to learning to play. Emily Patton may have pointed to this as early as 1877 in her statement in *Harmony Simplified for Popular Use* that many parents were both disappointed and puzzled that their children 'were unable on an emergency to strike correctly and with confidence a few extempore chords as an accompaniment to the voice'.[64] Ironically, Patton's publishers, Allan & Co., who became established publishers of sheet music after 1880, had much to gain from promoting musical literacy at the expense of systems such as hers which encouraged pianists to 'make up' their own music. However, it would be going too far, perhaps, to suggest that such local influential music publishers played an active role in downgrading the status of improvisatory accompaniment.

THE APPROVED GENRES BEFORE JAZZ

The Australian musical community struggled throughout the late nineteenth century to establish institutions and orchestras and to formalise and raise musical standards in the face of general apathy for the arts. With the emergence of Tin Pan Alley and its Australian equivalent around the turn of the century, the distinction between 'popular' and 'serious' music became sharply defined. Those who had taken part in the struggle for excellence and formal standards had little tolerance for the blemishes inherent in improvisation or the audacity of those who dared to spontaneously improve on what the masters had written. Nevertheless, there was still an occasional, almost nostalgic, call for improvisation in musical education. For the Australian musical establishment, however, novelties such as the pot-pourri belonged to vaudeville along with other 'trick' instrumental acts. Improvisation was now seen as that tinkling pianistic nonsense that seeped twice daily from an increasing number of corrugated-iron roofed suburban 'movie' theatres.

By 1918 – the time when Australian musicians began to play music described as jazz – improvisatory practice in the Approved genres was represented principally by the church organ tradition. To a degree the contingencies of vocal accompaniment also preserved improvisatory skills: the unexpected request for transposition or modulation on demand, the occasional unrehearsed encore accompanied from memory, or the need 'to be equal to all *contretemps*, such as the skipping of a line by a careless prima-donna or the tumbling down of the music.'[65] A similar enduring exception is the improvisation of musical accompaniments for ballet practice.

There were, however, (and always will be) individuals in the community who improvised in private or semi-private situations. Oscar Comettant, who visited Melbourne in the 1880s, casually mentions the virtuoso pianist he encountered who, after one drink too many, 'sat down at the piano and improvised for twenty minutes with a curious uneasiness penetrated by the skill of a musician who has learned his trade'.[66] The year following Comettant's visit a Melbourne musician wrote that he:

> was once spending a social evening where music was largely enjoyed, although the company were not all musicians. It was proposed that the writer should extemporise some short movement on the pianoforte illustrative of some sentiment, or incident, kept secret to himself until afterwards, and that each member of the company should try to guess what the 'meaning' of the music might be. He played a short impromptu strain for about four minutes.[67]

Students of the famous Melbourne orchestra founder and leader, Alberto Zelman, recall his private improvisations and how he once improvised a fugue on a motif under discussion.[68] One of these students, the pianist-composer (and former silent film accompanist) Esther Rofe, also recalls the enjoyment of privately performing extensive, free-structured, two-piano improvisations with another notable Australian pianist-composer, Miriam Hyde.[69] These examples are of course only a minute representation of informal improvisation for private creative expression.

It is significant to the remainder of this book that the forms of improvisatory practice already discussed represented a pool of skills, models and devices on which Approved genre musicians were often able to draw when working in the Anonymous genres. The most relevant of these are:

1. Melodic variation technique.
2. Interpolating and linking unrelated melodic segments.
3. Preluding, which can function as introductory, ending or filling-in material.
4. Ornamentation, which functions as the decoration or filling-in of rests, pauses or sustained notes.
5. Individual ornaments and special effects.
6. Keyboard accompaniment practice, which included many forms of harmonic and melodic elaboration.

Orthodox musical training offered pre-jazz musicians a systematic means of acquiring the basic building materials of improvisatory practice: scales, broken chord exercises, preludes, theme and variation models, cadences and so forth. The key element in this systemised training was transposition; models were provided in every key or the student was expected to transpose them to every key. Therefore, every rigorously trained musician had, at least in theory, the basis of variation and embellishment practice and, in the case of keyboard players, accompaniment practice. In the case of church organists the ability to realise technique and practical harmony as improvisatory practice was often highly developed – something that the silent cinema industry quickly recognised.

Of all these, two principles are crucial to subsequent discussion of African-American influenced improvisatory practice. The first is division: the concept of subdividing the basic beat as a form of improvisatory embellishment (e.g. with chord, passing and neighbour tones); and the second is interpolation: the principle of spontaneously interpolating musical patterns selected from a group of such patterns memorised in every key.

2 The Anonymous Genres

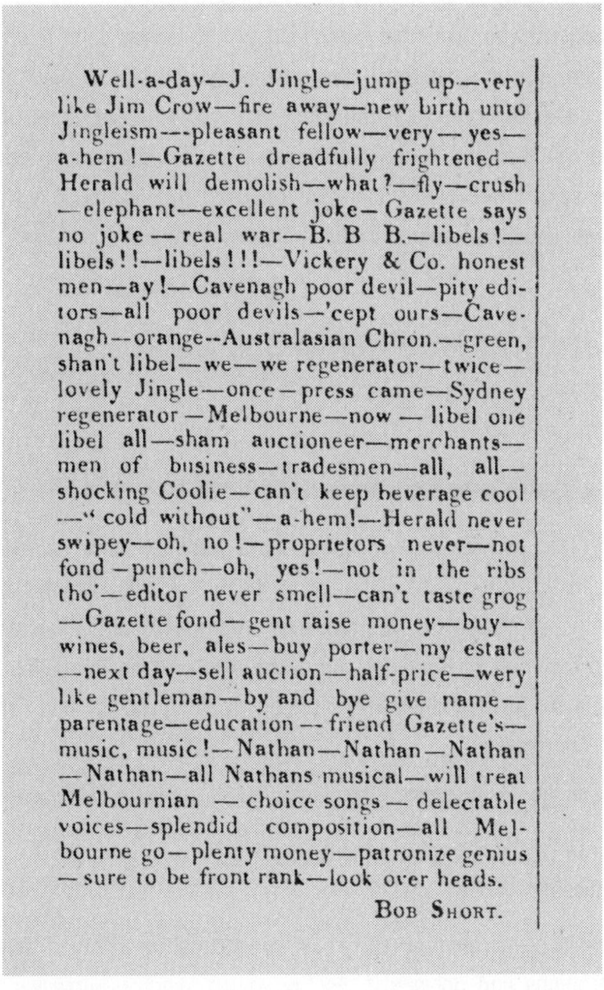

Well-a-day—J. Jingle—jump up—very like Jim Crow—fire away—new birth unto Jingleism—-pleasant fellow—very—yes—a-hem!—Gazette dreadfully frightened—Herald will demolish—what?—fly—crush—elephant—excellent joke—Gazette says no joke—real war—B. B B.—libels!—libels!!—libels!!!—Vickery & Co. honest men—ay!—Cavenagh poor devil—pity editors—all poor devils—'cept ours—Cavenagh—orange--Australasian Chron.—green, shan't libel—we—we regenerator—twice—lovely Jingle—once—press came—Sydney regenerator—Melbourne—now—libel one libel all—sham auctioneer—merchants—men of business—tradesmen—all, all—shocking Coolie—can't keep beverage cool—"cold without"—a-hem!—Herald never swipey—oh, no!—proprietors never—not fond—punch—oh, yes!—not in the ribs tho'—editor never smell—can't taste grog—Gazette fond—gent raise money—buy—wines, beer, ales—buy porter—my estate—next day—sell auction—half-price—wery like gentleman—by and bye give name—parentage—education—friend Gazette's—music, music!—Nathan—Nathan—Nathan—Nathan—all Nathans musical—will treat Melbournian—choice songs—delectable voices—splendid composition—all Melbourne go—plenty money—patronize genius—sure to be front rank—look over heads.

Bob Short.

Figure 2.1. A Bob Short text, *Port Phillip Patriot and Melbourne Advertiser,* 11 February, 1841, p. 3.

This curiously syncopated anticipation of stream-of-consciousness prose which I found in one of Melbourne's first journals warns against any assumption that early Melbourne was devoid of creative activity. More specifically it indicates that a known improvising musician, Isaac Nathan, had already reached Melbourne and that at least one element of imitation African-American culture, the stage caricature Jim Crow, a popular vehicle for improvised song verse, was familiar to its residents by this time.

This and other texts written under the alias of Bob Short demonstrate that artistic inventiveness in the nineteenth century was not always the province of the educationally or culturally privileged. These texts, several of which are published in *Compositions For Improvisers: an Australian Perspective* (1993), appear to have been the creation of an ex-convict who was once sentenced to 400 lashes: John Pascoe Fawkner (or possibly his ex-convict father), the co-founder of Melbourne.[1] His declamatory and often scandalous prose illustrates that rigid aesthetic, social, cultural and even political values could always be transgressed in a playful, spontaneous and fleeting manner. These same three words can also be used to describe the way improvisatory practice was usually presented in the Anonymous genres.

Part I: A Survey of the Anonymous Genres before Jazz

The Early Melbourne or 'Bearbrass' Period (1838-1851)

Early Melbourne or Bearbrass, as it was known, witnessed a gradual musical awakening which kept pace with the general development of the Port Phillip District. This awakening was accelerated at intervals by the arrival of enterprising and/or talented individuals from Sydney, Tasmania or Britain. A hint of the nature of music-making in Melbourne before 1841 is provided by a chronicler of early Melbourne, Edmund Finn, under the pen-name of 'Garryowen':

> Contemporaneous with the white settlement, there were musical amateurs in Melbourne, and at times they assisted at what were little more than tap-room entertainments, generally consisting of a wild chorus of songs, fiddling, and flute playing, aided by a hoarse, spasmodic piano.[2]

By the early 1840s organised instrumental and vocal concerts often included items such as theme and variations and pot-pourri. As Garryowen suggests, however, a separate 'lowbrow' mode of music-making was also present – one in which music was often mutated or modified (at least timbrally and rhythmically) by unorthodox improvisatory practice in performance.

The distinction between highbrow and lowbrow culture was relatively slow to emerge in small, isolated and entertainment-starved colonial communities such as early Melbourne. Nevertheless, even in this period of socially heterogenous performance environments, it is possible to identify several Anonymous genres, namely, dance music, theatre (including blackface minstrelsy) and early 'town band' music.

Dance Music

Dance and its musical accompaniment appear to have been a very important aspect of Melbourne social life almost from the start of the settlement. Soon after the publication of the first newspaper in 1838 mention is made of local balls; and advertisements offer music for balls and 'Quadrille parties' or lessons in 'all the fashionable dances now practised in Paris, London, and Edinburgh, viz: – Quadrilles, Waltzes, Gallopades, Mazourkas, &c., &c'.[3] In social contrast to these activities there were also reports of 'fiddling, shouting, singing, and dancing, nightly emanating from these haunts [taverns] of iniquity and vice'.[4]

The main social contexts in which dancing took place throughout most of the pre-jazz period were formal functions, private gatherings, small commercially operated venues (sometimes of dubious character) and dancing schools. In relation to the latter, colonial Australia inherited a tradition from Britain in which 'dancing academies' largely determined the type of dances that were adopted and the type of music that accompanied them. Colonial dancing masters were therefore agents of formality, standardisation and congruity in relation to both movement and music. By this means dance academies and their equivalents also gained much control over the level of improvisatory practice in dance music, a control they would maintain almost to the middle of the twentieth century.

The early years of Melbourne also correspond to a period during which major changes were taking place in colonial dancing. The fashionable dances mentioned above belong to two groups: 'sets' (Quadrilles) and 'closed couple' dances (in which the partner is held relatively close).* The latter group, including the most influential of these dances, the Polka, does not appear to have reached Melbourne until 1845. Apart from the Quadrilles, the most common colonial dances before this were the much older

* A point of usage should be noted here. Specific dances, such as the Polka, have been given an initial capital to differentiate the dance from the music associated with it. Thus cakewalk music is played for people who dance the Cake Walk.

English Country Dances, as well as Jigs, Reels, Strathspeys, Hornpipes and the Highland Fling.

A relationship between theatre and dance music can be traced back to these early years. In the tradition of British theatre, dances were frequently incorporated into melodrama or presented as 'entr'acte amusements'. The Sailor's Hornpipe and the Highland Fling, for example, were features of the first formal Melbourne theatrical performance (1842). Throughout the 1840s local theatre musicians provided the musical accompaniment for a wide range of novelty dances, including the Yankee Breakdown (danced by a 'black boy' brought from Sydney), the Tarantella, and the New-Fashioned Polka.[5] The convention of introducing the latest novelties in dancing and music to the colonial public via the stage was one that would have particular implications, later, for the introduction of ragtime and jazz into Australia.

Theatre Music

Nineteenth-century Australian drama is sometimes described as falling in two phases: 'strolling players' (or itinerant actors) and 'stock companies'.[6] The first phase roughly corresponds with the early Melbourne period and has special implications for improvisatory practice in theatre music. The increasingly formal and structured drama that characterised the second phase, during the Victorian era, is of less relevance to later discussion.

The serio-comic melodrama of early Melbourne theatre, which demanded constant role changes and offered few opportunities for rehearsal, had given rise to a relatively open-ended or improvisatory performance style. This style had its antecedents in British pantomime and in the London minor theatres (musical theatre in which the actors were not permitted to speak under the censorship regulations). It was therefore based, not on subtle relationships between characters, but on 'broad outlines, simplified characters, visual spectacle, and unashamed theatricality'.[7]

Colonial theatre emerged largely from tavern or hotel entertainment, and Melbourne hotels continued to feature theatrical amusements and British 'free and easy' or music hall style entertainments throughout the nineteenth century. The first Melbourne theatre, the Theatre Royal (first known as the Pavilion), was built in 1842, by which time theatre was already well established in Sydney, Hobart, Launceston and to a lesser extent, Adelaide. The Theatre Royal was dimly lit, leaked and apparently rocked alarmingly in a strong wind. It was 'opened with a musical performance, but of a very equivocal description, spiced with low buffoonery, ribaldry and interludes of riot and confusion'.[8]

Although the opening of the more substantial Queen's Theatre and the arrival of the actor and entrepreneur George Coppin in the mid-1840s resulted in an improvement in theatrical standards, episodes of riotous behaviour continued. The informality and disorder associated with early Melbourne theatre – particularly at the Pavilion – provided the freedom for musicians to react creatively and playfully with the stage action in a way not possible later. Finn's exhaustive account of the riotous behaviour of patrons and sometimes drunken actors makes for amusing reading: 'One fellow made at his neighbour, and butting him like a ram in the "bread basket," sent him spinning backwards amongst the musicians . . . A musical melange followed, which in some degree restored good humour.'[9]

In addition to the high level of informal interaction between stage and audience, the scenery, music, machinery, costumes, decorations and so forth often had to be hastily improvised for once or twice-only performances. Lack of local talent, continuous program changes and the indifference of actors to unappreciative and sometimes violently hostile audiences all contributed to parts often only half-learnt. The ability to 'gag' (to improvise dialogue) was a necessary skill for the itinerant actor of the period; and sexual innuendo or other impromptu dialogue was also frequently substituted for the written script. Farce and flexible commedia dell'arte forms like clowning, Jim Crow and the simpleton character Billy Barlow, also encouraged ad libbing. Coppin, for example, is reported to have varied each of three successive encores to his first Australian appearance as Barlow.[10] Moreover, audiences themselves often aggressively demanded spontaneous changes to the program such as a song or a dance. Musical accompaniment, in turn, had to be spontaneous and flexible enough to accommodate all of these contingencies. During one sixteen-week period in 1845 Coppin presented approximately 'one hundred different selections to the public':

> Included were nineteen tragedies, twenty dramas, fourteen comedies, fourteen farces, seventeen 'interludes', and sixteen specialities ranging from a full evening's concert to slack-rope performances by Frenchman M. Laurent, and dissolving magic lantern views.[11]

The entr'acte 'specialities' that separated the main items on a theatre program most commonly comprised vocal or instrumental items or novelty dances, but they also included gymnastics, conjuring, ventriloquism and less conventional items such as 'educated dogs'.[12] Thus, besides the special requirements of melodrama accompaniment, Melbourne theatre musicians were already providing musical accompaniment to some of the types of variety act that filled out the programs of later forms of popular entertainment in Australia such as vaudeville.

Other theatrical forms of the early Melbourne period which have particular implications for improvisatory musical practice are burlesque (including caricatures of other artists) and pantomime. The term burlesque was applied in a number of ways in nineteenth-century theatre. By the 1860s it was even being used to describe 'a compound of music hall, minstrel show, extravaganza, legs and limelight, puns, topical songs and gaudy irreverence'.[13] Here, however, I am principally concerned with burlesque as comic distortion – the highly exaggerated modification or distortion of a given model. Since the essence of burlesque in this sense is not imitation but 'Absurdity to the point of insanity', it clearly provides considerable latitude for improvisatory modification.[14] Where models such as ecstatic folk performances were burlesqued, as in early minstrelsy, spontaneous musical transformation was sometimes involved. This suggests that an incipient form of improvisatory music-theatre was present almost from the start of Melbourne.

Pantomime is significant because, although it comprised stock elements such as the Harlequin character and the 'transformation scene', its essence was fantasy and informality and its content was restricted only by the imagination. While we do not know the exact nature of the music devised for local pantomimes such as *The Goblin of the Gold Coast*, there is every reason to suspect that productions such as this, with its 'celestials', 'terrestrials', 'Demon of Discord', 'sound and fury', 'jumping and capering' and general suspension of disbelief, would have provided a wide latitude for imaginative textures and sound effects.[15] A claim that local pantomime audiences were 'infinitely amused' by backstage vocal farmyard imitations supports this suggestion.[16]

Early Melbourne theatre musicians had to cope with many more contingencies than their later counterparts and there was also far less uniformity of instrumentation and musical ability. To confuse matters, the term 'band' was applied to both professional theatre orchestras and the type of ensemble heard at public gatherings in the 1840s. The first 'town band', formed in late 1839, included two keyed bugles, two clarinets, two flutes, a piccolo, bass and tenor trombones, bassoon, 'large drum', side drum and triangle. A second 'very inefficient town band', formed in 1841, provided music for the first theatre productions.[17] This band, reportedly led by Mons. Gautrot, probably included one or two violins and a cello, fortified by the type of woodwind, brass and percussion instruments mentioned above, this being the most suitable ensemble structure for the accompaniment of scripted productions.

The first theatre production, in 1842, was accompanied by 'new music' arranged by the Town Band.[18] The occasional boast that a production featured 'original music' suggests that the early period was one in which the musical content of such productions was often cobbled together shortly before the performance or perhaps on the night itself.

A small professional theatre orchestra was brought to Melbourne in 1845 by Coppin, himself an experienced theatre violinist and musical director. This orchestra comprised at least two violins, a cello and, according to Coppin's diary, the 'first cornett and piston [sic] heard in Melbourne' and was its first 'professional band'. [19]

Town Bands

The history of Melbourne orchestral stage accompaniment can, in general, be said to date from the early town bands. Among their other functions, town and suburban bands continued to represent a major source of talented musicians for theatrical entertainments throughout the nineteenth and early twentieth century. The first town band (which incidentally included 'Black Jack', 'a man of colour') also had a dubious reputation as a dance band.[20] It therefore foreshadowed an important sociological and musical relationship between bandsmen and dance musicians. Indeed, Finn's description of the behaviour of this first band suggests an early precedent for the type of larrikin 'band boy' culture that has traditionally reinforced a concept of 'the band' as a male enclave.

By the late 1840s Melbourne also had a band comprising the newly invented saxhorns – the first 'brass band' as such. Hore's Saxe Horn Band, as this ubiquitous ensemble came to be known, played an important role in Melbourne musical development in the following years and was the harbinger of a Victorian brass band movement that would grow to massive proportions in the early twentieth century. This movement, with its direct and historic links to militarism (particularly through the volunteer movement in Victoria), subsequently became a major force for musical codification and conservatism (and oppositional to improvisatory musical practice). However, bands themselves continued to emerge in a fairly haphazard manner throughout the latter half of the nineteenth century, mostly comprising various combinations of brass and reed instruments. Before the Fortieth Regiment Band was stationed in Melbourne in 1852, military bandsmen seem to have played a relatively minor role in Melbourne's musical development, especially in comparison with that of the convict settlements of New South Wales and Tasmania.

It is important to note that the early Melbourne period overlaps with what band historians consider the 'plebeian' era of British wind band history. This was prior to the establishment of uniformly regulated band contesting, commercial brass band arrangements and the widespread distribution of the newly developed saxhorn family of valve instruments (which became the basis of the modern standardised brass band). The British historians, Vic and Sheila Gammon, note that:

> It seems certain, from the evidence we have considered, that the majority of instrumentalists active in the first third of the nineteenth century were ear players, who learnt their playing without reading the notes.[21]

Therefore, even the unfavourable reports of Melbourne's earliest town bands raise the intriguing question of how these bands really sounded. Was this just the music of ear-playing musicians attempting to sound like reading musicians or was it, in fact, that of a rich, variegated and improvisatory folk tradition, one eventually purged from cultural memory by a sweeping new popular movement centred on standardised brass band playing?

By 1851 all areas of music were much more firmly established in Melbourne. This was due in part to German immigration from 1849, which brought a wealth of musical talent and concepts such as the Liedertafel, a major influence on Melbourne instrumental and vocal music until the First World War. Many of these German musicians were capable of improvising and probably did so in certain circumstances, yet their influence in Victoria was generally towards uniform, precise and disciplined musicianship. The establishment of a local theatre orchestra and casual dance band tradition was, for improvisatory practice in the Anonymous genres, the most significant feature of the early Melbourne period. Of lesser significance was the establishment of a town band tradition and the advent of the first brass band.

The Goldrush Period (1850s)

The Victorian (and New South Wales) goldrushes brought a sudden and relatively massive influx of performers, notably from Britain and America. These were generally individuals or small troupes, attracted by the prospect of extracting gold dust or nuggets from the purses of an entertainment-starved populace. It also brought a substantial decentralisation of entertainment as tent and shanty towns sprang up around the goldfields. Geelong, Ballarat, Bendigo and Castlemaine became key destinations for touring troupes and individual performers like the improvising violinist, Miska Hauser. This period was also characterised by serious social upheaval, as whole sections of the rapidly swelling population moved around Victoria in search of gold or its by-product, wealth. The type of behaviour ascribed to early Melbourne audiences was also commonplace throughout the 1850s and particularly on the goldfields.

By the mid-1850s Melbourne had become sufficiently wealthy to sustain several theatres as well as additional places of stage and other entertainment such as the Cremorne Gardens at Richmond. There was also a number of less formal places, such as entertainment and dancing saloons attached to the very numerous hotels. One observer noted at the beginning of this period that:

> At some of these [Melbourne] taverns, as they are called, 'free and easies' are held three or four nights a week, where many get intoxicated, and all who like, sing what they like, to an extempore pianoforte and violin accompaniment. Between the singing, dance tunes and popular melodies are performed by the violinist and pianiste.[22]

During this period a conceptual distinction between 'amusements' and serious entertainment began to emerge. The Australian theatre writer, Alex Bagot, points to Coppin's Melbourne production of *Othello* in 1855 with the Irish tragedian G.V. Brooke as a turning point whereby 'legitimate' Australian theatre would ultimately emerge distinct from its popular counterpart.

> Good plays had been put on in the past, but nearly always in a melange with farce and melodrama. From now on, Australian theatre was to have a new character. Serious drama, including tragedy, had come into its own.[23]

Nevertheless, the type of melange described here, combined with a high level of interaction between audience and stage, remained fairly characteristic of Melbourne and goldrush district theatre throughout most of the period. Moreover, the production of absurd farce (burlesque) based upon almost any type of performance model (even *Othello*) had become particularly popular by the late 1850s.

The flood of immigration and visitors to Melbourne also led to the diversification of entertainment genres, which now included many new musical stage acts, blackface troupes, street entertainers (buskers) and circus.

Novelty Genres and Musical Acts

'Novelty! Novelty!! Novelty!!!' was the catch-cry of the goldrush period and theatre musicians were required to provide the accompaniment for an expanding array of novelty genres.[24] Rope dancing, juggling, acrobatics, animal acts, ballet and 'phantasmagoriceccentricities' (optical illusions) had reached the Melbourne stage before the goldrush. Astley's Amphitheatre Melbourne (1853-6) – in the tradition of Astley's Amphitheatre London of the 1770s – featured equestrian acts along with more conventional theatre fare. Charles Waller's book, *Magical Nights at the Theatre,* catalogues a surprising variety of original novelty acts that passed through Melbourne theatres, halls and hotels from 1854.[25] Many of these acts (conjuring, for example) required specialised musical accompaniment of a flexible, spontaneous nature.

Among the novelty genres that became popular during the goldrush were 'trick' musical acts. These performances featured conventional instruments played in unorthodox ways; exploitation of the timbral or technical possibilities of newly-invented instruments such as the saxophone; the demonstration of unconventional instruments;

or even new instruments invented specifically for an act. Notwithstanding the actual preparation involved, these visually entertaining trick musical acts ideally unfolded with a sense of spontaneity similar to conjuring. It can be assumed that these acts would almost always have been performed without visible reference to a score in order to achieve the cohesive fluidity required of the multiple-skilled stage entertainer.

Blackface Minstrelsy

'Negro delineation' or blackface acts (by white actors in black face make-up) such as Jim Crow, 'Billy Waters' and the 'Congo Minstrel' first reached the Melbourne stage during the 1840s.[26] These characterisations were solo performances, usually presented as single entr'acte items, and the musical content seems to have comprised mostly dancing or 'Negro melody' with 'bone castinett' accompaniment. 'Negro melody' and 'Ethiopian melody' usually refer to a genre of song with words that supposedly characterised African-American slave plantation culture. After 1850, however, complete blackface minstrel troupes, capable of providing a whole evening's vocal and instrumental entertainment, began to arrive in Melbourne.

Street Entertainers (Buskers)

Impromptu musical and non-musical street entertainment, or busking, flourished in the wake of Victoria's sudden influx of gold-seeking immigrants. Thirty years later Melbourne reportedly still had, among other forms of busking, 'its share of ladies and gentleman who play the barrel organ, violin, mandolin, banjo, flute, flageolet, and trombone.'[27] Busking has historic links with both popular theatre and circus and has a strongly aural tradition of music-making. In fact the term is still commonly used by Melbourne dance band musicians when referring to the practice of playing without a score. Melbourne street musicians are still described as 'buskers'.

Literature from the goldrush period provides very little detail of street entertainment. This is probably due, first, to the itinerant nature of the work and, second, to the fact that reasonably good performers would have been quickly absorbed into music halls and tent shows in the entertainment-starved goldrush, perhaps to reappear in the streets or local showgrounds when times were harder. Henry Mayhew's published series of interviews with mid-nineteenth-century London street entertainers does, however, provide direct insight into this genre.[28]

Mayhew's informants give detailed descriptions of the musical accompaniment for various forms of puppetry, itinerant actors, acrobats, rope dancers, stilt vaulters, jugglers, conjurers, street clowns, Billy Barlow and 'penny equestrian shows' among others. Street musicians (which Mayhew classifies as tolerable or intolerable) included hurdy-gurdy players, a violinist/farmyard imitator, multi-instrumentalists, pipers (Irish/Scotch/Italian), English street bands, German street bands, harp players, barrel organ players, Italian clarinet players, concertina players, tom-tom players, blackface minstrels, and ballad singers. The majority of these musicians are said to have played by ear.[29]

Circus

Edmund Finn described a performance in 1849 of the first Melbourne circus as:

> little more than the faintest semblance of a circus, the occasion scraping together all the scum and low villainy of the town; and during, and for hours after, the performances, the place, and its precincts witnessed scenes of riot, blackguardism, and outrage of every kind.[30]

This circus was quite short-lived and does not appear to have been replaced until the arrival of Noble's Olympic Circus in 1852, followed several months later by Rowe's American Circus, direct from California.[31]

Although early circus in Australia was undoubtedly directed towards colonial admiration for equestrian ability, it also included such things as novelty dances, vocal items, farce, pantomime, and blackface minstrelsy, along with various feats of daring, strength and agility. The musical accompaniment required for circus was therefore probably quite similar in function to that of the theatre music of the period. In 1852 Rowe employed Hore's Saxe Horn Band and thereafter circus in Australia became closely associated with town bands, travelling bands (notably German) and a slowly evolving Australia-wide brass band movement.

Dancing

Dancing became a particularly important form of entertainment for Victoria's restless and socially disoriented population during the goldrush. Almost any occasion was sufficient reason for a ball and these ranged from mammoth and highly formal civic affairs to those held in seedy entertainment rooms attached to ramshackle goldfields hotels. Small, commercially-operated dance venues sprang into existence throughout Victoria in almost every conceivable form. This development, in a sense, anticipated Australia's pre-First World War dancing boom.

Well-rehearsed and balanced string orchestras (string and wind) or all-wind bands could be obtained for important social occasions. However, the majority of Assembly

Hall, hotel annexe or bush dances were served by 'orchestras' comprising whatever instrumentation or talent was available.

By the end of the goldrush, theatre and circus were gradually becoming separate social and musical domains, as each genre became more diversified and acquired its own conventions, performance practices and employment networks. Nevertheless, a striking characteristic of the 1850s is the interconnection of various genres and the ease with which musicians and ensembles moved between them. Between the late 1840s and the early 1850s, for example, Hore's Saxe Horn Band played for ballroom dances, the circus, outdoor games, formal concerts and the first promenade concerts. It had also provided musical accompaniment to an early predecessor of silent film and was able to supply 'a strong string band, consisting of a violin, violoncello, flute, and cornet'.[32] Even the most highly respected local concert artists sometimes advertised their services as dance musicians.[33] Theatre musicians remained familiar with all the latest styles of dance music and therefore could and did take casual dance work.[34] Travelling circus bands also played for local dances and the German bands (itinerant immigrant wind bands) that were often employed by circus proprietors were particularly noted for their dance music.

The Post-Goldrush Period to the First 'Jazz Band' (1860–1918)

This period embraces the Victorian era which saw an increasing emphasis upon 'rational recreation' and the emergence of a conservative musical establishment preoccupied with fostering excellence, standardised musical education, uniform performance practice and music-reading skills. At a grassroots level this was paralleled by the slow emergence of an Australian brass band movement. British band historian Arthur R. Taylor comments that 'Brassbanding was, if you like to look at things in that way, yet another example of the Victorians' skill at codifying unruly sports and making them respectable'.[35] This was also the case in Victoria and to varying degrees in other parts of Australia. The most significant manifestation of this codification was the establishment of both the standard brass band (as opposed to the old mixed brass/reed bands) and in 1862, brass band contests, the most famous of these being the annual South Street (Ballarat) contest, established in 1900 (see Figure 2.2).

The Australian band movement's links with the volunteer military movement intensified its focus on uniform appearance, behaviour and musical standards. In a booklet published in 1902, *Chats on Amateur Bands*, J. Orde Hume explains some of the rationale for military-style uniformity: 'The effect rivets one for the moment, and our exclamation is – splendid! Everything is smart, clean, bright, and uniform to a degree;

The Quickstep Contest.

The appended table shows the points awarded by the judge (Drum-Major Longuehayes) in the quick-step contest at the City Oval on Friday last, and he gives notes on the marching :—

No	Band.	Music	Marching	Total	MUSIC
3	PROUT'S	30	38	68	UNDER. BANNER. VICTORY
8	BATHURST	32	31	63	BATHURST.
6	GEELONG	34	29	63	20th CENTURY
9	EAGLEHAWK	23	36	59	POSTMAN'S PARADE.
2	LORD NELSON...	28	30	58	POSTMAN'S. PARADE.
1	THIRD BATTALION	20	37	57	MOUNT. WASHINGTON.
5	HOPETOUN	24	32	56	ON. THE. WARPATH.
4	BULCH'S	24	29	53	THE. TYPHOON.
7	LAUNCESTON	20	16	36	PRIDE. OF THE. BATTERY

No. 1 BAND (3rd BATTALION).

General Appearance.—Very smart; men well set up, clean and tidy, evidently been well drilled. Intervals and dressing.—In turning to the left one man in second rank did not turn in rank, two men were out of line in wheeling to right Instruments and Accoutrements.—The instruments and accoutrements clean and in good condition. Marching.—The marching and countermarching was executed in soldierlike manner, for which they gained full points.

NO. 2 BAND (LORD NELSON).

General Appearance.—Good, clean, and tidy. Three men did not have their heels closed in front rank; two in No. 2 rank. Intervals and Dressing.—Lost 2 points for not keeping the proper covering, and 2 points for not wheeling properly to right. Instruments and Accoutrements.—In good and clean condition, with the exception of bass, trombone, and trombone dirty, 3 points. Marching.—Done correctly and to time.

NO. 3 BAND (PROUT'S)

General Appearance.—Splendid; no fault. Intervals and Dressing.—In wheeling to right two men were out of dressing. Instruments and Accroutrements.—In splendid condition; evidently well looked after. Marching.—Correct and to time.

NO. 4 BAND (BULCH'S)

General Appearance.—Fair. The band lost 3 points for having dirty boots. Intervals and Dressing.—Front rank not properly dressed, three men being out of line. They also lost 5 points for wheeling incorrectly, and properly covering when turning to the left. Instruments and Accoutrements.—Very clean. Marching.—Correctly done.

NO. 5 BAND (HOPETOUN).

General Appearance.—Smart, well set up Intervals and Dressing.—In turning to the left the band lost 3 points for not keeping proper intervals, and 2 points for not being halted with flag post opposite centre of band. Instruments and Accoutrements.—Instruments very clean; 2 lyres short. Marching.—Two points were lost for taking 62 seconds to clear red flag.

NO. 6 BAND (GEELONG TOWN).

General Appearance.—Smart, neat, and clean. Intervals and Dressing.—Very Bad. Lost 3 points in wheeling, 5 points for not properly covering and intervals. Instruments and Accoutrements.—Very clean. Marching.—Three seconds over time through not keeping proper intervals

NO. 7 BAND (LAUNCESTON).

General Appearance.—Very dirty; cross belts and pouches exceedingly dirty, and not properly put on. Boots, etc., very dirty. Intervals and Dressing.—Did not halt with centre of band opposite flag pole; 2 men out of dressing in wheeling. Instruments and Accoutrements.—Very dirty. Marching.—Drum-major kept too far to the left of band, and continued to do so.

NO. 8 BAND (BATHURST).

General Appearance.—Splendid. Intervals and Dressing.—Lost 3 points in wheeling to right. Instruments and Accoutrements.—Very clean. Marching.—One second behind time.

NO. 9 BAND (EAGLEHAWK.

General Appearance.—Fair. Two men's tunics partially unbuttoned. Intervals and Dressing.—Drum-major too far in front of his band; as he continued to keep too far ahead the band lost 2 points. Also not having centre of band opposite flag staff, 2 points One point in wheeling to right through not keeping dressing. Instruments and Accoutrements.—One bass dirty. Marching.—Correctly done.

SATURDAY CONTEST

NO. 1 BAND (BATHURST).

This band lost 12 points for not keeping proper intervals and dressing.

NO. 2 BAND (GEELONG).

Lost 21 points incorrect dressing and wheeling and not keeping correct intervals; also drum-major keeping too far to left of his band and not counter-marching correctly.

Figure 2.2. From the judges' report of the 1900 South St Band Contest. Note the emphasis upon appearance and demeanour.

but if we were to hear the same march by the same men, only with rusty looking instruments, the effect would be completely absent.'[36] To the circus bandmaster, the dance band leader, the variety theatre conductor and the cinema orchestra conductor (and subsequently the jazz band leader), the emerging band movement represented a burgeoning Australia-wide pool of homogeneously disciplined musicians, including many of exceptional talent. This points to a significant anomaly in the history of improvisatory practice. The brass band movement represented increasingly intractable musical conservatism, with its obvious impact on the notion of individual musical freedom of expression. A 1918 *Australian Band News* article, 'Mannerisms in Music', explains why individuality is undesirable in brass band playing.[37] Yet this same movement also produced many of the pioneers of Australian jazz.[38]

Post-Goldrush Theatre

After the goldrush subsided, a more orderly pattern of social development began to emerge. The establishment of musical organisations and increasing musical codification were accompanied by a growing taste for more formal, comfortable and sophisticated venues for entertainment. By the 1860s, several very large theatres, even by London standards, had been built and in subsequent years many notable actors and opera singers would visit Melbourne. Theatre producers still encountered major problems with the staging of plays, pantomimes and opera; nevertheless, staging and music were now much less haphazard and audience behaviour less disruptive. The overt audience-stage interaction and general informality that had characterised Australian theatre in the past was increasingly restricted to the cheaper forms of popular entertainment, such as the music or variety hall.[39]

The highly stylised serio-comic melodrama of early colonial theatre was, by now, considered something of bygone days and appeared only as farce or burlesque (although it was revived for silent film acting).[40] Much of the musical practice associated with the original form of melodrama had begun to become redundant much earlier as demand for unified (especially composed) accompaniment increased. The late nineteenth century also gave rise to a new 'realist' form of indigenous Australian melodrama that did not require the starkly overstated accompaniment of its predecessor.[41]

Variety and Vaudeville

The roots of Australian variety theatre – later called vaudeville – are located in early theatre entr'acte entertainment, the leasing out of theatres to circuses, blackface minstrel troupes, magicians and so forth and local variants of the English music hall tradition.[42]

As early as the 1860s Melbourne had a theatre called the Varieties that provided diverse popular entertainment. In the early 1890s the English entertainer, Harry Rickards, introduced a style of vaudeville to Sydney and subsequently Melbourne audiences that comprised a minstrel show in the first half followed by a program of variety acts in the second. Of the minstrel show segment, Charles Norman writes:

> In 1895 the stars of Mr Rickards' Tivoli theatre were Pope and Sayles, two negroes of exceptional talent. . . The set-up was a semi-circle of performers with the interlocutor in the centre, behind him and to either side sat the ladies of varying talents. The back row was filled with what were termed 'seat warmers'. These were ladies of little talent but well dressed and used mainly for decoration. . . There would be all sorts of ad lib fun from the comedians, vying with each other for local gags and jokes.[43]

What came to be known as Australian vaudeville therefore emerged in association with a much-diluted version of the minstrel show tradition.

By the beginning of the First World War the two main vaudeville formats in Australia were vaudeville/revue and 'straight vaudeville' (all variety). In vaudeville/revue the first half of the show, a sequence of variety acts, was followed in the second half by:

> a potted revue, in which a thin story-line was used to connect a series of comedy sequences, backed by song and dance numbers.[44]

At this time the two main vaudeville rivals in Melbourne were Hugh McIntosh's Tivoli Theatre (formerly the Opera House) and Benjamin Fuller's Bijou Theatre. The 'Tiv' and the Bijou both belonged to interstate circuits, which were also included on the big international vaudeville circuits. Other vaudeville networks were established to serve the smaller city, suburban and provincial town venues and these frequently featured both variety and cinema.

The performance practices associated with the musical accompaniment of straight vaudeville had to be flexible and spontaneous enough to accommodate a new set of speciality acts each week – usually on the basis of one very brief rehearsal with, at most, the bare bones of a score.

The 'revue' associated with Australian vaudeville was also often underpinned by talented comedians such as Nat Phillips and Roy Rene (Stiffy and Mo). Such artists were noted for their ad libbing and it is not difficult to imagine the level of playful, spontaneous musical interaction and burlesque that their 'pleasant gullible clowning' encouraged from the orchestra pit. The main musical collaborator in this respect was the theatre percussionist.[45]

American and African-American Influence

Theatre became a conduit for American popular culture and both white and African-American performance exerted an influence in Australian variety theatre, circus and dance music. Americans began to make their presence felt in Australia in the 1790s, when American whalers first began to invade the Pacific. It was only during the gold-rush, however, that this influence became really apparent. One early historian writes:

> of all the foreign elements then attracted to our young Colony there were none that took such hold, stamped it with a new quality of keenness, penetrated it with a new sense of energy and enterprise, as the American element.[46]

Americans were admired for their energy, forthrightness, inventiveness and for the many improvements and developments they initiated. Daniel and Annette Potts provide an invaluable account of early American theatrical influence in *Young America and Australian Gold*.[47] Two prominent examples of American influence in Australian theatre are the Irish-American opera entrepreneur William Lyster, who is given much of the credit for Australia's 'golden age' of opera in the late nineteenth century; and James Cassius (J.C.) Williamson, who was similarly influential as a theatrical entrepreneur.[48]

The Influence of American Circus

Perhaps because of their energy and success, Americans seem to have been identified almost immediately with display, boastfulness and exaggeration. Mark St Leon writes of the mammoth American circuses that visited Australia during the late nineteenth century:

> The size and splendour of American circuses quite eclipsed their Australian contemporaries. They gave colonial audiences a taste of Yankee culture. The menageries, the boastful advertising, grand parades, circus trains and other trademarks of the American circus were adopted by the St Leons and by a succession of the largest Australian circuses which gradually divested themselves of a staid British heritage.[49]

The non-musical characteristics of American circus that St Leon describes here are in fact analogous with the exuberant, starkly contrasting colours and exaggerated effects heard in late nineteenth and early twentieth-century American band music, notably the circus music of Fred Jewell, Karl L. King and Russell Alexander. A widely known example is Karl King's 'Barnum and Bailey's Favorite' (1913), which has become internationally synonymous with circus and is frequently used in screen or television productions.[50] Although similar qualities also existed to some degree in the transplanted British theatre music tradition, Australian musicians were doubtless impressed and influenced by the flamboyance and colour of touring American circus band music.

By the early 1890s, the big American circuses had ceased to visit Australia, leaving the field largely open to the the small to medium travelling bush circuses and several larger Australian circuses which served the burgeoning capital cities on a seasonal basis.

Late Nineteenth-Century Blackface and Black (African-American) Minstrelsy

The American blackface minstrel shows that reached Melbourne during the goldrush were characterised by informality, extroversion, spontaneity and risqué rapid-fire humour. Early minstrelsy offered a theatrical representation of the perceived primitive performance culture of African-American plantation slaves, but later minstrelsy in Australia was strongly influenced by the British-style 'Christy companies'. Christy-style minstrelsy generally sought to avoid offence and tended to emphasise orthodox instrumental and vocal musicianship.

The 1870s brought some resurgence of American influence in Australian minstrelsy, beginning with the Melbourne opening of Frank Weston's Opera House. This theatre was established by Weston, an American, as the first theatre in Australia to specialise in blackface minstrelsy.[51] Moreover, the establishment of a regular steamship service between San Francisco, Sydney and Melbourne in 1871 gave American entertainers fast, comfortable and cheap access to an affluent and expanding Australian market. 'American minstrel companies flocked to Australia as never before and the colonies became simply an extension of the western circuit'.[52]

African-American minstrel companies also began to arrive in the late 1870s and their novelty value ensured them a limited degree of popularity. The most notable of the early black troupes was Hicks' Original Georgia Minstrels, who collaborated with a local theatre company in a successful Melbourne production of the melodrama *Uncle Tom's Cabin*.[53] Although some black troupes continued to tour into the 1890s, generally speaking, this period marks the end of the main era of large black (and blackface) American touring minstrel troupes in Australia.

By 1900 minstrelsy had long ceased to be a novelty genre, but around 1903 the Cake Walk (an improvisatory, African-American influenced stage and social dance), cakewalk music (syncopated, march-like, dance music) and 'coon song' (syncopated song with textual reference to contemporary African-American culture) became the latest vogue in Australian popular culture. These forms are all subgenres of early ragtime music and dance.

Shortly before the First World War a world-wide craze for a new type of syncopated vocal music was precipitated by the success of Tin Pan Alley hits such as Irving Berlin's 'Alexander's Ragtime Band'. The popularity of the new 'ragtime' also resulted in the importation of numerous ragtime variety artists to Australia, most of whom were Americans.[54] The term ragtime, unless qualified (e.g. classic ragtime or 1910s ragtime song), is used hereafter as a generic term embracing the various genres of pre-jazz, African-American influenced music, as it did at the time.

Ragtime Dancing

The pre-War ragtime craze was also associated with the most important changes to occur in Australian dancing since the introduction of the 'closed couple' dances in the early 1800s. These changes include public dancing on a commercial scale, made possible by increasing urbanisation (as reflected in the construction of the original St Kilda Palais de Danse late in 1913) and a change in emphasis from specific steps to 'bodily rhythm' or moving the whole body to the rhythm of the music.[55] More importantly, the segmented 'vamp-like' nature of ragtime rhythm made it possible for dancers to ignore the overall unfolding of dance melody and form, and interact creatively with syncopated patterns such as ♫ ♫♫ ♫.

The outbreak of the First World War brought Melbourne's budding public dancing boom to a sudden halt. Established 'string orchestras' such as Rosenthal's or De Gilio's were able to find a thread of work through patriotic balls and similar functions but, at a time when Australian society was both fearful of the direction the War was taking and in bitter conflict over the conscription debate, these functions were often very formal and sombre affairs.

Ragtime dancing was often associated with the 'smart set' and the latest in fashion, but there is also evidence that it became identified with such things as youthful rebellion, pacifism, and left-wing and unpatriotic sentiments.[56] Indeed, newspaper advertisements sometimes declared 'Ragtime Dancing strictly prohibited'.[57] By the end of the War, Ragtime dancing had once again become fashionable – although in a more refined form. Melbourne's *Footlight Star* declared in 1919 that the One-Step or 'rag' was the most popular dance of the hour, but 'much more "classy" now'; at the same time warning that 'no freak innovations' should be allowed in this dance.[58]

Silent Cinema

> And her hands jump here and her hands jump there,
> While betimes with one she will fix her hair,
> But she keeps right on with the other hand,
> In a ragtime tune that is simply grand. . .
>
> From 'Lizzie Plays for the Pictures'[59]

Although the Edison Kinetascope (on which a loop of moving film was viewed through an eyepiece) reached Australia in 1894, the Australian silent film era is widely perceived to have begun in 1896 at the 'Opera House' in Melbourne, with the screening of a number of short, mostly unrelated segments of film as an item on the variety bill.[60] This event represents the beginning of a long screen/variety act relationship which initially comprised the screening of short films as a support to vaudeville or circus bills. Later this relationship was reversed and variety acts began to supplement the screening of film in the new cinemas. This second phase followed the pre-First World War establishment of a highly successful Australian and American-owned film exhibiting industry and the introduction of various improvements and changes to film exhibition, including the advent of full-length feature films and 'continuous exhibiting' (11am-11pm).

Just before the First World War the demand for cinema began to spread rapidly throughout urban and country Australia. Based on the mass-produced image and its technology (film and projector) rather than a finite pool of talented performers, the expansion of this new form of entertainment was seemingly unlimited. Film could be exhibited anywhere: an outdoor area, a prefabricated shed, a Mechanics Hall or a specially constructed cinema. There was not, however, an unlimited supply of versatile theatre-type accompanists to meet this expanding demand and exhibitors very often had to settle for whatever local musical talent was available.

Some idea of the number of musicians employed in the cinema industry is indicated by the fact that, even by the beginning of the War, people living in well-populated Melbourne suburbs usually had several permanent cinemas within walking distance, all of which would employ an orchestra of some description or a pianist. The situation was similar in regional centres such as Geelong and Ballarat. Those towns and communities that did not have some form of permanent cinema were served by travelling exhibitors who generally employed a pianist.

Cinema accompaniment ran counter to the attempts of Australian music educators, the brass band movement and other forces in the musical community to codify musical practice. Although cinema orchestras and pianists throughout Australia often accompanied the same popular films, the many variables associated with the task made the achievement of broad musical uniformity impossible. This is most apparent in the case of the solo cinema accompanist. Regardless of what the cue sheets may have suggested, once the film began to roll the solo pianist was really only limited by imagination, repertoire, technique and intuitive judgement. Rita Sheehan, whose parents managed an Australian silent cinema, recalls their pianist's music as:

> an incredible lucky dip of pieces that seldom matched the action. The maiden died in the hero's arms to a rousing rendition of 'Colonel Bogey', or the 'Teddy Bear's Picnic', depend-

> ing on the train of thought Smithy might be pursuing at the time. Often the cavalry charged over the hill to 'The Rustle of Spring' played, as a concession, in ragtime.[61]

American and to a lesser extent African-American influence was also a significant factor in cinema music, particularly after 1910, when Americans began to gain control over a substantial proportion of the Australian cinema industry. American cue sheets, orchestrations, collections of dramatic and 'descriptive' music and 'how to accompany' literature all had an influence on the type of music played in Australian cinemas. In fact, ragtime may have reached more Australians through the cinema than through any other performance medium in these pre-radio and recording industry days, for ragtime arrangements were a part of every up-to-date cinema orchestra library. Cinema pianists such as the one described by Sheehan could even make 'Rustle of Spring' sound modern and rhythmic by 'ragging it', that is, by embellishing it in ragtime style.

Part II: Improvisatory Performance Practice in Four Anonymous Genres

Dance Music

> 'Yes, my brother "musiker" was a valuable help, although he could not vamp to the songs strange to him. All he could do was to play 'toons out of his own hed, and wot he picked up wen he herd bands play at "Mayne" or "Rat".' By this, I presumed he meant Castlemaine or Ballarat.
>
> St John Caws, 'Experiences of a New Chum in Victoria in the Early Sixties'[62]

I first began to play dance music not with jazz musicians but with members of the Melbourne brass band community. A tradition of amateur brass band musicians who play dance music on a part-time basis can be traced back to Melbourne's first 'town band' and my experience of playing dance music with these brass band/dance band musicians provided valuable insight into the sort of improvisatory skills that were probably required of dance musicians before Australian dance bands began to play jazz.

Although these brass/dance band musicians always included some popular jazz 'standards' in their repertoire, in the form of slow or medium tempo Foxtrot or Quickstep dance tunes, they did not, generally speaking, identify with the jazz tradition or the freedom of jazz improvisation, which was aesthetically, socially and culturally at odds with their first love, brass band music. Yet many of these musicians were able to play almost any request (within certain stylistic bounds) without a part. They could also fake block harmonies or (to a lesser degree) counter-melodies and embellish or 'fill-in' in a minimal way where required. All they generally asked was for someone to 'call the tune and/or key' and 'count in'. I noted, for example, that a string bass player such as Teddy Ellis (a champion euphonium player of the 1920s) would never bother to look at the dance band parts. His explanation was that playing the string bass was just a matter of being able to hear down to the 'foot-note' of the chord.[63] While sight-reading was an important skill in this work it was equally important to be able to play without notation, or 'busk'.

For my own part, as a keyboard player, I had to learn quickly how to fake introductions, endings and modulations; spontaneously interpolate or leave out a section of music (particularly in dances with sequences of steps); transpose on sight or by ear; play accompaniments by ear; spontaneously 'fill-out' or otherwise modify a given arrangement to suit a particular ensemble structure or type of dance; spin out simple dance tunes by embellishing or otherwise varying each repetition of my solo or 'break' (for example, to give the sole trumpet player's lip a rest); and 'fill-in' gaps left by the lead instrument (e.g. at phrase endings or cadences). I also had to learn how to add metronomic propulsive dance rhythm to popular music.

Although this list of improvisatory practices may seem daunting it was, and still is, the absolute minimum for a pianist working in a casual dance music network. Furthermore, I would suggest that versatile 'all round' dance musicians have always needed most (and in the case of pianists, all) of the following: a memorised library of common repertoire; knowledge of the style characteristics of the music and dances to be performed; deeply-learned technique (scales, arpeggios, etc.); knowledge of the stock devices (introductions, endings, modulations, transposition, vamping, etc.); structural hearing (to be able to sense chord changes); theoretical knowledge (practical harmony and chord nomenclature); instrumental voice-leading ability (e.g. for faking block harmonies or counter-melody); and absolute pitch (aural recognition of individual pitches) or good relative pitch (the conscious or subconscious aural recognition of intervals). Putting aside natural talent and basic technical proficiency, the key factors in gaining these skills are the accumulation of an internalised repertoire (which also provides an expanding store of useful sound patterns); the ability to transpose (which gives one the ability to play these sound patterns at any pitch level); and professional opportunity (which constantly forces the musician to 'have a go').

These attributes were certainly required in the late 1890s. The memoirs of a Melbourne brass band musician record that, when introduced to the Melbourne casual dance circuit as a 'raw youth' from rural Victoria, his prospective employer, the pianist leader, said:

> 'You will need to be not only a good reader, but you must be able to 'fake' as well, for we have no cornet parts for quite a number of ditties which dancers ask for'. I told him that when in the country I did quite a lot of that sort of thing; in fact it was a rare thing ever to see cornet parts for this brand of playing – which was perfectly true.[64]

Musicians with more ability than is required for playing dance music often engage in playful improvisatory interaction, particularly where players are very familiar with each other's capabilities and share a common repertoire of dance tunes. Faking or busking also occurs where musicians cannot read music; where band parts are unavailable, inappropriate, illegible or poorly catalogued; or when other contingencies (other than lack of parts) arise. I have no doubt that these situations have always been a part of playing dance music in Australia.

Playing by Ear

> As the night deepened, a blaring band began to play, and the tramp of awful dancers' feet ushered in my first midnight in Melbourne. Tramp, tramp, tramp – thump, thump, thump – blare, blare, blare.
>
> From a journalist's memoirs of Melbourne in 1855.[65]

Illustrations of nineteenth-century dancing are particularly striking for the contrast they portray between the elegance and formality of ballroom scenes on the one hand, and on the other, the ecstatic musical and terpsichorean abandonment in, for example, the 'Miners' Dance' (see Figures 2.3a-b). It will be noted that the musicians in the less formal contexts often play without music and assume a demeanour not unlike jazz musicians.

There is no doubt that a considerable proportion of Australian dance music was played without reference to notation. While some rural dance music was provided by, say, the young, possibly formally-trained female pianist of the household or a cornet, violin and piano ensemble (possibly reading from Francis & Day or Wright & Round stock dance arrangements or their equivalent), the majority of 'fiddle' and, after the 1840s, fiddle and button accordion-type dance music heard throughout rural Victoria was provided by self-taught ear players.[66]

Pictorial evidence and the field-work of collectors since the 1950s, such as John Meredith, although conducted relatively recently, further support what is self-evident: that the isolation of colonial Australian life, and especially rural colonial life, fostered self-taught musicianship.[67] E.S. Emerson paints some vivid images of the performances

Figure 2.3a (above). W. Lacy, 'Miners Dance', *Illustrated Australian News,* 28 May 1867 (Courtesy La Trobe Library, State Library of Victoria).

Figure 2.3b (left). S.T. Gill's 'Subscription Ball, Main Road, Ballaratt' [sic]' (1852). (Courtesy La Trobe Picture Collection, State Library of Victoria).

of an ear-playing bush accordionist called the Rat, in his grossly nationalistic novel, A Shanty Entertainment (c.1909).[68] What can be observed in the unfolding of this music (depending of course upon the natural talent and experience of the performer) is a particular type of sonic open-endedness that cannot be fully represented by notation.

Variations

'Well, len's me accordyon', replied The Rat, 'an I'll give yers' 'Ome Sweet 'Ome with variations.'

From E. S. Emerson, *A Shanty Entertainment*, p. 59.

In the introduction to *Folk Songs of Australia*, Roger Covell and Patricia Brown point out that:

> elaborations of dance tunes within the correct metrical format of the dance. . . [are] an integral part of good dance accompaniment and always have been. . . Dance tunes are usually short. . . . They can be spun out by being linked to other tunes for the same dance and/or by being provided with nimble elaboration and other kinds of variation. Such elaboration should ideally spring from the itchy fingers of the player in that phase of his or her mastery of the tune when merely playing the basic notes leaves hands and mind with a feeling of being underemployed.[69]

Where bush dance music was based around simple popular dance tunes of the day, such as 'Pop Goes the Weasel', 'Nix My Dolly' or 'Jim Crow', there was an even greater natural invitation to clever variation.

Without sound recordings or transcriptions of nineteenth-century Australian rural music-making it is probably safest to assume that melodic elaboration comprised, at most, the symmetrical division of the beat with diatonic chord, passing and neighbour tones, while the melodic outline and rhythmic placement of melody notes was more or less retained. A transcribed example of a variation published in *Folk Songs of Australia* fits this description.[70]

Melodic elaboration or variations in nineteenth-century step-dances (e.g. Quadrilles) had to be fairly simple and symmetrical since the melody served as an aural map for the dancers. To transform a tune beyond recognition was to risk confusing inexperienced dancers. Variation would have also included the interpolation of various effects, for example, double stopping on fiddle, ornaments and various idiosyncratic rhythmic, timbral and pitch incongruencies associated with unorthodox technique.

Dance Pianists

Pianists have always played an important role in Melbourne dance music. At the 1839 Bachelors' Ball some women pianists among the guests took over from the town band which apparently was not up to the task of providing suitable dance music.[71] It was also very common for nineteenth-century pianists to compose their own dance music (see Figure 2.4). It will be recalled, for example, that Patton's *Harmony Simplified for Popular Use* provided 'skeleton forms' for the composition of waltzes, polkas,

BRAID'S Melbourne Assembly Rooms, Russell-street, corner of Little Collins-street.
The Proprietors beg to inform their friends and the public that their second grand monthly Subscription Ball will take place this evening, August 3rd, at the above Rooms. The following is the Programme, which contains some new and elegant dance music, composed expressly for these Rooms:—

PART FIRST

1 Quadrille—Hungarian ... ... Jullien
2 Polka—Bridesmaids ... ... Jolly
3 Spanish Valse
4 Lancers
5 Schottische—Original
6 Valse—Wild Flowers ... ... Jullien
7 Polka—Braid's Assembly ... ... Radford
8 Quadrille—Canotier Parisienne ... Bosisio
9 Schottische—Atherton
10 Galope—Flight of Haynau from Barclay and Perkins' draymen.

An interval of fifteen minutes.

PART SECOND.

11 Quadrille-Polka—Les dames de Varsovie
12 Valse a deux temps ... ... Jullien
13 Polka—Abbotsford ... ... Jones
14 Quadrille—Caledonian
15 Schottische—Hungarian ... ... D'Albert
16 Valse—Lucrezia Borgia ... ... Jullien
17 Quadrille—New ... ... Radford
18 Polka—Argus. ... ... Ditto
19 Country Dance
20 Galope—Spirit of the Ball ... ... D'Albert
21 National Anthem.

CHARLES & JOHN BRAID, Proprietors.
13012

Figure 2.4. Advertised program for a dancing venue, *Argus,* 2 May 1853. Note the reference to new music composed for this venue.

mazurkas, galops and schottische. It is fairly safe to assume that professional dance pianist-composers could both play and embellish their own music without the need of a score.

The considerable volume of surviving notated music by colonial pianist-composers (where it has not been purposely simplified) probably gives some idea of the type of accompaniment patterns and fills that these pianists applied to simple dance tunes 'on the job'.[72] The dance section of the song 'The Home of the Hardy Norsemen', from Marcus Clarke's play *Alfred the Great* (1878), suggests one type of embellishment late nineteenth-century professional musicians probably applied to popular tunes as dance music (see Musical Ex. 2.1). Note that the dotted note/triplet rhythmic paraphrase of the tune is identical to what I describe in Chapter Five as one form of 'jazzing up' popular music for dancing.

A key purpose of the numerous vamping systems published in Australia in the late

Musical Ex. 2.1. Third verse and two of the dance sections from the song, 'The Home of the Hardy Norsemen' (1878), by Fred Lyster.[74]

nineteenth century was to provide instruction in improvisatory accompaniment for dancing. For example, W.M. Perrier states in his *Art of Vamping* that:

> Any light music such as waltz or schottische airs, or preludes to song &c., may be accompanied. . . Step-dances may also be accompanied in the same way by playing any of the popular *hornpipe, jig, or reel airs* in the R.H., and accompanying with the L.H. chords, according to the *time* required. A good impromptu time may also be formed for *American breakdowns, &c.,* from the ordinary changes as marked in any of the keys in the diagrams.[73]

In his memoirs, 'Experiences of a New Chum in Victoria in the Early Sixties', the pianist St John Caws, who played in a goldfields hotel dance hall in the 1860s, generally refers to his playing as vamping or improvising and never mentions the use of sheet music. The type of contingencies Caws describes are those that have always faced pianists working in the more seedy establishments:

> I sat down to the claviers and attempted to run a scale in C ma[jor]. To my dismay none of the white keys in the four octaves right and left from the centre of the keyboard would reply, owing to broken strings or dislocated hammer-heads; moreover, there were the remains of several mice-nests, which I had to clean out before I tried again to get it to sound. In preluding, I discovered that the black notes had scarcely been touched, and that there were tuneful notes in the key of D flat, and that a melody or vamp could be 'knocked out' by judicious management. . . [75]
>
> [I was] called upon to provide improvised accompaniments to German, French and other foreign airs of which [I] had not the slightest idea of the tunes; but that did not matter; the vamp pretty well agreed with the vocalists' efforts. . . In a life long experience I invariably find that those who sing not by note sing in G flat major, and a knowledge of the common chord, with its inversions, will invariably pull one through, no matter what tune the singer by ear selects; and the key referred to is always a safe one to accompany unknown airs.[76]

Caws also complains that many customers seemed unable to dance to anything much more sophisticated than 'Pop Goes the Weasel'.[77]

One of the key functions of the piano in dance music is to supply strong rhythm. This became even more important in the twentieth century as dancing based on step patterns was superseded by dancing based on body rhythm. In an autobiographical article, the Sydney dance pianist Fred H. Gooch (who, like Caws, had to play on pianos 'minus a few strings, teeth and pedals'), recalls that:

> Dance music in those days [1890-1914] was invariably supplied by a solo pianist, although three piece orchestras, piano, violin and cornet were occasionally used, or, if the importance of the function demanded it, the orchestra was augmented by the addition of a flute or double bass . . . It was the usual thing for three or four hundred dancers to be perfectly satisfied with our [the solo pianist's] ability to fill the hall with volume and rhythm.[78]

Musical Ex. 2.2. The last 16 bars of 'The Squirrel Parade' by Warren Crosby.

Gooch also makes mention of pianists using the stock Francis & Day arrangements. As these were relatively skeletal arrangements, it can be concluded that pianists sought or invented their own techniques for creating fuller, more propulsive dance music (Musical Ex. 2.2). The solution to this problem, namely, the improvisatory interpolation of the 'full' or 'professional' bass, is discussed in subsequent chapters.

Another pre-war phenomenon was the so-called 'black note kings': solo dance pianists who avoided the white keys of the piano. Eric Pearce, who later led the renowned 2FC Studio Dance Orchestra of the 1920s, claims to have been a black note king before the First World War.[79] It is not clear whether this is a reference to playing ragtime, to the preference of some ear players for the black notes, or whether it is just a comment upon the poor condition of local pianos. Nevertheless, it points to the presence of some form of unorthodox improvisatory practice.

Performance practice and context

Since the beginning of social dancing in Melbourne, social context has been an important determinant of the degree to which music can be altered or embellished in performance. Music that functions to break down social inhibitions and generate ecstatic excitement is played differently to music intended to accompany serene, graceful dancing. Social informality encourages musicians to 'do things' to the music to make it more exciting and the dancers also feel encouraged to improvise. William Kelly, describing a Melbourne dance of the 1850s for example, records

> . . . the grotesque gymnastics of their dance, which resembled nothing in the world I can bring to mind so much as the awkward bobbing and jostling of empty bottles in a water-butt: polking [sic] with an Irish jig step, performing the schottische in the style of the Highland fling, and waltzing like so many Westmoreland wrestlers. I derived a wicked enjoyment in the corroboree. . . in a joyous spirit of mad revelry, I went in for a squeeze and 'double shuffle' with some spinsters, whose perfumery was beginning to succumb to odours of a very different nature.[80]

Another observation of dance music and dancing in Melbourne during the goldrush illustrates how the social context could encourage improvisatory interaction between musicians and dancers, with one spurring the other on to greater deviation from orthodox performance behaviour:

> At other of the public-houses, balls, such as would disgrace the very lowest pot-house in England, are of frequent occurrence. The ball-room is generally a rude, undecorated apartment; the scene one of wild confusion; here they dance grotesquely, there a quadrille, a sailor does a hornpipe in one corner; some Scotch reel, with arms a-kimbo in another; a posse of Irish merrily jig and hugh on the left, while seated on a long form on the right, men and women drink, curse and send everyone but themselves to perdition, the musicians all the time playing a popular nigger melody, or the like, as loud and fast as they can. Such are the everyday pot-house balls in Melbourne; need I add, that the fair dancers are the most degraded of their sex.
>
> The orchestra frequently consists of a violinist and a drummer, who each labour for the ascendency in a manner truly ludicrous. The violinist rasps and saws regardless alike of time, tune, or any one thing, but rendering inaudible the melody that is, or should be, streaming from his cremona, which, despite his exertions, is overpowered and crowned by the incessant thundering of the huge drum, while an occasional extra whack, enough to burst the drum's head in, electrifies the dancers, and sets them prancing away with their hob-nail boots, noisy as dray-horses, graceful as crocodiles. It would appear that the masses prefer noise to music: a cornet-à-piston, two or three horns, an ophicleide, and a couple of monster drums, all roaring away with little tune and no time, appear to enchant them.[81]

The level of spontaneous musical transformation can, however, be quite minimal, involving perhaps a slight shift in rhythmic accentuation or tempo, a more abandoned approach to tone production or the interpolation of an occasional surface embellishment.

Other important aspects of improvisatory practice in dance music are discussed later in relation to early Australian 'jazz', where I return to the topic of transformed ('jazzed up') music for dancing.

THEATRE MUSIC

Melodrama Accompaniment

Early melodrama accompaniment probably involved a considerable degree of improvisatory musical practice in the social contexts and under the conditions in which it was performed in pre-goldrush Melbourne. Yet so little has been written about the actual performance of early melodrama music that it is very difficult to determine just how this music was played or how much dependence was placed on detailed musical notation.

This accompaniment generally comprised music for specific songs and dances, segments of 'mood music' over which actors would speak, themes to accompany the entry or exit of each character, and separate 'effects' to accompany certain actions. For example:

> When the avenging hero, with dread purpose, cried: 'Die (followed by a crashing chord in the orchestra) traitor!' (followed by another), and the heroine cried out, 'No! (tremolo violins), no! (more tremolo), don't stain your hand with his blood!' (plaintive music). . .[82]

By the mid-nineteenth century these musical clichés had become so familiar to musicians and audience alike that they had virtually taken on linguistic meaning as descriptions in sound of certain events on stage. A description of a performance of the melodrama *Bluebeard,* for example, includes the statement 'then the music goes "Ha!-a!" as he draws back his sword'.[83]

The more common musical clichés have survived through literary description and music written specially for melodrama, such as Matthew Locke's famous music for Macbeth:

> an ominous rumble of the contrabass for the villain, a trumpet fanfare for the hero, flute trills for the heroine, and a ribald guffaw from the bassoon for the comic. . . the crash of brass at catastrophes, and the soft music for tender and pathetic scenes.[84]

It is easy to imagine how a musical program might have been assembled during rehearsal in quite a creative way, using a combination of scores, simple cues and memory. A small cohesive ensemble (such as the one Coppin brought to Melbourne in 1845) could conceivably have followed the action by sight, almost without preparation. The formularised nature of the musical gestures or 'effects' supports this suggestion as these well-known devices lent themselves to being played on the spur of the moment, even in an ensemble.

Certainly, later variety orchestra musicians are known to have been able to play a memorised stock of tunes, dances, run-offs and so on upon demand. Writing of her own experience in more recent times, the Australian variety artist Valantyne Napier, records that some specialty artists

> would rely upon musicians 'busking' [faking] something appropriate. Pit musicians had a wealth of music they could busk and they all had to be first rate sight readers.[85]

Another reason variety musicians had to be able to fake was because their music was often illegible. In Axel Christensen's *Instruction Books for Vaudeville Piano Playing, Book Five: Vaudeville Cue Music*, the examples are purposely made 'as "sloppy" and careless as possible, so that [they] may be a typical imitation of what a pianist has to expect in a vaudeville theatre'.[86] An Australian vaudeville manager complained in 1914 that 'nine-tenths of the Australian artistes never considered an orchestra . . . a more dilapidated mass of rubbish could not be imagined. Not only did it bear an unsanitary appearance, but a majority of it was so much torn in parts that it was impossible for the pianist to do anything else but fake'.[87]

Where detailed 'original music' for a play was available – and legible – this would probably have been played as written, to the degree that this was possible in the chaotic conditions described by Edmund Finn. In other cases, available scores would probably have been assembled on the music stands as a collage of musical segments that related to the action (this was common practice in silent movie orchestral accompaniment). The social and cultural climate of early Melbourne theatre would in any case have left a wide latitude for imaginative, if iconoclastic, musical play or jest, as the following, extremely rare, references to early Melbourne theatre accompaniment indicate:

> By-the-bye, these 'incurables', whilst mangling the 'Flaxen Headed Cow Boy,' produced such a discordant clamour (as if the first violin and the double bass were in hysterics, and the rest of the instruments enjoying the joke) that the risibilities of the audience were pretty generally and loudly excited.[88]

> Again we must call the attention of the management to the timeless and tuneless awkward squad who occupy that portion of the theatre commonly known as the orchestra. Every member of the band seems bent upon playing an air of his own, of which the leader appears to be in the most blissful state of ignorance.[89]

Novelty Musical Acts

Novelty musical acts can be traced back to Mons. Gautrot's performances in Melbourne in the early 1840s of 'Andante Varie on one string of the violin' and to earlier Sydney performances of a similar nature by Wallace.[90] Each new form of instrument introduced to colonial Australia was potentially a variety-act instrument. Among the earliest of these were the accordion, valved brass instruments (saxhorns), the banjo and the 'turkophone' (saxophone). 'Ali-Ben-Sou-Alle', almost a mid-nineteenth-century counterpart of later visiting star American jazz saxophonists, was in Melbourne in 1854–55. In addition to featuring (presumably improvised) 'fantasias' upon his own themes, he introduced a range of unorthodox timbral effects:

> Mr. Sou Alle made his debut in turkish [sic] costume, and being a fine looking man, with a magnificent beard, he did full justice to the dress. . . His performance upon the new instrument, the turkophone, was extremely successful; and he was vehemently encored no fewer than three times, each time returning with a different instrument; to the intense amusement of the audience. These instruments dwindled gradually away til the last was a mere squeaking pipe, with a sound precisely representing the bagpipe: and a few bagpipe tunes (if there be such things) were blown through very successfully and with a great deal of humour.[91]

Numerous instruments were similarly featured as stage acts, including some which remained nameless. Louis Haselmayer:

> played selections on an instrument of his own invention. Apart from the fact that it was triangular in shape, it was otherwise much like our modern xylophone. A pianist too, he introduced into his serious work the playing of the piano with a clothes brush.[92]

A prominent local novelty-act performer of the late nineteenth century was the ex-military band musician and remarkable multi-instrumentalist Richard Kohler, who moved with ease between solo concert performance, Lyster's Melbourne opera orchestra, the variety stage, the dance hall and even American blackface minstrelsy.[93] Harold Love suggests that Kohler was also an alcoholic. If so, this may have led to even more extended and humorous transgressions of musical orthodoxy than is suggested by Figure 2.5.

Musical imitation in the form of comic caricature, such as 'barn-yard imitations', maintained its popularity through the nineteenth century and later. There were also more precise imitations such as (the former Melbourne choirboy) Harry Atkinson's 1904 variety act, in which he used his voice to imitate 'a motorcar', 'a concertina with a broken note', 'a duet with the oboe and violin (pizzicatto and bow)' and 'in rapid succession an imitation of ten different instruments'. Atkinson also let the audience hear a comparison of his imitation with the corresponding instrument in the orchestra.[94]

The reverse of this is seen in the Stavordale Quintet act (harps and banjos) in which:

> By the use of suggestive settings and by taking such liberties with time and modulation as are usually reserved for vocal music, [the Stavordales] approached close enough to human tones to make the resemblance plain enough when a little imagination was called to aid.[95]

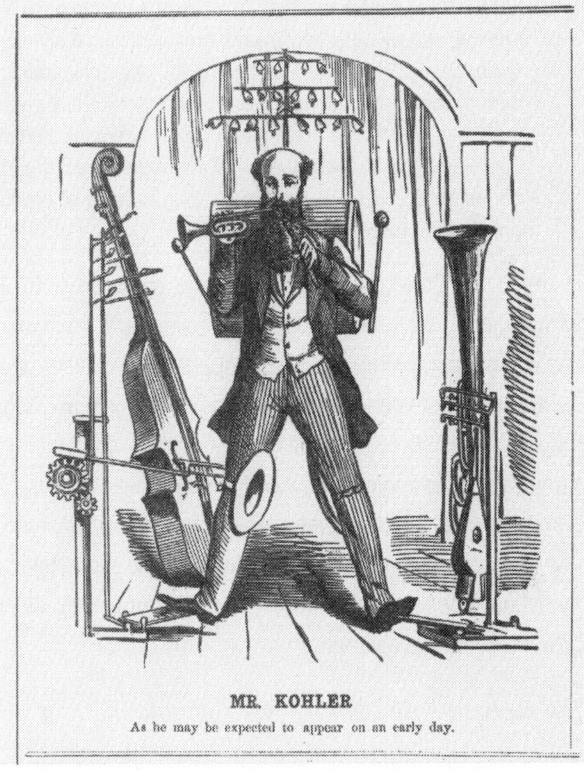

Figure 2.5. Richard Wildblood Kohler, a novelty musical act performer. *Punch* (Melbourne), 12 June 1862.

One novelty genre which became remarkably popular was the 'descriptive piece'. The *Argus* observed of 'Railway Gallop', performed by Hore's Saxe Horn Band in 1850, that 'From the bell for starting throughout all the rumble, clatter, shriek and whistle, the resemblance was perfect.'[96] Descriptive pieces often combined familiar musical segments, innovative textures and individual sound effects to represent a particular event in sound.

Some notable examples were performed in the early 1860s by Poussard (violin) and Douay (violoncello). The duo interpolated (sometimes improvised) variations on popular tunes and an array of unorthodox instrumental techniques to create complex and lengthy musical 'descriptions' of topical events. The following is an excerpt from a review of their musical description of the recent near fatal expedition of the Australian explorer John MacDouall Stuart:

> 'The start' followed, and the clatter of hoofs, the confusion of voices, and the rumbling of the wagons could all be readily distinguished; variations on *Cheer boys, cheer* were

> beautifully introduced in this part. The songs of the Birds followed, at the approach of the evening, and we need hardly say were given with a minuteness of imitation. . . 'The route' again renewed the clattering of hoofs and noise of starting afresh. 'The hot wind,' as might be supposed, was the most disagreeable part of the whole; now it whistled through the trees and now roared across the plain . . . The subsequent 'sufferings of the explorers,' their sighs, their cries, their low murmurs, their groans of pain and despair were eloquently described . . . How such sounds could be produced from two instruments like violin and violoncello was a marvel.[97]

In the 'Train Crash', a descriptive piece recorded onto a surviving wax cylinder at Warrnambool, Victoria in 1897, the 'celebrated drum demon' Herr Schoot, cleverly depicts the train journey and subsequent noisy catastrophe 'with his kit of 20 assorted drums and other sound effects devices'.[98] The colonial stage was therefore the context for an increasing number of novelty sounds combinations and effects. This was a significant development providing a locus for innovative, unorthodox and extended performance techniques that were not, nor could be, prescribed by conventional notation. These sounds and sound combinations were tolerated to varying degrees as functional effect or musical jest, even though they were largely at odds with the prevailing musical aesthetics.

Predecessors of Silent Movie Accompaniment

As a genre, silent movie accompaniment has a number of theatrical predecessors. In Australia these include the musical accompaniment to ballet, equestrian pantomime, unscripted variety acts and 'tableaux vivants' (posing to create striking scenes). The system of short cryptic instructions or cues on which the accompaniment to early Melbourne melodrama was often based also became the basis for much silent film accompaniment.

More direct predecessors include the practice of providing accompaniment for projected or painted moving images. As early as 1845 Coppin's theatre orchestra was accompanying 'dissolving magic lantern views' and the ubiquitous Hore's Saxe Horn Band accompanied a phantasmagoria depicting:

> the boa constrictor gliding into notice under the elegant tutelage of the Gabrielen, the King Vulture pouncing upon us in the midst of the rattle of the Rataplan, and the African lion being ushered in with the spirit stirring strains of the [D]rum-polka.[99]

Some months later the Melbourne pianist Mr Hemy provided 'musical accompaniment' for 'dissolving views' (optical illusions) and the 'revolving chromotrope. . . the brilliancy of the colours, and variety of the combination of which have never failed to excite the greatest interest'.[100] The Moving Panorama was another type of moving image supported by musical accompaniment. This comprised a long canvas painting that moved on vertical rollers across an opening on stage. Performances could also take place in front of the moving canvas. A panorama featured at the Queen's Theatre in 1851 depicted what was billed as a 'Terrific Storm – Two Females in Distress – Boat Wrecked upon the Rocks off the Gold Coast – Laidronetta preserved by the Serpent'.[101] A speciality of the previously mentioned 'drum demon', Herr Schoot, was the invention of all manner of sound effects for the lantern slide shows that were so popular before silent film. Schoot depicted one battle scene with:

> The roar of the field pieces . . . The cracking of the rifles, the whistling sound of the machine guns . . . the charge of the cavalry, the bugle calls, in fact all the din of a fierce battle'.[102]

Silent Movie Accompaniment

> Lizzie plays at the piano –
> Plays for the moving picture show.
> All the time must her fingers go
> With an endless whirl and a rhythmic flow
> And a ceaseless flitting to and fro;
> She fakes and vamps til her hands get cramps
> And there is no tune that she does not know. . .

From 'Lizzie Plays for the Pictures'.[103]

Silent movie accompaniment is the Anonymous genre that sustained the highest level of improvisatory practice in the immediate pre-jazz period. Although it was related historically, sociologically and musically to melodrama, vaudeville and circus accompaniment and similar forms of theatre accompaniment, the unique requirements of silent film exhibiting produced a genre with its own special characteristics.

At the beginning of the Australian silent movie era when the screening of short lengths of film was sandwiched between variety acts, conventional stage act accompaniment was quite adequate, particularly as these short reels often featured variety acts. By the time permanent cinemas and full-length films arrived, however, the unique problems, contingencies and variables of the silent film were more clearly defined.

Quick reactions and stylistic flexibility were required to synchronise the music with fast changing and highly contrasting screen events, such as an opera scene, a car chase, a wedding service, Ragtime dancing and a Hawaiian setting (see Figure 2.6). Musicians would often find that a film no longer corresponded to its synopsis after being cut by the local censor, and projection speed could alter unexpectedly according to the whim of the projectionist. Speeding up Indian attacks and similar action scenes

Figure 2.6. A typical advertisement for mood music from the cover of the orchestration of 'Chanson d' Amour', New York 1912 (from the Music Library of the Alhambra Cinema, Brunswick, Melbourne).

made them more exciting for patrons and also allowed the projectionist to finish early.[104]

The cinema musicians also had the task of providing human mediation between the audience and the non-responsive screen action. Unlike live stage or circus ring accompaniment in which the accompanists and the accompanied have flexibility to interact, screen action unfolds from beginning to end without pause. The accompaniment also had to be both loud and seamless enough to neutralise the noise of the machinery and the relatively uninhibited behaviour of an audience in a darkened environment. At the same time it had to be unobtrusive: music that was too loud, out of tune, out of phase or inappropriate could destroy the ambience of the 'dream palace'. Finally, silent film required a system of accompaniment that could accommodate continuous program changes with inadequate or no rehearsal.[105]

Cinema accompaniment was provided either by ensembles, in which the principal requirements were fast reactions, concentration, sight-reading ability and a highly talented director, or else by solo pianists or organists who, through improvising, reading or a combination of both, could substitute for an ensemble. The latter included brass or 'military' (brass and reed) bands; small to medium combinations of wind and stringed instruments; and in major 1920s theatres such as the Capitol Theatre (Melbourne) orchestras of perhaps twenty players. Allan's orchestral folio, *The Movies* (undated), lists what was considered a very adequate orchestra at the beginning of the 1920s: two violins, cello, string bass, flute, clarinet, cornet, trombone, piano and drums.

Within the structure of the cinema orchestra it was principally the director (often the pianist or lead violin) and the percussionist who brought a high degree of musical spontaneity and creativity to their work. It was the director's task to organise appropriate music for the film and ensure synchronisation during the screening under any circumstances. Ron Richards, a cinema violinist in the 1920s, described to me in detail the way orchestra members responded to the screen action. From his account it is clear that by the mid-1920s the procedures were so well established that, notwithstanding the types of contingency discussed, synchronisation was not difficult for experienced cinema musicians:

> You got used to the flash [which came at the end of each scene] so you moved onto the next [piece of music]. [Some conductors and leaders] were so experienced at doing it that they knew exactly where it was going to change . . . You were playing here and the screen was right above you – you couldn't look at the screen to see what it was. . . Soon as you got the flash. . . [the leader would indicate to] cut the sound and everybody would stop. . . the back of [his] bow would hit [the music stand] and soon as [we] heard that tap there was not another sound.[106]

The second category ranged through pianists who played by ear to piano teachers, highly-skilled amateur and professional pianists and church organists (including highly-paid, imported cinema organists).

Specific Performance Practices

> But the kids – how they used to scream when there were [chases]. There was always a chase in it, you know – the cowboys and the thundering hooves. Soon [playing] became absolutely unnecessary. I just took my hands off the keys and let the boys go on with it, and when they decrescendoed I took it up again, you see, and nobody knew the difference.
>
> Esther Rofe, a former Melbourne cinema pianist[107]

Cinema pianists and organists had one unique advantage: through improvisatory practice they were able to watch and synchronise their music with the screen action in a way that was denied the orchestra member.[108]

It is easy to get some idea of the main conventions used by cinema pianists and

Musical Ex. 2.3. From the original manuscript of the orchestral and band suite, 'At the Movies' (1920), by the Australian composer and cinema conductor Alex F. Lithgow. Intended for use as silent cinema mood music.

organists as many of them were formalised into the various methods published mostly in the last decade of the silent film era. Pre-War Australian cinema journals such as *Photoplay* provided some advice to cinema musicians and the American journal *Melody,* which was available in Melbourne by 1918 at the latest, featured regular articles directed at cinema pianists. In 1920 the *Age* carried an advertisement for formal tuition in silent movie accompaniment: 'Pianists trained for picture playing, with pictures in actual operation, numerous openings; introductions guaranteed.'[109]

The first relatively comprehensive work on the subject of keyboard accompaniment for screen was probably Edith Lang and George West's *Musical Accompaniment of Moving Pictures* (Boston, 1920).[110] Just how influential this method was in Australia is not known but the book probably summarises what were considered the main elements of ideal improvisatory keyboard accompaniment to screen action in 1920. Essentially, the Lang and West method was an adaptation of the basic features of theatre accompaniment to the new medium. The stratification of music into three levels, characterisation, moods and effects, was developed in live theatre genres such as melodrama:

> Musical characterisation. . . should be announced in the introduction, it should be emphasised at the first appearance of the person with which it is linked, and it should receive its ultimate glorification by means of total volume, etc., in the finale of the film.[111]

Mood music had to match the nature of scenes such as the 'Indian attack', 'the wedding' or 'the lovers' parting' (see Musical Ex. 2.3) as they unfolded. Individual effects such as the low trill, the glissando and the chordal 'crash' with sustain pedal, could represent individual screen events (as sound effects) or could be represented by commonly understood signifiers such as the fanfare.

Lang and West describe the following categories of improvisatory practice:

1. Varied or developed repetition of the main theme or themes.
2. Modulation.
3. Transposition.
4. Memorisation.
5. Spontaneous invention and harmonisation of melodic lines.

Thematic variation is intended to represent changes of mood associated with the main characters. This variation includes major/minor key changes, rhythmic transformations (including expansion, contraction and metre change), transformations of textural configurations (such as changing from melody and accompaniment to polyphony), ornaments and elaboration (subdivision of the basic pulse with chord, passing, neighbour tones, etc.), register change and, in the case of organists, distinctive timbral variation.[112]

Memorisation provides an instantly accessible library of musical segments, textures and effects that can be juxtaposed intuitively according to the screen action.[113] Modulations function as bridges of flexible duration between contrasting segments; and transposition enables a player to interpolate memorised musical segments at any key level.[114] Improvisation, according to Lang and West, is basically melodic invention and harmonisation at the keyboard (as in church organ 'preluding') and directly reflects standard late nineteenth-century works such as Frank Sawyer's *Extemporisation* (see Chapter One), which would have been familiar to pianists and organists with a reasonable practical and theoretical background.

Lang and West conclude that:

> *Mental alertness* and *musical resourcefulness* will enable one who is gifted with sufficient technique to give a most adequate musical interpretation of the pictured scene. With a certain facility in improvisation and a sense of dramatic values, the player may even hope to accomplish more than that, and really give the spectator that most illusive of all experiences, a thrill![115]

For more than two decades cinema pianists came from a particularly broad cross-section of the local music community and the majority of them were women. Whatever their level of expertise, they were confronted with the demand and also the opportunity for spontaneous and artistic inventiveness. This is contrary to the common notion of the legendary improvising male virtuoso of the romantic or jazz era.

Rita Sheehan provides a particularly colourful image of an Australian cinema accompanist:

> Smithy was our picture show pianist. She was a battler and chopped wood, milked cows, drove a high-stepping horse, plucked chooks, tended smelly ferrets, without – in show business terms – losing a spangle. . . Her cape was khaki-coloured and almost touched the ground. Coarse black hair, coiled and skewered, jet ear-rings swinging, she'd sweep in the side door with the aplomb of an opera star.[116]

Carmen Naylor

In 1986 I interviewed Carmen Naylor who, around 1910, had begun playing the piano for the smaller of two theatres in Bathurst, New South Wales. She continued this work until the decline of the industry in the late 1920s. What is interesting about Naylor is that her formal training consisted of less than a year of private lessons. Her previous musical experience had mostly comprised playing for home entertainment and dances. For her first engagement at Bathurst she was given neither synopsis nor sheet music:

> The orchestra [at the other end of town] – they had music, and a synopsis all [set] out for them . . . But you see, with me . . . they didn't have anything to give me to help me. They

> said to me: 'Look! we know you can play the piano all right – as far as we know – and you won't have to use music'. . . I started the first show and they were just thrilled with the music, and they said, 'How did you get the music . . . to combine . . . so it wasn't at loggerheads with the picture?' I said 'Well, to be strictly honest . . . I didn't play the music – I made it up'. . . Whatever came on the screen I'd play accordingly. If it was tears, you know, I'd just think of the doldrums and play all the sad little bits that would go through my mind. I had no music but I had the instinct in me . . . I'd improvise the whole show some nights.[117]

Even at one hundred years of age Naylor was able to demonstrate the type of music she played for mood changes. I was immediately struck by two aspects: its similarity to the dense texture of early piano-roll music with its characteristic embellishment devices (e.g. fast scale runs, arpeggiation and trills) and its nebulous or 'fantasia-like' nature. Naylor's formative musical background was principally the popular music of her era: Strauss waltzes, parlour songs, schottisches, cakewalk and other march-type music. Drawing on this music as a pool of textures, she was able to create a meandering impressionistic stream of sound in which recognisable tunes emerged and dissolved.

On a video tape in which she demonstrates the musical settings for different moods on request, one short segment ('music for a happy event') unfolds as follows:

1. A typical fast march introduction in 6/8 time.
2. The four-bar antecedent phrase of a slow waltz (ascending pitch contour), played very rubato with a florid arpeggiation at the half-cadence.
3. The consequent (answering) phrase (descending pitch contour) with florid arpeggiation at the full cadence.
4. Two hesitant melody notes which sound like the start of a new section of the waltz (but now in the relative minor).
5. A sudden, rapidly-accelerating march.
6. The still-accelerating march, rhythmically transformed with what resembles syncopated ragtime embellishment (see Chapter Four, Musical Ex. 4.3b).
7. The texture dissolved into a complex texture of fast two-handed cadenza-like runs – a type of dense 'rumbling' – ending on a minor chord, the tonic of this section.

All of these changes take place within twenty-five seconds.[118]

From my interview and brief observations, her approach falls into two main categories: an objective (imitative) or a subjective (emotive) response to the screen action. Her objective response to a dramatic event, such as a fight, was to interpolate the stock melodrama device of rumbling low tremolos and runs in the bass. A descending sword was denoted by a descending glissando. After several screenings of the same film these imitative musical responses would apparently become fixed or structural elements of the accompaniment to that film. However, much of her playing seemed to be quite subjective: a personal musical response to the changing action that would probably be quite different at the next performance. Of improvisation she says: 'You would just put your hand on the keys and play, or start in a certain key – and the key itself [pause] . . . I can't explain it to you.' And of modulation: 'I'd kind of slide out of one key and, before I knew where I was, I was over in a different key but nobody would ever notice it'.[119]

Naylor is therefore an example of a virtually self-taught pianist who developed an effective approach to cinema accompaniment in almost total isolation from broader musical and theoretical input. Her own descriptions and playing suggest that the limitations imposed by her musical isolation and lack of formal training actually assisted her to invent a style in which a small vocabulary of elements was reworked with infinite variation (as is the case of, for example, the more authentic forms of African-American blues).

Esther Rofe

In contrast to Naylor, Esther Rofe was a formally-trained musician who at nineteen became the accompanist to Alberto Zelman and is known today as a significant Australian composer of ballet music. Rofe played the piano in a Melbourne cinema orchestra in the 1920s and she describes this as 'a driving sort of ordeal', in which she had to be ready to fill in any missing instrument from the miniature cues provided on her score. She also played as a solo pianist for matinees and her approach to this work was probably very common in cinema accompaniment after about 1914, when special mood music albums became readily available (see Musical Ex. 2.4).[120]

> It was all cowboy things – and kids! – *screaming* from the balconies and *screaming* from the hall – it was wonderful! . . . There wasn't time for a single pianist really to turn over [the music], so you'd snatch your Sam Fox [film music album] and put it up and that would be in a way [the] nucleus of what you would work from. So now we come to the improvisation . . . I used to have about seven, eight or nine different [albums] and then I'd just snatch that over and then there would be the next sort of atmosphere. Then I could often improvise just a dreamy atmosphere – Pacific islands [music] or anything like that. You would just improvise something in that style . . . And then you'd come back [to your album].[121]

Sheehan recalls a similarly interactive soundscape:

> Oh, Armageddon! from all sides, the novelty noises would compete. Catcalls, falsetto voices imitating the hapless heroine. Ear-splitting whistles. A barrage of yaahhoos and

Musical Ex. 2.4. Introduction and the first 8 bars of 'Indian Attack' by J.S. Zamecnic (1915), *Sam Fox Moving Picture Music*, vol. 3.

> whaaackaroos! Then the steady thud of wooden seat flaps. Heartstopping sound of tough alley on the move.[122]

Equipped with a synopsis which indicated the type of music for each major scene change and a set of Sam Fox or Jacobs' mood music folios, it was only a matter of selecting and organising stock moods into a sequence that corresponded with the synopsis, and filling in where necessary with improvisatory practice (e.g. extended modulation, the invention of textures or the interpolation of memorised textures). There is no doubt that even the average pianist would soon play the stock moods from memory because of the need to follow the screen action. Nevertheless, it is easy to see the remarkable freedom for improvisatory creativity that was available in this genre.

Circus Music

The Melbourne opening in 1852 of Rowe's American circus with music provided by Hore's Saxe Horn Band marks the beginning of an association between circus music and an emerging and increasingly conservative Victorian brass band movement. Around the same time, Australian circus music also came to be identified with German musicians, members of an emigrant group renowned for their musical precision. The best known of these were the Wirth circus family and later (in the 1880s) Herr (Henry)

Von Der Mehden, who was both a famous circus cornet soloist/band leader and a highly respected patron of the Australian brass band movement. Such associations would seem therefore to greatly reduce the likelihood of a circus band tradition in which there was freedom to improvise.[123]

By the early 1900s travelling circus musicians such as Von Der Mehden and the Wirths were living legends (at least to the Australian brass band movement). Brass band culture stood for musical excellence, achieved by uniformity, precision and obedience to the score, the bandleader and the rules of the movement. Faking was abhorred; and yet, paradoxically, there is evidence that Australian circus did support a tradition of improvisatory practice.

Furthermore, there are historical and musical connections between Australian circus music and jazz. For example, both Australia's 'first' jazz band and the first Melbourne 'jazz' recording sessions featured Der Mehden's son and former circus musician, Harry Mehden, while Sydney's first recordings of an Australian jazz band feature two circus musicians, Harry Larsen and Harold Barlow (see Chapter Five).

German Musicians and Circus

The so-called German bands that played in the streets were, as the following quotation suggests, often employed by circus proprietors (see Figure 2.7):

> 'Twas in the early part of 1854 that our band, after a prolonged tour, which had carried us from our own homes in the Fatherland, throughout the length and breadth of Great Britain, and from thence to Australia, entered into an engagement with Messrs. Noble, Jones, and Foley, circus proprietors, for a lengthy season at Ballarat . . . Our band consisted of five pieces – an F flute, E♭ clarionet, B♭ cornet, E♭ horn and B♭ bass . . . We never played for less than £1 per hour.[124]

This account also mentions that another German band had just been arrested for busking in Ballarat. In the late nineteenth and early twentieth century the term 'German band' was virtually a euphemism for noise. William Kelly claims that the German band music he heard in Melbourne in the late 1850s would 'drive swine into anguish, or turn a whole brewery of Barclay and Perkins into vinegar'.[125] Another Melbourne description of a German street band reads:

> First of all they play as well as they can, which is sometimes not too badly; but if their victim does not immediately search his pockets for the ransom money, they start to play out of key, out of time, and so horribly that at last the exhausted, despairing, almost maddened listener gives in and hands over money without even counting it. Their goal achieved, the band stops and goes off somewhere else to carry out their musical warfare.[126]

Accounts and illustrations suggest that itinerant German bands often played without music, especially under the conditions of street playing. It is also possible that colonial 'town bands' employed by circus proprietors were able to fake. It has already been claimed that the majority of early nineteenth-century English village band musicians played by ear. One known Australian counterpart was the 1860s Echuca Borough band which:

> could on occasion play without any music whatsoever. The leader would call the tune and instructing the various minor players what notes to accompany with, the band would ring forth merrily.[127]

Another account mentions that Nat Hallas' town band (also known to have been a circus band), having lost their music on the way to an engagement in 1871, 'had to fake a day and night's playing'.[128]

It is also known that German bandsmen Von Der Mehden and Wirth brothers, Philip and John, had both aural and general musical ability far in excess of that needed for playing straightforward circus accompaniment.

Figure 2.7. Illustration of a German band in late nineteenth-century London.

Of all the players not one was known
With such a range, such wondrous tone...

Obituary to circus band musician Herr Von Der Mehden (1920).[129]

Von Der Mehden came to Australia in the 1880s with Chiarini's Royal Italian Circus and subsequently led Fitzgerald's Circus band for many years. Fitzgerald's billed him as Australia's 'premier cornetist' and he was particularly noted for his vast range, outstanding tone and fast triple-tonguing.[130] He also seems to have been extremely versatile. It is claimed that he played the lead violin with the Sydney Opera orchestra and he is cited in an 1890s vaudeville program as a solo performer on tuned glasses, xylophone and 'cornet-à-piston'.[131] A letter published in the *Australasian Bandsman* in 1920 describes Von Der Mehden, shortly before his death in 1919:

> tearing off 'jazz music' in fine pep style, at a dance from 9 p.m. to 3 a.m... with the same apparent ease and contentment he invariably displayed in his younger Australian days... Whenever some quite unexpected, and appropriate air or tune was requisite for the occasion, to Mr Von Der Mehden the musicians always turned to start the melody from memory, and he was always 'right on the job' for he seemed to remember any named tune right off the reel. The band then of course took it up from him... and so he was in great demand as an artistic cornet player, a tune-faker, a reliable and 'good' musician and a gentleman.[132]

Intriguingly, the description above mirrors other recollections of his performance behaviour from a time long before jazz:

> The wonderful work he was capable of and the ease with which he did it... [won't be forgotten]. He had a remarkable memory, for he rarely used music, he would stand cornet in left hand, or in right as the whim took him, using either to conduct his [circus band]. If he did hold his instrument with one hand while fingering the pistons with the other – as he would do at times when a dainty bit of solo work was to be played – he would slightly sway his body from side to side.[133]

Far from a model of rigid German orthodoxy, this description suggests someone unlikely to have been content to play the same music, show after show, without creative modification. As a skilled arranger and composer, Von Der Mehden possessed technical and aural ability, theoretical knowledge and a creative impulse – all the attributes needed to cleverly embroider repetitive accompaniment music.

Alex F. Lithgow dedicated 'Le Cirque' (Musical Ex. 2.5) to Von Der Mehden in 1907. Although this piece may be only an impressionistic representation of circus music, the accenting, among other things, may suggest how expert circus musicians modified their music to generate excitement and attract attention.

Much of the evidence of the musical ability of the Wirth Circus family (notably Philip

Musical Ex. 2.5. A and B sections of the solo cornet part from Alex Lithgow's 'Le Cirque' (1907).

and John) comes from a history written by a family member, George. He claims that their father, John, a German bandsman who reached the Victorian goldfields in the 1850s:

> was a musician of great ability, able to play any instrument from a piano to a Jew's harp, or from a clarionet to a double bass. Wind string or ivory instrument was all the same to John Wirth, senr. And therein lay the genesis of the Wirth Circus.[134]

George also claims that his brothers, John and Philip:

> were at that time [late 1870s] Australia's leading players. John was the best cornet player, with his wonderful double-tonguing polkas and high register, while Philip was an all round musician, playing any brass instrument well. They were both excellent readers and composers, and were equally good at playing by ear.[135]

It is difficult to verify these claims. However, Harry Larsen, one of Australia's most respected trombone players and teachers of earlier years, heard Philip Wirth playing three or four decades after the period referred to above:

> I remember him coming in one day and asking if he could play something on my euphonium. Well, he just paralysed me when he started to play, I thought I was a good player![136]

Therefore, while these leading circus music performers played brass instruments and were admired by many in the brass band movement, they were both capable of, and likely to have expressed their ability by improvising.

Family Bands

> It might be asked 'who were the circus bandsmen?' 'Where did they come from?' Well, for the most part they were born of circus parents. Many had neither professional nor amateur band experience, yet time and time again they were complimented by professional musicians on the way they handled the difficult programmes.[137]

The influence of the many American circuses who visited Australia in the late nineteenth century notwithstanding, Australian circus also developed its own characteristics in response to local conditions. There was, for example, the intense Australian admiration of equestrian ability, the hardship of travelling in the Australian bush, the post-goldrush economic collapse and the rise of nationalism (and consequent decline in demand for imported culture). There was also the special contribution of Aboriginal Australian performers. Travelling circus families often adopted very young Aboriginal children and their equestrian capabilities became a feature of Australian circus.[138]

The most significant factor for improvisatory practice in circus music, however, was the phenomenon of the small to medium travelling family circus bands (see Figure

Figure 2.8. Seymour's family circus band, from Fred Lord, *Little Big Top.*

2.8).[139] For economic survival alone it was fairly important that every family member could take on several jobs including band musician. It therefore became a convention that the children, as well as learning circus acts, had to 'have a go' at playing an instrument at a very early age:

> While I was wiggling the costume over Madge and pulling one arm of the dress on her, she was expected to grip an instrument with the other hand and go on playing, just as Lulu and Win sometimes do in similar circumstances . . . Everyone had to do their stint in Seymour's Family Band as well as in Seymour's Family Circus.[140]

The musical proficiency of these children depended of course upon their natural ability and learning environment. The St Leons, for example, were tutored by Von Der Mehden and subsequently produced what is claimed to have been an outstanding band. Reginald St Leon, the most musically accomplished of this family, became noted for some exceptional feats of aural and technical ability. It is claimed that he could transcribe a full band arrangement on the basis of one or perhaps two hearings of a live performance.[141]

Other travelling circus children were less fortunate: their musical training was often limited to what knowledge the older family members could pass on. Mervyn King, who joined the St. Leon family circus in 1915, has described how, as a circus child, he was given a brass instrument and allowed to sit in with the band and contribute by simply reinforcing the basic pulse.[142] Learning to play this way is a trial and error process in which the ear could be more valuable than the eye.

The social structure of the travelling family circus band came to comprise musicians ranging from highly experienced, although not necessarily technically proficient, senior family members to young children just learning to play; hired circus performers (also usually from circus families) who doubled as band musicians; and (depending upon the finances) one or more professional theatre or outstanding local brass band musicians to augment the band and generally raise musical standards.[143]

Because the musicians had multiple functions in the family circus, the band constantly changed in size during the program and those still playing had somehow to fill in for absent players.[144] Sid Baker and George Wirth both described their experiences:

> one by one they would leave the bandstand to go into the ring and do some act or some other chores until finally only Jimmy Perry on trumpet and myself on the sousaphone would be left to play the acts until the others returned.[145]

> We could all play pretty well any brass instrument. The [three piece] band inside underwent all sorts of changes, because of the work we had in turn to do in the course of the performance. This included tumbling, horizontal bars, Roman rings, contortion, club-swinging, single trapeze, and double trapeze. I was the contortionist.[146]

Published arrangements for a 'military style' (mixed reeds and brass) or standard brass band would often be too heavily scored or contrapuntal for a small circus band with a drastically changing structure.[147] This would probably leave the leader of a small circus band with three options: to score specially for the changes in band structure during the program;[148] to use some sort of flexible or 'elastic' scoring system;[149] to rely upon the experience of players to fill out or fake some of the simpler sections of the program; or to use some permutation of all three.

The often extreme difference in ability between the musicians in family circus bands meant that some had technical and aural ability far in excess of what was needed for the basic circus program. Given the relatively informal context of circus and the frequent repetition of the pieces within a program and over a whole season, it is very likely that travelling circus musicians often indulged in playful musical interaction or embellishment, possibly even along the lines of variation development in the popular cornet solos of the day (see Musical Ex. 2.6). At the very least, the fast double and triple-tonguing that was the hallmark of the competent brass player would have been easily applied spontaneously to embellish crotchets or minims in pieces of moderate tempo.

Among the many famous brass band musicians known to have played with circus bands are Thomas Volver Short, Arthur Stender, Hughie McMahon and as already mentioned, Harold Barlow and Harry Larsen.[150] As champion brass band soloists, such musicians would have intentionally internalised many of the devices of brass band

Musical Ex. 2.6. Variations on 'Swanee River' by T.E. Bulch, *Bulch's Cornettist*, Melbourne (published by T.E. Bulch before 1920 but possibly written two or three decades earlier).

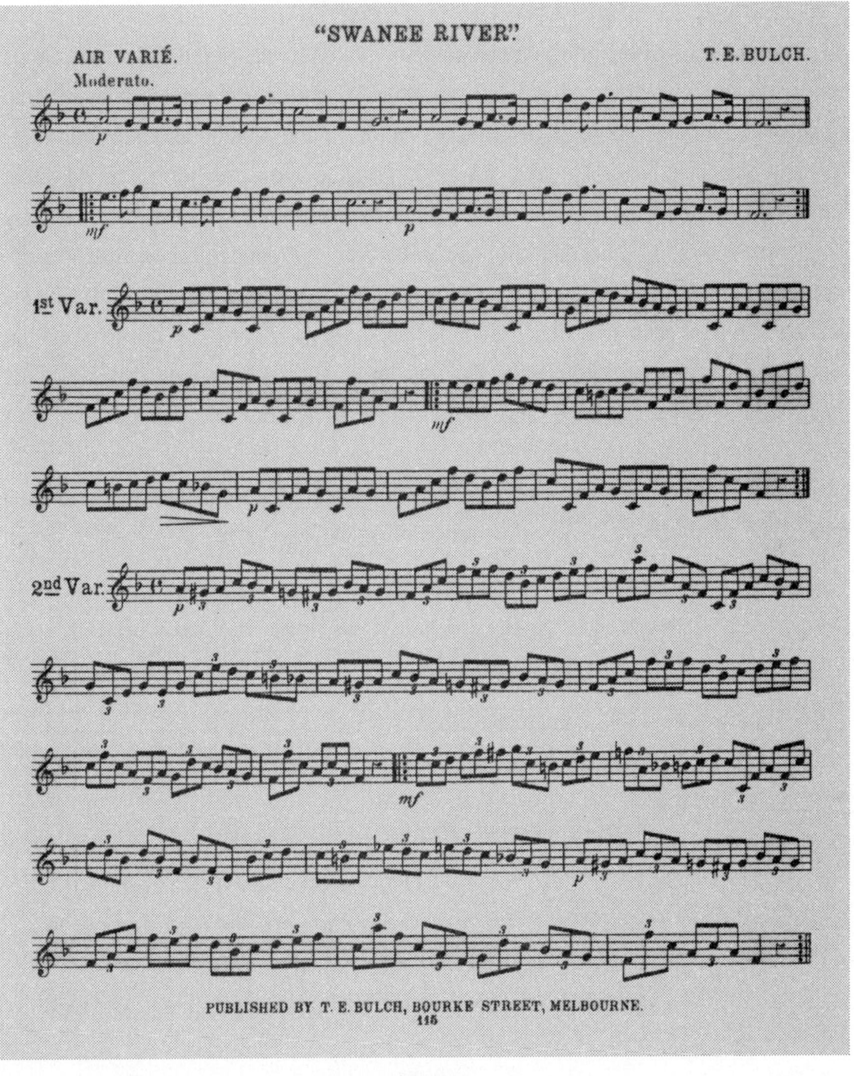

music in the process of preparing for contests. These devices included the very common diatonic sequences in melodic thirds, various ornaments, extended cadenzas over the dominant and so forth. The distinctive style of counterpoint that is characteristic of the euphonium's role in brass band music can eventually be internalised and become manifest in the ability to invent a counter-melody spontaneously.[151] Counter-melody can also be presented as a type of variation on the original theme. In addition, the extremely thorough and systematic approach to learning technique presented in published brass methods gave the diligent student control over all the basic melodic patterns, ornaments and devices in every key.[152]

Effects

As circus is a form of theatrical amusement, the professionals who filled out the circus bands brought with them influences from other forms of stage accompaniment such as novelty trombone glissandi (or 'smears') and 'laughing' trombone or saxophone.[153] The 'smear' occurs almost by default on the trombone and is the perfect sound effect for musical clowning, circus 'clown bands' or for representing up or down motion (e.g. sliding down a rope). It became a principal element of American circus music 'razzamatazz' and notated trombone glissandi are the identifying characteristic of the 'circus trombone' pieces such as *Slidus Trombonus* (M. Lake, 1915) that also became popular in Australia. The improvisatory smear is a very important link between American circus music and American ragtime and jazz (smears were even called 'rags' and later 'jazzes'). Unfortunately there are neither recordings nor known written documentation of the use of trombone smears as improvisatory practice in pre-jazz Australian circus music. The emphasis on novelty percussion effects in 'Le Cirque' (bird warbler, sleigh

Musical Ex. 2.7. Upper system: the eight-bar 'trotting effect' section of the solo cornet part of 'Bucephaleon' (1904). Lower system: the interlocking pattern from the same section of the soprano cornet part.

bells, triangle, cymbal, tambourine, castanets) suggests that these may have been used regularly in Australian circus music. The eight-bar novelty 'trotting effect' (the octaves) in Von Der Mehden's 'Bucephaleon' (Musical Ex. 2.7) indicates that he also favoured imaginative novelty effects.

'Playing up the octave' was often used on stage by touring cornet virtuosi such as Paris Chambers and was another effect that was probably employed by circus musicians.[154] References to the remarkable range of Australian circus musicians such as Von Der Mehden imply that they were either playing specially written parts or were playing up the octave. An early Australian Salvation Army musician, Tom Robertson, known as 'Mudgee the Marvel' or the 'freak cornetist', is claimed to have developed a range of five-and-a-half octaves, after he 'chanced to hear a player in a travelling circus performing in an extraordinarily wide range'.[155]

Ear players

Mervyn King is one of the few Australians, if not the only one, in a position to comment on early circus music from first-hand experience. As a circus child with St Leon's Great United Circus, King was expected to play an instrument in the band.[156] He recalls that there were circus musicians of exceptional ability who would 'have a little bit of a play around'; and he names several who could 'put in a few extra notes of their own here and there if they wanted to and it would still sound all right'. He also mentions that some players would 'take a roundabout course' (simulating double-tonguing) to fill-in melodically while waiting.

King was adamant that many circus musicians played by ear: 'Most of our good reputation players were ear players and that always puzzled me how they could be so good'.[157] As well as listing the notable musicians who were ear players, he also pointed out that, since lighting was inadequate and frequently failed during performances and the circus repertoire was standardised across the industry, even good readers seldom bothered with music once they had played it through once or twice.

Arthur Stirling expressed what may have been a common view among members of the brass band movement in the early twentieth century. He recalls that circus musicians were very 'clever' at negotiating fast changes and feats of technical ability (which 'only one out of ten brass band players could do'). However, he also felt they were basically 'lug merchants' – they relied too much on their ears.[158] This was something that was not acceptable to the reading-oriented brass band movement.

More Recent Circus Music

The Australian champion cornet player and conductor Arthur Withers joined Bullen's Circus band in 1956, when the Australian circus band tradition was already in decline (see Figure 2.9). However, he believes that the basic procedures and routines he encountered there had been handed down from circus to circus. Because his prestigious banding career had kept him more or less isolated from jazz and other contemporary forms of improvisation, his account of improvisation in circus band music is relatively unprejudiced by fixed ideas of what can be described as improvisation. It is also a vivid illustration of many of the practices discussed so far:

> Cornet or trumpet players would be playing off 'legit' [fully scored] parts and it depended on the complement how you played the music. 'Cocka' Newman on euphonium, who was the leader – he improvised nearly all the time. They might start the march off together [as written] and then he would 'go off'. Davey Greenhorn would even do much more vamping and [so forth] on the tenor cor – he'd go all over the place . . . Allan Jolly the trumpet player, he'd warm up on a high F and Jeff and I would be amazed; [but] he wasn't so good on the technical playing of the legit music, of the charts . . . which from memory wasn't greatly of variety . . . What Allan would do is play up the octave and do a bit of 'gliding around' and that sort of thing – not what you would call extemporizing . . . Most times [the run-offs] were played with a quick tempo; I recall that two or three of those closes or run-offs [were played] just from memory – we got to know which ones to play.[159]

Figure 2.9. Philip Wirth and Wirth's Circus Band, *Music Maker,* 20 April 1948, p. 36.

No Circus Complete Without A Band

VERSATILITY is the keynote of Wirth's Circus Band, which is called upon to play for any and every type of act from trapeze artists to performing horses.

In the accompanying picture Philip Wirth gives some last-minute instructions to its members—front row, left to right: Bill Horshman, Stan Rogers, Ern Pilkington. 2nd row: Mario Booth, Alf. Foletta (Bandmaster), Dave Beasley. Back row: Al Anderson, Vic. Wilson and Bob Banks.

Withers seems to be describing a form of collective improvisation/ embellishment that does not fall easily into any category of twentieth-century professional music-making: not jazz improvisation but spontaneous decoration or musical 'play' on traditional circus favourites. He also discussed circus accompaniment in a broader sense. Circus music, he claimed, had a special quality that is difficult to define, principally because it is heard in a context saturated with powerful visual, tactile, olfactory and aural messages.[160]

The experience of a circus performance is more than just the observation of ring action. It is the experience of a total environment, a moment in the complex daily life of the circus. This includes some events that are partly controlled and others that cannot be.

The sonic environment of the circus tent is a rich, multi-levelled and constantly changing complex of sounds which includes machinery, children, gasps, laughter, wild animals, galloping horses, billows of applause, changing props and outside noise. The circus music interacts with these layers of sound in complex ways. Even when the music has only a passive relationship to the ring action (when the band continually repeats a section, for example), the intermittent waves of audience response provide a sonic link between ring action and music. Nevertheless, the circus bandmaster can use a combination of musical intuition and experience to gain some control over this complex environment. The most dramatic example is the abrupt and extended pause, which instantly throws the non-musical elements of the sonic environment into dramatic relief.

The music itself is sometimes described as circusy, blaring, brassy, stirring, 'having a special ring' and so forth, but its main quality springs from the role indeterminacy plays in the event as a whole. The musical accompaniment to the ring action must be responsive to constant variation in human or animal reaction and to the loop of interaction between audience and performer. The musicians must therefore respond spontaneously to both very subtle and dramatic changes in mood with or between acts.

Withers describes the type of quick, intuitive responses required of the musicians, individually and as a group, to cope with the indeterminate aspects of the performance and the way various parameters of the music – tempo, dynamics, textural density – are altered spontaneously to create mood changes:

> We watched quite a lot, especially in the high wire act. Sometimes they would look down and you would play very quietly while they were getting ready for the double somersault, or whatever – or then you might 'cut out'. You had to start quickly – be on the alert. . . 'Cocka' would stand up in front of us and (direct with his elbows) while he was facing the act, and then at certain times he would turn around and say 'A bit slower lads in the next

> verse' – he would give verbal instruction . . . The grand parade [for example] – that could change its length without you realising it . . . timing wasn't definite on any piece of music; you would have to sense it [by] watching the act. The high wire – that varied a lot because if they missed their catching, or took extra time just to settle down, you would have to keep repeating or . . . You just had to get used to variations of tempo at quick notice. You might be doing a waltz at one speed for a while and suddenly the act changes. Then you either faded out or sped it up, or then went very quiet – which was different to what was written on the music. It was like a gigantic rubato effect – dynamics or tempo. . .[161]

The demands of life in the travelling circus fostered a culture in which musical spontaneity, versatility and unorthodox practices were both permitted and necessary. Therefore, at the very time that the Australian band movement was moving in the direction of total musical codification, the circus band tradition was embracing practices and conventions which were the antithesis of the other's aims, the most unorthodox being the persistence of an aural tradition. The social structure of the family circus band also preserved the tradition of the skilled performer able to work across a variety of media.

3 Early Blackface Minstrelsy

This and the following chapter examine some of the diluted forms of African-American musical culture that were present in Australia before jazz. It explores performance practices that pre-empted the type of 'jazz improvisation' first heard in Australia and suggests how blackface minstrelsy might have influenced later Australian attitudes towards improvisatory practice in popular music.[1]

Few people would disagree that jazz was the main locus for improvisatory music during the first half of this century. It is far more difficult however to argue that Australian jazz has its own Australian pre-history. The most notable characteristics of early jazz, such as blues tonality and form, improvisatory polyphony, the rhythmic vamp and call-and-response patterns, can be related separately to pre-jazz African-American forms such as the spiritual, work-song and field holler or remnants of West African or Caribbean dance music.[2] These were of course not present to any degree in pre-jazz Australia and therefore could not have greatly influenced Australian musical development. Furthermore, style development in American jazz itself is known to have centred largely around the musical vitality and originality of African-American musicians such as Buddy Bolden, King Oliver, Louis Armstrong, Jelly Roll Morton; and later Duke Ellington, Thelonious Monk, Ornette Coleman and Miles Davis.

For some years now jazz scholars have been making serious attempts to acknowledge the black contribution to jazz. But perhaps out of shame over earlier white disregard for this contribution, several significant aspects of white influence on the emergence of jazz have been by-passed or played down. It is rarely stressed, for example, that the mid-nineteenth-century blackface minstrel show, a form greatly responsible for creating and defining the role that African-Americans would later play as entertainers, was largely developed by white actors, virtually excluding African-Americans during its initial stages of development.

Similarly, the importance of later popular American theatre and Tin Pan Alley as the principal conduits and popularisers of ragtime (in the broadest sense of the term) is usually glossed over or ignored. More importantly, it is rarely acknowledged that most composers and arrangers of ragtime were white or that most of the people who played ragtime in the period leading up to jazz were white. Amongst the latter were the countless young women who played the piano as one of the 'essential accomplishments' required of their gender.[3] In America the practice and teaching of 'ragging' or 'ragtime improvisation' (the spontaneous rhythmic transformation and embellishment of popular music) was most widely associated with white musicians. This suggests that the specific types of blackface minstrelsy and ragtime that reached Australia before jazz had musical characteristics that anticipated improvisation in early Australian jazz.

Readers unfamiliar with the literature of the period may be disturbed by the quoted terminology and images presented in this and the following chapter. However, the social attitudes that produced these terms and images are linked intrinsically to the ways that African-American performance culture was perceived and adopted in Australia. To omit them would be to present an inadequate and misleading, if more palatable, history.

The Emergence and Nature of the Early Minstrel Show

In American theatres and circuses before the 1840s white actors in blackface make-up commonly performed solo acts representing various aspects of African-American culture. They often claimed to play the instruments of African-American music-making, such as the banjo, bone castanets, tambourine and fiddle, in an authentic manner. Similar claims were often made for their dancing, singing and use of dialect. American audiences were therefore treated to an exhibition of what they were led to believe was a 'correct' representation of the idiosyncratic behaviour and natural abilities of the African-American, presented in the form of talented and humorous white acting, or 'Negro delineation' as it was called.

Blackface music and dance were commonly syntheses of African-American and European forms. So-called Negro minstrel song frequently combined popular British melody with words depicting white perceptions of African-American life and dialect.[4] The dances were generally a combination of long established European folk forms such as the Hornpipe or Jig and imitations of African-American forms. They also drew

Figure 3.1. Thomas Rice in Blackface. Reproduced in Harry Reynold's *Minstrel Memories*.

upon Anglo-American folk forms. The most influential of the early Negro delineators was Thomas D. Rice, whose Jim Crow routine, supposedly based on his observation of a peculiar performance by a deformed African-American, represents the beginning of a genre of dance and song that soon became world famous.[5] Rice, probably more than anyone, contributed to the definition of the African-American's future role in performance as typically 'grotesque, shuffling, peculiar, eccentric, jumping, loose-limbed, awkward, funny and, of course, rhythmic[al]'.[6]

In 1843 a group of blackface performers billed as the Virginia Minstrels performed a complete program of 'oddities, peculiarities, eccentricities, and comicalities'.[7] This was, in effect, the beginning of the minstrel show as an independent entertainment genre.

> The Virginia Minstrels inadvertently began to shape the conventions of the minstrel show when they structured their performances. To improve the coordination of the show, they arranged their chairs in a semi-circle, with the tambourine and bones (simple rhythm 'clackers') players on the ends; to give the performance the aura of a real party and to provide continuity, they interspersed comic repartee between the otherwise unconnected songs and dances; to add laughter they closed the first part of their two part show with a stump speech (a humorous address on a topical subject delivered in heavy malaprop-laden dialect); and to stress their authenticity as 'Ethiopian delineators,' they concentrated on songs and dance about Southern Negroes . . . Besides that, the instruments they used – the fiddle, banjo, bones and tambourine – became the core of the minstrel band. But, minstrelsy still had only minimal structure. From its inception, it had such versatility and flexibility that it could immediately respond to its audiences' preferences in both form and content.[8]

A few black performers, most notably the famous black dancer, Juba (William Henry Lane), played an active role in determining the content of minstrelsy. However, genuine black minstrel troupes did not even begin to evolve until the mid-1850s, more than a decade after the structure and conventions of the show had been established. After the

Civil War minstrelsy provided the main entry-point for African-Americans into the entertainment industry but it also represented a dilemma. Black minstrels could not gain much credit from white audiences for their cleverness as actors or delineators because they were perceived to be the 'real thing'. They were therefore more or less limited either to imitating the already popular structure, conventions and exaggerated racial stereotypes provided by white minstrelsy or promoting their own authenticity. Yet those who adopted the distorted stereotypes of the white minstrel show and claimed authenticity only reinforced the existing white perception of the African-American as a naturally grotesque, spontaneous, gifted musical clown or buffoon 'playing the music of nature untrammelled by art or any degree of affectation'.[9]

The significance of nineteenth-century black (African-American) minstrelsy to jazz development is already acknowledged in works such as W.C. Handy's *Father of the Blues.* Yet, as this acknowledged predecessor of jazz was based significantly on procedures and performance practices of an earlier, white theatrical invention – the blackface minstrel show – then white minstrelsy, the only form of 'Negro minstrelsy' of any influence in Australia before 1876, must have included some practices which anticipated jazz improvisation.

The following table offers some orientation to the history of the relationship between American, British and Australian minstrelsy in preparation for subsequent discussion. It corresponds to general discussion of events as recounted in significant secondary sources such as Robert Toll's much cited *Blacking Up: the Minstrel Show in Nineteenth-Century America* (1974), or Richard Waterhouse's *From Minstrel Show to Vaudeville* (1990). (see Table next page).

Minstrelsy as Aesthetic Subversion

The early minstrel show in America was both socially and musically subversive. The informality of the minstrel show's presentation and format returned to its working-class audiences the interactive freedom the elite had sought to deny them through the increasing formality of nineteenth-century theatre and concert performances. The content of minstrelsy also often mocked authority, formality and politics. Waterhouse describes the minstrel performance in terms of 'a 19th century leftover of Carnival, a modern equivalent in Peter Bourke's words of "a time of institutionalised disorder, a set of rituals in reverse"'.[10] The minstrel show in Australia followed this pattern by frequently mocking 'high art' such as opera and gave Australians a taste for a form of artistic expression that was, in certain respects, diametrically opposed to the prevailing aesthetic and direction of musical development of the period.

AMERICA	BRITAIN	AUSTRALIA
Early Nineteenth century: Individual blackface entertainers. **Early 1830s:** Rice's Jim Crow routine achieves fame.	**Early Nineteenth century:** Occasional Negro characterisation seen on the British stage. **1836:**Jim Crow craze reaches Britain.	**Early Nineteenth century:** Occasional Negro characterisation
1843: Virginia Minstrels herald the minstrel show craze.	**Early 1840s:** The Virginia Minstrels and other American troupes reach Britain. Local troupes are formed.	**c. 1840:** Solo blackface entertainers appear on stage (often local actors).
Mid-1850s: A few black minstrel troupes appear. **Post-Civil War:** (1) White minstrel shows move increasingly from Negro delineation towards larger, more lavish, 'respectable' and tightly structured variety programs. (2) Authentic black minstrel troupes present a challenge to pre-Civil War style white minstrelsy, but also follow changes in white minstrelsy.	**Late 1850s:** 'Christy Minstrels' troupes appears in Britain. ('Christy-style minstrelsy was more structured and 'refined' with an emphasis on musical content.) **Early 1870s:** Black troupes begin to reach Britain but do not greatly influence the nature of British minstrelsy: a minimal emphasis on African-American authenticity.	**1850s:** Small British and American troupes arrive. Some local troupes are organized. **1860s:** Minstrelsy dominated by Christy-style minstrelsy. **1870s:** Larger American troupes begin to arrive. **Late 1870s:** First black troupes arrive. **1880s:** Minstrelsy reaches height of popularity, but the minstrelsy content of large shows becomes secondary to burlesque and specialty acts.
Late 1890s: The minstrel show is now largely superseded by vaudeville and other entertainments. Early 'ragtime' in the form of syncopated 'coon song' and Cake Walk dancing and music become popular on the variety stage partly through emerging black musical theatre.	**Late 1890s:** Syncopated 'coon song' and Cake Walk dance and cakewalk music become popular.	**1890s:** Minstrelsy becomes a standard component of Australian vaudeville. **1899:** McAdoo's and Curtis's African-American troupes popularise syncopated 'coon song' and Cake Walk dance and cakewalk music.

Admiration for the formal, clean, simple, unadorned, symmetrical and beautiful in music, the 'classical' aesthetic, is a recurrent theme of colonial music critics. By the mid-1850s musical development in Australia was already pointing towards rational recreation and musical congruity as reflected in such phenomena as the burgeoning of mass (tonic sol-fa method) trained choirs. In place of formality, symmetry, beauty, rationality and orthodoxy, however, the first British and American minstrel shows to reach Melbourne offered spontaneity, absurdity, unorthodox instrumentation and modes of performance, and 'grotesque' distortion.

The term 'grotesque' is widely encountered in American, British and colonial Australian reviews of minstrelsy and has two related meanings in this context. It refers to what was perceived as the inherently primal nature of African-American plantation-slave performance and, more commonly, comic distortion or exaggeration.

The grotesque aspect of the minstrel show is most evident in the portrayal of the African-American as 'peculiar and grotesque musically as well as physically'.[11] It has been noted, for example, that the concept of Jim Crow, minstrelsy's first significant Negro stage stereotype, is a burlesque of a deformed Negro (a racial group already perceived to be intriguingly grotesque by many whites of the period). This burlesque comprises (in addition to improvised song verse) a set of dance movements which unfold in time in a distorted or grotesque way, including a bizarre syncopation in the form of the famous Jim Crow 'jump'.[12]

When blackface minstrels imitated what they believed to be the characteristics of African-American performance within a context of clowning, buffoonery and burlesque, they were actually improvising various unnatural travesties or 'grotesqueries'. In doing so they established in the Australian public mind a conceptual association between African-American culture and the notion of grotesque or comically distorted music and dance performance. It is is easy to see why improvisatory performance behaviour in early Australian ragtime and jazz improvisation was perceived as musical clowning or travesty.

Improvisatory Performance Practice in Minstrelsy

Performance practice in blackface minstrelsy, including the type that arrived in Melbourne two decades before the first African-American troupes, indicates the presence of various elements that related to improvisatory practice and, in some cases, to the type of jazz improvisation first heard in Australia. The principal elements were 'head arranging', playing by ear, musical burlesque or clowning, extended vocal techniques and instrumental variations. This is in addition to the fluid and indeterminate nature of the minstrel show structure, resulting from interaction between audience and stage entertainment.

Head Arrangements

Although piano and vocal arrangements of minstrel music were published during the mid-nineteenth century, much of the musical material used in the shows was probably the end product of what today might be called creative workshopping. Musical acts in minstrelsy functioned as on-stage theatrical entertainment and therefore represented a bonding of musical inventiveness with acting skills. Furthermore, minstrelsy evolved in a period when the practices of gagging (improvising dialogue) and improvised song verse was still common. Therefore new material for the show, whether musical or non-musical, would have often emerged from intuitive group or individual responses to situations and problems arising out of live performance or rehearsal, especially as early troupes in Australia (such as Rainer's Original Ethiopian Serenaders) sometimes advertised a 'change of program every evening'.[13] Whereas standard theatre could draw upon a vast repertoire of stock dramas or farces, the early minstrel show was in the process of creating a new genre and was therefore often forced back upon its own limited resources to create or synthesise new material.

Playing by Ear

The minstrel shows that toured Victoria in the 1850s were generally made up of four or five multi-skilled performers who played overtures and provided musical accompaniment to opera burlesque and other components of the minstrel show. However, their totally unorthodox 'orchestras' usually comprised violin or flautina (button accordion) or concertina, banjo, bone castanets and tambourine. It is therefore very unlikely that scored musical arrangements were ever used in the preparation of the accompaniment for new program material.

As the early minstrel show required performers with multiple skills it frequently threw together aurally-oriented and formally-trained musicians, as was the case with travelling Australian family circus bands. Given the nature of the core orchestra's instrumentation, the need for physical mobility, the elasticity of the program and perhaps the need to sound 'authentically grotesque', 'playing by ear' (or by memory) was probably the norm. The ear was really the only means by which the idiosyncrasies of such unorthodox instrumental music as bones playing could be learned or imitated.[14] Ear playing was also prevalent with the later African-American troupes.[15] In his memoirs, the former black minstrel W.C. Handy even complained of certain musicians who 'bowed to the authority of the printed note' and could not 'fake' and 'sell it', like minstrels.[16]

In a sense, the blackface minstrel troupe has its closest counterpart in the present-day rock band. The successful rock band performance is of necessity a multi-medium show: a fluidly structured, self-contained piece of musical theatre. Emerging rock bands (at least those that aspire to originality) generally assemble such a show in progressive layers through an intuitive and fairly democratic group process: what works is kept, what doesn't is discarded and nothing really needs to be written down. It could be said that the successful rock musician is, ideally, a clever multiple-skilled performer who can sing, dance, ad lib dialogue and play African-American influenced music by ear.

Musical Burlesque

The informal and sometimes riotous context of the minstrel show must have translated frequently into exaggerated and possibly imaginative musical buffoonery. Minstrels performed numerous forms of musical burlesque including grand opera. For example, the Backus Minstrels' first Melbourne performance included vocal burlesque of 'Chinese song', 'Hungarian vocalists' and 'Miska Hauser's [violin] variations of the Carnival Of Venice'. It also included 'choral participation in a banjo trio' and 'extraordinary imitations of the bagpipes and of other wind instruments, in a solo on the violin'.[17]

Opera burlesque was sung in imitation Negro dialect and included the interpolation of humorous dialogue; and absurd liberties were probably often taken with vocal range, timbre, fermatas, cadenzas and so forth. A later Australian reviewer (1863) notes that:

> Sometimes the original air is carried out, sometimes it is ludicrously changed . . . [They] are exactly the kind of entertainments that one would imagine the 'darkies,' with their remarkable imitative faculties would concoct, after having, from the 'Negro Tier,' witnessed the representation of an opera.[18]

The musical buffoonery heard in the Melbourne minstrel shows during the gold rush was therefore often a valid and functional form of improvisatory embellishment: the spontaneous (or seemingly spontaneous) variation upon well-known musical models.

Extended Vocal Techniques

Minstrels, in their roles as musical clowns, utilised various unorthodox or extended instrumental techniques in the production of humorous sound effects or novelty 'noise'. Vocal sounds were, as already indicated, a particularly important way of producing entertaining effects and included 'extraordinary' falsetto.[19] Rainer's Original Ethiopian Serenaders, who reached Melbourne in 1852, claimed to 'give forth Inimitable Entertainment illustrative of Negro life and character'. One of their items was an

'"Ethiopian Dirge" displaying a compass of voice truly astonishing'[20] This description brings to mind the haunting and melismatic African-American 'field holler' although it probably refers to something quite different. The extent to which blackface minstrels of the colonial era imitated the improvisatory nuances of African-American vocal technique is not clear, but the minstrel music scholar Hans Nathan writes that:

> In imitating the Negro's manner and speech, [Negro delineators] must have also imitated his way of singing which was characterised not only by a specific timbre, but, as it still is, by pitches outside our tonal system, 'slides from one note to another, and turns and cadences not in articulated notes'.[21]

Early cylinder recordings of Negro delineators such as Len Spencer often feature these characteristics.

Instrumental Variations

In addition to novelty sound, the minstrel show provided a context for more active forms of musical variation. Local programs often featured an instrumental 'solo with variations' or, less commonly, a 'fantasia' upon an unspecified theme.[22] This is of no great significance in itself as similar items are cited in Melbourne concert hall, circus, and variety hall programs of the period. Yet some of the forms of musical variation presented in the minstrel show, such as banjo variations, were specific to minstrelsy,

Figure 3.2. The Ethiopian Serenaders (1846). Reproduced in Harry Reynolds, *Minstrel Memories*. This is the type of ensemble that reached Melbourne in the early 1850s. Note the absence of the violin.

or at least to its core instruments. Therefore, to the degree that these variations were supposed to represent the performance characteristics of African-Americans, they are an explicit historical link with the white jazz soloist of later years.

The Core Minstrel Band

The prototype 'orchestra' for the early minstrel show was the fiddle, the banjo, the bones and the tambourine. Rhythmic hand-clapping and minstrel dance were similarly related to the core of the minstrel show. Nathan provides a score which he suggests approximates the 'manner of performance' of the early minstrel bands. His reconstruction is based upon a published vocal/piano score of the minstrel song 'Twill Nebber Do To Gib It Up' (by Dan Emmett) and information regarding minstrel banjo accompaniments which he gleaned from later banjo methods. In this reconstruction the fiddle follows the solo voice (often playing a semiquaver behind the vocalist), while the banjo embellishes this same line. Nathan explains:

> The parts of the tambourine and the bones are mere skeletons; they allow any number of shakes and syncopations . . . Finally, the banjoist should tap his foot to the music – four times within a measure.[23]

In an earlier description of such a band he mentions that:

> The tones of the banjo died away quickly and therefore could not serve as a solid foundation in the ensemble. On top was the squeaky, carelessly tuned fiddle. Add a dry 'ra, raka, taka, tak' of the bones and the tambourine's dull thumps and ceaseless jingling to the twang of the banjo and the flat tone of the fiddle, and the sound of the band is approximated: it was scratchy, tinkling, cackling and humorously incongruous.[24]

In Musical Example 3.1 I have reconstructed an approximation of an early minstrel orchestra performance of the song 'Old Rob Ridley'. The banjo line would also include syncopated patterns arising from off-beat stresses on particular notes, as explained in the following discussion of minstrel banjo playing. The staves, from top to bottom, represent vocalist, fiddle, banjo, tambourine and bones.

The Fiddle

Very little information survives on early blackface minstrel fiddle style, although Nathan suggests:

> the fiddler may have played the tune straighter than the banjoist, though with occasional variants including dotted notes and syncopations, and with open strings as drones, as is still the custom in the backwoods.[25]

He also notes that the accordion frequently substituted for the violin (perhaps because

Musical Ex. 3.1. My reconstruction of an early blackface minstrel ensemble performance based on an example of minstrel song ('Old Rob Ridley') with banjo accompaniment from *Phil Rice's Correct Method for the Banjo: With or Without a Master.*

it was more of a novelty than the latter). This was the case with several of the touring minstrel shows that performed in Melbourne before 1855.[26] The 'orchestra' of the locally formed (and reformed) Barlow's Sable Minstrels was sometimes led by a violinist. Their programs include violin, or 'fiddle', variations and potpourris on popular tunes, violin and banjo duets and 'trickery on one and two violins'.[27]

Changes which are said to have taken place in minstrel violin performance practice from the formation of the Virginia Minstrels onwards illustrate the tendency of blackface minstrels to distance themselves from the old-fashioned delineation of 'grotesque' Negro performance. Another leading minstrel music scholar, Robert Winans, writes:

> I suspect that [violin solos] were based on 'plantation' material towards the beginning of the period . . . Towards the end of the decade [by the early 1850s], however, the evidence suggests that violin solos were serious music, played seriously, to show virtuosity.[28]

Melbourne minstrel show programs from the mid-1850s indicate that bagpipe imitations and so forth on violin still had entertainment value but reviews of conventional concerts testify that 'carelessly tuned', 'flat', 'scratchy' and out of time violin playing was no novelty to long-suffering colonials. Nevertheless, the violin remained a core instrument in the minstrel show orchestra throughout the remainder of the century and the ability to play convincingly in authentic 'grotesque' or 'characteristic' style (it would later be called 'hot' style) was still required of minstrel fiddlers in 'plantation sketches', 'Negro song' accompaniment, and similar situations.

The Accordion or Concertina

Early minstrel button accordion and concertina playing raises further questions about improvisatory practice in early minstrelsy, as performers on these instruments were often complimented by Australian critics on their virtuosic variations or 'fantasias'.[29] Nathan suggests that, in the minstrel ensemble, the accordion 'probably played no chords but merely the main melody' and here he cites some early 1840s accordion methods.[30] As a button accordion player of many years' experience, I believe that virtuosic players, such as those mentioned in colonial reviews, would have developed many clever ways of elaborating the melodic line in their quest to be entertaining. The most significant aspect of virtuoso minstrel accordion or concertina playing is that it takes a step away from 'grotesque' or 'authentic' plantation delineation.[31]

The Bones

Even before the gold rush the bones were played by local 'Congo Minstrels' in Melbourne as self-accompaniment to 'Negro melody'.[32] An 1849 Melbourne advertisement for the Congo Minstrel suggests an early colonial appetite for 'hot' percussive rhythm on the bones.

Winans describes the bones as:

> flat, animal rib bones, slightly curved, or hardwood facsimiles. Two pairs were used, one in each hand, held between the fingers and played with a rapid wrist action to produce a castanet-like sound capable of great rhythmic complexity.[33]

Colonial programs show that bones solos often involved drum and 'horse race imitations' or participation in, as one program describes,

> a Musical description of a Fashionable Sleigh Ride, with the departure – Race on the Road – the Arrival at the Hotel – the ball.'[34]

The former minstrel and minstrel-show historian, Harry Reynolds, claims that 'quite remarkable effects have been obtained at times by expert players'.[35] A Melbourne observer of the 1850s was less forthcoming in his comment that a particular minstrel 'handles the bones skilfully and contrives to knock music out of those primitive instruments'.[36]

The Tambourine

Another core instrument, the tambourine, was often featured in conjunction with the bones to create a more complex rhythmic and timbral texture. In the hands of an 'expert' player, however, the tambourine was capable of producing complex rhythmic

Figure 3.3. Advertisement for the Congo Minstrel, *Argus*, 24 April 1849.

and timbral embellishments. One 1845 American program description of a 'Solo On The Tambourine' claims that the performer would:

> go through his imitative powers on the Tambourine, particularly where the locomotive runs off the track and bursts the Boiler, also the rattling of the Cannon in the distance, his Reveille beating the Troops to quarters, his imitations of a celebrated French drummer, executing single and double drags in perfect time – his Grist Mill grindings showing the power of steam, (of course) and the rattling of a Cotton Mill and machinery. Language cannot convey any idea of his brilliant rapidity of execution on his Tambourine.[37]

As the performance practices of bones and tambourine playing were aurally transmitted, we cannot be certain just what techniques are represented by this description. It is significant, however, that the way these instruments were used represents an important antecedent to the jazz 'break'. One of Mayhew's London minstrel informants says, for example, that 'we've real bones, rib-of-beef bones, but some have ebony-bones, which sound better than rib-bones – they tell best in "Goin ober de Mountain," for there's a symphony [a break] between every line'.[38] Expert 'endmen' on the bones and tambourine developed a sufficient degree of rhythmic complexity on these simple percussion instruments to thrill nineteenth-century audiences, perhaps to the degree that contemporary audiences are thrilled by an impressive jazz or rock drum break.[39] One example is provided by the versatile goldfield entertainers, Mr and Mrs Pendleton, who were acclaimed for their 'inimitable' bone and tambourine act in the 1850s. A Melbourne review of the San Francisco Minstrels, who toured Australia in 1858, commends a local musician (Richard Kohler) for his performance on the 'American pine sticks' (the bones).[40]

Patting Juba

Another type of percussive, rhythmic minstrel music that was probably familiar to Melbourne audiences in the 1850s was hand-clapping. They would have encountered this form of accompaniment through the 'plantation dances' mentioned on local programs and the 'plantation scenes' in the numerous Australian productions of *Uncle Tom's Cabin* (which from the late 1870s often featured African-American performers). An early nineteenth-century description of this 'patting juba' records that the rhythm comprised:

> a slap of one hand on the left knee followed by the same stroke and noise on the right, and then a loud slap of the two palms together. I should add that the left hand made two strokes in half-time to one for the right, something after the double stroke of the left drumstick in beating the kettledrum.[41]

The mention of 'dance-time' in the following reference to patting juba in the late nineteenth-century suggests a simple inactive texture with something 'clever' added to make it 'hotter':

> the spatting of dance-time with the outspread palms on the knees . . . [which if] cleverly executed . . . will set the saltatorial nerves in motion as quickly as the catchiest music.[42]

Nathan suggests that both hands were clapped together overhead, or sometimes one hand was clapped against an elbow.

Minstrel Dancing and Improvisatory Practice

Minstrel dance interacted with the music to produce audible rhythmic patterns something like the percussion sounds produced by tambourine, bones and minstrel hand-clapping. For example, a Melbourne reviewer noted in 1863 that one minstrel 'produces with his feet sounds which harmonise with the musical accompaniment to a really extraordinary extent'. [43] This dance included improvised or seemingly improvised rhythmic variations. Nathan points out that:

> Percussive rhythms were emphasised from the early forties on, when clogs began to be used occasionally. The taps were heard as accompaniment to the dance, and sometimes appeared as inserts as well. For example, in a minstrel song of the forties, 'heel solos' briefly interrupted the music, thus at once varying the motion and furnishing a literal illustration of the question in the text: 'who dar knocking at the door?'.[44]

Minstrel dancing as a popular ingredient of Melbourne entertainment can be traced back to the 'Yankee Breakdown', mentioned in Finn's description of Melbourne theatre before the goldrush. Most of the better known forms of minstrel dance reached the Melbourne stage after 1850.[45] An early Melbourne handbill for Charles Coppin evokes intriguing images of unorthodox sound and rhythmic movement:

> Mr Coppin will appear as the Old Kentucky Nigger and screech the celebrated Nigger melody Jim Brown, with his unequalled CYMBAL POT-LID ACCOMPANIMENT and extraordinary LOUISIANA JUMP and OLD KENTUCKY GRAPE VINE TWIST making a display of toe and heel genius 'surprising to de white folk and sartin death to all Long Island Niggers.'[46]

The American dance writer Marian Hannah Winter points to a 'definite continuity of terminology' between the use of the term 'lick' (a short improvised interpolation) in minstrelsy and its later use in jazz. She cites the billing for one famous mid-nineteenth-century American blackface minstrel which mentions his 'Unheard of, Outlandish and inimitable Licks, what is Death to all de Long Island Darkies'.[47] She also notes that the sense of timing and the rhythmic breaks that are integral features of jazz were equally a part of African-American dance.[48] 'Breakdown' was the generic term for minstrel dance, even in colonial Australia; and this notion of 'breaking down' (assuming that the term breakdown refers to the breaking down or subdivision of the basic beat) corresponds to one of two basic approaches to improvisatory practice (the second being the improvisatory insertion of stock devices). Isaac Goldberg, who spoke with former minstrels such as W. C. Handy, writes:

> Before the Negroes called these tunes and dances by the name of rag, I believe the word was 'breakdown.' It is helpful, in this connection, to recall the word, 'break', as used to designate the improvisations characteristic of the later jazz bands. To break down the rhythm, to rag it, would mean simply to pep it up with off-beat rhythms and effects of syncopation.[49]

Ironically, the notion of breaking down would seem to be much more closely related to the European conception of rhythm (divisive rhythm) than that of African-American plantation slave culture, which might be expected to have embodied the more modular conception of rhythm found in West African drum ensemble music.[50]

Another connection between jazz improvisation and dance may be found in the Plantation Walk Around, a common minstrel closing item (Figure 3.4). The 'Walk Around' foreshadows the jazz 'jam session' when each performer takes a turn to improvise the chorus. In this dance routine each member of the minstrel troupe would apparently:

> walk down stage from the semi-circle, walk around for sixteen bars of the music and do one step of a reel, finish with a break, then resume his place in the semicircle as another stepped out and repeated the performance, varying, though, with a different step.[51]

The following account is reminiscent of the final chorus of a collective improvisation in early jazz style:

> . . . and to the concluding instrumental music, the solo performers began to dance in a circle with boisterous and grotesque steps and rowdy gestures.[52]

In the Cake Walk dancing that reached the Australian stage in the late 1890s, the short exhibitionary solos of the Walk-Around finale had become the improvisatory flourishes of individual Cake Walking couples as they competed for 'the cake' in the Cake Walk finale (see Chapter Four).

It has been argued that before the introduction of the syncopated Buck and Wing (i.e. Soft Shoe: a combination of clogs, jigs, song and dance) in the late nineteenth century, all the blackface minstrel dances 'lacked swing in the jazz sense'.[53] The following colonial description, however, illustrates that they did not lack swing in the sense of maintaining precise rhythmic cohesion with the musical accompaniment.

Figure 3.4. Concluding dance of a Walk-Around (1859). From an American playbill reproduced in Hans Nathan, *Dan Emmett and the Rise of Early Negro Minstrelsy.*

Note also the reference to the insertion of breaks, the short catalogue of devices and the playing of an 'accompaniment' with plated heels:

> We are unacquainted with the technical or rather artistic varied terms of the Terpsichorean or saltatory movements: the toe and heel, double shuffle, back slide, tremolo, double tremolo, where every inch of flesh, every fibre and muscle seems to quiver . . . His perception of time is marvellous . . . no matter what the movement, what his position, or what innovations he may introduce on each cessation [break], not the sixteenth part of a semiquaver is he behind or before the accompanying musician. And at length the acme is reached amidst the loudest exclamations, when, after a series of extraordinary multipedlian gyrations, he gives a series of measures to popular melodies, the accompaniment to which he plays with the plated heels of his own boots.[54]

Blackface minstrels in their role as delineators attempted to represent the supposedly grotesque ('primal') nature of African-American folk dancing through forms such as the Juba (similar to a jig with variations) or the Grotesque Essence; or Essence Of Old Virginia (the origin of Soft Shoe), which was much more African-American in origin (see Figure 3.5). The grotesque aspect of minstrel dance became much less relevant in later blackface minstrelsy which was increasingly oriented towards variety theatre. In 'The Rise and Fall of Early Negro Minstrelsy' (1915) Brander Matthews states that eventually 'Clog Dancing became more intricate and mechanical – and thereby more remote from the buck-and-wing dancing of the real Negro'.[55] By the late 1880s Melbourne had at least one 'Dance Academy' which taught Clog-Dancing and organised competitions, a sure indication of increasing codification of stage dance practice.

Figure 3.5. 'Old Rob Ridley': a sketch of a blackface minstrel dancer. Reproduced in Harry Reynolds, *Minstrel Memories*.

Nathan states that:

> the stage demanded planned variety and it encouraged showmanship. The dancer was expected to excel in precision, speed, near-acrobatic flexibility, and endurance, and to stress jolliness and clownishness for their own sake.[56]

Where blackface minstrels took a 'break' on stage, this was improvisatory primarily in the sense that it was skilfully assembled in performance time from a select stock of personal devices or 'licks'. A comparable form of imitation ecstatic performance practice is described in the following chapter in relation to the procedures of ragtime improvisation practised by white musicians. The arrival in Australia of new forms of African-American inspired dance such as the Cake Walk heralded a new age of less inhibited improvisatory self-expression through dance.

Incipient Ragtime and Jazz Improvisation In Early Minstrel Banjo Style

> The history of jazz has now been extended backward. It does not begin with ragtime, Negro spirituals, or the songs of the early popular theatre, but with a few dozen [blackface minstrel] banjo tunes which have the flavour of the plantation. Although originating about one hundred years ago, they furnished the basic elements of an idiom of surprising contemporaneity.[57]

Early minstrel show music was overwhelmingly vocally oriented, and simple minstrel song was the aspect of minstrelsy most rapidly absorbed by colonial Australian culture. Yet some significant connections between minstrel instrumental music and later instrumental ragtime and jazz (such as the mutual emphasis on 'hot' percussive rhythm) have already been indicated. Further to this, Nathan, Winans and other American scholars point to a particularly important relationship between the melodic and rhythmic content of early minstrel banjo playing and that of ragtime and jazz. This means that the type of banjo music that began to be played in Melbourne from about 1850 onwards included what might be described as incipient jazz improvisation.

The early minstrel banjo, which supposedly represented the instrument played by plantation slaves, was played quite differently, sounded different and was physically different to the banjo of today:

> The main differences were a larger diameter body with a deeper but thinner rim and a fretless fingerboard; its five strings were gut, tuned, as a whole, either a third or a fourth below modern pitch, depending on the key to be played . . . Surviving banjos from the period have a mellower, fuller, more resonant sound . . . In the minstrel ensemble the banjo was a melody instrument; it did not provide chordal accompaniment, as might be assumed.[58]

The percussive 'plunk' produced by even the modern banjo does not sustain and banjo playing is therefore improvisatory, in the sense that banjo players, and ear players in particular, must fill in pauses and sustained notes with embellishment.

In his much-cited analysis of surviving manuscript versions of early minstrel banjo tunes, Nathan demonstrates the presence of a rhythmic language which anticipated

> the principle of pitting highly irregular accentuation in the melody, chiefly produced by melodic rather than dynamic means, against a precise metrical accompaniment, which characterises all American dance music up to the present [1962].[59]

He lists eight 'rhythmic features of banjo music' which were absorbed into jazz and compares short musical examples from ragtime and jazz literature with complete examples from the banjo literature.[60] Among these features are:

1. Omission of a tone from one of the beats to create off-beat stress.
2. Successive repetition of identical tones on off-beats.
3. Repetition of adjacent tones in quick succession with changing accentuation.
4. Premature phrase entry.
5. Alternate single tones and simultaneous tones to create off-beats.
6. Dotted notes and triplets in a context of duple notes.
7. The primary ragtime pattern ♪♩♪

Nathan mentions that 'the banjoist liked to vary the main melody by inserting into it the open tones of his two highest strings' and that 'motion was intensified by omitting tones on accented beats, creating a type of syncopation which existed in print already in the forties'.[61] More importantly, he points to a connection between minstrel banjo music and ragtime improvisation in observing that 'the omission of the tone on the first beat was a landmark of ragtime'. Here he is citing the first published method on ragtime improvisation (published in 1897) devised by the famous vaudeville pianist and self-proclaimed originator of ragtime, Ben Harney (see Musical Ex. 3.2).[62]

Nathan acknowledges the plantation origins of the 'preference for off-beats' found in the minstrel banjo repertoire and suggests that some of the minstrel tunes may have been appropriated from plantation musicians.[63] Winans supports this in his comment that 'banjo pieces seem always to have been 'plantation' material; that is, more or less in imitation of the dance music of the Southern plantation.'[64]

In his article 'The Banjo In Ragtime' Lowell Schreyer discusses *Briggs' Banjo Instructor* (1855) by the American blackface minstrel, Tom Briggs, which explains:

> a more subtle means for inner rhythm – the banjo stroke technique. This style was common to minstrel banjo playing of the period. It produced shifts in emphasis, not always apparent in notation, by differences in timbre of notes within a phrase.[65]

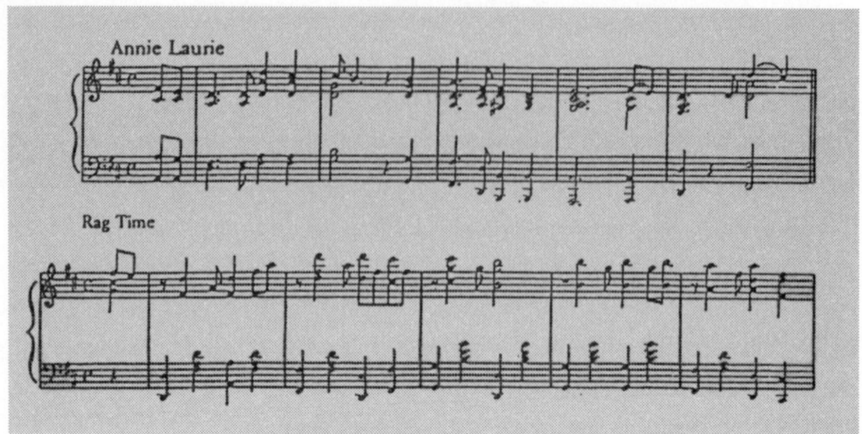

Musical Ex. 3.2. Exercises 1-2 of *Ben Harney's Rag Time Instructor*, (arranged by Theodore Northrup, 1897). The second system of no. 2 illustrates the system of 'ragged' transformation or ragtime improvisation.

Schreyer describes the result as a regular on-beat pattern over which is superimposed:

> a variant in irregular rhythm . . . In concept this was not unlike West African drumming, which lay in the past, or ragtime which was to come.[66]

He also provides a notated example from Briggs' instructor (Musical Ex. 3.3) to which he adds his own notation of the superimposed pattern of syncopation (not included). Here the fingerstrokes (F) create a stress on each quaver while the finger slides (-) and the thumbstrokes (X) superimpose a distinctive off-beat pattern, thereby producing a polyrhythmic pattern. The Melbourne five-string banjo player, researcher and collector, Ray Jones, provided me with a tape of himself playing tunes such as 'Bones in de Barn Yard' from Briggs' instructor and the superimposed stresses described by Schreyer are immediately audible.

Schreyer also discusses the relationship between nineteenth-century 'banjo imitations' on piano and early banjo style, noting that 'this technique of breaking-up

Musical Ex. 3.3. Bars 1-2 of the B section of 'Briggs' Jig'. F represents the right hand index finger; the slur below the notes and the underlying dash represent sliding with the index finger; X represents the right hand thumb.

chords to create piano ragtime is explained in *Ben Harney's Rag-Time Instructor* of 1897.'[67]

In his essay 'The Folk, The Stage and the Five String Banjo', Winans discusses minstrel banjo style in far greater depth than either Nathan or Schreyer and gives a detailed description of the 'strike' system which was used to fill out or embellish a given melody with repeated notes or neighbour, passing or chord tones (Musical Ex. 3.4).[68]

Since the banjo was played in unison with the violin and the vocal line, in minstrel banjo style the basic tones of the original melody were stressed, while sustained tones and rests were filled-in with a secondary level of melodic embellishment. Where the rhythmic placement of notes was displaced (i.e. syncopated) to represent the

Musical Ex. 3.4. 'Darling Nellie Gray' from *Phil Rice's Correct Method for the Banjo: With or Without a Master.* Compare the banjo line with the vocal line.

'grotesque' character of plantation music, the result is comparable with ragtime and jazz embellishment practice. The complex polyrhythm resulting from the uneven dynamic stress and timbre produced by the early minstrel stroke (or strike) technique reinforced the grotesque nature of the music and was a further anticipation of ragtime and jazz.

The Banjo in Melbourne Minstrel Shows

> . . . two parties of Ethiopians hav[e] suddenly invaded us; making this whole town alive with the notes of the banjo and the rattle of the bones; and leading us in our astonishment as [to] the extent of the sable invasion, to exclaim with the poor o'd lady who had a long day's washing spoilt by the smoky chimney, 'Oh drat 'em, how the blacks is fell'.
>
> *Argus*, Melbourne, 17 July 1850, p. 2.

Although the Melbourne public was familiar with blackface minstrels before 1850, the almost simultaneous arrival of the two rival troupes mentioned above represents the introduction of both the minstrel show as such to Melbourne and the banjo as a major instrument of popular entertainment. By 1854 it could be remarked that blackface minstrelsy 'seems to have become a "staple of amusement in Melbourne"'[69] Listed below are most of the blackface minstrel shows that appeared in Melbourne up until 1855. Although some returned several times, I have cited only their first appearances:

1850	Waterland and Readings Band	British
1851	Howard's Ethiopian Serenaders	British
	American Black Serenaders	Local?
1852	Rainer's Original Ethiopian Serenaders	American
1853	Barlow's Sable Minstrels	Local
1854	Totten's Harmoneons	American
1855	Backus Minstrels	American[70]

Shortly before the Howard and Waterland troupes appeared in Melbourne, the Theatre Royal in Geelong featured what seems to have been a largely local troupe, the Ethiopian Serenaders. They were directed by the 'celebrated banjoist' Troy Knight, who had been introduced to Geelong audiences several months earlier as a vocalist. The critic of the *Geelong Advertiser* noted that:

> Unlike most of our own colonial 'Ethiopians', Mr Knight really brings music out of that primitive instrument the banjo, and does it too with a lightness and swiftness of touch, absolutely astonishing. His success in his 'nigger' personations [sic] accompanied by this instrument was complete, and bestowed a great fund of comic humour into them.[71]

A review of the Waterland troupe (who claimed to be the 'Original Performers on the American Banjo in New South Wales') suggests a high level of energy and spontaneity, but reveals nothing of banjo performance practice; although the reference to the 'ultra-grotesque' suggests it included some unconventional musical transformation or embellishment. The *Argus* reviewer described the show as:

> a constant succession of songs and choruses accompanied by the banjo, the bones, the tambourine, and flautina [button accordion], ranging through all grades from the most deeply pathetic to the ultra-grotesque, filling the intervals with a running fire of conundrums, jokes, and anecdotes; and presenting together a most amusing sketch of nigger life.[72]

Very little is reported of the Melbourne performances of Howard's Ethiopian Serenaders. The *Geelong Advertiser* had previously noted that they had 'more efficient command over their instruments' than the local troupe which they had just superseded and also commented upon the energy and immediacy of their show:

> The *bon mots*, riddles, conundrums, and the equivoques which were poured out in succession and jostled one against the other last evening, intermixed, with such drollery, humour, and facetiae succeeded in keeping the audience in one continual roar.[73]

Figure 3.6. From the program for Howard's Ethiopian Serenaders. *Geelong Advertiser*, 20 July 1850, p. 3.

It can only be assumed that the banjo in Howard's Ethiopian Serenaders or Waterland and Reading's Band played a similar role in the minstrel orchestra to that described by Nathan.

Howard's Ethiopian Serenaders' Geelong program, in Figure 3.6, claims that their performance was an accurate representation of African-American characteristics. It is therefore disappointing that Geelong reviewers do not compare the 'authentic' banjo technique of this troupe with that of Troy Knight. The third troupe to arrive in Melbourne (in August 1851), the American Black Serenaders, also featured banjo solos in their programs, but again these are ignored by reviewers.

The programs of Rainer's Ethiopian Serenaders who arrived in Melbourne in 1852 provide clear evidence of banjo variations and (unspecified) banjo embellishment technique. As advertised in the *Argus* from 1852 to 1854 this troupe featured items such as 'Solo-Banjo with oddities,

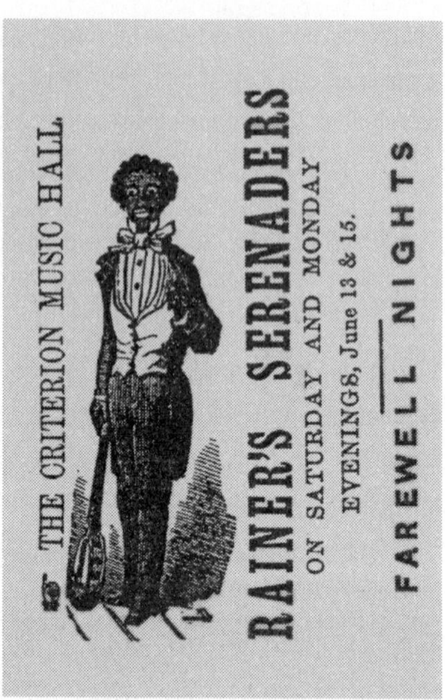

Figure 3.7. A typical 1850s advertisement for Rainer's Serenaders, Castlemaine, Victoria (undated).

absurdities, comicalities, profundities, contradictories, incongruities, probabilities', 'Solo-Banjo – Polka with variations', 'Banjo solo with variations', 'Banjo solo (original – first time)', 'Characteristic [African-American] Banjo Trio' and 'Solo – banjo – grand medley with variations introducing harmonic march family polka'.[74]

In 1853, programs for the locally formed Barlow's Sable Minstrels featured a 'Duetto (Banjo and Violin) – Old Folks at Home with Variations'. The banjo player, Mr Barlow, also performed a 'rock harmonicon solo', a bones solo, various songs and the Dance of Lucy Long. Baker and Clark of Totten's Harmoneons, who arrived in Melbourne in 1854, often featured banjo solos on their programs, but the *Argus* reviewer seems to have been more intrigued by the button accordion fantasias of another troupe member, noting only that Clark's banjo playing was 'richly-toned'. One of the banjo solo titles on the Harmoneons' program, 'Hard Times', is by Tom Briggs, author of *Briggs' Banjo Instructor*. Winans describes 'Hard Times' (which he recorded for World Records) as:

> a typical banjo solo of the first decade [which] illustrates some of the features of banjo pieces that Nathan discusses, especially the repetition of brief motives with slight variations, the use of triadic figures, and the general emphasis on rhythmic rather than melodic complexity.[75]

He also states that, in America, banjo solos were often omitted from the program. Melbourne programs may, therefore, under-represent the amount of banjo soloing that actually took place in local minstrel shows. It can be assumed that the 'banjo solo', 'banjo solo with variations' and 'characteristic' banjo items listed in Melbourne programs were often plantation delineation material, along with 'Hard Times', 'Gravy on their Taters' and others which are also cited. Other plantation tunes such as 'Root Hog or Die' and 'Grape Vine Twist' are mentioned as minstrel dances and would have been accompanied by the banjo.

The important thing, however, is not that plantation tunes were played, but that the early minstrel banjo style, which was soon formalised in banjo methods such as Briggs' (1855) and Rice's (1858), transformed even the simplest popular tune into something different – something 'hotter' and more exciting. Nathan states that 'minstrel music stirred popular imagination in the nineteenth century, particularly in the first half, with the same intensity as jazz does in our own time'. The impact this new sound had upon Melbourne audiences in the 1850s, given their isolation, was possibly even more intense.[76]

After the mid-1850s references to banjo 'eccentricities' become less common; but this also corresponds with the overall post-goldrush trend in Australian mainstream audience taste towards more 'refined' entertainment, as already discussed. By the 1860s, however, the banjo was a relatively commonplace instrument and Australian reviewers had very little reason to comment on its use in a minstrel show. Both the Court Minstrels and Christy Minstrels featured 'comic' banjo items on their Melbourne programs in the 1860s but a reviewer of Emerson's Californian Minstrels' opening Melbourne performance in 1873 states bluntly that the 'banjo eccentricities might have been dispensed with without prejudice to the merits of the performance'.[77] A detailed review of the Beechworth Amateur Minstrels in 1878 discusses with enthusiasm an 'air and variations' on violin while ignoring the 'banjo eccentricities' performed on the same program.[78]

It becomes very difficult to trace the residual influence of early minstrel banjo up to the Australian ragtime era for the following reasons. From the 1870s the old-style fretless minstrel banjo was gradually superseded by improved fretted versions (increasingly with steel strings) which brought, in turn, the new 'guitar' or 'classic' finger-style and a burgeoning repertoire of banjo compositions and transcriptions, including classical works such as the 'William Tell Overture'. These changes were assisted by the efforts of manufacturers, teachers and music publishers to distance the banjo from its long associations with 'grotesque' plantation style performance and comic eccentricities and elevate its performance practice and repertoire almost to 'art music' status. As a result the banjo became a widely popular instrument, independent of its minstrel show associations. The establishment in Australia of banjo academies, societies and banjo 'orchestras' from the early 1880s further distanced banjo playing from the old 'grotesque' banjo style.

Classic style was primarily a notation (not tablature) based performance tradition, but Melbourne banjo teachers offered to teach classic style by reading music or 'by ear' and it is claimed that Australia's best known classic-style player, Bessie Campbell, learnt to play by ear in the 1880s from the resident African-American minstrel and banjo virtuoso, Hosea Easton.[79] Classic style also embraced improvisatory characteristics such as the use of harmonics, plectrum tremolo, turns, shakes and 'rolling playing': chordal patterns that players could 'introduce into accompaniments and solos as pleasure'.[80] However, highly significant aspects of the old minstrel banjo technique, such as the subtle rhythmic embellishment described by Schreyer, gradually receded from the minstrel show sound or became overlaid by the new classic techniques, except where this sound was required for old-time plantation sketches and so forth.

Yet the virtuoso classic players associated with this second phase of banjo technique, such as Campbell, often played minstrel jigs, cakewalks and other ragtime related music. Some idea of the extensive ragtime embellishment techniques used by this generation of banjo players can be gained from the acoustic recordings of early American-style leaders such as Vess Ossman and Fred Van Eps or British counterparts, such as Joe Morley or Olley Oakley. Recorded examples of early Australian adoption of banjo ragtime technique are, to date, sadly lacking.[81]

Melbourne and Sydney had fledgling commercial recording enterprises before 1910. One of these enterprises advertised 'records of local artists giving the latest songs as sung at the Tivoli and other Sydney theatres; and Local Bands and instrumentalists'. Early wax cylinder recordings of banjo music made in Australia feature Alfred Ringwood (recorded in June, 1899) and R. Hall (recorded c. 1907) playing 'Dreams Of Darkie Land'.[82]

Local banjo playing can be heard on recordings of Australian jazz made from 1926 onwards. By this time, however, the five string finger-style banjo playing of the classic era had been largely displaced by four-string tenor banjo playing in plectrum style and resident American 'jazz specialists' such as Will Squires had already been an influence on local style for several years. The tenor banjo's function in popular music was principally non-melodic, namely, the provision of propulsive chordal backing to dance band music, albeit interspersed with improvisatory jazz embellishments or 'fills'. Furthermore, a new generation of Australian banjo players, including women such as Thelma Ready, were making their mark in this new style of popular music.

Nevertheless, an American banjo-mandolin beginner's method (copyright 1922)

E-Z METHOD FOR MANDOLINE OR BANJO-MANDOLINE 29

Ragtime And Jazz

These are popular terms for describing what is called syncopation. Any melody can be played syncopated by merely changing the accented notes or altering the accented beats in a measure. Here are some examples

Musical Ex. 3.5. From the *E-Z Method For Mandolin Or Banjo Mandolin.*

which was published in, and sold widely throughout, Australia, demonstrates a simple ragtime embellishment system which is markedly similar to the practice described in the early banjo instructors (Musical Ex. 3.5.). In both methods the integrity of the original tune is retained while the basic beat is subdivided by related tones. Not surprisingly, some of the simple rhythmic devices found in the early banjo jigs are also apparent, for example, the alternation of single and double notes (jazz variation 4), omission of a tone to create off-beat stress (jazz variation 6) and the basic ragtime figure (variation 6). This method presents the idea that any unsyncopated melodic model can be transformed into imitation African-American music by selection from a small library of rhythmic possibilities, a concept explored further in the next chapter.

While minstrel banjo playing is a very significant example of early African-American influence performance practice in Australia, broader aspects of minstrel show music must also be considered when evaluating the influence of the minstrel show on later Australian performance culture. The following aspects represent what was perceived to be most 'grotesque' about the early minstrel show:

- an emphasis on percussive rhythm
- the ecstatic improvisatory (abandoned or 'happy darkie') mode of performance
- an emphasis upon rhythmic embellishment (e.g. the break)
- 'incongruous' (or 'primitive') ensemble, instrumental and vocal sound.

Interest in the portrayal of 'untutored', 'undisciplined' or 'natural' African-American performance practice certainly waned as audiences became increasingly accustomed to the often dazzling precision of international variety acts. What did not fade, however, was the Australian association of African-American culture with comic absurdity. Moreover, percussive rhythm remained in the sound of the banjo, bones, tambourine and the rhythmic footwork of the minstrel dancer; and blackface minstrel singers continued to take liberties with the perceived characteristics of African-American song and vernacular. Even after conventional instruments had taken over the function of the old core minstrel band instruments, the 'noisy' minstrel overture of the large touring shows retained the grotesque, incongruous or 'primitive' characteristics of early minstrel orchestra music. And while plantation-style music did not remain the focus of the minstrel show, it persisted as a speciality in Australian minstrelsy up to and well beyond the ragtime era. However, the arrival of black (African-American) minstrel shows in the last quarter of the century and their role in early Australian ragtime development, discussed in Chapter Four, greatly complicate the question of how much plantation influence actually survived the early blackface minstrel show in Australia.

4 Ragtime and Ragging in Australia

Part I: Ragtime before 1910

> In all the arts a striving is visible towards the inner spirit of things, blended with a desire to break down old devices and build on their ruins a structure that will express the complexities, energy and novelty of present-day conditions of life.
>
> Henry Tate, 'Modern Musical Tendencies', Melbourne, 1918[1]

The significance of ragtime to improvisatory music in Australia is due to its immense popularity in the first two decades of this century. Ragtime in its various forms became a conduit for the widespread importation of unorthodox, even iconoclastic, sounds, rhythms and practices which changed the direction of musical development in Australia. Even when frozen into notation, ragtime was the musical characterisation of improvisatory African-American performance practice and as such carried the seeds of a new form of musical liberation: jazz improvisation. The dances imported along with the music were also improvisatory in character and the social contexts and soundscapes in which such dancing took place often invited uninhibited and improvisatory interaction between the dancing and its musical accompaniment.

Tin Pan Alley-Style Ragtime

American ragtime historians commonly focus on the development of 'classic' piano ragtime (the sophisticated, fully-composed ragtime of Scott Joplin, Joseph Lamb and associates) and its transition into early black jazz. A second, less common, view on this history centres around the popular stage, Tin Pan Alley, the public dancing boom (which began before the First World War) and the emergence of a world-wide brass band movement. This perspective is the one most relevant to the history of ragtime in Australia.

The Australian history of ragtime primarily concerns the importation, consumption, reproduction and synthesis of white American and British ragtime music and performance behaviour models. The emergence of ragtime music in Australia can also be viewed as a complex arena of cultural negotiation between American and Anglo-Celtic/Australian popular culture. Yet there was also some degree of performance-culture contact between African-Americans and Australians via popular entertainment, particularly through the black jubilee singers and ragtime artists who performed in Australia or could be heard on imported sound recordings and hand-played piano rolls. Discussion of ragtime in Australia is made even more complex by the fact that the terms ragtime, rag-time or rag embrace many forms of popular music besides the familiar classic piano ragtime of Joplin and others.

Vaudeville Piano Ragtime

> Ben Harney was the pioneer of ragtime music. Modern jazz and swing stemmed from the same syncopation. His playing led to the ragtime craze and the cakewalk craze using the same tempo.[2]

From the perspective of American Tin Pan Alley music, the history of ragtime is considered by many to have begun in 1896 with the white vaudeville entertainer, Ben Harney, mentioned previously as the author of the first publication to describe ragtime improvisation.[3] Harney, a blackface minstrel, pianist, coon-singer, dancer and self-proclaimed 'Inventor of Ragtime', played a role similar to the Virginia minstrels half a century earlier and Elvis Presley a little over half a century later. He was in effect a remarkable cultural receiver, with the ability to decode elements of white and black musical culture and transmit a synthesis palatable to white taste.[4] Some historians even deny that Harney was white.[5] Harney toured Australia in 1911 but his main significance to this chapter is his earlier role as the catalyst for the white school of ragtime performance:

> while most of the real blacks in show business were putting on the swallow-tail coats of minstrelsy, Ben Harney was rag-dragging the rustic part of American popular culture into an urban future.[6]

Harney also popularised the notion of ragging (embellishing/syncopating) unsyncopated music through his onstage piano improvisations. He would, for example,

> play such numbers as Rubenstein's Melody In F, Mendelssohn's *Spring Song*, the Intermezzo from Mascagni's *Cavalleria Rusticana* and similar [works] . . . as originally written and then . . . in his special brand of ragtime.[7]

Following on Harney's success, a community or 'school' of white ragtime instrumentalists, composers and arrangers came into being which greatly influenced the development of piano ragtime style in both vaudeville and the closely associated Tin Pan Alley. Harney provided a model for the razzle-dazzle, exhibitionist style of ragtime improvisation, or ragging, that was adopted by famous white American pianists such as Mike Bernard, Rube Bloom, Jimmy Durante, and Charlie Straight (who toured Australia several years after Harney).

The basic principles of ragged transformation are described in instructors published at this time. These include *Ben Harney's Rag Time Instructor* (1897), *Christensen's Rag-Time Instruction Book for Piano* (1904 and later editions) and *Winn's How to Play Ragtime* (1913 and later editions).[8] Christensen, the self-proclaimed 'Czar Of Ragtime', claimed that his system made it possible to 'play ANYTHING in happy, snappy Rag-Time'.[9]

Where ragging is based on fully harmonised Tin Pan Alley-style sheet music, the original upper voice is transformed rhythmically by the intuitive selection and interpolation of memorised rhythmic motifs or clichés. Musical Example 4.1 from Christensen's method shows only three basic possibilities. Winn's system, however, provides a greatly expanded library of rhythmic clichés and places more emphasis upon what is termed 'discord bass' (contrapuntal and syncopated bass).

In this type of ragging, the original melody is heard as the upper voice of the musical texture with particular melody notes rhythmically displaced (syncopated) or 'ragged'. These off-beat melody notes are further emphasised by the addition of a lower chord tone (usually a sixth or an octave below) to create the characteristic 'double-note' effect of ragtime. An entire composition can be embellished in this way but ragging sounds most effective when restricted to filling in at sustained notes, rests and cadences.

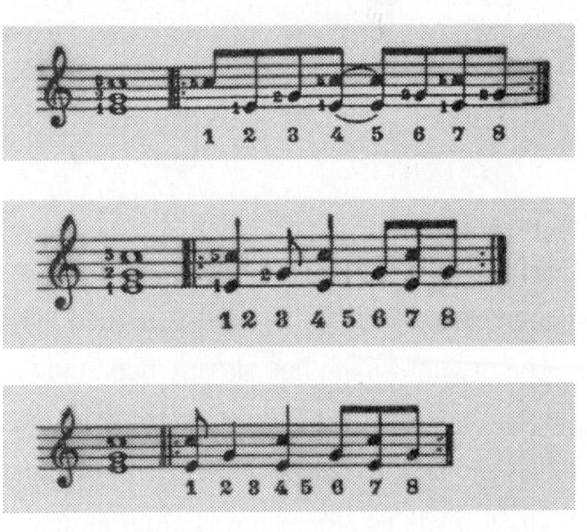

Musical Ex. 4.1. The three basic 'movements' from Christensen's *Rag-Time Instruction Book for Piano*, no. 1, (reprinted 1919) pp. 7-10.

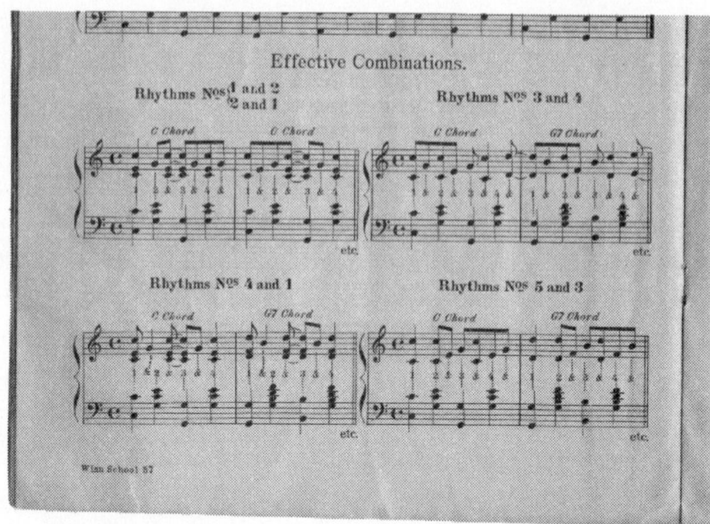

Musical Ex. 4.2a. Rhythms 1-5 in combination from *Winn's How to Play Ragtime.*
Musical Ex. 4.2b. 'Discord Bass', from *Winn's How to Play Ragtime.*

This practice of inserting fills was, as has been noted, common musical practice before ragtime, the difference being that ragged fills featured 'hot' rhythm.

Hot rhythm, which has already been mentioned in relation to minstrel music, is the quality that most distinguishes ragtime improvisation from non African-American influenced improvisatory practice. The rhythmic tension results from idiomatic off-beat or cross-rhythmic stress and is often associated with, but is not to be confused with, hot timbre (expressively variegated or percussive timbre), another strong characteristic of African-American music.

The notated repertoire of so-called classic ragtime features many variants of this basic hot figure . These include the use of tied syncopation and even more complex rhythmic devices such as off-beat phrasing (Musical Ex. 4.3a) and implied polyrhythm (Musical Ex. 4.3b) – devices that are also characteristic of the West African drum ensemble tradition.

Another gesture back to West African or plantation culture commonly found in (but far from exclusive to) classic ragtime is the 'rhythmic vamp': a distinctive, continuously repeated rhythmic pattern. Joplin's famous 'Maple Leaf Rag', for example, can be heard as a long sequence of cleverly juxtaposed rhythmic vamps (see Musical Ex. 4.3b). This aspect of ragtime was particularly significant in dance music because, as already suggested, a strong repetitive rhythm encouraged dancers to interact creatively with the music.

Published Ragtime Methods in Australia

Since Australian 'Anonymous genre' musicians had to stay abreast of developments in popular music, they often subscribed to American music journals or purchased them locally, instead of relying on information recycled within the (decontextualised) Australian music community. The name L.F. Collin, Melbourne, is even incorporated

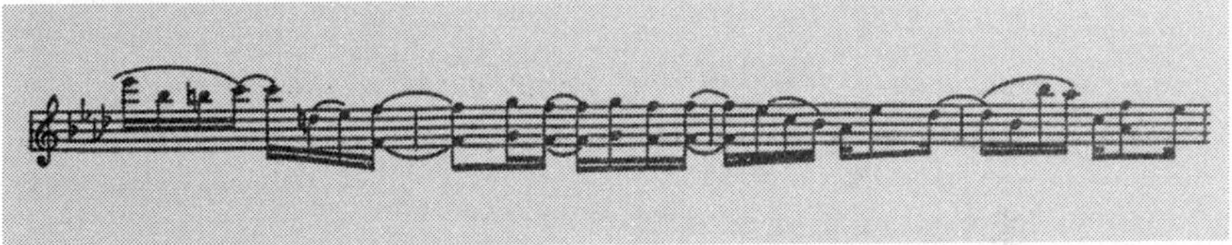

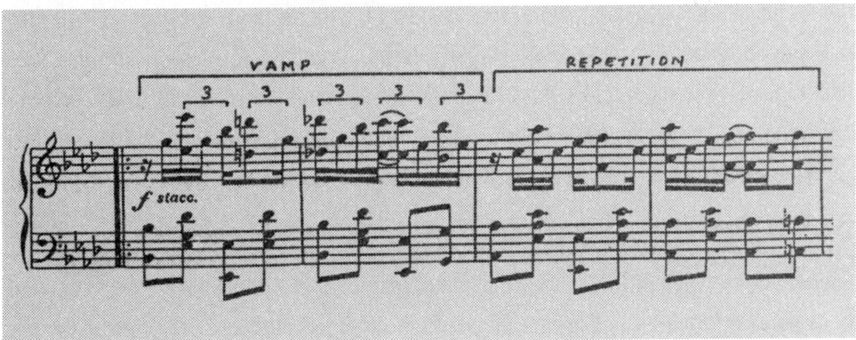

Musical Ex. 4.3a. Bars 13-16 of Scott Joplin's 'Gladiolus Rag': (1) a variant of the basic ragtime figure, (2) off-beat phrasing.
Musical Ex. 4.3b. Bars 1-4 (B section) of Scott Joplin's 'Maple Leaf Rag': (1) implied polyrhythm, (2) the rhythmic vamp, (3) syncopated broken chords.

into the masthead of a ragtime era copy of the *Metronome Orchestra Monthly* sent to me from America, suggesting that Melbourne was a substantial outlet for the journal. Furthermore, Collin's music house, Melbourne, and W Deane's music house, Sydney, are listed as official agents for Winn's ragtime journal *Melody*.

Winn's extensive ragtime course certainly reached Australia before 'jazz', since Winn's *Ragtime Piano Playing: a Practical Course of Instructions for Pianists* and his series of articles, '"Ragging" the Popular Song Hits', appeared in *Melody* from its first issue in January 1918. *Melody*'s predecessor, *Tuneful Yankee*, also featured 'Ragtime Piano Playing'. Advertisements for subscriptions to Christensen's *Ragtime Review* appeared regularly in *Etude*, a popular monthly magazine sold through Allan's and

Figure 4.1. Masthead of the *Metronome Orchestra Monthly*, November 1920.

METRONOME

INFORMATION FOR SUBSCRIBERS

Receipts for subscriptions are not sent unless requested.

If magazine fails to arrive by the 15th of the month, notify us and duplicate will be mailed at once.

If you intend to change your address please give us three weeks' notice and mention old address as well as new.

A memorandum bill enclosed with your copy shows that your subscription expired. If memorandum bill is received after subscription is renewed disregard it.

ORCHESTRA MONTHLY

Established 1885 and devoted to the interests of Music and Musicians in General

GUSTAV SAENGER, Editor
GEO. H. HILBERT, Manager

Entered as second-class matter at the post-office New York, N. Y., under act of March 3, 1879

Copyright, [illegible], by the Metronome Publishing Company, New York

AUSTRALIA L. F. COLLIN PTY LTD. MELBOURNE

SUBSCRIPTION PRICE FOR THIS MAGAZINE

Issued Once a Month

Per Year in the United States . .
Canadian Postage . . . . . .
Foreign Postage . . . . . .
Single Copies . . . .

Published Monthly by
THE METRONOME PUBLISHING CO.
GEO. H. HILBERT, Treasurer
[illegible] Cooper Square New York

numerous other Australian outlets.[10] Articles by Christensen and advertisements for his ragtime correspondence course also appeared regularly in *Melody* and its predecessors. Christensen had been promoting his system since the turn of the century and by late 1914 he was the director of a chain of around fifty ragtime schools across America as well as an international mail-order course.

Ragtime Song

The two other types of ragtime that became influential in Australia were ragtime song in its various forms and cakewalk music. Both emerged directly from popular theatre and became principally associated with white performers, but they also had strong connections with the black musical theatre that emerged in America during the 1890s in the wake of minstrelsy.

The earliest form of ragtime song was 'coon song', an extension of the minstrel song tradition. Coon song was associated with a particularly cruel caricature of the African-American that emerged in America after the Civil War. By the mid-1890s coon song began to be identified as a strand of the new syncopated American popular music, 'rag-time'. An important characteristic of coon song was the parody of black vernacular. Coon song lyrics generally characterised the 'hot coon' as urban, ugly, 'uppity', violent, treacherous, fast-talking, flashy, uncontrollably impulsive (particularly with regard to food and sex) and very rhythmical.[11] Some African-Americans were able to gain a foothold in popular theatre and Tin Pan Alley by exploiting the popularity of this stereotype. White entertainers, however, were responsible for its invention and most of its initial popularisation as an early form of ragtime song. An early landmark was May Irwin's 1895 performance of the 'Bully Song' (a song about razor-wielding African-Americans) in the Broadway musical *Widow Jones*.[12] By describing herself as a 'coon shouter' Irwin provided the model for generations of white coon or rag shouters:

> Your coon-shouter was a lusty, rounded lady. She was all curves. Her voice was a wild, raucous yell, and perfect intonation was her least concern.[13]

Harney's appearance in vaudeville the following year was an even more significant landmark for white coon shouters:

> Ben Harney had the huskiest voice most people had ever heard in a human being, and this quality made his voice just right for ragtime singing. It had queer breaks in it that affected the words as well as the music. Broadly speaking, he might even be called the first of the crooners. He would sustain certain notes, for special effect, to extravagant, breathtaking lengths; others he would break in a way that he alone could manage.[14]

The popularisation of ragtime song and cakewalk music was also directly associated with the emergence of black musical theatre in the 1890s in the wake of the declining minstrel show tradition. The most significant of the early black musicals was the operetta *Clorindy; or, the Origin of the Cakewalk* (1898), with music by Will Marion Cook in the 'new ragtime style' and a special emphasis on Cake Walk dancing. This show (which played exclusively to white audiences) featured the black coon song singer and composer, Ernest Hogan, who was already famous for his coon song composition, 'All Coons Look Alike to Me' (1896). In 1899 Australia felt some of the impact of this new African-American creative activity with the arrival of two large African-American minstrel troupes.

'All Coons Look Alike To Me' is possibly the first item of published sheet music to carry the designation 'rag'. Moreover, the sheet music itself demonstrates that a key principle of jazz, the 'hot' or 'ragged' chorus, was an element of Tin Pan Alley ragtime by 1896. Musical Example 4.5 is an optional ragged version of the basic chorus (Musical Ex. 4.4) arranged by Witmark & Sons' house arranger. Comparison of the two versions reveals how an unsyncopated song chorus accompaniment could be played hot or ragged.[15] In fact, the chorus sections of most published ragtime songs have notated chorus accompaniments that are 'hotter' (e.g. more syncopated) than the verse, reinforcing the idea of the hot chorus.

The 1911 publication of Irving Berlin's Tin Pan Alley hit 'Alexander's Ragtime Band' ushered in a new and final phase of ragtime song. A significant feature of the new ragtime song was its unambiguous projection as 'modern American music'. As such it no long needed to parody black vernacular.

Musical Ex. 4.4. Bars 1-4 of the chorus of 'All Coons Look Alike to Me' (1896; straight version).
Musical Ex. 4.5. Bars 1-4 of the optional chorus of 'All Coons Look Alike to Me' with 'Negro "Rag" Accompaniment'.

The American ragtime scholar, Edward Berlin, also notes that:

> Irving Berlin's hit tune seems to have shown that syncopation was not necessary, and from 1911 on there was an increase in both vocal and instrumental rags that feature dotted notes instead of syncopated rhythms.[16]

A significant transformation had thus taken place within the mainstream of popular music: a shift from a stiff, straight quaver rhythm towards a more ambiguous dotted note/triplet rhythm that anticipated the relaxed push-and-pull of jazz. This tension between the old and the new ragtime rhythmic treatment can be heard clearly, for example, in the Sousa band's 1912 recording of 'Alexander's Ragtime Band'. The performance time transformation of straight quaver to dotted note or triplet rhythm was used much earlier for adding excitement, energy and propulsion to dance music.[17] After 1911, however, the dotted note/triplet feel and playful shifting between straight and ambiguous rhythm became increasingly characteristic of both written and improvised ragging of popular music. A typical example is the notated juxtaposition of dotted notes and straight quaver syncopation of the chorus in Irving Berlin's 'Everybody's Doin' It'.[18]

Improvisatory Practice in Ragtime Song

The aesthetics of even the earliest ragtime song, which tolerated considerable ambiguity in pitch, timbre and the rhythmic placement of sounds, were much closer to jazz improvisation than instrumental ragtime. In fact ragtime song sheet music is probably only marginally more useful than blues sheet music as a source of information about how the music was actually sung.

The most significant aspect of vocal ragging is the convention of breaking-up words with nonsense syllables to create what could be described as incipient scat or rap singing. The musical effect is comparable to the plunking timbre of banjo or piano ragging in which, for example, various note values of the original tune can be broken down into quavers, dotted notes or syncopated figures. This practice was first popularised by Ben Harney and is even transcribed into the published version of his song 'The Cake-Walk in the Sky'.[19] It can be heard in the recordings of the white vaudeville artist Gene Greene, the most influential ragtime singer to visit Australia in the pre-jazz period (see Musical Ex. 4.20b).

Vocal ragging can also include the rhythmic displacement of notes in association with trombone-like portamento, unorthodox timbral alterations (growls and so forth) and a subtle rhythmic independence from an often vamp-like rhythmic accompaniment. Musical Example 4.6. is the transcription of the vocal line from the closing bars of 'I've Been Floating Down the Old Green River' (1915) sung by Billy Murray, another American ragtime recording artist who was popular in Australia.

The type of rhythmic independence heard in this example foreshadows the subtle and sophisticated phrasing often heard in jazz instrumental and vocal lines. Yet in ragtime song it was also associated with rubato, something quite atypical of jazz.

The success of ragtime song helped to deflect ragtime musical development away from complex, multi-thematic forms such as that found in classic ragtime towards simple popular song form (e.g. verse/chorus), which openly invited varied repetition. Furthermore, just as the vamp-like rhythm of ragtime offered a level of creative freedom to dancers, it also gave the ragtime singer the freedom to phrase, articulate and

Musical Ex. 4.6. Transcription of the last bars of Billy Murray's vocal line in 'I've Been Floating Down the Old Green River (1915).

experiment with timbral variation in a fluidly independent way. Therefore, ragtime singers not only improvised but also provided a model of creative freedom for ragtime instrumentalists. These factors take on a proportionately greater significance in Australia, where other aspects of African-American derived musical culture were largely absent.

One aspect of ragtime represents an important link between pre-jazz African-American influence and later discussion of improvisatory experimentalism in Australia. The white impression of ragtime – whether as 'frozen' (notated) or performance time improvisatory practice – included the notion that it was a potentially liberating form of 'free music'. Rupert Hughes wrote in 1899 of 'a new and free use of the old device of imitation', predicting also that 'In this beautiful independence of motion the future contrapuntalist will revel'.[20] In 1913 an article in *The Times* described the 'effect of a perfectly free declamation' and the 'free rhythm' of ragtime.[21] A Melbourne theatre pianist and director, Fred Dennett, claimed in 1919 that 'Ragtime may not be classical music, but it is music all the same. It has cut out a new era in the brighter forms of music, by the free use of the syncopated note, and it is so fascinating that it has come to stay'.[22]

The vertical non-alignment of bass and treble in ragtime created new levels of temporal and harmonic dissonance. Even classic ragtime when played as dance music (percussively) reveals the iconoclastic (and prophetic) level of dissonance or 'noise', that most enraged early critics of ragtime (see bar 1 of Musical Ex. 4.2b). Hughes wrote of 'lawless' harmonic progressions and dissonance 'hardly to be represented by any conventional notation'.[23] A key feature of Winn's method was his single or double 'discord bass' which, he claimed (if exaggeratedly), could open up 'opportunities for considerable originality'.[24] This 'dissonance', when refined for white popular taste, could represent the 'brightness' mentioned by Dennett above. Yet it also represented public mass-conditioning to new levels of temporal and harmonic dissonance at the very time (in the late 1910s) when Australian musicians were confronting alarming new levels of 'dissonance' in art music.[25] Moreover, at this time improvisation itself represented a type of 'social dissonance', a refusal to bow to the printed note or to foster musical conformity. Ragging incorporated all of these forms of dissonance.

African-American Ragtime-Style Minstrelsy in Australia

> At one time many American minstrel companies enjoyed highly prosperous seasons in Australia, but for a long time we have not had one. The popularity of the coon song and the cake walk in the United States has produced a boom in minstrelsy, and we are now to partake in it.
>
> *Sydney Mail,* 24 June 1899[26]

The popularisation of ragtime in Australia was given impetus late in 1899 by the arrival of two large African-American minstrel troupes: Orpheus McAdoo's Georgia Minstrels and Alabama Cake Walkers and, two weeks later, Curtis' Grand African-American Minstrel Carnival. These were the first large African-American minstrel troupes to arrive since the Hicks-Sawyer Minstrels a decade earlier. McAdoo was best known to Australian audiences as the leader of a professional black chamber choir, the Jubilee Singers (sometimes erroneously called the Fisk Jubilee Singers), which first visited Australia in the late 1880s. The Curtis troupe was headed by the coon singer and comedian, Ernest Hogan. Only one of these troupes, McAdoo's Georgia Minstrels, came on to Melbourne following their opening season in Sydney. The most important thing about these minstrel troupes was their introduction to Australia of the new ragtime-style black minstrel theatre they brought to Australia which had, as already mentioned, found full expression the previous year in the New York production of *Clorindy; or, the Origin of the Cakewalk.*

It is not possible to reconstruct Australian audience perceptions of these mammoth African-American minstrel shows on the basis of a few brief newspaper reviews. Nevertheless, the following sketch of a late nineteenth-century minstrel show opening evokes some sense of the general context:

> followed by a noisy overture, including cymbals, banjos and drums, the performance would begin with a scene of assorted brilliance, colour and apparent noise which, however, would finally assume a tranquil and engaging mobility abounding in humour, side-splitting jokes, grotesque song and dance steps, quaint dialogue and tidbits.[27]

The white colonial audience was confronted by thirty to fifty 'coloured' performers who acted, sang, danced and perhaps even performed their variety acts to the new 'rag time' music. Taken at face value, this situation seems comparable with Bruce Johnson's speculations on the impact of 'Australia's first jazz band' on Sydney audiences nineteen years later:

> If the audience laughed, they were also disturbed – it is, when visualised even at this distance, a disturbing spectacle. The knowledge that this was Negro music prepared the spectators for an ambiguous *frisson*, a glimpse into a fascinating but disquieting darkness.[28]

The program of the McAdoo troupe of thirty 'star Negro performers' included 'coon song' by the 'Hottest Coon in Town', the 'Extraordinary Pas-Ma-La Dance', and 'The latest American and English craze, The Coon's Cake Walk'. Curtis' massive troupe of fifty performers featured Hogan as the 'Originator of "Rag Time" Music in America'. Their program included 'coon song' by Hogan and others, 'Smith's Pickaninny Band', 'Alexander's Imperial Orchestra', the 'Rag-Ma-La dance' (Pas-Ma-La), 'America's Latest Fashionable Fad, Rag Time Opera' (opera burlesque) and the 'Grand Southern Cake Walk'. Of these, the presentation of the Cake Walk, Rag Time Opera and Pas-Ma-La dance were declared to be the first in Australia.[29] Excluding traditional minstrel show elements and variety acts such as Ferry the Human Frog, the contents of the Curtis show in particular seem to have been drawn substantially from the African-American musical theatre productions, *A Trip to Coontown* (1898) and *Clorindy*.

Towards the end of the Curtis troupe's Sydney season, their program announced that 'every Lady attending will be presented with a magnificent Music Album, containing Rag-Time Negro Melodies, as sung by and composed by Mr. Ernest Hogan, the unbleached American'. By this means, these colonial women became the first wave of Australian amateur ragtime performers.[30]

McAdoo's Georgia Minstrels opened for a season at Melbourne's St George's Hall with an augmented troupe of '40 Coloured Star Artists'.[31] At the beginning of their Australian tour a reviewer commented that:

> Recently the value of the cake walk for show purposes has been suggested by the success of the coon singers, and now it is a rage of London and the States. It is intensely funny, and we are likely to see it introduced to some of our social dances.[32]

PROGRAMME.
WEEK COMMENCING JULY 1, 1899.

GRAND FIRST PART
Showing the interior of the Palace of the Emperors of Ministrels gathering of the Mastodon Senate. Grand Opening Overture by E. Smith's Piccaninny Band, and Professor Charles T. Alexander's Imperial Orchestra.

INTERLOCUTORS.
Miss VINCENT BRADLEY. TOM LOGAN.

BONES.
BILLY McCLAIN
GEORGE JONES
LADSEN B. ALSTON
TURNER BASKETT
MASTER LIVERS

TAMBOS.
ERNEST HOG
MASTER BLU
WILLIAM JO
AMON DAVIS
NEEDHAM W

VOCAL CORPS.
ROBERT C. LOGAN, TOM LOGAN, LAURENCE CHENAULT,
H. SAULSBURY, MISSES MARION BLAKE, LAURA C.
CARRIE CARTER, KITTIE CARTER, MURIEL RINGOLD,
LUELLA PRICE, VINCENT BRADLEY, SIREN NAVARRO.
PRIMA DONNA ASSOLUTA - - MISS MADAH A.

POT POURRI OF POPULAR COON MELODIES,
By M. B. CURTIS'
SWEET SINGERS from the SUNNY SOUTH

GRAND INTRODUCTORY OVERTURE ... ENTIRE COM
"Tapioca" ... GEORGE J
"She was bred in Old Kentucky" ... Miss MARION B
"Johnny Frasier" ... MASTER BL
"Because" ... LAURENCE CHEN
"I Guess I'll Have to Telegraph My Baby" ... BILLY Mc
Comic Song (original) ... ERNEST H
"Hello, Ma Baby" ... SIREN NAVARRO, McCLAIN & H
"Asleep in the Deep" ... ROBT. C. L
FINALE—"La Duel de N'Oirville."

INTERMISSION OF FIVE MINUTES.

OLIO.
KATIE CARTER
MURIEL RINGOLD
THE KENTUCKY FOUR
MASTER BL
MASTER LIV
One Thousand Pounds Challenge to the WORLD to produce their equals in Buck and Wing Dancing.

MADAH A. HYER, the Bronze Patti, in Operatic Selections.
SIREN, the Lilliputian Creole Contortion Danseuse.
ERNEST HOGAN, the Unbleached American.
BLACK DANTE (the Original "Dante the Great.")

RAG TIME OPERA.
(Published by Witmark & Sons, New York City, U.S.A.)
A NEGRO LOVE STORY, IN ONE ACT
PERSONAE.

M. Dispute, who thinks he is a Bosom Friend of Albert Prince of Whales	BILLY McCLAIN
...	BLUTCH JONES
... a Leader of Coloured Society	LAURENCE CHENAULT
... Tatties (henpecked)	L. B. ALSTON
... Jenkins	WILLIE JONES
... (his Pal)	AMON DAVIS
...	GEORGE JONES
... Pete (a Bad Man)	LAURENCE CHENAULT
... Smith	MASTER LIVERS
... Waite	JAMES SPRANGLES
... Lotts	FRANK WATTS
... Importance	NEEDHAM WRIGHT
...	TURNER BASKETT
... Moss	CHAS. KENNEDY
... Howard	TOM LOGAN
... Peterman	MADAH A. HYER
...	VINCENT BRADLEY
... Tatties (a Gossip)	CARRIE CARTER
... (Dispute's Sweetheart)	SIREN NAVARRO
... Babb	KATIE CARTER
... Flip	MURIEL RINGOLD
...	LAURA MOSS
... Dora	MARION BLAKE
... Ann Dooley	LUELLA PRICE

ERNEST HOGAN as RASTUS HOTBONE THE INTERLOPER
CONCLUDING WITH
THE GRAND CAKE WALK,
...ted in by Sixteen Devotees of Delsarte, who stand ready to defend their claims as Champions on the merits of Style, Grace, and Execution.

Box Plan at Nicholson & Co.'s George Street.
Curtain at 8 p.m. sharp; Carriages, 10.45.

EXECUTIVE STAFF FOR M. B. CURTIS.

... of Amusements	ERNEST HOGAN
... Manager	BILLY McCLAIN
... Stage Manager	TOM LOGAN
... and Electrician	H. S. STAFFORD
... of Properties	THEOPHILUS WAY
...	AMON DAVIS
... of Wardrobe	MISS REYNOLDS
... Director	PROF. CHAS. F. ALEXANDER
...	PROF. E. CLARK SMITH
... Representative	LIONEL SOLOMON

Printers, York-street.

Figure 4.2. Program for Curtis' 'Grand Afro-American Minstrel Carnival', 1 July 1899. Criterion Theatre Sydney (Programs and Playbills Collection, Mitchell Library, State Library of NSW).

Thus, in 1899, the Australian dancing public was on the verge of embracing a style of dancing which invited improvisation of imaginative body movements to music. McAdoo's Cake Walk is described by one journalist as follows:

> The 'Cake Walk' which the company introduced in Australia . . . has only been done by individual artists previously. In this figure the 'coons' of either sex are separated, and are posing and swaying in characteristic manner. In other figures they set out in pairs, and 'walk,' and prance and dance and posture as suggests itself to their sense of humour after the fashion of a grotesque minuet in a fashion intensely laughter-provoking, each pair striving to outdo all the rest and catch the approving eye of the judges.[33]

Melbourne's first reaction to the Cake Walk is interesting as the dance was first presented, not by McAdoo, but by the white Hoyt and McKee Company which had arrived shortly before them with the musical show *A Trip to Chinatown*. Their cast included three dancers who performed a coon song and a Cake Walk routine based partly on material from *Clorindy*. One reviewer notes that 'The influence of the "Coon song" and the "Coon walk" is evident all through the "business" of the piece'.[34] A Melbourne review describes their performance as follows:

> To the strains of a lively march, they cross and recross the stage, with sundry nimble

> contortions, many flexions of the body, sometimes singing, sometimes chattering volubly in what is probably meant to be coons' dialect.[35]

While their first Sydney performance of the Cake Walk is described as 'very finished', a Melbourne reviewer comments:

> The dance contributed by Mr. Sam Marion and the sisters McCoy pleased the audience by its grotesqueness and acrobatic skill . . . The 'cake walk' in which these young ladies figure is perhaps a little 'caviar' to Australian audiences. To appreciate a caricature we need some familiarity with the type burlesqued.[36]

While these comments do not refer to musical improvisation directly, they may provide insight into the process or criteria by which culturally isolated colonials chose to assimilate or reject deviant performance models. Deviation and distortion (grotesqueness) were acceptable, but only as light-hearted travesties on relatively familiar models. Also reflected in Australian references to the Cake Walk dance is the essentialist notion that African-American performance practice (by African-Americans) was something natural, spontaneous and inimitable:

> Mr. McAdoo's cakewalkers will be full-blooded negroes who have inherited the traditions of this peculiar prancing movement . . . as a matter of fact white people cannot reproduce the queer gestures of this strange contest.[37]

> . . . with their natural inclination for the ridiculous the slaves in their enjoyment turned the walk from a mere imitation into a howling caricature.[38]

> . . . each couple dance in their own characteristic manner, in many instances exhibiting a crude kind of gracefulness peculiar to negro-dancing.[39]

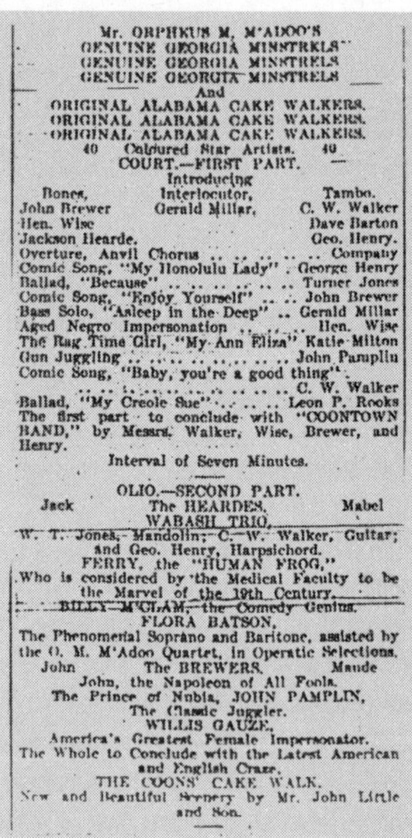

Mr. ORPHEUS M. M'ADOO'S
GENUINE GEORGIA MINSTRELS
GENUINE GEORGIA MINSTRELS
GENUINE GEORGIA MINSTRELS
And
ORIGINAL ALABAMA CAKE WALKERS.
ORIGINAL ALABAMA CAKE WALKERS.
ORIGINAL ALABAMA CAKE WALKERS.
40 Coloured Star Artists. 40
COURT.—FIRST PART.
Introducing

Bones,	Interlocutor,	Tambo.
John Brewer	Gerald Millar,	C. W. Walker
Hen. Wise		Dave Barton
Jackson Hearde.		Geo. Henry.

Overture, Anvil Chorus .. .. Company
Comic Song, "My Honolulu Lady" . George Henry
Ballad, "Because" .. .. Turner Jones
Comic Song, "Enjoy Yourself" .. .. John Brewer
Bass Solo, "Asleep in the Deep" .. Gerald Millar
Aged Negro Impersonation .. .. .. Hen. Wise
The Rag Time Girl, "My Ann Eliza" Katie Milton
Gun Juggling .. .. John Pamplin
Comic Song, "Baby, you're a good thing".
.. .. C. W. Walker
Ballad, "My Creole Sue" .. .. .. Leon P. Rooks
The first part to conclude with "COONTOWN BAND," by Messrs. Walker, Wise, Brewer, and Henry.

Interval of Seven Minutes.

OLIO.—SECOND PART.
Jack The HEARDES. Mabel
WABASH TRIO.
W. T. Jones, Mandolin; C. W. Walker, Guitar; and Geo. Henry, Harpsichord.
FERRY, the "HUMAN FROG,"
Who is considered by the Medical Faculty to be the Marvel of the 19th Century.
BILLY M'CLAM, the Comedy Genius.
FLORA BATSON,
The Phenomenal Soprano and Baritone, assisted by the O. M. M'Adoo Quartet, in Operatic Selections.
John The BREWERS. Maude
John, the Napoleon of All Fools.
The Prince of Nubia, JOHN PAMPLIN,
The Classic Juggler.
WILLIS GAUZE,
America's Greatest Female Impersonator.
The Whole to Conclude with the Latest American and English Craze,
THE COONS' CAKE WALK.
New and Beautiful Scenery by Mr. John Little and Son.

Figure 4.3. McAdoo's Melbourne Program. *Argus*, 5 August 1899.

Ragtime Song Performance

That some Australians were aware in 1899 of a distinction between the old style coon song and the new style 'ragtime' is indicated by a reviewer's comment that the song 'Zizy-zy-ze-zum', performed by a member of the white Hoyt and McKee company, 'imitates and tells of the craze o[f] the "Coon-rag-music", a development of the "Coon Song" craze in the States'.[40] The main ragtime singers in the McAdoo and Curtis troupes appear to have been Hogan, Billy McClain and to a lesser extent Katie Milton and Blutch Jones. Only McClain and Milton reached Melbourne in 1899 with the McAdoo troupe. Hogan, Jones and others from the Curtis troupe arrived later as individual variety artists.

Australian commentary on the two troupes does not reveal how or to what degree McAdoo's and Curtis' artists ragged their songs. It does, however, refer to unspecified forms of exaggerated performance behaviour or 'fooling around' with the music. One Australian newspaper article on Hogan notes that he 'writes "coon" songs and he sings them with a wealth of "business" and expression'.[41] A review of his performance states that 'a program of coon melodies was well carried out, and Mr Ernest Hogan, said to be a pure-blooded negro, fairly eclipsed all others in the art of the amusing'. The same review refers also to 'some excellent fooling' between Siren Navarro, McClain and Hogan in the coon song 'Hello Ma Baby'.[42]

American sources are more specific. Rupert Hughes states in the 1899 article, 'A Eulogy of Ragtime':

> I heard Mr. Ernest Hogan sing . . . 'All Coons Look Alike to Me,' with an impudent determination to keep out of key and out of time that was simply fascinating. Another curious feature of the singing of these songs is the interpolation of the syllable 'a' till they sound like the broken English of an Italian. I have even heard this extreme case: 'I'm a hust-a-ling-a coon-a, and-a that's-a just-a what-a I-a am.'[43]

It can be assumed that McClain and other coon song artists in these troupes aspired to Hogan's successful style.

Musical Accompaniment

It is intriguing to speculate on the type of instrumental music these early black ragtimers brought to Melbourne in 1899: whether, for example, the musical accompaniment to the Cake Walk dance provided by McAdoo's 'parade band/orchestra' was played with brass band precision or was humorously burlesqued into some incipient form of jazz improvisation.

On the one hand, we have many images of ecstatic music-making by African-Americans on, for example, early ragtime sheet music covers. On an American cylinder recording of a cakewalk made the following year (RCA Black & White Series, vol. 190) we hear an anonymous white studio imitating musical abandonment. We also know of the ability of minstrel musicians to 'fake and sell it' and of the direct association of cakewalk music with trombone smears or 'rags'. On the other hand, the professionalism required of McAdoo's black theatre musicians probably discouraged them from playing in a way that would sound too unruly to late nineteenth-century Melbourne theatre audiences, unless the performance was presented unambiguously as musical jest or caricature.

It is interesting however that two of the only three clear Australian references to musical accompaniment by the McAdoo orchestra are complaints against musical extroversion:

> ballads and coon songs of various kinds, [were] accompanied by an effective orchestra comprising the members of the 'Parade Band' which the company has brought over.[44]

> On the whole the show went off splendidly and the only thing we heard [sic] found fault with was the somewhat too vigorous play at times of the very fine orchestra and its accessories.[45]

> Many novelties were introduced, and a fine orchestra of a dozen players assisted materially in the success of the evening, although the instrumentalists would do better if they subdued their playing when accompanying the vocalists.[46]

All that is known with any certainty is the type of melodic models, forms, rhythmic patterning and in some cases, the textures over which improvisatory transformation or embellishment could have taken place. In coon song accompaniment, improvisatory performance behaviour most likely occurred in the repeated chorus sections, to reinforce the notion of the hot chorus. In cakewalk accompaniment, it is most likely to have corresponded with the final section of the Cake Walk where the dancing couples begin to invent steps and body movements.

An 1899 musical transcription, by the conductor of the Palace Theatre (Sydney) orchestra, of a 'Cake Walk Dance' as 'played and danced by the Georgia Minstrels with great success' gives some idea of what McAdoo's 'effective orchestra' may have played as accompaniment to the Cake Walk (Musical Ex. 4.7). This 'Cake Walk Dance' is typical of the genre of cakewalk music favoured by brass bands (i.e. multi-thematic, a singable melody, one or more sections in a minor key) and even includes a brass band type bass solo. Syncopation is minimal by classic ragtime standards and in section A the characteristic cakewalk syncopation ♪♩♪ sounds very inactive against the stodgy bass vamp. Section B (r.h.) features banjo-like fills and has the feel of a 'break' in minstrel dancing (note how rests are used to intensify rhythmic activity). In section C, another form of rhythmic instability is introduced with the interpolation of a syncopated vamp in the right hand part.

Published vocal/piano versions of the ragtime songs performed by McAdoo and

Curtis troupe members give a very general idea of the type of ragtime song musical accompaniment provided. The accompaniment to 'I Guess I'll Have to Telegraph My Baby' (Musical Ex. 4.8a), which was sung regularly by Billy McClain, features a sparse distribution of arpeggiation and broken chord fills. Note the prominent use of the basic cakewalk figure and its expansion ♪♩ ♪ to generate underlying rhythmic tension. Note also the resemblance of the last two bars to Harney's transformation device in 'Annie Laurie' (Musical Ex. 3.2). The optional chorus to Hogan's popular 'All Coons Look Alike To Me' (Musical Ex. 4.5), is an example of another fairly common type of coon song piano accompaniment: the continuous right-hand vamp. The optional chorus to 'Anne Elizer, the Ragtime Girl', performed by Katie Milton of McAdoo's troupe, features a similarly relentless syncopated or 'ragged' vamp.

It is difficult to generalise beyond these types of observations. 'Hello Ma Baby', for example, features minimal syncopation, while 'Who Dat Say Chicken in This Crowd', has an almost unsyncopated 4/4 dotted note verse and a syncopated 2/4 chorus.[47] The most common feature of the examples I have examined is the simple verse/chorus form with syncopated introduction and chorus. The very consistency of the syncopated final chorus in coon song suggests that even white orchestral musicians playing from detailed scores would have tended to apply surface transformations such as exaggerated or altered rhythm, dynamics or timbre to the final choruses of coon song accompaniments. This is very explicit in, for example, the orchestral accompaniment heard on the recording of Gene Greene's 'King of the Bungaloos', discussed below. Furthermore, as already indicated, the simple, repeated two-part form of these coon songs invited improvisatory variation much more than multi-sectional cakewalks such as the 'Cake Walk Dance' (Musical Ex. 4.7).

Cakewalk instrumental music and coon song with syncopated accompaniment, two very influential forms of early ragtime music, had definitely reached Australia by 1899 as part of the ragtime-style minstrelsy brought here by the McAddo and Curtis troupes, but writings of the day give no indication that a 'rag craze' of any sort had arrived.[48] The minstrel show concept itself was very dated by 1899 but blackface and authentic African-American 'coon specialists' remained a popular component of Melbourne stage entertainment for another decade. Many significant African-American ragtime artists, including members of the disbanded McAdoo and Curtis troupes (and influential permanently resident artists such as Charlie Pope and Irving Sayles), performed in Melbourne in the following years and each brought at least some vestige of the practice of ragging: the hot elaboration of popular music or its rhythmically related art, dance. Duke Johnson, who came to Australia in 1911, was noted for 'the extraordinary

THE CAKE-WALK DANCE.

Composed by Braham and Rhodes.

Arranged specially for "Tivoli Album," by T. W. Rhodes, Conductor of Palace Theatre.

Played and Danced by "The Georgia Minstrels" with Enormous Success.

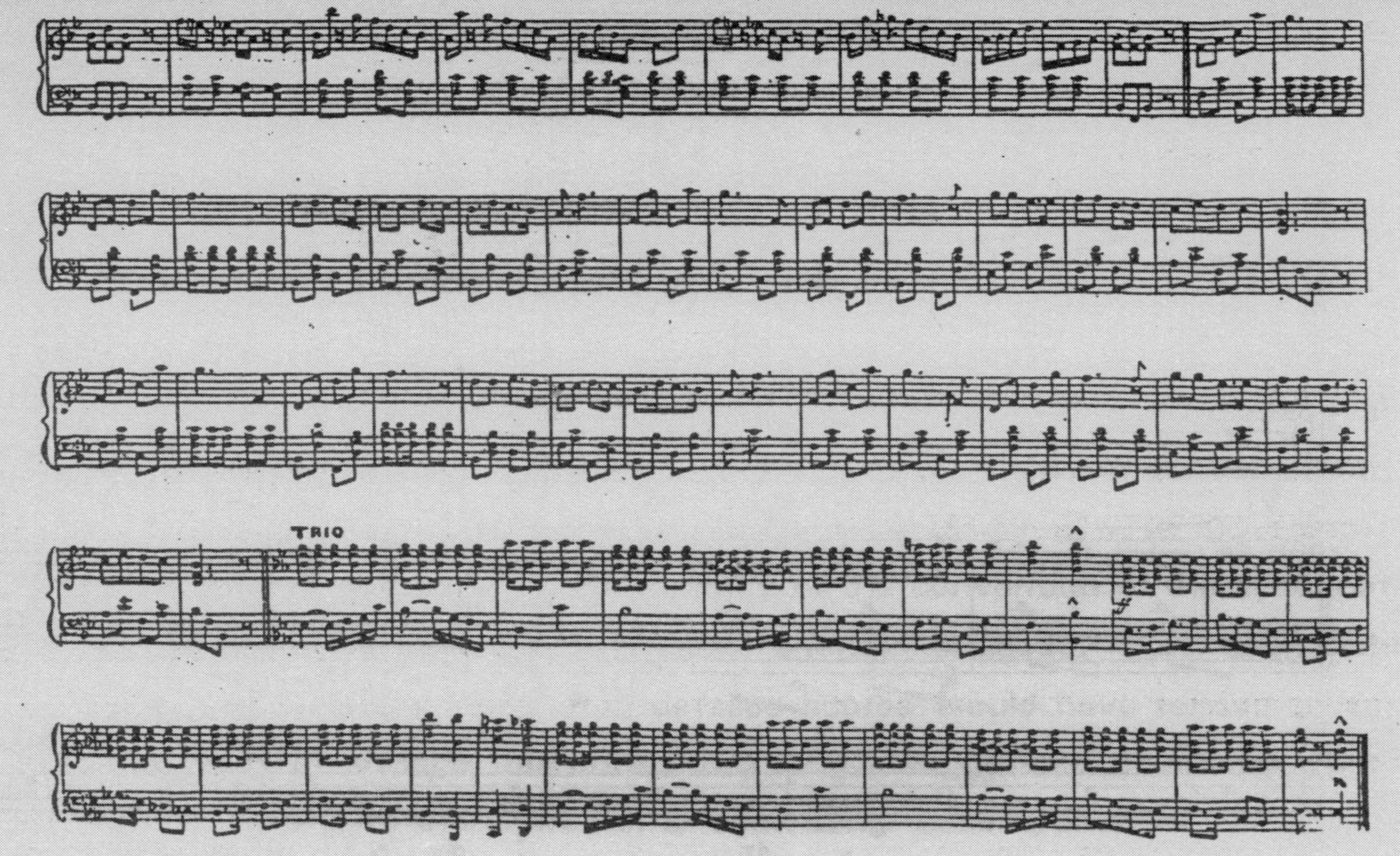

Musical Ex. 4.7. 'The Cake Walk Dance' (1899), arranged by T. Rhodes, *The Tivoli Album,* no. 9.

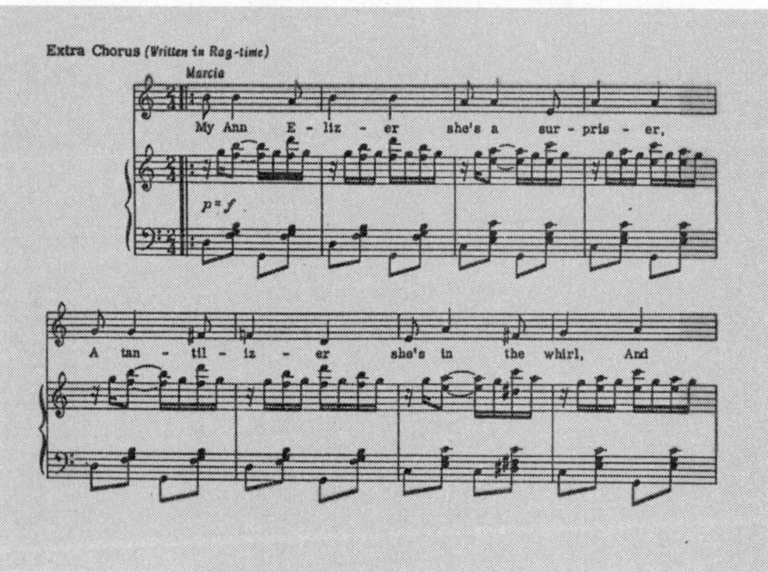

Musical Ex. 4.8a. Bars 1-14 of the chorus of 'I Guess I'll Have to Telegraph My Baby' (1898), by George M. Cohan.
Musical Ex. 4.8b. Bars 1-8 of the optional chorus of 'Anne Elizer, the Ragtime Girl' (1898), by Malcolm Williams.

banjo-like quality' of his voice,[49] while Leah Clark, who came with the very last big African-American minstrel show to tour Australia, is described as 'a robust member of the company [who] sang in coon style in a manner that aroused the audience', a description fitting the coon-shouter or rag-shouter.[50] Ironically, an Australian theatre writer claimed in 1913 that the only person to have sung 'the real negro broken time' in Australia was the white artist Ben Harney.[51]

The Cakewalk and Coon Song Craze

The first development that could be described as an Australian ragtime craze seems to have begun around 1902 as a cakewalk and coon song craze. T.A. Ricketts, a theatre conductor in the early 1900s claims that:

> it was to the credit – or maybe the discredit – of the World Entertainers, a very clever combination under the direction of Lee and Rial . . . [that they] release[d] the floodgates of syncopated music in the form of cakewalks, which proved an instantaneous success . . . It was my privilege to conduct an excellent orchestra for [their] opening season . . . The popular dance bands of the period were quick to take up the craze which followed when the World Entertainers carried it to Melbourne [in late 1901] . . . These were the precursors of jazz, jive, and modern eccentricities.[52]

One manifestation of this craze was the Amateur Cake Walk Competitions in 1904 held at the Tivoli Theatre in Melbourne. From around 1903, Melbourne publishers such as Allan's and Cole's began to include cakewalks in their dance music albums. In addition, Allan's published two Cake Walk Albums (1903 and 1905) and a dance tutor which contained instructions on how to dance 'that latest society craze the "cake walk"' (see Figures 4.4a-4.4b).[53] The instrumental cakewalks played in Australia ranged from

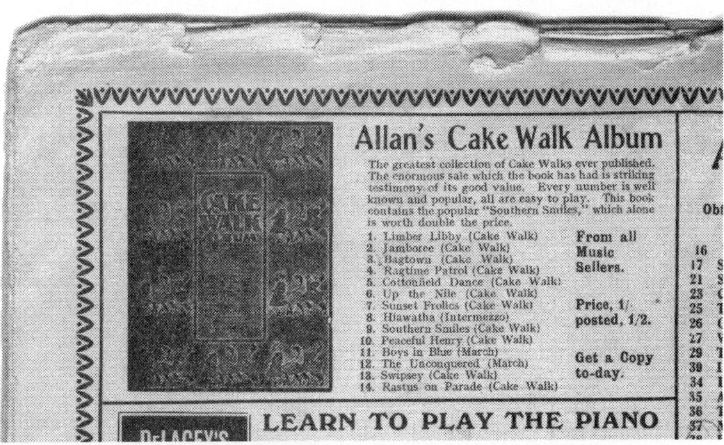

Figure 4.4a. Advertisement for *Allan's Cake Walk Album* (1903).

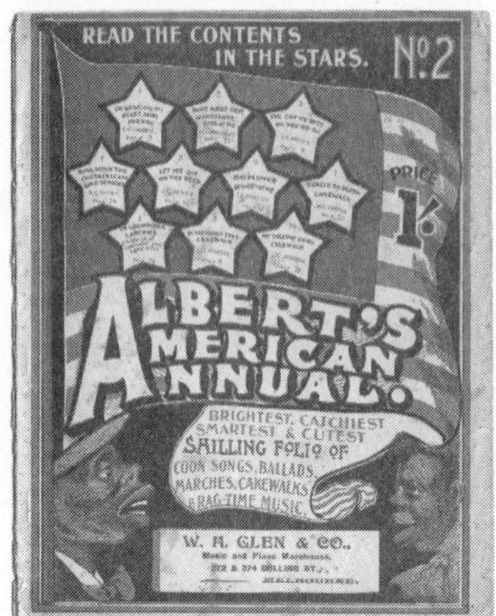

Figure 4.4b. Front cover of *Albert's American Annual* no. 2 of 'coon songs, ballads, marches, cakewalks and rag-time music', Sydney: Albert & Son, 1904.

characteristically syncopated pieces such as Kerry Mills' popular 'At a Georgia Camp Meeting' through to others which, although labelled 'cake walk', contain virtually no syncopation.[54] In the twelve months following June 1903 the *Argus* published advertisements for five new cakewalk albums and another five containing cakewalks, not to mention numerous individual items of cakewalk sheet music.

Cakewalk music was also very popular with theatre orchestras and circus, military and civilian brass bands. One Melbourne brass band musician recalled that in 1905 the Collingwood band became very popular after adopting 'the stirring old march "Creole Bells" . . . for street marching purposes'.[55] The St Leon family circus even had a Cake Walking Pony act in the early 1900s. By then the prolific local brass band composer, arranger, publisher and conductor, T.E. (Thomas) Bulch, had written several cakewalks and edited and arranged others for standard brass band.[56]

Given the nineteenth-century Australian perception of African-American culture, it is not surprising that what appealed to brass band musicians and their audiences was

Musical Ex. 4.9. Bars 7-16 (A section) of 'Dance of the Dandy Coons', by the Geelong/Melbourne composer by Thomas E. Bulch (c. 1903).

the supposed comic grotesqueness of the music. Around 1905, for example, the Melbourne publisher Sutton's was promoting its cakewalk arrangements for brass band (mostly by Thomas Bulch) as follows:

Coon Band Contest	A really forgivable bit of musical nonsense on one of those catchy American hits.
The Coon's Patrol	Will catch on like wildfire. Quaint, grotesque.
King of the Coons	Brimful of life, fun, and go.
Rastus on Parade	It's charmingly grotesque, a real topsy turvy happy lucky conceit.
Sambo's Birthday	An Americanism-droll, with that humorous character that these broken time items should always have. The public like Two Steps, the bandsmen like them; they are so bright and cheerful . . . [57]
Angelina from Alabama	A quaint 'good luck happy dark[ie]' grotesque piece of music.[58]

The 'grotesque' aspect of this music does not appear to have had strong social or political implications for Australians before the 1910s. To band musicians of this time, cakewalk music was probably the musical equivalent of the golliwog: a highly stylised and benign caricature of the mythical 'happy darkie'. An extract from a Melbourne newspaper article, the 'Carnal Cake Walk', illustrates however that American-style racist rhetoric had reached Melbourne by 1904:

> All the lynchings of blacks in America are punishments for bestiality; and some of the nigger bestiality manifests itself in the 'Cake Walk' which respectable Australian mothers allow their daughters to learn and perform. [59]

Cakewalk Music and Improvisatory Musical Practice

Although cakewalks such as 'At a Georgia Camp Meeting' subsequently became important vehicles for collectively improvised Australian jazz, there is no evidence to suggest they were the basis of comparable forms of collective improvisation in Australia before jazz. The simple 'melody and accompaniment' texture of cakewalk made it relatively easy for a band to 'fake'. Yet, this does not imply anything beyond the improvisatory behaviour already discussed in relation to circus, minstrel, vaudeville and dance band music in Australia. More importantly, the syncopated melody of the typical cakewalk does not lend itself easily to further rhythmic transformation or melodic embellishment without altering the quaintly stilted quality that appealed most to Australian musicians and their public (Musical Ex. 4.10). It is more likely that unsyncopated music was sometimes transformed into cakewalk-style music through rudimentary rhythmic paraphrasing techniques (e.g. by transforming ♩♫ to ♫♩). Charles Wallace, a popular Australian stage pianist of this period, is cited as playing

Musical Ex. 4.10. The last section of 'Coon's Ragtime' (1902), by François Albert (of Albert's Music, Sydney).

the tune 'Poor Old Joe' in turn as a polka, waltz and cakewalk.[60]

The popularity of cakewalk music did, however, strengthen a perceptual link between African-American music and improvisatory embellishments. Through their association with so-called circus-trombone 'smears' featured in cakewalks such as Arthur Pryor's 'Coon Band Contest', one of the most popular cakewalks to reach Australia. As Tin Pan Alley arrangers began to give the trombone a more independent role in popular music, these comic smears became idiomatic of ensemble ragtime. The improvisatory insertion of smears was, as already mentioned, described as ragging and later as jazzing.

Piano Ragtime and Song Accompaniment before 1910

By 1904 Australia had become a dumping ground for the ragtime song products of Tin Pan Alley. As well as directly importing the latest ragtime songs from Witmark, Francis & Day and other major overseas music houses, local publishers such as Allan's, Sutton's and Cole's published overseas items under licence as well as pieces composed or arranged by local musicians such as Fred Hall, George McIntosh and Thomas Bulch (see Figure 4.5). Coon songs composed or arranged by Melbourne or Sydney musicians give some idea of the style of ragtime accompaniment that Australian

Figure 4.5. Cover of *Allan's First Coon Album*, 1904.

composers and house arrangers considered appealing to the public of the time (see Musical Ex. 4.11a-b).

Most pre-1910s examples of locally composed or arranged piano ragtime feature the simple melodic and rhythmic characteristics of cakewalk music. Two exceptions are 'Happy Hits Lancers' arranged by the Sydney dance band leader, L.P. Purnell (Musical Ex. 4.12a) and 'Georgia Ragtime Waltz' (not shown) by François Albert (1907), both of which feature the characteristic double-note syncopation of piano ragging.[61] Of those published in Australia under licence or imported before the 1910s, the most pianistic is Musical Ex. 4.12b. This is from the dance section of a 'ragtime song' 'Oh, Go 'Way Man', attributed to an S. Joplin and is of course the B section of Scott Joplin's famous 'Maple Leaf Rag' (transposed to E♭). It presents a remarkable contrast to the other items in *Allan's First Coon Album* (1905) in which it is found.

Musical Examples 4.12a-b demonstrate ragtime devices that stage or dance pianists applied in performance to make their music more modern, rhythmic or hot, whereas an example such as 'My Dainty Blackbird' (Musical Ex. 4.11b) is only the skeletal outline of what the professional accompanist or dance musician would be expected to play. Published ragtime sheet music suggests that Australian pianists preferred a style, or styles, in which only rests, pauses and cadences were ragged. This was only a minor extension of earlier embellishment practice. The simple syncopated chordal vamp was probably also commonly used to rag accompaniments.

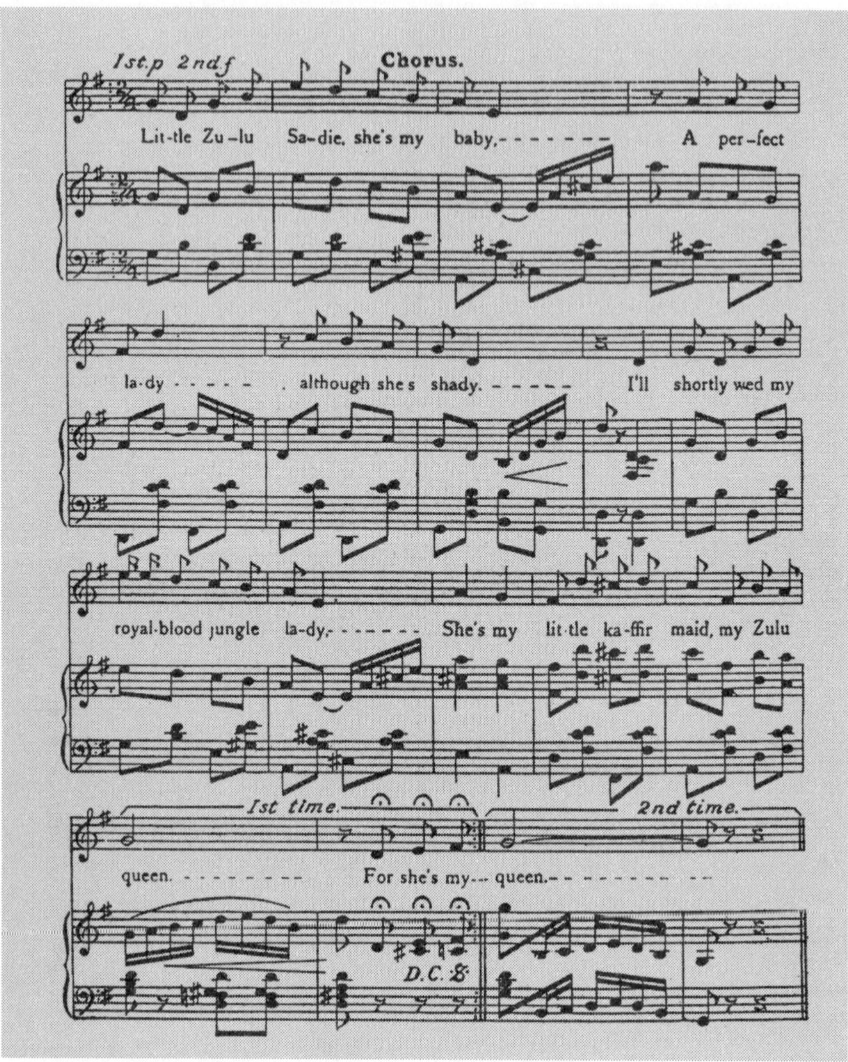

Musical Ex. 4.11a. Chorus of 'My Pretty Little Zulu Queen' (1904), by Jerome and Byrne and arranged by Owen Conduit.

Ben Harney's 1911 visit to Australia underlines the problem of defining early ragtime piano performance in Australia. Harney was still describing himself as 'the originator of ragtime' and his ragtime piano playing is mentioned in a relatively extensive Australian article, 'Ben Harney – and Ragtime'. Yet Melbourne reviews give no indication that there was anything out of the ordinary in his performances. His piano ragging must therefore have been either beyond comprehension or so familiar as a musical practice that it did not even warrant a mention.[62]

Musical Ex. 4.11b. Bars 1-7 of the chorus of 'My Dainty Blackbird' (1904), by Barney Fagan and arranged by Allan's house arranger, Fred Hall. Note the rhythmic displacement in the left-hand part and the rudimentary nature of the right-hand part.

The degree to which non-specialist, professional and amateur ragtime singers attempted to represent African-American performance characteristics must have varied greatly. There are some fascinating clues suggesting the early Australian adoption of vocal ragging, such as the 1903 Australian composition 'De Stammering Coon' by Horace Gleeson with its 'ad lib' stammering (ragged) chorus.[63] Melbourne theatre advertisements and reviews indicate that the increasing popularity of coon song produced a commercial theatre which supported not only 'coon impersonators' and authentic African-American artists. It also supported an expanding group of artists who sang 'dainty coon songs' such as 'Oony Oony Oon' or 'Slumber Little Coon' simply because they were popular, not to mention the countless amateurs who performed this music as home entertainment. A broader exploration of ragtime in Australia during this period could, in fact, separate the work of local 'coon specialists' such as John Gardner and visiting American specialists, such as Harney and Blutch Jones, from the more watered-down forms of ragtime song performance.[64]

Musical Ex. 4.12a. The last section of 'Happy Hits Lancers' (1907), by L. P. Purnell.
Musical Ex. 4.12b. The dance section of 'Oh, Go 'Way, Man' by S. Joplin (1904).

Musical Ex. 4.13. Bars 1-12 of the chorus of 'My Coal Black Dixie Queen' (1902), a 'hot-time darkie song' by May Irwin and Malcolm Denold, showing simple, syncopated fill in figures.

Part II: The 1910s

The 'Great Wave' of Ragtime

According to Jack Davis of the Sydney music house, Davis & Co., the 'great wave of ragtime' started in Australia after his firm published Irving Berlin's Tin Pan Alley hit, 'Alexander's Ragtime Band', in 1911.[65] Melbourne's first-hand response to Berlin-style ragtime song did not occur until late 1912 when J.C. Williamson's Melbourne production of the pantomime *Puss in Boots* opened, which featured this and other Berlin hits such as 'Ragtime Violin', 'Mysterious Rag' and 'Everybody's Doin' It Now'.

In early December 1912 Williamson's advertisement for *Puss in Boots* announced that the show would include 'exhilarating "hustle music" named as "rag-time" – at present the craze in England and America'.[66] By the end of the month the *Puss in Boots* advertisement was describing the new music as the craze of Melbourne and Sydney and Allan's phonograph department was offering several ragtime titles from the show on record. As in 1899, local reviewers made no attempt to provide an objective description of the new music the pantomime introduced. 'Incidental music' arranged for the show by a local musician in the new ragtime style was dismissed as 'slices of Ragtime Opera for the purposes of which some well known composers were sadly mutilated'.[67] This would indicate that by late 1912 such syncopated transformations of popular music were not particularly novel to Melbourne audiences. Nevertheless, *Puss in Boots* was clearly a manifestation of the same shock wave that had reached London earlier that year, prompting newspaper headlines such as 'Ragtime Craze Hits London: Real Hustle Music from America'.[68]

Shortly after *Puss in Boots*, Australian readers of *The Times* would have encountered an extensive article, 'What is Ragtime?', that set out to analyse this new music and even included some brief notated examples. Some months later, part of this article was reprinted in the Australian journal, the *Lone Hand*.[69] Although the musical analysis is naive, the article expresses what I have suggested was a common Australian perception of things American:

> Now of the character of 'rag-time' there can be no doubt – it is absolutely characteristic of its inventors – from nowhere but the United States could such music have sprung; it is the music of the hustler, of the feverishly active speculator; of the 'sky-scraper' and the 'grain elevator.' Nor can there be any doubt about its vigour – vigour which is, perhaps, empty sometimes and meaningless, but, in the hands of competent interpreters, brimming over with life.[70]

This article also distinguishes clearly between the notion of 'Negro delineation' and current ragtime performance practice. For example, it states that '"Rag Time" music . . . started probably as a debased imitation of the genuine negro song . . . But these conscious imitators did not quite understand what they were imitating'.[71] At the same time, the writer presents contemporaneous white ragtime performers as entirely in control of the language of this new synthesis: ' . . . this peculiar specialisation in rhythm which seems to fit in so absolutely with the American character'.[72] In relation to performance practice it comments:

> Nor is this syncopation a mere academic accomplishment; it connotes a special frame of mind, an eagerness, a desire to be beforehand [to anticipate the beat] which is eminently characteristic of the nationality of its performers. With a good 'rag-time' singer the hearer

> is not conscious of mechanical crossing of rhythms; the total effect is that of a perfectly free declamation which by some miracle coincides exactly with the absolutely strict time of the accompaniment.[73]

There is no reason to believe that Australians in 1912 were any more likely than their British peers to attribute this exciting 'new' musical development to black Americans.

1910s Ragtime Music and its Performance

In this new musical era the term 'ragtime' became synonymous with 'modern' and 'popular' and the musical influence of the new style of ragtime deeply permeated Australian popular entertainment. The craze quickly became manifest in burgeoning public demand for sheet music, recordings and piano rolls, Ragtime dancing and ragtime variety acts or other forms of theatrical entertainment which incorporated the 'new' ragtime sound.

Sheet Music

A large proportion of the new Tin Pan Alley ragtime song was published in a form that served both as piano music and vocal music with piano accompaniment. As time passed more complex forms of piano ragtime began to appear, including a few examples of genuine classic piano ragtime. Allan's (Melbourne) published three classic rags in their annual dance albums during the 1910s.[74] Among the other forms of piano ragtime to reach Australia were the numerous quasi-rags churned out by the publishers of music folios for silent movie accompanists and, later, the flashy, novelty-style piano pieces popularised by composers such as Zez Confrey.[75] Musical Examples 4.14a-c provide a broad sample of the types of piano ragtime published in Australia before the 1920s, although they do not necessarily indicate how local professionals or competent amateurs preferred to play. It must be emphasised, however, that ragging is not ragtime composition itself, but the ragtime-style embellishment of compositions.

A published partial listing of Australian ragtime compositions based on titles that include the word 'rag' illustrates that most Australian ragtime compositions were in fact ragtime song with piano accompaniment. Only five of the forty-four pre-1920s items are listed as piano solos. Australian composers often appropriated the ragtime idiom for nationalistic purposes, giving no recognition to the African-American or American origins of the idiom. This may also represent the desire of composers or publishers to distance themselves from the anti-American sentiments that emerged in the early years of the First World War. Consider for example the titles, 'Budgery Fellah Rag', 'Chinkee Chinee Rag', 'Fix Bayonets Rag', 'The Corroboree Rag', 'Commonwealth Rag',

D7
G
D7
G

Red Pepper.
A SPICY RAG.
HENRY LODGE.
Piano.
Also Published For Military Band and Piano Solo arr. by W. C. O'Hare.
Modto (Not fast)
603
cresc.

'Ragtime Kangaroo', 'Swastika Rag', 'The Diggers Rag', 'By The Big Blue Billabong: Australian Rag', 'Can't We Have a Rag about Australia', 'Let Er' Rip Rag', 'Golden Wattle Rag' and 'Coo-ee'.[76]

The piano parts for ragtime songs such as 'Corroboree Rag' (Musical Ex. 4.15) are little more than a simple harmonisation of the syncopated vocal line in song form. In contrast, the piano rags shown below are multi-thematic, relatively pianistic and very carefully composed. 'The Jazz Band Rag' and 'Sharps and Flats' (Musical Ex. 4.16a-b) feature a mix of dotted notes and straight quavers, reflecting the rhythmic transition from the straight march rhythm of early ragtime to the ambiguous triplet rhythm of the emerging jazz style. The playful musical interchange between straight quaver and dotted rhythms in these examples further suggests that Australians acknowledged this to be ragging which could be applied in performance to 'pep', 'spice', or 'ginger' up popular tunes (see Musical Ex. 4.16a).

'O-O-Meo', a ragtime song about the Victorian town of Omeo by the prolific Melbourne composer and publisher Reginald Stoneham, is another example of this ragtime-to-jazz transition (Musical Ex. 4.17). Again, the title indicates that the ragtime idiom was undergoing deep acculturation in Australia. This is but one of numerous compositions that, while containing some rag elements, will probably never be listed as ragtime in any catalogue of Australian ragtime compositions. The very full, syncopated bass of 'Jazz Band Rag' (see bars 1-3, Musical Ex. 4.16a) and to a lesser extent 'O-O-Meo' suggest how local professionals may have filled-out the left hand of Tin Pan Alley arrangements. Stoneham himself played and even recorded as a professional accompanist on occasions.[77]

These compositions indicate some familiarity with syncopated bass patterns of the type presented in the Winn and Christensen ragtime methods. There is also some similarity between the texture of Field's 'Sharps and Flats', Harris' 'Jazz Band Rag' and the ragged transformations featured in Winn's regular article in *Melody*, '"Ragging" the

Opposite top to bottom:
Musical Ex. 4.14a. Bars 1-8 of the A section of 'Black and White Rag' (1913), by George Botsford (see the Allan's advertisement in Figure 4.6). This very popular rag helped to familiarise Australians with the 'triplet overlay' or 'secondary rag' sound (i.e. the third and sixth semiquavers of bar one and the first and fourth semiquavers of bar two sound as accents, creating a secondary triplet pattern as in Musical Ex. 4.3b above). This later became a cliché of jazz.
Musical Ex. 4.14b. Bars 2-15 of the piano part of the A section of 'Red Pepper' (1910), by Henry Lodge (see the Allan's advertisement in Figure 4.6). The small notation (r.h.) functions as a guide to the pianist leader.
Musical Ex. 4.14c. The last eleven bars of the trio of 'Ragged Edges' (c. 1912), 'a real ragtime classic', by Otto Frey. This segment is more or less representative of the cakewalk-like nature of the remainder of the work.

Figure 4.6. Allan & Co. advertisement for piano rags. *Australian Musical News*, November 1913, p. 140.

Popular Song Hits', which was available to these musicians in the late 1910s (see Musical Ex. 4.18). On the other hand, it is clear that the multi-thematic 'Jazz Band Rag' and 'Sharps and Flats' are not notated transformations of popular tunes but cakewalk-like compositions in their own right. Winn's transformations frequently employ syncopations which cross the barline, whereas the only Australian example I have found is in the cakewalk 'Coo-ee!', by the Melbourne music experimentalist, Henry Tate.[78]

Australian ragtime compositions from the 1910s rarely feature the alternate single/ double-note syncopated patterns that were noted in two Australian compositions from an earlier period and typify the Winn and Christensen systems. It should be noted, however, that Winn uses these patterns very sparingly in his sample transformations published in *Melody*.

The relatively simple nature of local or imported ragtime is more likely a reflection of local popular taste – and a reluctance in the market to move away from formulaic 'easy to play' ragtime – than any lack of ability among local composers and professional pianists. Australian popular taste still favoured the unambiguous in music: a simple melodic style with a strong stable rhythm. A significant characteristic of this music is that syncopation rarely extends beyond manipulation of the same very small group of simple syncopated and unsyncopated figures. The most common of these were the cakewalk figure in its normal ♫♩ and expanded forms ♪♩ ♪ and the tied syncopation ♪♩ ♪♫♫ .

Sound Recordings and Piano Rolls

The advent of recorded sound provided local musicians with models – albeit mostly decontextualised white models – for the nuances of improvised performance practice which previously could only be learnt by direct observation. Before the phonograph, a local artist may have had one or two opportunities in a decade to catch the act of a particular visiting variety artist. By contrast, access to a standard cylinder phonograph

Musical Ex. 4.15. Vamp section and bars 1-6 of the verse of 'Corroboree Rag' (1916), by Vince Courtney. 'Corroboree Rag', written for the pantomime *The Bunyip*, is typical of syncopated show tunes of the period and the vamp features a harmonic cliché of Tin Pan Alley ragtime.

provided local artists with an almost unlimited opportunity to appropriate the style of any performer on record. The availability of sound recordings was such that by the 1910s, interested musicians were able to obtain a wide variety of ragtime sound recordings.

Even by the late 1890s phonographs were widely available in Australia, and both instrumental ragtime and coon songs, such as Hogan's 'All Coons Look Alike To Me', performed by both white and black American artists, were marketed here. The Edison phonograph was introduced to Melbourne around 1890 and was apparently 'selling well' at Allan's by 1899.[79] By 1912 Edison alone had released 150 or more 'coon' type songs by the white 'coon specialist', Arthur Collins, and these were often available in

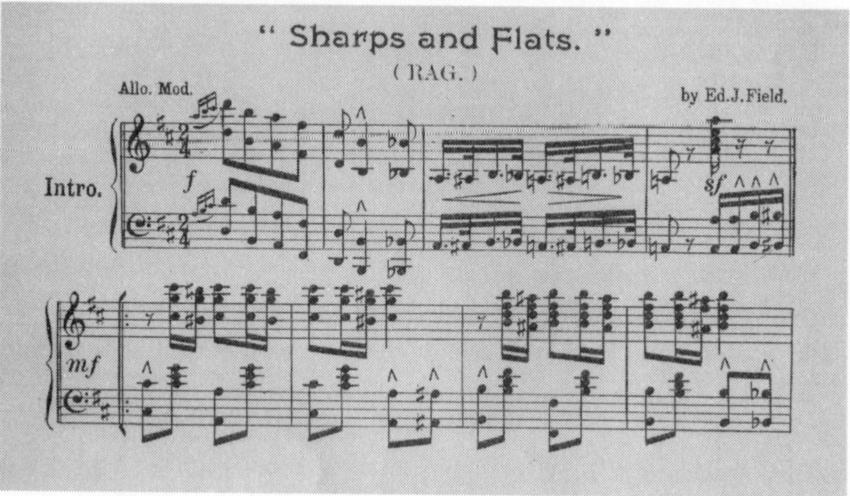

Musical Ex. 4.16a. The last 20 bars of the last section of 'The Jazz Band Rag' (1918), by S.H. Harris.
Musical Ex. 4.16b. Introduction and bars 1-4 of the A section of 'Sharps and Flats' (1918), by Ed J. Field.

Musical Ex. 4.17. Introduction, vamp and bars 1-3 of the A section of 'O-O-Meo', by Reginald Stoneham and C.J. Garis (c. 1921). Note the rhythmic instability created by the contrasting straight semiquavers in the vamp and the dotted semiquavers in bars 1-3 of the A section.

Melbourne only months after their American release. Although, as already mentioned, Melbourne and Sydney had their fledgling commercial recording enterprises, the 'coon song' content of their output remains to be confirmed.

Just before the First World War, private ownership of play-back equipment became much more common. The Melbourne historian Les Barnes vividly recalls the impact of hearing a 1911 recording of Irving Berlin's 'Alexander's Ragtime Band' (Edison 10522) for the first time on cylinders purchased for the family phonograph in 1914.[80] Recordings of many of the leading white ragtime singers of the 1910s reached Australia, including Billy Murray and Gene Greene. Greene had already recorded sixty-four issued titles for the Pathé Company with his ragtime accompanist, Charlie Straight, before his 1913–14 Australian tour. These recordings were heavily promoted and sold fairly well in Australia, despite being playable only on Pathéphone phonographs. Two expatriate Australians, Billy Williams and Albert Whelan, also made ragtime song recordings which sold well in Australia.[81]

Instrumental ragtime recordings made before the 1910s are mostly Tin Pan Alley-style band or orchestral ragtime, or banjo solos in the ragtime idiom. Recordings of solo piano ragtime were rare until the 1910s, a fact historians often attribute to inferior

Musical Ex. 4.18. Bars 1-20 of Edward Winn's ragged transformation of 'On the Rockin' Rosa Lee', from *Melody* 2(1) January 1918, p. 25. Compare with Musical Ex. 4.16a-b.

recording technology. Yet piano accompaniment to ragtime song can be heard clearly on recordings that reached Australia, even before 1900. Recorded ragtime accompaniments, in fact, provide more information about piano ragging than recordings of ragtime compositions played as written, as thc accompanist's ragging is heard in contrast to the Tin Pan Alley vocal line.

It was easier for local pianists to learn the techniques of ragtime embellishment from piano rolls because a novice could play the roll at slow speed and watch the piano keys for these embellishments. More importantly, piano rolls recorded in Australia provide valuable information about ragtime embellishment practice here. Both hand-played and arranged rolls (i.e. rolls which were not created by a performer in performance) normally contain many embellishments not shown on the published Tin Pan Alley scores, which usually appeared on the market in advance of the roll. Some of these embellishments are more or less idiomatic to the piano roll medium:

> An early technique was simply to double both bass and treble to achieve a fuller sound. Other embellishments were short fill in runs, and extensive use of the tremolo. The most popular device was the mid-range melody in tremolo with flashy embellishments carried on in the upper ranges.[82]

Another effect was the use of out-of-sync attacks on left-hand octaves and chords to create a strummed banjo or guitar effect. The presence of idiomatic effects, some of which were hand-played and others 'cut', can of course confuse a listener who is seeking to understand the procedures of playing ragged embellishment.

According to Barclay Wright, proprietor of the Mastertouch Piano Roll Company, the early history of hand-played piano roll performance in Australia began in the mid-1910s with two talented young Sydney duo-pianists, Laurel and Edith Pardey. Around this time Laurel began to play onto a recording machine built by a resident American organ builder, George Horton. These early sessions represent the beginnings of a piano roll recording enterprise which, in 1923, became the present-day Mastertouch company.

Wright saw the Pardeys play and had many discussions with Laurel about these early years of recording.[83] She told him that in her youth she was 'right into ragtime' and took part in at least two ragtime competitions in or around Sydney. As it was considered improper for women to enter these competitions, she dressed as a man and used the name James P. Taylor, a pseudonym found on her piano rolls. In attempting to describe Pardey's approach to ragging popular tunes, Wright could only say that she interpolated (he used the word 'imitated') 'rag breaks' into the introductions, endings and other appropriate places.[84]

With one or two exceptions all of the rolls cut before 1919 by Laurel, or Laurel and Edith Pardey as duo-pianists, appear to have been lost. However, many of her post-1919 rolls are still available from Mastertouch and Wright supplied me with several examples which demonstrate the embellishment practice he described. A further significance of this neglected primary source on African-American influenced performance in Australia is that it preceded sound recordings of locally performed 'jazz' by several years and therefore reveals aspects of the early Australian conception of jazz not previously considered by Australian jazz historians. These will be discussed in the following chapter.

The Melbourne pianist Len Luscombe, former child prodigy, Melbourne theatre conductor and founder (c.1919) of the Melbourne Anglo-American Player Roll Company, is claimed to have hand-cut (not played) the first piano rolls ever made in Australia. Unlike the Pardeys, Luscombe had spent some time in America and his 1920s style of playing on piano roll was greatly influenced by the famous American 'novelty-style' pianist Roy Bargey, with whom he was associated.

Ragtime Music and Dancing

> a string band did its best with rag-time airs . . . on several occasions the syncopations and cross-rhythms of the tunes were too much for the musicians, and finally . . . a piano was brought down . . . to reinforce the strings.
>
> Review of a Melbourne Tango Supper, 1914.[85]

The performance behaviour of dance musicians is generally regarded as utilitarian and unworthy of comment and this is particularly true of the period before Australian dance musicians began to play jazz. On the other hand, pre-jazz social dancing in Australia was of great public interest and the performance behaviour of social dancers – particularly if it did not 'conform' – was often commented on. It should be remembered that in certain social contexts the performance behaviour of dancers and the musicians that accompany them can form a loop of interactive behaviour – each spurring the other on to exaggerated and even inventive behaviour.

An examination of ragtime era social dancing in Melbourne demonstrates that transgressive and inventive behaviour, or 'breaking out', in popular music and dance began to occur long before the advent of Rock 'n' Roll dancing or even 1920s jazz dancing. Calls to rebel against terpsichorean and social orthodoxy were clearly encoded in the spontaneous performance behaviour of ragtime dancers and recognised as such. African-American inflected dance, with its emphasis on body movement and intensified rhythm, provides a special invitation to improvise movement and steps. The Melbourne article, 'Carnal Cake Walk', quoted above indicates that by 1904 the potential for personal improvisatory expression inherent in African-American influenced social dancing was already identified with moral transgression:

> But the Cake Walk is an exaggerated American nigger Can-can dance, stripped of all artistic evolution and reduced to low sensuous suggestion of a wild saturnalia. Every movement in the 'Cake Walk' has an indecent meaning, and is a representation, from beginning to end, of a couple who are working out with frenzy a licentious sexual scheme in front of spectators . . . For purposes of sociality, the valse, quadrille, lancers, polka, schottische, and barn-dance should suffice.[86]

A remarkable feature of pre-war Melbourne was the public enthusiasm for dancing; thirty or forty daily advertisements for venues can be found in Melbourne newspapers of late 1913. Such was this enthusiasm that entrepreneurs were prepared to face fierce, conservative opposition and possible financial ruin to construct the first St Kilda Palais de Danse. The Palais was considered a 'dangerous experiment' in informal public dancing which critics claimed would result in immorality, rowdyism and 'extravagance in conduct'. Moreover it was only allowed to open on the strict condition that there would be 'no Turkey Trots, Bunny Hugs, Tangos or other abominations'.[87] Newspaper references to (post-Cakewalk) Ragtime dancing began to appear shortly before the opening of the Palais late in 1913. These came first in the form of advertisements offering lessons in the so-called Ragtime dances: the One-Step, Turkey Trot and Tango. By the end of 1913 one Melbourne theatre was screening 'dancing films introducing the Tango and Turkey Trot'.[88] Some months later Jennie Brenan's dancing school began to offer lessons in 'Ragtime Dancing'.[89]

There appears to have been considerable confusion in Australia about what Ragtime dancing was. A dance tutor written here in an attempt to standardise local practice claims that most Australian ragtime dancers simply invented their own steps. In *How to Learn the Turkey Trot, Hesitation Waltz & Tango*, George Salinger writes:

> In the present mixed condition of dancing, any kind of dance may be called any name. Those who are, unfortunately, unfamiliar (which consists of the majority of people at the present time), believe that any contortions of the body or movement of the feet will fill the bill for a Turkey Trot or a Tango. For all I know, they may have various names for all these contortions, such as the 'Horse Trot,' 'The Aeroplane Dip,' 'The Monkey Wrench,' the 'Fish Walk,' 'The Kangaroo Glide,' etc., etc. . . . when a proper process of standardisation is working there will be definite, clear cut dances, definitely named and meaning the same to people everywhere.[90]

Putting aside the influence of the Cake Walk on the emergence of creative freedom in Australian social dancing, there seems to have been a period around 1913–14 in which dance academies struggled to control and negate the potential for creative body movement released by the new Ragtime dancing craze. In this battle for conformity and control Salinger uses the same deterrent against individual creative expression that was applied earlier to Cake Walk dancing and later to Jitterbugging, Rock 'n' Roll and so forth, namely, the claim that it was anti-social. He writes:

> Immoral dances have never been invented, but one can not refrain but noticing that an immoral element can easily put their own construction on a dance and create in the mind of the refined the impression that these dances are not fit for their private homes or any ballroom.[91]

To give some idea of the complexities faced by Australian dance academies in the standardisation of Ragtime dancing, Salinger's instructions for 'The Turkey Trot Or Ragtime Dances' begin in the following manner: 'This dance is distinctly American, and has about a dozen steps and features, these steps being again divided into numerous variations'.[92] He then proceeds to painstakingly describe the components and variations of the Turkey Trot. Interestingly, Salinger informs his Australian readers that Ragtime dancing was invented in San Francisco as a refinement of a Texas cowboy dance (which in turn borrowed from the 'Negro Buck and Wing dance'), a further example of how African-Americans were now being denied even the previously meagre acknowledgment for their contribution to American popular culture.

An earlier Australian dance instructor, *Robert's Manual of Fashionable Dancing*, dismisses Ragtime dancing as a collection of 'freak dances':

> The Freak Dances known as the 'Turkey Trot,' 'Judy Walk,' 'Grizzly Bear,' 'Duck Waddle,' 'Wobbly Walk,' 'Bogey Walk,' 'Bunny Hug,' 'Puppy Hug,' 'Parish Pump,' 'Crabbing the Crab,' 'Terrapin Trundle,' 'Fuzzy Wuzzy,' 'Catch as Catch Can,' 'Rough and Tumble,' 'Piccanniny Dandle,' and 'Scullery Lancers' are objectionable absurdities, detestable and ludicrous in the extreme . . . Many of them seem to be a combination of a tired nigger's shuffle, and a demonstration of Hackenschmidt in training, and an occasional Kangaroo jump thrown in for picturesqueness . . . Freak dances are mostly characterised by swaying movement of the hips, a dipping of the body, a few inelegant aggressive arm thrusts, sudden clutches, and close contact . . . it is indeed as if some mischievously disposed persons were to add offensive details to a chaste piece of classic sculpture, and thereby cause the statue to appear indecent. Can anyone explain how it is that ordinarily inoffensive young Australians, when they dance, suddenly develop the spasmodic automatism of the coloured coon, combined with the suppressed fury of the Paris Apache?[93]

Local dance orchestras such as Allietti's did play instrumental rags from stock orchestrations, but Ragtime dancing seems to have been most commonly performed to particular Tin Pan Alley ragtime song hits such as 'Waiting for the Robert E. Lee'. The presence of a strongly accented two beat feel (2/4 or 2/2) was clearly of great importance, but Salinger also considered syncopation critical. In describing the first movement of the Turkey Trot, the 'walking glide', he states that 'it is a case of sliding on the toes, dropping the heel to each beat of the music. It is absolutely essential that one first learns the syncopation of Ragtime music'.[94] He later notes that 'in many cases Two-Steps are being used for Ragtime [dancing] – this is essentially wrong, as the Two-Step does not give the time or the syncopation that is embodied in Ragtime'.[95]

Salinger's instructions propose a system in which musical patterning and body movement are almost mechanically interlocked, allowing for only the most minimal forms of variation in each. Dance proprietors also had some very practical reasons for desiring uniformity of body movement. Important among these is that uniform dancing takes up less floor space. Yet ragtime dancing and music offered musicians and dancers exciting new levels of creative freedom, if they were prepared to transgress the bland congruity that the dance industry establishment was attempting to impose.

The Influx of American Ragtime Artists

The greatest boost to ragtime in Melbourne came with the arrival of numerous white American ragtime artists, including the Primrose Four, Josephine Davis and, most notably, Gene Greene and his accompanist, the accomplished ragtime pianist, Charlie Straight. Greene introduced 'Ragtime Contests' to Melbourne, with gold and silver medals and cash prizes for the best local ragtime song performers. Ragtime instrumental acts also became popular. These featured not only the more conventional instruments (piano, xylophone, cornet, violin, banjo, etc.) but also, in the tradition of variety, novelty instruments and unconventional ensembles such as six cornets and a trombone.[96]

From late 1913 to late 1914, somewhere between sixty and one hundred ragtime artists (or artists who made a special feature of ragtime) appeared on the principal Australian variety circuits. These artists were predominantly vocalists and all ragtime vocal acts required complementary ragtime accompaniment, which was provided either by the vocalists themselves at the piano, an accompanist belonging to the act, the theatre orchestra pianist or the theatre orchestra.

The popularity of Irving Berlin-style ragtime song had ushered in what was perceived as an entirely new era of Australian vaudeville. 'Old style' vaudeville was now finished. In this new era an act could be brought up to date and given 'class' simply by the inclusion of ragtime music either in the act itself or its musical accompaniment. One Sydney pit band on the Fuller vaudeville circuit (discussed below) was even billed as the 'Grand American Ragtime Orchestra'.[97]

Vaudeville Ragtime Artists and Accompanists

The presence of many expert American 'ragtimers', together with what some considered the inordinate demand for the music, compelled local stage performers to familiarise themselves with any performance practices that could sustain them against the impressive American competition. The most obvious way for local artists to learn how to rag was simply to ask visiting Americans, for which there was ample opportunity, given the high level of social and artistic interaction between American and Australian artists. For theatre musicians this interaction differed very little from what occurs at a present day 'jam session' or typical musicians' party, during which impromptu performances take place, ideas are exchanged and performers demonstrate their skills with an eye to soliciting work and expanding their network of contacts. Quotations and references 1-7 below, mostly from the vaudeville trade journal, *Australian Variety*, refer to vaudeville industry parties and outings in Melbourne and Sydney and illustrate situations in which knowledge of ragging would have been sought and passed on:

1. Mel Brewer did a Charlie Straight act at the piano and Dave Fanton Melba-d [danced] to a marked degree.
2. Nelson Storey . . . gave a fine exposition of 'ragging' on the piano, when he put through George Murphy's gladiator music to great applause.
3. Prior to leaving the slip, Harry Hart got to the piano and hit up some ragtime. Turkey-Trots and Bunny Hugs were indulged in by several members until the launch left.
4. At 11.30 pianist Peck got busy and for the next hour [there was] ragtime dancing, singing and a few monologues . . .
5. A reference to the 'Two Bobs' as the 'life of the party' with their ragtime playing and singing.
6. A reference to Gene Greene's impromptu vocalising with other artists at a social gathering.
7. Harry Hart presided, to be followed later by Harry Stone, who gave an almost perfect imitation of George Sharratt's clever pianologue at the National.
8. [Baroness D'Astreel's] burlesque opera singing of 'mysterious rag' was a real riot.
9. Jack Kearns has a parody on 'a ragtime band,' which has a finish some of the 'heads' ought to go and listen to . . .
10. A reference to acts featuring parodies on ragtime song by Denis Carney, Russell Carr, Tom Leonard and other artists.[98]

As already noted, the appropriation, imitation or burlesque of style characteristics was an integral element of the popular stage. References 1 and 7-10 indicate that the characteristics of ragtime performance practice were commonly transferred in this way.

Quotations 11-17 below, about instrumental acts, use the terms 'ragging' or 'rag' as verbs, or suggest performance practice beyond the mere reading of fully scored ragtime.

11. Stan Stanley, a local product who 'rags' the piano and puts over several character numbers to success.
12. [Violinist, Jack Prince] gets away from the usual run of syncopated instrumentalists . . . Several 'rag' numbers are introduced with wild abandon . . .
13. Billy Gellor at the piano caused a furore with his playing of 'Robert E. Lee' in double ragtime.
14. Miss Josephine Davis . . . assisted by a young man [Billy Gellor] who has acquired the dreadful habit of ragging ragtime and beats the piano like a musician at a suburban hop.
15. Corona can still rag some on the cornet . . . [Corona was billed as 'The man who makes the cornet talk'].
16. [Rosa Roma's violin] selections included the 'Swanee River,' with ragtime variations . . .
17. In [Lizzette's] playing of ragtime the trombone becomes a ragged harsh medium of crudely broken notes that are absolutely jarring to the ear [from the conservative *Theatre Magazine*].[99]

The casual use of the term 'double ragtime' (reference 13 above) indicates that readers of *Australian Variety* were already quite familiar with this key concept in ragging (see

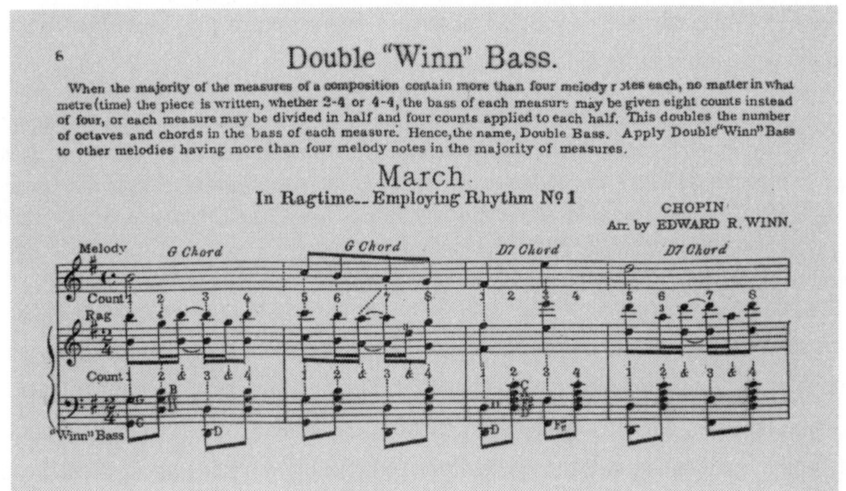

Musical Ex. 4.19. Instructions for 'double ragtime' from Winn's How to Play Ragtime.

Musical Ex. 4.19). For example, the aim of Edward Winn's method, described below, was to show

> how to convert ANY piece of music into the most intricate, complex syncopated rhythm at sight and [furnish] a complete course for the highest technical and artistic performance of single and double ragtime.[100]

Vocal Ragging

One of the better documented instances of Australians directly appropriating ragtime performance practice can be found in references to the ragtime competitions introduced by singer Gene Greene during his six week season at Rickard's 'Opera House', Melbourne, in late 1913. Greene's visit seems to represent the first manifestation of an Australian youth culture based around African-American derived, vocally oriented music. Although the momentum of this early 'wave' was greatly retarded by the First World War, Greene's visit was nevertheless a harbinger of a much later Rock 'n' Roll youth culture.

Melbourne variety reviews – traditionally brief, cryptic and utilitarian – give little indication of the cultural impact of Greene and other ragtime artists. Ian Whitcomb, however, provides a useful account of the ragtime 'invasion' in Britain around the time Greene was in London, 'scat-singing his way nightly through his big American hit, "King of the Bungaloos" to the car-chase rag piano of Charlie Straight of Tin Pan

Alley'.[101] Whitcomb cites a youthful observer's impression of the American ragtime artists who visited Australia, such as Greene:

> I instantly became, at a callow 16, an avid fan of the real American ragtime. Not for me the wet and weedy British imitations! When those Hedges boys let loose with their eccentric hand gestures and torso gymnastics I had to be physically restrained by ushers so excited had I become. Why, these lads were no older than I! There and then I wanted to talk American, walk American, and dress American.[102]

The performance practice of new-style American ragtime singers was, like blackface minstrelsy, a synthesis of perceived African-American performance characteristics and popular stage performance craft blended for current white taste. To the Melbourne public, however, the African-American contribution to this synthesis was of no particular interest. Ragtime was simply the newest product of American popular theatre and Tin Pan Alley.

References to vocal ragging, however, although far from conclusive are much more common than to instrumental ragging. A first review of Greene's Melbourne performances in the *Argus* gives a fair indication of the nature of his act. It also describes performance behaviour that included various mannerisms and the spontaneous ragging of popular songs:

> [The audience] showed an inclination to keep him singing the quaint stringhalt [spasmodically contracting] melodies as long as his throat – and the management – would stand it, and he had difficulty in escaping . . . after 'ragging' for half an hour. Clad in dapper dress suit and silk hat, he inadiated [sic] ragtime from features, legs, feet, arms, and fingers. With an infinite capacity for making weird noises he combined clear enunciation. At the end of his own songs and storics he took calls from the audience for tunes to be 'ragged' . . . Not a little of the success of the turn was due to the piano accompaniment of Charlie Straight.[103]

Straight was expected to provide ragtime accompaniment to the audience's requests without a score or any other form of preparation. The *Age* review also notes the interdependence of Greene and his accompanist and comments that 'Greene, in brisk and showy style, led off with a number of striking songs, and afterwards 'ragged' others in an equally airy manner, at the will of the audience'.[104]

Both papers note the remarkable audience response to Greene. It would be easy to mistake the following review for first impressions of an early rock 'n' roll star:

> on Saturday crowded audiences at both matinee and evening performances called him back more than half a dozen times . . . In the convulsive movements which accompany his singing of ragtime: and, in fact, in everything he sings, says and does, Gene Greene shows himself to be a thorough artist.[105]

In regard to Greene's ragtime contests, however, the *Argus* comments: 'Whether Mr Greene is doing a kind thing to Australia in encouraging its youth to develop the ragtime habit must be left to his conscience'.[106]

The criterion for these contests seems to have been the reproduction of Greene's own performance behaviour. Jim Fraser, first prize winner of the competition in Melbourne and also later in Sydney, is described as 'closely allied' to Greene in voice and mannerisms.[107] Immediately following Greene's departure to Sydney, Fraser became a feature of the Melbourne Opera House program where 'he gave further indication of his 'ragging' abilities'.[108] Australian ragtime artist, Edith Huxam, says that she was tiring of her work until she 'took up ragging' after having her first lessons from Greene. 'It was more than interesting, and it inspired me again [and] gave me new life and 'go' in my work'.[109]

The most significant elements of Greene's performance practice – the model for Fraser, Huxam and his other Australian 'understudies' – can be summarised as follows. Vocalisation was combined with rhythmical body movements and other idiosyncratic physical gestures. The spontaneous or seemingly spontaneous breaking up of words was combined with the interpolation of nonsense syllables, rhythmic displacement, rubato, portamento and novelty effects, such as the deep growl heard in 'King of the Bungaloos' (see Musical Ex. 4.20b). They also included spontaneous or seemingly spontaneous interaction between the vocalist and piano accompanist.

Whitcomb points out that as Irving Berlin-style syncopated song emerged from everyday American speech patterns, it sounds unnatural in other accents, 'And so from 1912 onwards, after the Invasion had conquered, British singers who wanted to ride American songs tended to adopt an American accent'.[110] It can be assumed that many Australian ragtime song performers did the same.

Greene was in Australia for approximately six months during which time he gave Australian artists many opportunities to appropriate his style through public performances, private interactions and ragtime competitions. His recordings for the Pathé label ensured that they could continue to do so after his departure. Nevertheless, it must be remembered that the ragtime song tradition was an established part of Australian theatre long before Greene. He was simply the most entertaining exponent of the style to reach Australia by 1913.

The leading researchers of early Australian sound recording have so far failed to unearth any examples of 1910s ragtime song recorded in Australia. However, some later Australian recordings demonstrate aspects of earlier Australian ragtime performance practice. The ABC radio broadcaster, jazz pianist and researcher, Tony

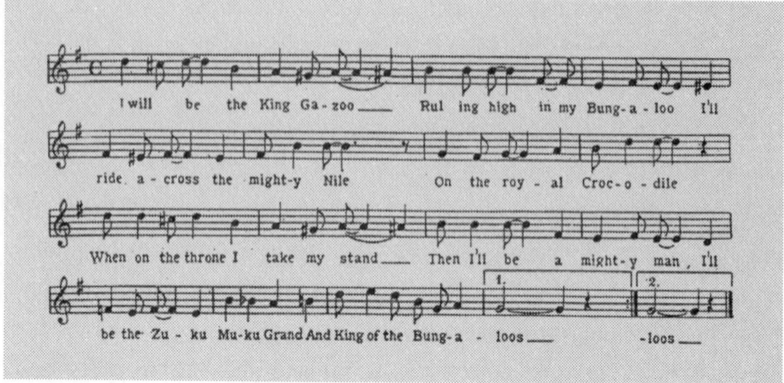

Musical Ex. 4.20a. The vocal line of the chorus to 'King of the Bungaloos' (1909), by Charlie Straight (Greene's accompanist). From the sheet music (voice and piano) published in Australia during Greene's 1913-14 tour.

Baldwin, provided me with some examples recorded in 1929 which preserve a style that he claims was already old-fashioned by 1920.[111]

These recordings feature the Australian vaudevillian George Sorlie, who was described shortly after Greene's tour as 'easily one of the most natural ragtime singers in Australia'.[112] The four tracks, 'Ida Sweet as Apple Cider', 'Ragging the Baby to Sleep', 'Down on Bullfrog's Isle' and 'If You Only Had my Disposition', are sung by Sorlie in a style which sounds strange to ears accustomed to jazz singing – particularly in the 'patter' (spoken sections) in which Sorlie's distinct Australian accent sometimes surfaces.[113] The straight quaver interpretation used in 'Ragging the Baby to Sleep' gives the vocal line a muted banjo or piano-like quality (Musical Ex. 4.21a), although this effect results more from the absence of the familiar fluid triplet/dotted note interpretation used in jazz than the specific application of rhythmic embellishment. The stilted rhythm and simple triplet embellishments of the trumpet solo in 'Ragging the Baby to Sleep' reflect a pre-1920s approach to embellishing popular song on single line instruments.

These examples have other distinctive characteristics which probably represent what was the common conception of ragging around 1913, when Sorlie was establishing his reputation as a ragtime singer. Among these are melisma (including unexpected intervallic leaps within a single syllable), the interpolation of syllables, extensive use of rubato, vibrato on sustained notes, the singing of nonsense syllables in unison with the piano, ambiguous pitches and, in particular, subtle shifts from straight quaver to dotted note rhythms (see Musical Ex. 4.21b). Sorlie combines clear

Musical Ex. 4.20b. Transcription of the final two choruses of a 1917 recording of Gene Greene singing 'King of the Bungaloos'.

enunciation with vocal effects in a striking way, as also noted in Greene's Melbourne performances (see the review quoted above). A distinct shift from dotted note to straight quaver rhythm is also heard in the final eight bars of the piano accompaniment to this example, 'Down on Bullfrog's Isle'.

The comment about Sorlie's 'natural' style is fully sustained by these recordings. The rhythmic sophistication featured here gives the impression, unlike many other Australian 1920s recordings of African-American influenced performance, that it is based upon deeply internalised experience: something very close to what I have defined in the introduction as ecstatic improvisatory practice. The fact that Sorlie's part-Carib-

Musical Ex. 4.21a. Transcription of the vocal and trumpet part of the chorus of 'Ragging the Baby to Sleep', sung by George Sorlie.

bean descent had given him the opportunity to work with visiting African-American artists such as Josephine Gassman and Billy Brown could partly account for this. In the 1910s, Australian theatre reviewers continued to note the naturalness or spontaneity of such African-American artists. This was, unfortunately, usually in the familiar terms of the supposed primal nature of the African-American.[114] Even a very favourable 1914 Melbourne reference to Gassman's expressive transformation of a Tin Pan Ally ragtime song is shocking to present day sensibilities:

Musical Ex. 4.21b. Transcription of the first verse and final chorus of 'Down on Bullfrog's Isle', sung by George Sorlie.

> Miss Gassman opened up [her act] by singing 'You made me love you,' and her rendering made it a different song to that hackneyed air with which we all are familiar. The expression of primal passion and burning desire put into it was a marvellous demonstration of savage feeling, and it fascinated the civilised white audience, that looked and listened spellbound.[115]

Orchestral Ragtime

Local dance and cinema orchestra libraries of this period were built largely on what was popular: old and more recent favourites and the latest ragtime hits. Probably about a fifth of the average Australian professional dance band or cinema orchestra music library comprised ragtime, or what was considered ragtime, namely, cakewalk/two-steps, syncopated one-steps, instrumental versions of ragtime song show hits (see Musical Ex. 4.22) and Tin Pan Alley instrumental rags, all of which vary greatly in their resemblance to the, now, more familiar sound of classic ragtime.

Since the orchestrations used by 1910s dance, silent cinema and live popular theatre orchestras had to be highly standardised and easy to play in order to accommodate frequent and often drastic changes to ensemble size and personnel, the instrumentation of ragtime orchestration is usually the same for any other commercial orchestration of the period. The 'small orchestra' folios comprise first and second violins, viola, cello, bass, flute, clarinet, first and second cornets, trombone, piano and percussion. The 'large orchestra' folios also include a second clarinet, oboe, bassoon and horns. These professional scores are organised in such a way that allows even the large orchestra sets to be played with a skeleton ensemble – with or without piano. The ragtime 'sound' produced by these arrangements is of course greatly mutated by the expediency of an arranging system based on the need for simplicity,

Musical Ex. 4.22. Bars 1-5 of the verse (piano part) of 'The Dusty Rag', Note the instrumental nature of the vocal line.

ff

Instrument	Function
Flute	Upper Melody
Oboe Clarinet 1&2	Upper Harmony & Doubling
Violin 1	Melody
A Cornets	Mid Range Harmony & Doubling
F Horn Bassoon Cello	Lower Harmony
Violin 2 Viola	Off Beats
Piano	Off Beats
	On Beats
Trombone String Bass	Bass
P'cussion	Rhythm

Musical Ex. 4.23. Bars 1-4 of the A section of the orchestration of 'Freckles Rag' (1906), by Larry Buck (arr. Daniel Dore), which I have arranged to show the function of the various instruments.

Musical Ex. 4.24. Upper stave: bars 1-4 of the first violin part of 'Freckles Rag'; lower stave: an unragged reduction of this part.

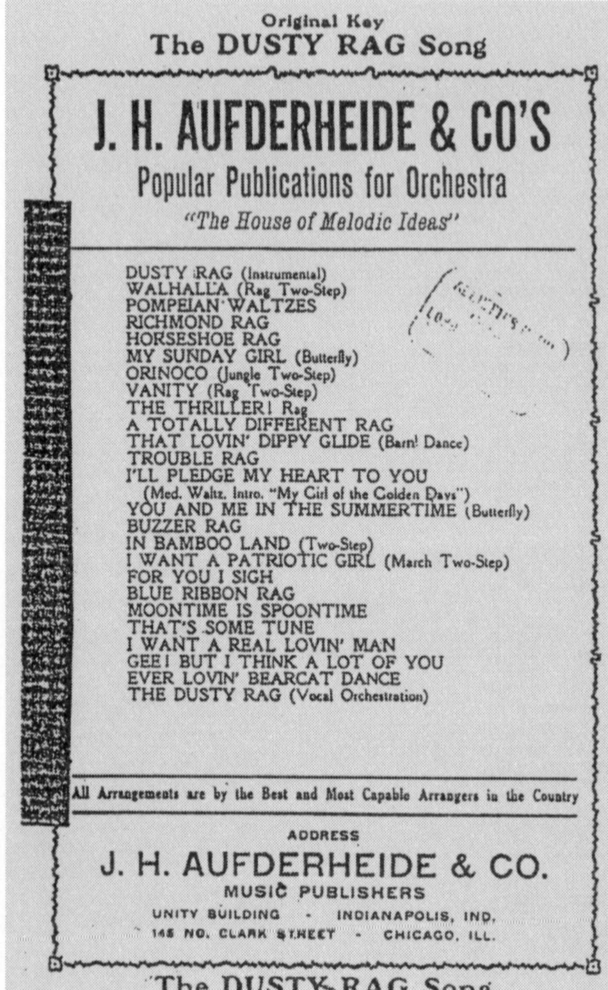

Figure 4.7. The front cover from the orchestration of 'The Dusty Rag' (ragtime song) (1912). From the Allietti dance band library.

standardisation and musical consistency across a whole range of musical genres and combinations of instruments (see Musical Ex. 4.23).

Appropriation of Ragtime Style: Pit Musicians

Pit musicians had to adapt to the increased demand for ragtime at a time when the appearance of smaller local pit ensembles and a universal shift from first violinist/leader to pianist/leader were placing the vaudeville pianist in a more prominent role. As for performance practice, this would have varied greatly between small and large ensembles and different classes of variety venue (between, for example, the Melbourne Tivoli and a small suburban cinema/variety house). In considering the question of ragging by variety show pit musicians, it must also be remembered that they were renowned for their general versatility and ability to fake, transpose and fill in.

There are no detailed Australian accounts of ordinary brass, string or reed pit players ragging the melody parts assigned to them, but circumstantial evidence suggests that they must have done so in specific situations. Australian popular theatre musicians had been familiar with ragtime from around the turn of the century. Lead players (first violins, first clarinet and cornet in particular) were very familiar with characteristic ragtime lines and syncopation (see Musical Ex. 4.24).

In 'Band and Orchestral Ragtime', Thornton Hagert describes a procedure used by large ensembles in the performance of pre-jazz orchestral arrangements which is, in effect, a spontaneous restructuring of the published version. Hagert writes:

> If doubling of the parts allowed performance by a smaller group, it also gave the fuller orchestra the option of a considerable variety of combinations. Even during a performance, the leader could assign the prominent parts to one of several instruments, thereby producing a more varied effect.[116]

He also mentions that such an orchestra 'may have *several* first violins, playing melody in unison or with one or more ad-libbing harmony parts or counter parts' and that an instrument which dropped out to leave a new instrument a clear field 'might fake a harmony part, counter part, or *obbligato*'.[117] Similar procedures are still used by old-style Melbourne dance bands, such as Ron Richard's Rhythm Kings.

Since pianists and 'rag shouters' ragged simple unsyncopated music to produce a hot, exciting, modern sound, the orchestral musician assigned a simple unsyncopated lead part (e.g. a popular song melody) would have been tempted to do likewise – if only as a clever or humorous theatrical effect. Whether they did, of course, depended on the musician's ability, the formality of the context, the function of the music and the disposition of the leader. The procedure outlined by Hagert, in which a player dropped out to give the soloist a clear field, suggests the most common situation in which single line players would have ragged. Probably the most commonly heard form of instrumental ragging was the idiomatic trombone smears mentioned above.

One pit musician who probably often ragged his lines even before the First World War was the trombone player, Harry Mehden (son of Von Der Mehden). Mehden had played in venues on America's Barbary Coast with pianist Al Tatro shortly before they, with Mehden's brother Carl, took the pit job at Sydney's National Theatre, billed as the American Ragtime Orchestra. Working alongside a ragtime expert such as Al Tatro in such a limited combination (piano, trombone, drums) Mehden had to fill out his part with any device at his disposal, including ragging. Reviews of the band confirm that they had some difficulty providing satisfactory accompaniment for variety acts. A 1918 review, discussed in the next chapter, specifically mentions Mehden's trombone ragging as part of a stage act. Another pit player clearly capable of ragging a chorus was the variety artist Corona. Only a month after being commended for his ability to 'rag', he joined the pit orchestra of the Melbourne Bijou.[118]

Vaudeville Piano Playing

In a small pit orchestra a vaudeville pianist who was able to rag could – potentially – provide a full active texture in many items, thereby compensating for missing instruments. This is probably how Al Tatro managed to lead a pit band comprising only three instruments. How much piano 'ragging' of vaudeville music actually took place depends partly on the degree to which Australians adopted the type of performance practice described in American vaudeville literature.

An important question that still needs to be resolved concerns the extent to which Australian vaudeville pianists followed the old practice of playing from hand-written single line 'lead sheets' (leader's sheets – usually a first violin part). The American Mike Bernard, for example, gained great public admiration for the way he could rag a variety act's lead sheet and otherwise fill out an entire musical program with improvised elaboration.[119] Some American literature indicates that this was still common practice in the early 1910s. An obvious advantage of playing from lead sheets was the elimination of the task of writing out a full piano part. The pianist/leader could also follow cues, direct and play simultaneously without page turns; and lead sheets had more space for handwritten cues. The fundamental practicality of this system suggests that it was probably standard practice in international variety shows until the early 1910s, if not later.

Christensen's Instruction Books for Vaudeville Piano Playing (1912) provide precise instruction on how to improvise from lead sheets:

> In accompanying songs, it does no harm to embellish your part, 'fill in,' and elaborate it, *provided* you have, first of all, good taste, experience, and a sufficiently accurate technique to make the part interesting. Songs in two-step or fast march form and some others are frequently made more interesting by 'ragging' them, if you have the ability to so treat them.[120]

In addition, he warns:

> Do not introduce a lot of ridiculous embellishments and flourishes, runs, arpeggios and four-flushing stuff of that kind unless you want to be 'called down' and 'bawled out'. Fill

> in solid harmonies, as we have said before, a few judicious ornaments here and there, using ragtime when it can be used to the best advantage.[121]

Playing from lead sheets involves a type of harmonisation and embellishment technique similar to that described in Patton's *Harmony Simplified for Popular Use* or other nineteenth century practical harmony manuals. Yet vaudeville pianists also improvised syncopated music on the basis of a method commonly associated with contemporary jazz musicians and their 'Fake Book', which contains the upper voice of 'jazz standards' with chord indications. The vaudeville pianist, however, often had to get by without the latter. Finally, in considering this seminal question of lead-sheet playing, it must also be recalled that the 1910s was the central decade of the era of improvising silent cinema pianists, some of whom were cited as ragging in Chapter Two. Moreover, cinema pianists had to provide ragtime accompaniment to the live vaudeville acts that were a normal feature of silent film exhibiting in the 1910s and 1920s. I believe that in Melbourne alone there would still have been numerous theatrical entertainment pianists capable of improvising from lead sheets in the manner described by Christensen.

Much is yet to be discovered about the extent to which ragging occurred in vaudeville accompaniment music, but there is no doubt that the vaudeville circuit functioned as a conduit for various forms of this practice. Some of the aspects discussed here also apply to other theatrical genres that featured variety and burlesque, such as the Pierrot shows and revue companies. It was the notion of presenting a constant variety of entertainment that made vaudeville both a particularly important conduit for new musical ideas, sounds and practices and also a performance environment in which improvisatory accompaniment practice could survive. Discussion in Chapter Five of what can be described as the ragtime-to-jazz transition (c.1918-23) throws further light on Australian ragtime performance behaviour.

5 Jazzing

The first five years of Australian jazz (1918-23) are intriguing because this was the period in which, following a deeply traumatic war, local musicians had to negotiate a transition from ragtime to jazz in considerable isolation from overseas developments and performance culture. This was before the first visiting (white) American and British jazz bands and before recordings of jazz (other than Tin Pan Alley-style) were imported in quantity. It was also a time when the dance band – which became the primary site for jazz-inflected performance in Australia – underwent a major transformation in structure and sound. This chapter explores the improvisatory characteristics of the earliest forms of Australian jazz and also discusses a perception of jazz improvisation that persisted until the beginning of the so-called Australian Swing era of the late 1930s: that jazz improvisation was the 'jazzing' or 'jazzing-up' of popular music.

Australian jazz writers tend to use the term 'jazz' as a noun or an adjective; jazz is discussed as a type of music, an era, a dance (the Jazz), a concept, a complex of influences, a vigorous intangible impulse and so forth. It is essential to note, however, that the term 'jazz' was also used as a verb. 'To rag' had long been the ragtime era term for transforming and/or embellishing music in accordance with the ragtime idiom and 'to jazz' became its jazz era counterpart. Early 'jazzing', I believe, offers the clearest insight into the nature of the earliest Australian jazz.

It has already been shown that even before the jazz era local musicians regularly consulted American musicians' journals such as the ragtime journal *Melody* and the *Metronome Orchestra Monthly*. Figures 5.1a-c illustrate that advice on the type of jazzing appropriate for white orchestral musicians was available long before 1923.

JAZZING on the TROMBONE a CINCH

BY THE HENRY FILLMORE METHOD

A unique treatise in book form on Jazzing. Gives all the practicable Trombone Jazzes. Shows how and where to fake a jazz into a plain trombone part. Contains a department of Jazz Solos. A self-instructor so clearly and thoroughly explained by word and examples that any ordinary trombonist should in three or four weeks become a R-E-A-L Jazz Artist. SPECIAL PRICE, $1.00.

FILLMORE MUSIC HOUSE, CINCINNATI, OHIO

Learn to Jazz on the SAXOPHONE

A complete method on ragging the Saxophone explains by new system of models how to fill in sustained notes, how to play variations, etc.

Thompson's Simplified Chart of Fingering also included in this book. ORDER NOW.

Price $1.00

FRANK J. HART SOUTHERN CALIFORNIA MUSIC COMPANY

Figure 5.1a. Advertisement for Henry Fillmore's *Jazz Trombonist*. *Metronome Orchestra Monthly* 36(11), November 1920, p. 77.

Figure 5.1b. Advertisement for K.L. Thompson's *Rag-time Saxophonist*. *Metronome Orchestra Monthly* 36(11), November 1920, p. 90.

Figure 5.1c. Advertisement for the 'Virtuoso School': a saxophone course including lessons on jazzing. *Metronome Orchestra Monthly* 36(11), November 1920, p. 75.

SAXOPHONISTS

BEGINNERS AND ADVANCED

Our new Mail Course covers the entire field of Saxophone playing and reveals the SECRETS of Low and High Tones, Tonguing, Tone Control, Correct Tone, Transposition, Fingerings, Jazzing, Solo Playing, etc.

Write for full information. Sent FREE.

VIRTUOSO SCHOOL Buffalo, N. Y.

Furthermore, as early as 1918 Melbourne and Sydney journals were attempting to inform Australian readers on jazz performance:

> 1. . . . and then a portion of the tune, usually half of it, is played again, the players generally managing to introduce some novel features in this repetition, sometimes creating very pleasing effects. (1 June 1918)
> 2. The jazz band is a combination of clarinet (playing violin parts) cornet, trombone (playing all the slides in his power – and blue notes), a good piano player who can improvise and Rag and a good snappy drummer who can originate, read and fake. (1 July 1918; a reprint)
> 3. There is no music used, they all fake and make up their own combinations. (5 July 1918)

> 4. There is some music that only Americans can play. This is their new medium – jazz, an extension of ragtime, it is a spontaneous music . . . Certain instrumentalists, like the clarionet player are given a free hand, and it is according to how they feel that they embroider and elaborate a theme. This 'free sound' is never twice the same. (2 December 1918)[1]

What, then, was the approach of local musicians to playing 'jazz' before the arrival of the first visiting jazz band in 1923 – an event which Frank Coughlan, a notable early jazz trombonist, described as 'the great turning point in the development of jazz in this country'?[2]

Stage Jazz

Before the mid-1920s, when resident radio station 'jazz bands' such as Melbourne's The Statics began to emerge, live 'jazz bands' were generally heard either as variety stage acts or, more commonly, as dance bands. Jazz stage acts were nevertheless a very important influence on the way jazz and jazz improvisation were initially perceived in Australia.

A vaudeville act called 'Australia's First Jazz Band' made its debut in mid-1918 on the bill of Ben Fuller's Sydney vaudeville house, the National Theatre. At its first appearance it featured a:

> lady baritone [accompanied by] highly excited and eccentric musicians, a fiddler, saxophonist, trombonist, pianist, and drummer with complete outfit, who 'Jazzed' for the best part of 25 minutes.[3]

The band (henceforth referred to as the Jazz Band) was initially fronted by Belle Sylvia, who had only recently arrived in Australia for a season at the Sydney Tivoli where she was billed as 'London's foremost lady baritone', a 'strict departure from the conventional'.[4] Sylvia may well have brought with her some knowledge of 'early jazz' (collectively improvised style jazz), but there appears to have been little general awareness of this music in Britain until the arrival of the Original Dixieland Jazz Band (ODJB) from America the following year.[5] It is more likely that she fronted the Jazz Band as a so-called 'coon-shouter' or 'rag-shouter', in the theatrical tradition first popularised in white American society by May Irwin, in the mid-1890s.[6]

After its Sydney season the Jazz Band appeared at Fuller's Melbourne venue, the Bijou theatre, where Sylvia was almost immediately replaced by another lady baritone, Mabelle Morgan. Morgan was an Australian with American stage experience who had already appeared in the 1911 London revue, *Hullo Ragtime*.[7] She did not accompany the Jazz Band on the remainder of its Australian tour, which included Adelaide and Brisbane. There are no sound recordings or musical arrangements to suggest how the band sounded and written observations are generally meagre, second-hand or other-

Figure 5.2. A Melbourne advertisement for the Jazz Band. *Herald,* 25 July 1918, p.8

wise problematic. However, the above reference to the drummer who jazzed for twenty-five minutes provides one important clue.

The Jazz Band and 'Early Jazz'

It is important to consider whether the jazzing of the Jazz Band was something similar to the collectively improvised style of playing that the ODJB introduced to London audiences the following year. If the Jazz Band did, in fact, attempt to play in something resembling the style of the ODJB in mid-1918, it would probably have been the most stylistically advanced white ensemble in the world outside America. Furthermore, it would have introduced a style of jazz improvisation which many believe did not emerge as a performance style in Australia until the end of the 1930s with the Melbourne formation of the famous Bell Band.

The basic ensemble of the Jazz Band was violin (the American leader, Billy Romaine) saxophone and clarinet (Jock Thompson), trombone and probably cornet (Harry Mehden), piano (Wally Smith), drummer (Don Royal) and the vocalists mentioned above. An ensemble with this instrumentation could conceivably have attempted to play in collectively improvised style, perhaps by using a recording of the ODJB as a model. The ODJB's seminal recordings, 'Dixieland Jazz One-Step' and 'Livery Stable Blues', had been recorded over a year earlier (Victor 18255, May 1917) and although there is no evidence of this record's release in Australia before the time of the Jazz Band, individual copies may have been brought here by visiting American or returning Australian artists or agents. Some unspecified 'jazz-band' recordings (also described as 'real American Ragtime') had reached Australia by June, 1918.[8]

If the Jazz Band did, perchance, base their act on recordings of the ODJB, they would probably have adopted the musical characteristics that are most audible on these recordings. A very perceptive observer of the Jazz Band's performances might, therefore, have noted that violin, saxophone (or clarinet) and trombone (or cornet) created a sequence of complex polyphonic textures, backed by loud, heavily syncopated drumming and a pianist who frequently paraphrased or 'ragged' the melody in the right-hand. In each textural permutation one particular melodic or 'front line' instrument would have been heard presenting the main melody, while the other two weaved above and below it in what would have seemed an ambiguous and discordant but clever way. Even a less aurally perceptive observer would at least have noted that the front-line instruments formed themselves into various unfamiliar, 'noisy' combinations.

In a detailed reference to the Jazz Band, William Deane, a leading Australian music publisher, wrote 'There is no music used, they all fake and make up their own combinations'.[9] This may seem significant but careful reading suggests that Deane could be referring to jazz bands in general at this point in the text.[10] However, a Melbourne reviewer also mentions the formation of unusual combinations:

> in the music played by this band eccentric combinations are made to out-rag ragtime. The instruments played are piano, violin, saxophone, trombone, drums, with effects provided by cowbells, pistol shots and other noises, musical and unmusical. Perhaps the best number was that in which the noises of a farmyard were cleverly imitated.[11]

The above reference to 'noises' seems only to relate to percussion effects, but other references could indicate a more collective form of 'noise making'. For example, an Adelaide reviewer noted that:

> The band reminded one of the old-time nigger minstrel bands. For the most part the members made more noise than music – simply 'jazzed' away for all they were worth, but it was patent to see that they were all experts in their various department.[12]

A prominent feature of the 1917 ODJB recordings and many other examples of early collectively improvised early jazz is the weaving of novelty sound effects, including animal imitations, into the texture. It could therefore be significant that reviewers repeatedly refer to the Jazz Band's so-called 'farmyard selection', which included 'chicken sounds' on violin, a 'zoological saxophonist' and 'cattle lowing sounds' on trombone. A Melbourne reviewer noted that the 'Jazz bander should be ready for anything, from an acrobatic exploit to the imitation of a flock of geese or the roar of a jungle beast'.[13]

However, there are many factors that detract from the possibility that the Jazz Band played in collectively improvised style even before the ODJB had reached Britain. The playing of conventional instruments in unusual combinations was a relatively common feature of musical variety acts. Therefore, the term 'combination' used by Australian reviewers may simply refer to combinations of instruments considered relatively unorthodox at the time: the inclusion, for example, of a saxophone or unusual percussion instruments. The playing of conventional instruments in unconventional ways to produce humorous or novel sound effects can be traced back to mid-nineteenth century colonial variety acts, pantomime and blackface minstrelsy and does not necessarily indicate that the Jazz Band was modelled on any particular white or black American jazz band. There were also other models of 'noise making' ensembles available, two obvious examples being the circus 'clown band' and the minstrel show 'orchestra'. Note that in the quotation above the 'noise' of the Jazz Band is compared to 'old-time' minstrel show music. Finally, although terms used to describe the Jazz Band's music, such as 'absurdities', 'eccentricities', 'riot', and 'madness', could be taken for first impressions of collective improvisation, they are also standard variety review language of the period.

Collective improvisation involves idiomatic forms of voice leading which produce considerable dissonance. Yet the band is sometimes commended by reviewers for its tunefulness and in its Melbourne and Sydney performances the instrumental music appears to have functioned mainly to support the vocalist. The Jazz Band act was presented not as a showcase for a specific type of music but as a sequence of contrasting musical variety items (e.g. ragtime song, 'ragtime opera burlesque', the 'farmyard selection' and a finale featuring the drummer). Accounts of the emergence of indigenous jazz in Britain strongly suggest a parallel with the Australian situation but, as I discuss below, this early British jazz does not appear to have included collective improvisation.

So, if the Jazz Band's jazzing was not the collective improvisation of early jazz, what was it?

Jazzing as Musical Burlesque

San Francisco, a city which already had its own fledgling jazz community, had particularly close ties with Australian vaudeville. By mid-1918 vague descriptions of jazz bands were, as previously noted, beginning to appear in the Australian literature. The model for the Jazz Band may therefore have been only a written description or even a drawing, a photograph or some faded, personal recollection of black or white American jazzing.

Burlesque was an especially popular form in the Australian popular theatre of the 1910s. About four years before the Jazz Band's debut, local variety artists had found it very profitable to create humorous burlesques of the new vogue, ragtime.[14] Moreover, blackface minstrelsy had long since established a strong conceptual association in the mind of the Australian public between African-American performance culture and the notion of grotesque or comically-distorted performance. From this perspective, it is likely that the Jazz Band was in the nature of a clown, revue, Pierrot or blackface minstrel band, improvising a musical burlesque or 'send-up' of a model virtually unknown to their audiences – and possibly only vaguely known and understood by Jazz Band members themselves. It is described, for example, as an 'eccentric combination of instruments [that] do their work in comedy style' and 'a combination of mirth and melody'.[15] (See Figure 5-3.) This likelihood is a pointed reminder of the decontextualised environment of much Australian performance practice.

The Jazz Band and Ragtime

The ensemble music played by the Jazz Band probably did not deviate much from the popular music of the day: instrumental ragtime and ragtime song in straight quaver rhythm or the increasingly fashionable dotted note rhythm. Individual parts were probably adapted and memorised from familiar stock orchestrations or worked out from piano/vocal arrangements. In Tin Pan Alley ragtime ensemble playing of the 1910s, the first violin normally took the lead line with the first clarinet playing upper harmony or doubling the main melody. The trombone sometimes reinforced the bass line, but it also played melody and counter-melody. In the Jazz Band itself, the violin probably doubled and thus reinforced the vocal line, while other front-line instruments took a role similar to that described above. If the voicing of the Jazz Band instruments was, as I suspect, an adaptation of standardised ragtime arranging procedures of the period, it would have sounded very different to collectively improvised jazz. It would, for example, have been relatively unvaried in texture and much less contrapuntal. One reason for

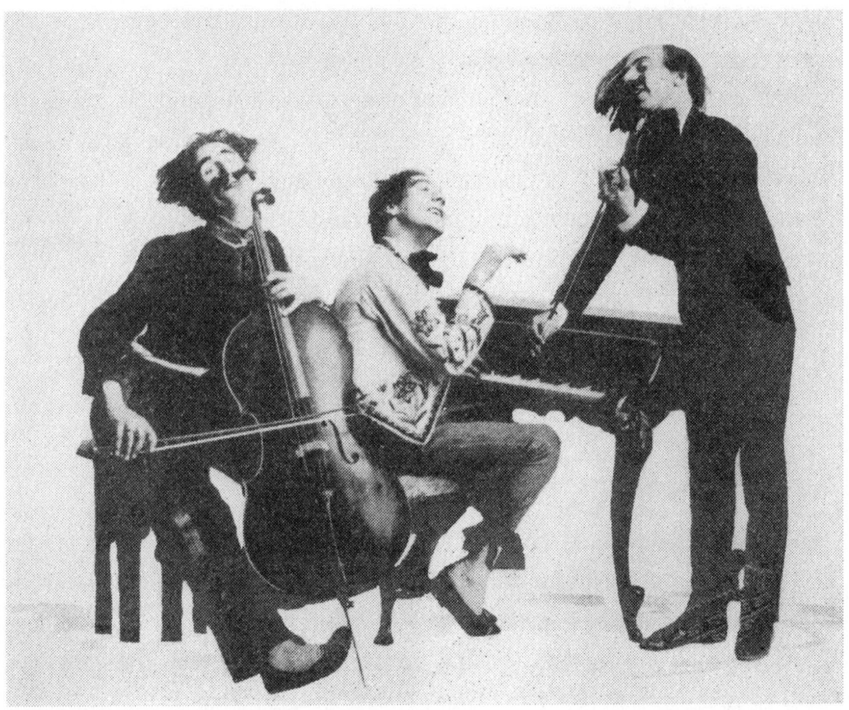

Figure 5.3. Blue Hungarian Band Burlesque, a popular Melbourne burlesque band of the 1910s that included the ragtime piano player Fred Dennett (La Trobe Library, State Library of Victoria).

this is that ragtime arrangements are often modelled on the melody and accompaniment texture of piano ragtime.

A memorised framework or head arrangement of minimally syncopated, Tin Pan Alley instrumental ragtime or ragtime song could then have been embellished in performance through the application of a flexible veneer of novelty sound effects. Trombone 'smears' (which saturate the ODJB's music) were already characteristic of orchestral ragtime and even written into stock arrangements of the period. As the essence of burlesque is not imitation but absurd misrepresentation, any one of a vast array of instrumental effects known to these musicians (the jaw shake, flutter-tongue, laughing trombone, multiphonics, and so forth) was probably good for a laugh.

The likelihood that the Jazz Band played Tin Pan Alley ragtime embellished in various ways is supported by the fact that ragtime was still highly fashionable in 1918, when the Jazz Band was formed. *Melody* (which had Melbourne and Sydney agencies) had only just begun to publish its instructive monthly article 'Ragging the Popular Song

Hits' and Australians to compose ragtime that even marginally resembled the more sophisticated forms of American instrumental ragtime.

Romaine, Mehden, Royal (and possibly other instrumentalists in the Jazz Band) were also ragtime performers of many years standing; playing familiar ragtime standards from memory would have left them free to concentrate on jazzing. Three of the four items in their Melbourne program were rags: 'Ragging the Scale', 'Oh You Drummer!' (described elsewhere as a rag), and 'Ragging the Miserere'.[16] Moreover, a reviewer mentions that Morgan 'appeared for the first time, assisted with popular ragtime songs', later noting that '[Morgan's] jazz band, which, despite unusually vigorous execution and unorthodox attitudes, continues to turn out real melody of the ragtime type'.[17]

Jazzing and Ragging

There is also ample evidence that in riotously improvising a burlesque on jazz, the Jazz Band's music involved some form of ragging. A Sydney review states explicitly that the Jazz Band 'did quantities of ragging. Even the *Trovatore* Miserere Scena was ragged, the fiddle taking the soprano and the trombone the tenor'.[18] A previously cited Adelaide review also mentions the Band's efforts to 'outrag ragtime', while another states that the Jazz Band's '"ragging" is exceptionally fine'.[19] A review of the Jazz Band's first Melbourne performance refers to a 'a tall powerfully-built brunette [Belle Sylvia], whose vigorous vocal portraits, with elocutionary embellishments, fit in with the general breezy Americanism of the Jazzers'.[20] The 'elocutionary embellishments' were probably vocal ragging, popularised in Australia by American vaudeville artist Gene Greene on his 1913–14 Australian tour and widely imitated by Australian artists.

None of the performance elements which I have so far suggested were associated with the Jazz Band were new to Australian audiences. Yet unquestionably the Jazz Band was considered a novelty.

Jazzing as Rhythmic Physical Movement

Reviews of the Jazz Band place particular emphasis on the highly stylised physical abandonment and grotesque gesturing of its members. They note, for example, their 'unusually vigorous execution and unorthodox attitudes',[21] and that:

> The Jazz Band players keep time to their music. Every note brings an accompanying movement of foot, arm, leg or head. Every musical phrase has an accompanying facial expression.[22]

A later writer claims that in their concluding rag 'the band apparently went mad, playing with head, arms, and bodies swaying to the music'.[23] This tendency to eccentric or exaggerated movement during musical performance was not new to imitation African-American performance practice. Frenzied movement, eccentric hand gestures and torso gymnastics were quite characteristic of 1910s ragtime singers such as Gene Greene. Furthermore, dancing ragtime instrumentalists were a common feature of Australian variety.

An article reprinted in the *Australian Musical News* in 1918 mentions that in jazz performance 'the swaying of the orchestra helps the dancers to keep in time'.[24] In the review cited above the Jazz Band is also described as keeping in time to their music. These movements, which visually reinforced the rhythmic aspect of the music, were probably perceived as a novel and important element of jazzing. Jim Godbolt, an historian of early British jazz, mentions that 'Because many of these acts [with jazz titles] included dance routines it was generally thought that jazz was a dance'.[25] This raises the further possibility that the Jazz Band members' movements were seen as 'jazz dancing', which also became known as 'jazzing' in Australia.

The Drummer and Jazzing

The most significant references to the Jazz Band are undoubtedly those which point to the dominating nature of loud percussive rhythm and the seemingly (but not necessarily) arbitrary selection of timbral effects. This is illustrated by the following quotations:

1. The Jazz Band still has too long an innings – 18 to 20 minutes would have been more satisfactory, likewise a little less drums.
2. . . . a string of percussion instruments which included a frying pan and saucepan . . . a realistic accompaniment of thunder and lightning, with a few revolver shots thrown in, just to add to the general din.
3. What is it all about no one seems to know except the drummer and Mabel[le], who does her best to tell you but only commits vocal suicide.
4. It is 'sound the trumpets, beat the drum' at the Bijou, where the Jazz Band does its level best to drive home, by means of Mabel[le] Morgan and – the DRUM, some curious airs, which amaze, astound and eventually cause some hearty laughter.
5. . . . the drum, it runs the band. The tune gets lost in drum. Belle Sylvia's deep voice gets in at intervals.
6. It is good to watch the skilful drummer with his haphazard methods, throwing away one musical instrument after another when he has utilised them.[26]

By 1918, theatre 'trap drummers' had long enjoyed a reputation as versatile, spontaneous and imaginative creators of unusual sound effects and reliable generators of rhythm. In his memoirs, the Australian variety artist Charles Norman highly praises the ability of 'traps' to 'ad-lib' and 'always proudly come up with a yes whenever you asked for an odd sound you needed for effect in your routine'.[27] These sentiments are echoed by another Australian variety artist, Valantyne Napier.[28] For percussionists, their often illegible (and sometimes missing) drum parts generally represented only a basic musical skeleton on which all manner of alterations and embellishments were overlaid, using a varying combination of hastily pencilled-in cues, memory and musical instinct. It should also be noted that in numerous Australian cinemas orchestral percussionists provided accompaniment to all manner of apocalyptic events on a daily basis.

The Australian drummer Eric Sheldon wrote in 1932 that just prior to the First World War it was discovered that:

> drums, and drummer's effects were a great asset, cow-bells became immediately popular because of their amazing propensities for making a lot of noise. Drummers became gunmen, they would rattle off volley after volley of blank cartridges.[29]

William Ludwig Jnr (of Ludwig Drums Co.) states that between 1910 and 1920 the so-called trap drummer's

> freedom of expression was given even greater reign. Ragtime was new and exciting. The tempo was fast and the syncopation catchy . . . Though they frequently did play without printed parts, they could read, understand musical moods, and, most important, perform with great showmanship thus bringing the drummer definitely into the lime-light.[30]

It is clear from these and similar references that an increased emphasis on drumming and special percussion effects began shortly before the First World War. This corresponded to a more general increased emphasis on rhythm in popular music and dancing. Note, however, that 'rhythm' does not necessarily mean complex syncopation.

The pre-war success of Irving Berlin's 'Alexander's Ragtime Band' had popularised a musical model which, instead of evolving further towards the complex cross-rhythms of classic ragtime, emphasised a strong, basic dance rhythm supporting a simple formulaically syncopated melody. In playing this music at the piano, for example, it was mainly the ability of the pianist to provide a powerful, metronomic, so-called professional, 'full' or 'jazz' bass with two or four-to-the-bar pedalling that separated the dance pianist from the 'straight' pianist. Bringing the basic dance rhythm to the foreground in this idiomatic way was in itself perceived to be a form of 'ragging' or 'jazzing' (and later 'swinging') of popular music. Therefore, the loud drumming described in reviews of the Jazz Band probably functioned to exaggerate or 'jazz' the underlying pulse, among other things.

In *Jazz in Britain*, Godbolt cites various references which indicate that our principal peers, the British, first perceived jazzing to be largely associated with highly unorthodox and extroverted percussion playing: the striking of as many different sounding objects as possible in the shortest possible time.[31] Such perceptions are also certain to have reached Australia (which commonly waited for London's approval of new American fashions) through popular variety papers such as *Encore*.

The foregoing discussion suggests that what was perceived to be most novel about the first so-called jazz heard in Australia was simply the presence of a trap drummer playing an amusing array of sound generators, including kitchen utensils. The other attractions were probably the unprecedented emphasis on timbral variety, strongly emphasised rhythms and the notion of the previously relatively anonymous drummer as showman. This extroverted percussion playing was undoubtedly perceived as a key element in the jazzing of popular music. It is therefore not surprising that the drummers' traps were subsequently often advertised and described simply as 'jazz' in the 1920s Australian literature (see Figure 5.6c). Of course, not being harmonically restrained, the drummer had more freedom of expression than other band members.

The references cited above could imply that the jazzing of the Jazz Band drummer was little more than the arbitrary generation of noise or 'din'. Today, however, it is more widely understood that a skilled and imaginative percussionist (as many professional trap drummers undoubtedly were/are) can organise a seemingly incongruous collection of sound generators (and the subtle range of sounds that can be extracted from each) into a remarkably extensive, personal, timbral language – a musical system with its own internal logic. In other words, potentially useful sounds are explored and mentally catalogued to become a vast internalised 'palette' or 'scale' of sound objects. These 'objects' can be ordered in advance or intuitively during performance as a percussion solo; or skilfully applied as pre-determined or improvised timbral embellishment or accompaniment.

One feature of the drumming that might have seemed particularly arbitrary or chaotic was the interpolation of solo percussion 'breaks' at appropriate places in the texture. The practice of filling in at phrase endings and other textural gaps had always been a common convention in popular music (most notably for pianists) and the interpolation of complex percussion breaks into popular music was already long familiar to Australian audiences through the bones, tambourine and audible dance-step breaks of blackface minstrelsy.

A 1917 recording (Folkways RF22) featuring the English variety drummer, James Lent, provides an insight into early percussion breaks. In the recording of Lent's 'The

Ragtime Drummer' one hears the skilful interpolation of short (two bar) breaks comprising semiquaver patterns played over a wide variety of sound generators (at about 120 crotchet beats a minute). The effect produced by the very rapid juxtaposition of contrasting timbres (e.g. wood-metal-skin) can be described as timbrally generated ragtime syncopation, an effect that is also characteristic of vocal ragging (see Musical Ex. 4.20a). The Jazz Band's riotous finale, 'Oh You Drummer', may have featured incipient jazz percussion breaks quite similar to those heard in Lent's Ragtime Drummer act, which had been around the variety circuit since 1904.

Overall I have argued that the Jazz Band was basically a send-up of the latest American craze, jazz, in the long popular tradition of burlesque on new vogues. As such, there was probably little concern for authenticity, since in burlesque the most ridiculous stage misrepresentation was often rewarded (as in the case of the Jazz Band) with 'a riot of laughter'. In its relatively short existence (around four months), the Jazz Band probably gave the impression that jazzing was playful musical interaction, vocal and instrumental ragging of popular music, the interpolation of novelty sound effects, faking, imitation ecstatic physical movements to music, improvisatory fills or breaks (particularly on percussion) and exaggerated drum rhythm and showmanship. However, the possibility that some attempt was made to imitate collectively improvised style jazz cannot be entirely dismissed.

The sudden appearance of an Australian ensemble representing what was in fact the harbinger of a new age of freedom in music and dance (i.e. jazz) in the form of confronting cacophony and grotesque body movement would seem to have very important socio-cultural and musical implications. However, the overall tone of Australian observers suggests that any iconoclastic meanings encoded in the Jazz Band's gestures were lost on wartime Australian audiences. They seem to have been taken simply as clever musical and theatrical clowning, forgotten the instant the Boxing Kangaroo (the next act on the bill) came on stage.

What remains most intriguing about the Jazz Band is its emergence at such an early time in jazz history in the extreme geographic and cultural isolation of wartime Australia. It can probably be assumed that, in this isolated context, the music changed and evolved over the several months of its existence through the processes of repeated performances and programming variations and the need to accommodate the successive departures of Sylvia and Morgan. Therefore, there is a distinct possibility that by the end of its tour the Jazz Band was jazzing in a way that sounded more distinctively Australian than any Australian jazz to follow.

Jazzing in Later Variety Acts

Other 'jazz acts' appeared on the Melbourne popular stage before the arrival, late in 1923, of the first of the imported jazz/dance bands. In fact, the Jazz Band was followed only weeks later by a novelty instrumental 'turn' by the comedians Tom Rees and Eileen O'Neil which included 'American "Jazz" music upon the cornet, violin, piano, trombone and other instruments'.[32] In January 1920, an American teenage jazz band (part of a large troupe of teenage performers, the American Boys) appeared at the Strand Theatre. While making no comment on improvisatory practice, a reviewer noted that:

> They possessed features peculiarly their own and bore an unmistakable Americanism. The Jazz Band was an orchestra of [a] novel kind, but it captivated the audience. To the unaccustomed ear there was a certain weirdness about the music at first, but as it was listened to it became strangely fascinating.[33]

Interestingly, this inference that there was something genuinely new and strange about the music is notably absent from reviews of the Jazz Band.

There are a few passing references in the theatre literature to improvisatory practice by stage jazz musicians in these years. For example, Linn Cowen of the Cowen, Bailey and Davis Trio (piano, banjo and saxophone), who reached Melbourne soon after the American Boys, claimed that his trio was 'strong on improvisation . . . Bill Bailey adds a few extra notes to the measure on the banjo and I interject several bars of music to every one shown on the staff'.[34] This does not, however, imply anything beyond the types of piano and banjo embellishment practice mentioned in preceding chapters.

A similarly isolated example is that of the eccentric French-Canadian pianist (ex-circus clown and 'improvisation artist'), Herschel Henlere, who may have been one of the earliest artists to introduce blues vocals and piano to Melbourne. Unfortunately this aspect of his performance is not described in detail. Henlere, who interestingly was described as 'essentially a modernist', employed a device rediscovered decades later by the experimental music pioneer, John Cage. Henlere 'prepared' his piano by placing metal plates on the strings to produce what were described as 'very original Egyptian embellishments'.[35] These were employed in the performance of his own compositions, such as his 'Arabian Fox Trot' and 'Kismet'. A description of his act states that he 'jazzes the classics unmercifully and by contrast turns jazz into the classics with equal ease'.[36] Fortunately, a sample of Henlere's playing survives in piano rolls he made during his visits to Australia in 1923 and 1925. These include 'Mocking the Classics' (musical parody) and 'Operafox[trot]', the latter played as a duo with Laurel Pardey, the Mastertouch Piano Roll Company's house pianist.[37]

The most successful of the early jazz acts was the 'home grown' Linn Smith's Royal

Jazz Band. Although this five-piece band did not appear on the Melbourne vaudeville stage until a few months before the arrival of the first overseas band (Bert Ralton's Havana Band) in December 1923, it is the earliest Australian stage 'jazz band' for which relatively substantial information is available. It is clear that the Smith band musicians were able to 'fake'. Their trombonist Dave Meredith states, for example, that neither their leader and pianist, Smith, nor their drummer could read music.[38] Frank Coughlan recalls their act as the 'epitome of jazz' and describes it as 'the popular music of the day jazzed up'.[39] This jazzing included 'weird' sound effects, which on trombone alone included comic slides, the 'laughing trombone effect', the 'turkey gobble' and 'hand in bell' vibrato. Meredith claims to have independently developed both his 'hand in bell' vibrato and the use of a hand-held crystal glass in special trombone effects such as the 'turkey gobble'.[40] Promotion for the band states that:

> [Meredith] presents a slithery-footed inebriated trombone, which joins in the happy hysteria led by the reckless saxophonist (Paul Jeacle), shrieking in delight and giving the impersonation of an educated turkey gobbler.[41]

The violinist, Arthur Curnick, who played a Stroh violin (horn amplified violin), is described as being capable of 'almost making his violin talk – it certainly shrieks at one'.[42] Like Henlere, Smith was unwittingly making a gesture towards the so-called experimental music of a much later era when he:

> played the theme and accompaniment of 'O Star Of Eve!' with his left hand and repeated by plucking the strings of the grand piano for the theme with his right, while he accompanied with his left on the ivories.[43]

As Smith's program did not change frequently, there was ample opportunity for the players to add progressive layers of embellishment, performance by performance, in a similar way to that described by the circus musician Arthur Withers (see Chapter Two). In full-on ensemble pieces such as 'Gundagai' , the trombone appears, from Meredith's description, to have often been employed (apart from playing 'weird effects') in providing a euphonium style counter-melody and interpolating breaks. The drummer's function (apart from clowning) was to provide timbral effects and to 'balance' the band by adding weight to an otherwise relatively weak rhythm section (piano with the intermittent addition of trombone and tenor banjo). In addition, the drumming is certain to have included percussion breaks and the almost mandatory solo chorus on xylophone with some form of elaboration. Some idea of what the Smith band sounded like can probably be gained by listening to famous American jazz burlesque bands of the 1920s, such as the Jumping Jacks.

The saxophonist Abe Romain, who joined Smith's band later in the 1920s, told the

Australian jazz historian Bruce Johnson that they sometimes worked from a 'score' comprising a numbered sequence of short sections (or 'loops') of music with repeat signs.[44] A section could be played repeatedly or substituted by any other segment selected in performance time. This description resembles some of the scores developed for improvised performance in the 1950s. Regardless of the intended function of this practice, the musical effect would have been an improvisatory collage. However, as already discussed, procedures similar to this were not uncommon in theatrical entertainment accompaniment where the duration of acts was indeterminate.

It appears, then, that there was considerable continuity of performance practice from pre-jazz theatrical entertainment through Australia's First Jazz Band (1918) to the later Linn Smith's Royal Jazz Band (1923). Important aspects of this continuity are 'non-linear' development (e.g. Meredith's invention, or unwitting reinvention, of certain effects), imitation ecstatic physical and musical abandonment, an aural tradition (e.g. head arranging, faking) and that elusive quality of attention-seeking exaggeration that distinguishes 'show' music (particularly American show music) from so-called legitimate music. Moreover, the stage 'jazz' musicians of this first period brought to their music all their earlier knowledge of ragtime performance practice.

Jazzing Dance Music

Early Jazz Bands for Dancing

> Nearly everyone in Melbourne is dancing today – or jazzing. The two things are almost synonymous. It may be a symptom of protracted rejoicing at the declaration of peace . . . The fact remains that dancing has become an "all embracing craze." On the principle that it is a poor heart that never rejoices, people are waltzing, one-stepping and jazzing from Richmond to Toorak, from Footscray to Heidelberg.
>
> 'The Craze of the Dance: Going Mad to Music', *Age* 10 April 1920, p. 20.

There are some specific connections between the first Australian 'jazz bands' for dancing and theatre music. Before the post-war palais boom made it viable for orchestral musicians to specialise in dance music, many theatre orchestra musicians supplemented their income by playing in dance bands. One such musician recalled that around 1919 he and other members of the Melbourne Tivoli orchestra 'were in demand for outside casual "jazz jobs"'.[45] As the term 'jazz' seems to have been strongly associated with the idea of theatrical sound effects and stage antics, it follows that those with theatrical entertainment experience were the best equipped to invent a passable burlesque of this style in their dance work (see Figure 5.4). In particular, the ability of theatrical drummers to improvise, their array of novelty sound generators and, more importantly, their experience in the 'manipulation' (specialised physical handling) of percussion implements placed them in great demand. It could therefore easily be assumed that the music of 'jazz bands' for dancing referred to in immediate post-war Melbourne literature was quite similar to that of the stage 'jazz bands'.

Although early Australian 'jazz bands' for dancing were obviously influenced to some degree by stage 'jazz acts', the term 'jazz band' was virtually synonymous with an up-to-date dance band. The veteran Melbourne dance band leader Ron Richards states, for example, that when he started dance work in the mid-1920s a dance band with up-to-date instrumentation and a popular music repertoire *was* a jazz band.[46]

The dance band industry, which had burgeoned just prior to the First World War, began to revive even *before* the appearance of the Jazz Band in mid-1918. Long established Melbourne bands such as Allietti's, Rosenthal's, De Gilio's, Nellie McEwan's and many others simply carried on into the 'jazz era', bringing with them the experience of the ragtime era and, in the case of many individual musicians, the theatre. Some pre-1923 Melbourne 'jazz band' leaders already had overseas experience. Through local entertainment papers it is also possible to follow the process by which local dance orchestras gradually came to terms (possibly with some reluctance) with the notion of 'jazz', not so much as a genre of music but as a new

Figure 5.4. Nellie McEwan's Jazz Band. *Graphic of Australia,* 13 November 1919, p. 13 (La Trobe Library, State Library of Victoria).

McEWAN'S JAZZ QUARTETTE IN A BURLESQUE MOOD.

fashion in dancing. This was the Jazz, which required 'appropriate' musical accompaniment (see Figure 5.5).

In early 1919, orchestras such as those mentioned above are sometimes cited playing at functions at which the Jazz was danced. By late 1919 many of the same leaders were describing their orchestras as 'jazz orchestras' and ensembles derived from these orchestras as 'jazz bands'. As indicated in Figure 5.5, the Jazz was a specific dance, but it was also a commonly held opinion that 'practically all modern dances – the one-step and two-step and fox trot – are really jazz dances provided that the band plays the proper jazz music'.[47]

There was considerable confusion over what music was appropriate for the new fashion in dancing. Initially local bands appear to have simply played any popular tune

HOW TO JAZZ.

For this Popular Dance a variety of steps are indulged in, but those which are most popularly used are set out below. Other figures can be substituted at the will of the dancer.

20 bars strain. In 4/4 time.

POSITIONS.

Lady stands with back towards line of dance. Gentleman facing. Gentleman's right arm round lady. Lady's right wrist held in gentleman's left hand across front of lady.

Gentleman starts with left foot. Lady back with reverse foot.

	Bars.
First Part—	
Intro.	4
Two walking steps forward (count 1 and 2 and)	1
Chase (count 1 and 2 and)	1
Repeat, commencing with right foot	2
Second Part—	
Step across with left foot over right (count 1 and)	
Point right foot to right (count 1), dip (count and)	1
Repeat, beginning with right foot over left	1
Repeat the whole	2
Third Part—	
Step forward with left (count 1), close right foot to left (count and), round left foot to back (count 2), pause (count and)	1
Repeat, commencing with right foot	1
Repeat the whole	2
Fourth Part, Roll—	
Step with left foot across right (count 1) step to side. With right foot (count and), pivot to left (count 2)	
Close left foot to right (count and)	1
(Lady moves her right foot behind, and in pivoting will turn to right, both swaying the body)	1
Repeat, commencing with right foot	6
Repeat the whole	
Bars	20

(Repeat *ad lib.*)

Figure 5.5. Instructions for the Jazz. *Allan's Jazz Fox Trot Album*, Allan & Co., (c. 1920).

in 2/2 or 4/4. In late 1919 two visiting Jazz dancing experts even complained that 'many returned men who have learnt to jazz in London are finding themselves all at sea in the Australian ballrooms owing to the fact that they are expected to jazz to fox trot music'.[48] As time passed, however, it became apparent that dancers were more willing 'to jazz' if the music itself was appropriately jazzed up. It is therefore important to explore some early Australian conceptions of jazzing in dance band music.

Jazz Music for Dancing and 'Noise'

The early Melbourne 'jazz band' leader Nellie McEwan commented in 1919 that:

> Many people suppose that Jazz is all noise, but that is a mistake. It has all kinds of effects, as an aid to the music, judiciously worked in, but never overdone. Some of the effects are very fine.[49]

Given the male orientation of subsequent Australian jazz subculture, it is interesting to reflect here on the possibility that in 1920 McEwan may have led the most progressive 'jazz band' in Melbourne. A 1920 reference to McEwan's band at the newly opened Olympia Jazzola Palace also mentions that:

> Novelty is the keynote of the Jazzola Hall, and novelty is what the restless world is asking for. Even the band comes as a surprise, not only in the riot of its jazz discordance, but also in the variety of its dances and the dance music it plays.[50]

Such views notwithstanding, most contemporaneous references to the noisy, discordant or cacophonous aspects of local 'jazz' bands take the form of severe criticism. Early in 1920 the society and entertainment paper *Table Talk*, for example, began to publish pointed remarks about the 'hideous jazz effects' of McEwan's band and others.[51]

The following colourful account of a jazz band in a Melbourne dance venue appeared in the *Age* in early 1920:

> Night after night halls in the suburbs and the city echo to the swish of skirts, the shuffle of feet – they do not tap in modern dances – and the remarkable din of the energetic jazz musicians, contorting themselves in the effort to play the tricky, syncopated music of the 'rags' . . . Probably the first thing that the casual visitor will notice is the band and its music. Strauss introduced some quaint 'effects' in his orchestra, but he never conceived the original idea of using a kerosene tin as a 'percussion' instrument. The jazz composer does this, however. He goes further, and adds a saucepan lid and a hammer; a motor horn, a whistle, a megaphone, a revolver and a set of cow bells, in addition to the ordinary band instruments . . . The jazz expert may also place on the walls some such motto as this: – 'Oh boy, listen to that drum! Can you beat it?' Having thus set the stage, he starts up his band, and away go the couples in a fox trot or a one-step, while the band plays ragtime . . . The saxophone player blows till his cheeks are like balloons; the violin bows

> flicker and flash. A cow bell clanks; a whistle screeches, and 'bang' goes a hammer upon a tin lid. Then, carried away with the exuberance of ragtime, a player rises and shouts a few syncopated sentences of the ragtime song through a megaphone. He jerks to and fro and tosses his long hair. The music becomes faster and more tricky. The trombone roars and the gongs clash. A musician dashes in a frenzy on to the floor and dances with the public, playing frantically the while; a whistle screeches, a pistol shot rings out, and with a final crash the music jerks to an end, and the couples congratulate themselves upon having safely negotiated the 'pep-step' or the fox trot and prepare for the next dance.[52]

To the extent that this description can be taken at face value, it reinforces both the notion of a ragtime/jazz transition period and of the drummer as the principal generator of what was perceived to be the cacophony in jazzing. Many other references point to percussion as the principal element of 'jazzing up' popular music for dancing at this time. The two visiting Jazz dance experts mentioned above claimed that:

> Australia has not yet learnt the first principles of jazzing . . . To dance the genuine ballroom jazz the correct jazz music is essential and the drummer is an important feature of the orchestra.[53]

Also, in a 1920s article referring to the formation of Ken Hallam's first 'jazz band' in 1918, it is mentioned that:

> the introduction of jazz drums to the drum section of the band was a great novelty, and the demand for bands under this talented conductor became so great that on many occasions it was necessary to have as many as six different bands out on one evening.[54]

Advertisements and reviews of the period also make it abundantly clear that the drummer's 'jazz effects' were the primary generator of 'jazz'. Therefore, references to cacophony or 'jazz discordance' in early jazz probably had much less to do with the improvisatory practice of the instrumentalists who played the melody or harmony than might be imagined.

Dance Band Percussion Playing as Jazzing

By mid-1920 the term 'jazz band' appears to encompass any ensemble capable of embellishing popular fox-trots, one-steps, waltzes and other fashionable dance tunes with the appropriate jazz effects. It was already well recognised that a fully equipped

'Phone, Windsor 2969 for
ALLIETTI'S ORCHESTRA.
FEATURING JAZZ EFFECTS, DANCES,
WEDDINGS, ALL FUNCTIONS.
"Como," York Street, St. Kilda.

Figure 5.6a. Advertisement for Allietti's Orchestra. *Table Talk*, 8 July 1920, p. 25.

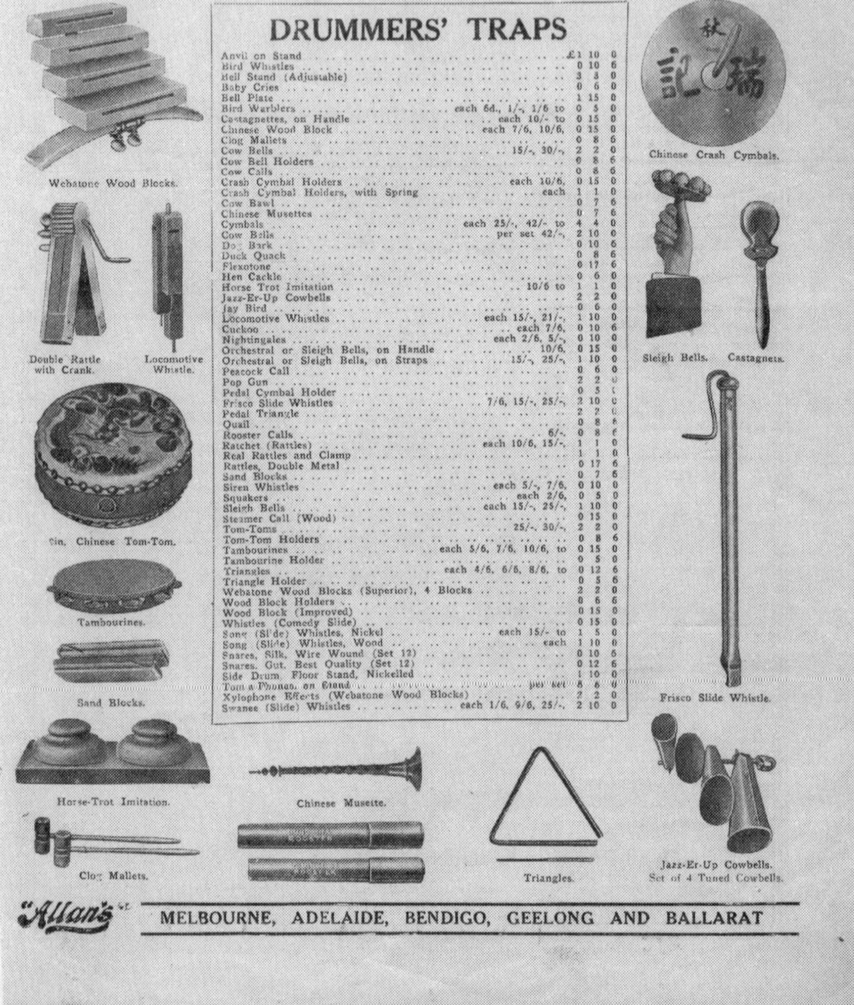

November 26, 1925. AUSTRALIAN BAND AND ORCHESTRA NEWS. iii.

LEEDY
DRUMMERS' TRAPS

DRUMMERS' TRAPS

Anvil on Stand		£1	10	0
Bird Whistles		0	10	6
Bell Stand (Adjustable)		3	3	0
Baby Cries		0	6	0
Bell Plate		1	15	0
Bird Warblers	each 6d., 1/-, 1/6 to	0	5	0
Castagnettes, on Handle	each 10/- to	0	15	0
Chinese Wood Block	each 7/6, 10/6,	0	15	0
Clog Mallets		0	8	6
Cow Bells	15/-, 30/-,	2	2	0
Cow Bell Holders		0	8	6
Cow Calls		0	8	6
Crash Cymbal Holders	each 10/6,	0	15	0
Crash Cymbal Holders, with Spring	each	1	1	0
Cow Bawl		0	7	6
Chinese Musettes		0	7	6
Cymbals	each 25/-, 42/- to	4	4	0
Cow Bells	per set 42/-,	2	10	0
Dog Bark		0	10	6
Duck Quack		0	8	6
Flexotone		0	17	6
Hen Cackle		0	6	0
Horse Trot Imitation	10/6 to	1	1	0
Jazz-Er-Up Cowbells		2	2	0
Jay Bird		0	6	0
Locomotive Whistles	each 15/-, 21/-,	1	10	0
Cuckoo	each 7/6,	0	10	6
Nightingales	each 2/6, 5/-,	0	10	0
Orchestral or Sleigh Bells, on Handle	10/6,	0	15	0
Orchestral or Sleigh Bells, on Straps	15/-, 25/-,	1	10	0
Peacock Call		0	6	0
Pop Gun		2	2	0
Pedal Cymbal Holder		0	5	0
Frisco Slide Whistles	7/6, 15/-, 25/-,	2	10	0
Pedal Triangle		2	2	0
Quail		0	8	6
Rooster Calls	6/-,	0	8	6
Ratchet (Rattles)	each 10/6, 15/-,	1	1	0
Real Rattles and Clamp		1	1	0
Rattles, Double Metal		0	17	6
Sand Blocks		0	7	6
Siren Whistles	each 5/-, 7/6,	0	10	0
Squakers	each 2/6,	0	5	0
Sleigh Bells	each 15/-, 25/-,	1	10	0
Steamer Call (Wood)		0	15	0
Tom-Toms	25/-, 30/-,	2	2	0
Tom-Tom Holders		0	8	6
Tambourines	each 5/6, 7/6, 10/6, to	0	15	0
Tambourine Holder		0	5	0
Triangles	each 4/6, 6/6, 8/6, to	0	12	6
Triangle Holder		0	5	6
Webatone Wood Blocks (Superior), 4 Blocks		2	2	0
Wood Block Holders		0	6	6
Wood Block (Improved)		0	15	0
Whistles (Comedy Slide)		0	15	0
Song (Slide) Whistles, Nickel	each 15/- to	1	5	0
Song (Slide) Whistles, Wood	each	1	10	0
Snares, Silk, Wire Wound (Set 12)		0	10	6
Snares, Gut, Best Quality (Set 12)		0	12	6
Side Drum, Floor Stand, Nickelled		1	10	0
Tom-a-Phones, on Stand	per set	8	6	0
Xylophone Effects (Webatone Wood Blocks)		2	2	0
Swanee (Slide) Whistles	each 1/6, 9/6, 25/-,	2	10	0

"Allan's" MELBOURNE, ADELAIDE, BENDIGO, GEELONG AND BALLARAT

Figure 5.6b. Advertisement for Leedy drummer's traps. *Australian Band and Orchestra News,* 26 November 1925.

Figure 5.6c. Advertisement for Collin's Jazz-Er-Up outfit. On the back cover of Collin's dance orchestration, 'The Southern Cross', Melbourne, 1927.

or 'traditional' jazz band featured a banjo, saxophones and brass. But even a stringed orchestra, large or small, could conceivably become a 'jazz band' by employing a trap drummer (see Figure 5.6a). Some idea of the remarkable range of jazz effects that were available to dance drummers by the mid-1920s can be gained from Figure 5.6b. The 'Jazz-Er-Up' outfit shown in Figure 5.6c appears to have become standard by 1922 or earlier and to this, glockenspiel or xylophone plus additional jazz effects were often added.

An early source of information on jazz drumming available to Melbourne musicians was a 1919 article published in the *Metronome Orchestra Monthly*, 'Ragging and Jazzing', by the American symphony orchestra percussionist and author of several methods, Carl Gardner.[55] This article, which seeks to explain and justify the modern dance hall drummer's freedom to improvise, does not attempt a clear distinction between 'ragging' and 'jazzing' from a technical standpoint (except to underline the jazz drummer's emphasis on clowning and 'ludicrous noises'). Gardner does, however, provide some clues to what was expected of the modern orchestral musician who played for dancing. He points to the incapacity of notation to convey the correct rhythm and mentions that foreign musicians are often unable to 'render the figures with the particular swing which the American-born naturally associate with the ragtime'.[56] Here he is referring particularly to the way white Americans (in imitation of African-Americans) 'are likely to give strong [unnotated] artificial accents upon the second note of the pulse quadruplet'.[57]

In relation to drumming, Gardner comments that:

> No rules can be made for jazz drumming – much of it is improvised upon the spur of the moment, and its effectiveness is measurable by the ingenuity of its originator . . . One of the most common stunts is an after-beat accent; this is sometimes done in a rapid sequence of notes, sometimes during a long roll, and sometimes with crushed ruffs [discussed below]. Single and double strokes in a rapid succession are often mixed, thus giving a peculiar lilt to the rhythm. Similarly, short breaks of one pulse or less are made in a long roll during which rapid triplets or quadruplets are played.[58]

He is also careful to point out, however, that while the dance drummer should be able to improvise:

> [h]is technique should be under perfect control, and he can draw upon the beats in military drumming as well as those in legitimate drumming . . . To avoid chaotic and meaningless jumble, the drummer should make logical repetitions of interpolated figures and phrases . . . The printed sheet may be followed in order that the prevailing figures, the phrase lengths, and period construction may serve as a background for the interpolations.[59]

Gardner's article also illustrates that Melbourne dance drummers and other instrumentalists of this period were increasingly required to master an imported idiom that combined orthodox technique with skills that could only be learnt though aural transmission and personal experimentation.

Some idea of how jazz drummers (and other jazz instrumentalists) played for dancing in the first phase of the Australian jazz era can be gauged from dance band orchestrations of the period. Several private collections of published orchestrations include some rare items written in Australia before the arrival of the first American dance/jazz bands.[60] I am assuming that these pre-1923 arrangements are typical of what was considered appropriate and functional for up-to-date Melbourne dance bands at that time. It should be noted, however, that since the dance industry was competitive, it was (and remained) incumbent on leading bands to improve on stock arrangements in any way possible, as a comparison of stock arrangements with recordings will often indicate.

The most noticeable thing about these arrangements is their simple formal layout which has particular implications for improvisatory practice. The layouts commonly comprise introduction, vamp (a short repeated section), verse and repeated chorus, and there is often no change of key signature. The following examples (all arranged in Melbourne) will suffice for subsequent discussion.[61]

Title	Arranger	Date
1. Oh, Mother, I'm Wild	Fred Hall	1921
2. Arkona	Maurice Guttridge	1922
3. June	Neil McBeath or Guttridge	1922
4. Julio	Jack O'Hagan or Fred Hall	1922
5. Fool's Paradise	Fred Hall	1922

Ex.	Intro	Vamp	Verse	Chorus	Time	Key Changes
1.	8	4	24	40 x 2	2/4	none
2.	8	4	24	32 x 2	4/4	chorus in rel. major
3.	8	2	16	32 x 2	2/2	none
4.	4	0	24	32 x 2	2/2	chorus in rel. major
5.	8	2	24	32 x 2	2/2	chorus in rel. major

The instrumental 'routines' (the ordering of solos, ensemble section, key changes, etc.) which map over these layouts are also often extremely simplistic, as the following routine for 'Oh, Mother, I'm Wild' illustrates. The instruments which take the lead line enter as follows:

intro:	flute	1st violin	cornet	
vamp:		1st violin		
verse:	flute	1st violin	cornet	
chorus 1:	flute	1st violin	cornet	bells (bars 1-14)
chorus 2:	flute	1st violin	flute	bells (bars 1-14)

(Key of E♭ throughout; clarinet plays counter-melody throughout.)

This routine stands in contrast to standard routines of the late 1920s, with their many contrasting segments and frequent modulations. Compare, for example, the routine for Jack O'Hagan's 'All that I Want is a Stay at Home Girl' (arranged by Lionel Corrick, 1929):[62]

intro (key E♭):	lead: piano	1st violin 1st trumpet	
chorus:	lead: piano	1st violin flute	1st sax
short modulation to C:	saxes 2 bars	brass 4 bars	saxes 2 bars
verse:	brass section	(saxes take last two bars)	
chorus:	tenor solo	(includes brass interjection & tutti section)	
chorus:	clarinet solo		
hot chorus in F:	saxes 16 bars	trombone solo 6 bars	
	saxes 2 bars	tutti 12 bars	

This comparison shows that devices used later in the 1920s to 'jazz up' popular music, such as the skilful use of colour contrast, sophisticated chromatic modulations and idiomatic sectional voicings, were not a part of the earliest Australian conception of jazzing up. Unlike the complex and tightly segmented structure of later jazzed up popular music, the simple repetitive forms of the early arrangements openly invited any form of jazz effect or variation capable of providing structural contrast and variation of surface detail (as long as it did not distort dance tempo or basic dance rhythm). An imaginative trap drummer with an array of jazz effects could provide at least a rudimentary level of structural contrast and surface embellishment without alteration to the basic arrangement. In 'Fools Paradise', for example, the drum part becomes a xylophone solo in the chorus section and therefore the drummer had to 'ad lib' the drum part in subsequent choruses. It is also clear from the skeletal nature of these

Musical Ex. 5.1. The last 22 bars of the drum part for 'Oh, Mother, I'm Wild' showing accented 'crushed ruffs'. Arranged by Fred Hall.

Musical Ex. 5.2a. The last four bars of the drum part of the chorus of 'Rachety Coo' (1915).
Musical Ex. 5.2b. The last four bars of the piano part of the chorus of 'Rachety Coo' (1915).

arrangements that the interpolation of jazz effects (including cymbal work) and breaks was mostly ad lib.

Many of the drum rhythms in these arrangements are so rudimentary as to be irrelevant to an experienced musician. However, some are detailed enough to provide a starting point for mapping out the details of common practice for filling in and embellishment technique. A detailed article on drum notation in the *Australasian Band and Orchestra News* shows that the notated pattern marked with an asterix in Musical

Example 5.1 is what Gardner described above in his article, 'Ragging and Jazzing', as the 'common stunt' of using 'syncopated accents with crushed ruffs'.[63]

In surviving orchestral drum parts from Australian dance and theatre libraries assembled before 1918, percussion syncopation is often reinforced in other orchestral parts (see Musical Ex. 5.2a-b). It is therefore reasonable to assume that early 'jazz' drummers in Australia continued the well-established conventions of providing a solid, basic 'two to the bar' rhythm on bass drum, subdividing the main beat in various ways (e.g. the hemiola) on the higher pitched percussion such as woodblocks and reinforcing the syncopated rhythmic clichés of straight quaver or dotted note/triplet ragtime. In addition to the increased emphasis on novelty effects, the existing convention of reinforcing syncopation in other instrumental parts through the use of cymbals is certain to have become even more prevalent in jazzing.

Keyed Percussion Elaboration

Generally, xylophone, bells and glockenspiel solos are written out in the same manner as other lead lines. In performance, however, the xylophone part in particular was embellished in various ways to compensate for its lack of sustaining power. The most common form of embellishment was the intervallic tremolo, a practice that is described as 'extinct' in Australia by the 1930s.[64] A notable Australian theatre and dance percussionist wrote in 1932 that 'the main point to remember is to avoid staying on a note. By this I mean to fill all the sustained notes and also the gaps' (see Musical Ex. 6.14). He also notes that 'the triplet has always been and still is a most effective form of rhythm on this particular instrument, and can be used unsparingly'.[65] Glissandi are a special feature of this instrument and it could be assumed that they were often used as a jazz effect. A dance music tradition of assigning 'all kinds of droll variations' to the xylophone extends back into the nineteenth century and the 'novelty' variations heard on 1920s and 1930s recordings relate back to this tradition rather than to any African-American source.[66]

Orchestral Coloration as 'Jazzing Up'

While the inclusion of a chorus on the 'bright and agreeable' glockenspiel or the humorously 'grotesque' xylophone was one means of 'jazzing up' dance music, the interpolation of additional 'jazz instruments' could fulfil a similar function.[67] Although Melbourne dance orchestras before 1918 were usually string-oriented, standard orchestrations included cornets, clarinets, trombone, string bass and drums. The most significant additions to dance bands in the jazz era were the banjo, with its cutting,

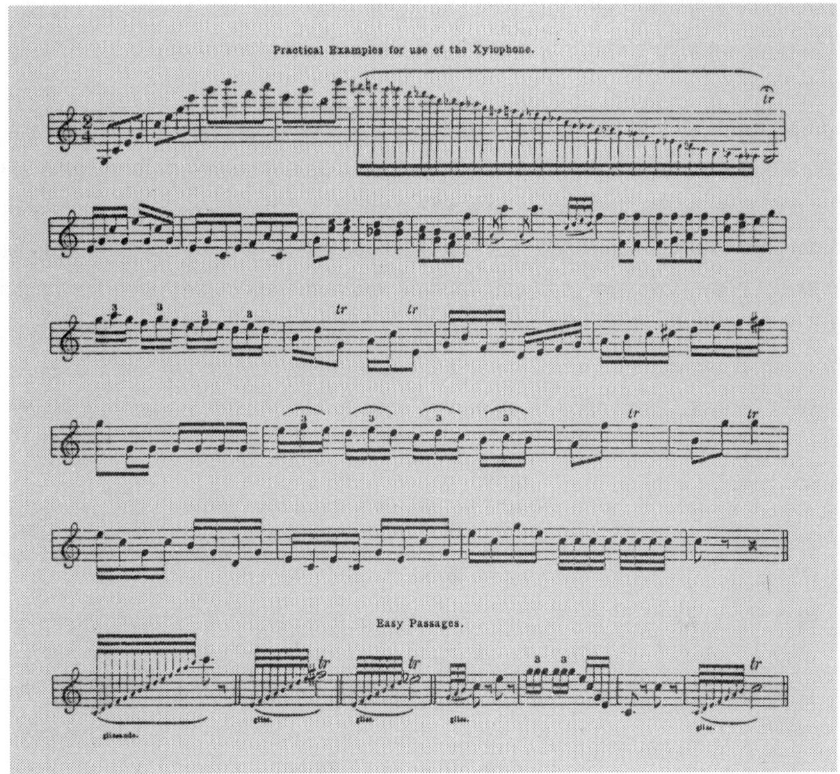

Musical Ex. 5.3a. An illustration of idiomatic xylophone patterns and devices from H. Kling, *Kling's Modern Orchestration and Instrumentation.*

propulsive percussiveness, and the saxophone, with its penetrating sound and vast potential for timbral richness, variety and technical facility. The basic sounds of both instruments were reasonably familiar to Australians through variety acts (both had reached Melbourne by the mid-1850s) and the banjo's role in the minstrel orchestra. The saxophone, however, was best known as part of the 'concert' or 'military' (mixed brass and reeds) band. The saxophone and the banjo, together with the increased emphasis on the trombone and cornet or trumpet as lead instruments, offered new potential for exciting forms of timbral incongruity that could jazz up music.

Imitation Ecstatic Body Movement as Dance Band Jazzing

Some published photographs and illustrations from this period suggest that local dance musicians indulged in the same sort of musical clowning and imitation ecstatic movement as 'jazz' variety act performers and their blackface minstrel predecessors (see Figure 5.7). The 1926 Australian silent film, *Greenhide*, also briefly captures jazz musicians weaving and posturing to the rhythm of the unheard music in an almost ecstatic manner.[68]

Such evidence can be misleading however. Most photographs of 1920s Australian bands actually show relatively formal and sombre groups of musicians (see Figure 5.8). Band and orchestra literature of the 1920s continued to reinforce the association between disciplined demeanour and musical excellence; and the notion of abandoned 'ecstatic' body movement is certain to have met with strong resistance from many dance band leaders and individual musicians. Palais musicians working from dance band arrangements had to channel most of their energy into maintaining the level of musical cohesion demanded. The image (Figure 5.7) of the dance musician in dress

Musical Ex. 5.3b. Bells chorus from 'Arkona' (1922)', arranged by Maurice Guttridge. Note the rudimentary drum pattern (lower stave) and the instruction to fill in sustained notes in the upper stave with 'trem[o]lo ad-lib'.

Figure 5.7. Front cover of 'Jazzin' the Blues', c. 1920.[69]

suit and bow tie, contorted in grotesque, imitation ecstatic posturing, is a reflection of the predicament of the early 1920s orchestral musicians who jazzed popular music. They found themselves poised awkwardly between orthodoxy and an emerging jazz culture with an, as yet, undefined potential for personal freedom of expression.

Variation and Jazzing

The quotations cited at the beginning of the chapter show that even by 1918 Australians were being informed that varied repetition was an important aspect of jazzing. Choruses were probably repeated many times over the duration of a single Foxtrot, One-Step or Waltz, giving performers an opportunity for variation not possible in later arrangements. There is in fact a 1923 reference to a 'decided improvement' in the

Figure 5.8. George Arnold's band at the St Kilda Palais c1920. *Australian Music Maker and Dance Band News,* 1 May 1939. Don Banks, father of the Don Banks discussed in Chapter Seven, is the tenor sax player (Courtesy of Mitchell Library, State Library of NSW).

dance music when the jazz band of the Carlyon's Hotel (probably Melbourne's most progressive 'jazz band' at the time) played several different numbers for each dance instead of continually repeating the one.[70] The concept of continuous variation of a simple repeated song form is manifest in a 1923 Australian piano roll performance of the Pardeys' version of 'Chicago' (Mastertouch S9121), in which each of the many repetitions of the tune introduces an imaginative new paraphrase or variation.[71]

Before 1923, published dance band arrangements featured neither specially designated ad lib sections nor the piano or banjo chord indications which later lead players (e.g. trumpet, trombone or saxes) could pencil in above a written chorus as a guide to improvisation. However pre-1923 Melbourne band leaders such as Maurice Guttridge who were known to have written special (unpublished) arrangements for their own bands may have included such sections. Furthermore, any early leader could convert a stock dance arrangement into a 'hot' arrangement simply by pencilling 'solo ad lib' over the appropriate section of a player's part (which is still a common practice). In later stock arrangements with specially designated ad lib sections, the basic melody is still present (see Musical Ex. 5.4). The later players were therefore faced with the same option as earlier players: to apply, according to circumstances, some level of embellishment or transformation to the notated melody or to forfeit the opportunity and just play the part as written. The following discussion focuses on forms of jazzing mostly likely to have been used by early lead instrumentalists to create variety in repeated choruses or elsewhere (as designated by written instruction or direction during performance) in a routine.

Musical Ex. 5.4. An ad lib section from the second saxophone (tenor) part of 'I Wonder What's Become of Sally', by Milton Ager, arranged by Ralph Gordon, 1938.

Rhythmic Transformation as Jazzing

The gradual transition from the rhythmic concepts of Tin Pan Alley ragtime to those of Tin Pan Alley jazz makes it difficult to determine the rhythmic conception of jazzing held by improvising dance musicians in the first years of Australian jazz. One way of establishing what first distinguished jazz rhythm from ragtime rhythm is to examine the first Australian compositions of dance music that include the word jazz in the title or description. Below are details of thirteen such piano scores by Australian composers, most of them published in Melbourne.[72]

Composer	Title	Time	Date	Jazz Fox Trot
1. F. Hall	The Jazz Lancers	6/8 & 2/4	c.1918	
2. S. Harris	Jazz Band Rag	2/4	1918	
3. S. Harris	Jazzarino	2/2	c.1919	*
4. C. Ryder	Jazz-O-Mine Waltz	3/4	c.1920	
5. A. Lithgow	Mischievous Tom March ('jazz march')	2/2	1920	*
6. R. Stoneham	Deva Jazz (p.1 only)	2/2	c.1920	*
7. R. Stoneham	Jazzin' the Blues	2/4	c.1920	*

Numbers eight to thirteen below are all from *Allan's Jazz Fox Trot Album.* These and number six above contain instructions for dancing the Jazz.

8. J. Rolfe	Ragging Chopin	2/2	1919	*
9. W. Clark	A Ragtime Dream	2/2	1919	*
10. A. Clifford	That Haunting Strain	2/2		*
11. H. Penn	Honolulu Girls	4/4	1917	
12. H. Penn	Mysterious Melody	4/4	1917	
13. F. Hall	Billo	4/4	1918	

The time signatures of most of the examples point to one element which may have distinguished the music of the Jazz Fox Trot from the ordinary Fox Trot in the minds of local musicians and dancers: emphasis on a two-beat feel. While three of the pieces in *Allan's Jazz Fox Trot Album* are labelled 'Fox Trot' and are written in 4/4 time – and indeed, instructions for dancing the Jazz provided in this album give 4/4 as the correct time for the dance – it may be that the different time signatures reflect local confusion about the relationship of two-beat instrumental ragtime to jazz, or that a two-beat feel was applied to playing Jazz Fox Trot music, regardless of the 4/4 signature.

This latter possibility is reinforced by early Australian piano rolls and other evidence. For example, it can be heard clearly in the Pardeys' performance of the fox trot

Musical Ex. 5.5a. Bars 1-5 of the A section and bars 1-6 of the B section of 'Ragging Chopin'. *Allan's Jazz Fox Trot Album.*

'Chicago'. In white and African-American jazz band performances recorded before 1923 which feature vocals, the feel often shifts from four to two-beat when ensemble jazzing takes over from the vocalist. This can be heard very distinctly in the final choruses of Gene Greene's 1917 recording of 'King of the Bungaloos'.

The only other rhythmic feature common the above-mentioned piano scores is a continuous or interjected filling-in with dotted notes (Musical Ex. 5.5a-c). In other words, what had been a growing tendency in ragtime rhythm throughout the 1910s

Musical Ex. 5.5b. Bars 1-7 of the B section of 'Jazzarino'.
Musical Ex. 5.5c . Bars 1-8 of the C section of 'Jazzin' the Blues' (c. 1920). Note that the right-hand stave of the piano part is virtually a 'ragged' or 'jazzed' filling-in of the song line (except for bar 4).

became the defining characteristic of what was most fashionable in dance music rhythm.

Although the syncopated paraphrase subsequently became a principal means of jazzing popular music, these examples suggest that it was of less importance around 1920 than the filling-in of the basic pulse with dotted notes. This returns us to the

Musical Ex. 5.6. The last 22 bars of the Trio of 'Jazz-O-Mine Waltz'.

notion that a line (or break) could be made into something more rhythmically exciting by simple transformation (ragging or jazzing) into an unsyncopated dotted note feel (as heard in Greene's ragging). At a time when there was still general confusion about how to dance the Jazz, this new/old rhythmic device gave popular music a propulsive feel while reinforcing the basic dance beat. It can be assumed that other dance times (waltz time for example) were often jazzed up in a similar way (see Musical Ex. 5.6).

Other ragtime rhythmic concepts were still valid and fashionable at this time, particularly through the continuing popularity of the One-Step or Rag and its acceptance as one of the 'jazz dances'. And as late as 1923 some American sources still reinforced a conceptual link between ragging and jazzing. In the foreword to his *Winn Method of Popular Music: Rag, Jazz, Blues and Novelty Piano Playing* (1923), Winn states that 'Jazz refers particularly to music of a syncopated (ragtime) rhythm, generally played for dancing, in which novel harmonic and tonal effects are introduced' (see Figure 5.9).[73]

Repeated choruses in early Melbourne 'jazz' were therefore probably often varied by a rudimentary rhythmic paraphrase technique, the transformation of crotchet and straight quaver patterns into dotted note/triplet feel and, to a lesser degree, the

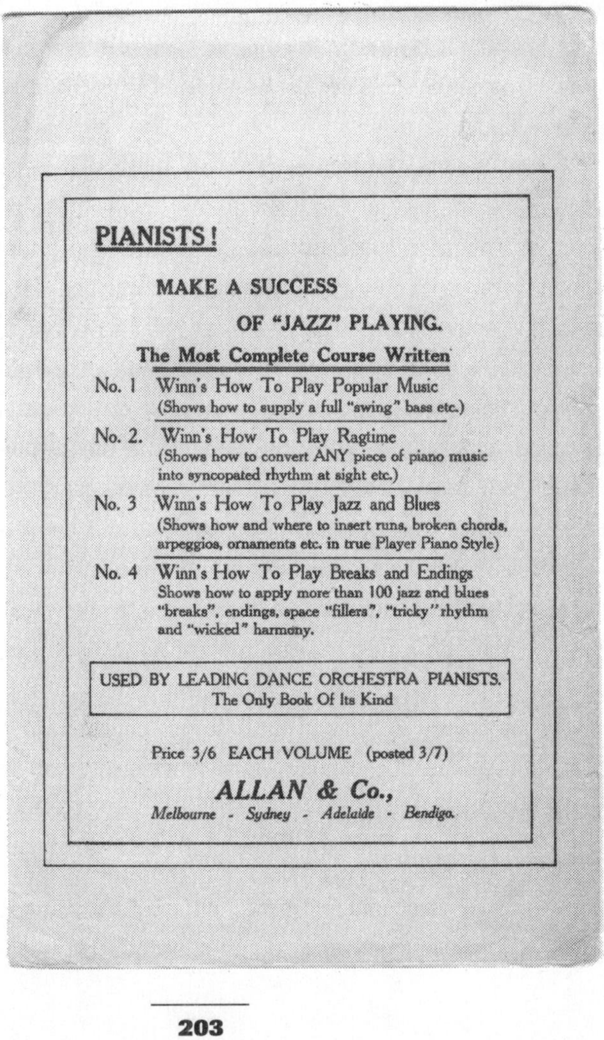

Figure 5.9. Advertisement for Winn's method from the orchestration of 'Sweet Hawaiian Sands' by Jack O'Hagan, 1926.

PIANISTS!

MAKE A SUCCESS OF "JAZZ" PLAYING.

The Most Complete Course Written

No. 1 Winn's How To Play Popular Music (Shows how to supply a full "swing" bass etc.)

No. 2. Winn's How To Play Ragtime (Shows how to convert ANY piece of piano music into syncopated rhythm at sight etc.)

No. 3 Winn's How To Play Jazz and Blues (Shows how and where to insert runs, broken chords, arpeggios, ornaments etc. in true Player Piano Style)

No. 4 Winn's How To Play Breaks and Endings Shows how to apply more than 100 jazz and blues "breaks", endings, space "fillers", "tricky" rhythm and "wicked" harmony.

USED BY LEADING DANCE ORCHESTRA PIANISTS.
The Only Book Of Its Kind

Price 3/6 EACH VOLUME (posted 3/7)

ALLAN & Co.,
Melbourne - Sydney - Adelaide - Bendigo.

syncopated rhythmic transformation associated with instrumental ragtime. It is clear from piano rolls played by Edith and Laurel Pardey, for example, that in 1923 both dotted note 'feel' and basic ragtime syncopation patterns were still being used in Australia to jazz up dance music (see Musical Ex. 5.7a-b). The preservation of a ragtime era sound is particularly explicit in some of the piano breaks heard on late 1920s recordings of Australian 'jazz'/dance music (discussed below).

While it can be assumed that solo choruses often reflected the new rhythmic conception of the transition period, it is much more difficult to comment on the conventions of spontaneous rhythmic transformation in ensemble work, among which I include the idiomatic use of exaggerated stress to generate hot rhythm. I can only speculate that interpretation would have been influenced by the universal shift towards the dotted note/triplet feel and the formularised hot (syncopated) paraphrase that was increasingly being scored into arrangements of popular music to 'jazz' them. The 1919 article, 'Ragging and Jazzing' (cited above) makes it clear to readers that the correct 'swing' in ragtime or jazz could not be obtained simply by playing what was written on the score.

It is also important to consider the very substantial oppositional influence brass band training and playing had upon the development of a more fluid conception of rhythm by Australian musicians, especially given that the same popular 'jazz hits' played by local dance bands were commercially arranged for and played by local brass bands. This factor influenced the way brass band players working in or leading dance bands interpreted very similar dance orchestra arrangements of these tunes.

The general approach to rhythm in brass band playing is characterised by the direct translation from notation to physical production of precise note durations. A common result of early brass band training is a deeply conditioned rhythmic response that becomes manifest in what was once commonly called 'tucky' playing: idiomatic rhythmic inflexibility. Rhythmic inflexibility can also result from orthodox musical training but, for technical and other reasons, it is particularly characteristic of brass band musicians. The Melbourne trumpet player Mervyn Simpson recalled that even by the 1930s tucky playing was still a great problem for dance musicians.[74] Traces of this idiomatic stiffness are present in some of the first recordings of jazz by Australians and it is certain to have been a common rhythmic characteristic of pre-1923 attempts at jazz improvisation by brass players.

Harmonic Conventions of Early Jazzing

Two particularly important influences on the local harmonic conception of jazz improvisation came largely *after* this early period. One was imported recordings by

Musical Ex. 5.7a. Transcription of the B section of a piano roll performance of 'Bees Knees' by Laurel and, probably, Edith Pardey (after 1922). Compare with Musical Example 5.7b and note the level of embellishment.

influential white American musicians featuring distinctive, easy to imitate jazz breaks. The other was the blues. The impact of a third influence, the so-called 'novelty piano' style, is less clear-cut since this style was also an extension of existing piano ragtime practice.

Musical Ex. 5.7b. B section of the published sheet music for 'Bees Knees' (1922), by Ted Lewis and Ray Lopes.

In an article published in *Melody* in March 1918, Winn discusses his written-out ragged elaboration of a popular song, mentioning that:

> The continued vogue of jazz and blues effects – effects which are leading us where no one is even brave enough to hazard a guess – is such as to demand recognition, and these are given due consideration.[75]

A comparison of this jazzed transformation with earlier ragged transformations by Winn shows that the 'jazz and blues' effects to which he refers are the attention-getting, chromatically altered dominant ninths. These 'exotic' harmonic effects featuring exposed tritones (the dissonant interval that occurs between three whole tones), shown in the second bar of Musical Example 5.8a and the second time bars of Musical Example 5.8b, seem to be intended as the equivalent of the novelty coloration of 'jazz' percussion effects. They are novelty dissonance or benign, controlled 'noise'. As already suggested, 'to jazz' could simply mean to 'brighten up' popular music and such non-structural harmonic devices do just that.

Musical Example 5.9 illustrates another form of controlled dissonance: the use of glissandi to 'brighten' the music and generate propulsion (as in the use of ragtime trombone smears). This was of course a feature of ragging, but it seems to have become particularly characteristic of jazzing and is a notable feature of the Pardey piano rolls.

The 'novelty piano' genre which became very popular in Australia in the early 1920s placed even more emphasis on 'weird' dissonance. Emphasis on the tritone is found in earlier ragtime, but prominent tritones together with right-hand runs in parallel fourths became the clichés of the novelty style. By this time the 'licks' (devices) of this genre had been codified into 'jazz' methods, such as *Zez Confrey's Modern Course in Novelty*

Musical Ex. 5.8a. Bars 1-10 of the chorus of a ragged transformation of 'Somewhere in France is Daddy' (1918).
Musical Ex. 5.8b. The last nine bars of 'Somewhere in France is Daddy'.

Piano Playing (1923) or the *Winn Method of Popular Music: Rag, Jazz, Blues and Novelty Piano Playing* (1923). Many of these methods seem to have reached Australia (see Musical Ex. 5.10a-b).[76]

In addition, numerous 'novelty piano' compositions such as Confrey's 'Tricks' and 'Stumbling' were published here, including some which are orchestrated for dance band. Novelty piano style also became a means of showcasing 'crack' band pianists, but the more general popularity of pieces such as Confrey's 'Kitten on the Keys' (1921) also had a strong cumulative influence on local musicians. This style, which was a direct extension of the white school of ragtime performance, was considered to be an exciting and authentic aspect of jazz idiom. It was probably perceived by most Australians as either a new white American innovation or another example of how white musicians, from the blackface minstrels onwards, had been able to improve, standardise and make coherent what were considered the raw elements of African-American music. A Melbourne article on jazz from 1922 states that:

> Jazz originated in the Southern American States, where the negroes . . . would work up a sort of 'musical excitement' by verbal interjection or clapping of hands. From this humble

Musical Ex. 5.9. Introduction and verse of the first violin part for 'Sleepy Seas' (c. 1921), by Reginald Stoneham, arranged by Will Finlay.

> source the jazz idea was taken by men of musical learning or talent and applied to compositions of more or less merit, which anyway had greater attractiveness than the simple nigger folk songs possessed. Great possibilities in novel musical effects were perceived . . . It made for brightness, cheer and happiness. It went abroad . . . Jazz [was] brightened, polished up, and brought to perfection.[77]

It seems, then, that Australian musicians probably became aware around 1918–19 of a trend in popular music towards attention-grabbing harmonic devices or effects, notably, chromatic coloration, distinctive breaks or fills, the dominant ninth chord and other surface decorations. The notion of surface decoration in popular music was of course far from new. In fact, in another 1918 *Melody* article, Winn spells out what were already the standard improvised embellishment devices of the period:

> For the most part, they consist of passing notes, embellishing the melody and connecting the tones of the chords in the accompaniment; diatonic, chromatic and combination scale passages; grace notes both melodic and harmonic; broken octaves and 'rolling' bass in tenths, broken chords and arpeggios. These in fact are the representative stock inventions used by the majority of pianists, and are therefore the most familiar.[78]

Nevertheless, the degree of emphasis on particular devices such as jazz effects was new; and musical references to chromaticism by means of superficial decoration (e.g.

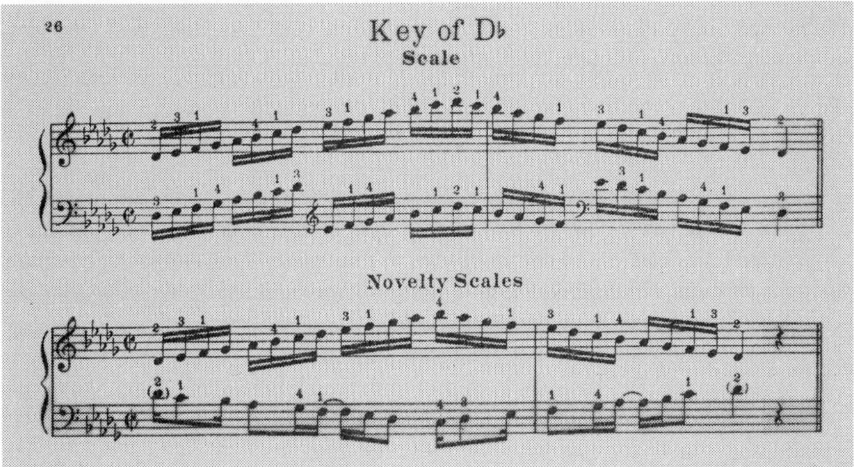

Musical Ex. 5.10a. An example showing how to jazz-up a diatonic passage. *Zez Confrey's Modern Course in Novelty Piano Playing* (1923).
Musical Ex. 5.10b. An example showing how to 'jazz' popular music with 'novelty scales'.

chromatic passing tones or dissonant simultaneities) or the more frequent appearance of the tritone became increasingly prevalent after 1918. Furthermore, the increased use of tonal ambiguity was possibly a parody on the perceived tonal ambiguity of early jazz (particularly of blues tonality). Many of these devices can be heard on the Pardey piano rolls, some of which feature surprising levels of what could be called 'novelty dissonance' or 'chromatic inflection as jazzing'.

'Blueing' as Jazzing

Apart from the use of chromatic jazz effects, it seems unlikely that early Melbourne dance musicians would have attempted to apply authentic blues tonality, such as the flattened or ambiguous third, fifth and seventh scale degrees, much before 1923. Although many of the earliest jazz or quasi-jazz recordings have blues titles and/or characteristics (e.g. 'The Chinese Blues' (1916) and the ODJB's famous 'Livery Stable Blues' (1918)), I am unable to point to any significant Australian public interest in the blues as a musical style until around 1923.[79] Sheet music with blues titles was published and even composed in Melbourne before 1923 (e.g. Reginald Stoneham's 'Jazzin' the Blues'), but the blues does not appear to have become fashionable as music until 1924, when it was featured as the accompaniment to a new dance step, the Blues. For example, in April 1924 a special feature of Carlyon's (Melbourne) was 'the latest world-wide dancing vogue "the blues"'.[80] It was also announced that Carlyon's Hotel would conduct a 'blues dancing competition' and that their band was 'now featuring up to the minute blues numbers'.[81] The following Melbourne description may not be too far removed from the general level of understanding about this music by the beginning of 1924:

> There is a class of music comparatively little known in Australia and in most cases little understood, namely 'blues' music which is even more languorous than the slowest of foxtrots . . . 'Blues' can be distinguished by a rather mournful and almost religioso strain, together with a rhythmical vamp bass mostly in fifths, consisting of four beats to the bar. Some numbers with the 'blues' strain which have been published lately are 'Home Again Blues,' 'When You Walked Out,' 'Homesick,' 'I've Got Those Yes, We Have No Bananas Blues'. On the other hand, there are a lot of numbers published as 'Blue' . . . which are ordinary foxtrots and do not contain the strain of blues as their titles would suggest.[82]

Further on in this article the writer also gives grudging recognition to the African-American origin of the blues 'strain'.

It should also be noted that two important style carriers of the period, the piano and piano rolls, were unable to express the micro-tonal ambiguity inherent in the blues. By the time the above article was published, however, there were American bands and American jazz specialists in Australia who could demonstrate something of the use of pitch inflections in blues performance. American jazz recordings were now more generally available to those who sought them, although this availability was mainly restricted to white jazz. Along with the popularity of the Blues as a dance, an enthusiasm also developed for 'blueing' popular music.

'I've Got Those Dinkum Aussie Blues' (1923-4), arranged by Maurice Guttridge, indicates that local musicians already knew how to jazz up popular music in the latest, most fashionable mode through the specific forms of pitch alteration associated with novelty blues (see Musical Ex. 5.11).[83] The art of the blues, however, lies substantially in the seemingly unsystematised recycling of certain motives with continuous subtle and skilled micro-variation of pitch, timbre and duration. The application of harmonic and rhythmic clichés such as those found in 'novelty blues' could at best only produce a travesty of this fundamentally African-American sound art form. Yet, regardless of what Guttridge personally understood or felt about the blues, his arrangement is certain to have been shaped by his awareness of what type of music was best for dancing the Blues and most palatable to decontextualised white Australian musical taste.

Breaks as Jazzing

After 1923 Australian dance musicians had begun to gain access to recorded examples of jazz breaks by white American musicians which were both recognisably 'modern' and also corresponded to their own musical aesthetic. They were symmetrical, melodic, coherent and played in a way that did not disguise the considerable level of orthodox technique demonstrated. Being relatively unambiguous, they were also easily memorised; and being symmetrical, they were easy to interpolate into the new, more highly structured arrangements.

Musical Ex. 5.11. The 'vamp' section and the first seven bars of 'I've Got Those Dinkum Aussie Blues'. Note the typical Zez Confrey break.

Break Methods

As with previous Australian importations of imitation African-American music, the watered-down, more congruent, white American product was taken as an authentic model. The white American trombonist Miff Mole, for example, whose breaks were apparently a major influence on Australians at this time, is described by one local admirer as the 'father' of modern trombone playing: 'Miff devised a new style of playing, and freed the trombone from the rag-time influence that was given it by every other trombone player of the time'.[84] Frank Coughlan refers to Mole's 'impeccable licks' and to how his band was 'never unmusical, haphazard or crude, like other improvised jazz of those days'.[85]

As with some earlier white syntheses of African-American improvisatory practice, the breaks of Mole and other pioneers of white-style jazz were frozen into notation and systematised into jazz break methods for all jazz instruments. Many of these methods had reached Australia by the late 1920s and some were published here under licence. Music houses such as Allan's used the covers and margins of band parts to advertise them. One such advertisement describes *100 Jazz Breaks for Trombone by Miff Mole* (1926) as 'a literal Education in How to Jazz'.[86]

What is most apparent from a comparison of these methods is their basic similarity to each other as well as to pre-jazz improvisation systems. Moreover, their widespread distribution (and, presumably, use) could only have fostered a bland congruence of style among dance musicians. In *Bass Noodles* (1929), for example, the same 100 breaks are transposed for tuba, trombone, mellophone, string bass and baritone saxophone.[87] From a stylistic perspective the use of these breaks would have often resulted in considerable incongruence through their juxtaposition with unrelated motivic material.

The conventions for the insertion of jazz breaks described in these methods summarise what were also the pre-1923 conventions for filling-in. The following quotation from *Jazz Breaks, Tricks, Blues, Endings* (1925) covers most of them:

> A BREAK is usually inserted in the chorus of a popular song at the 15th and 16th bars, as the melody note of the song at this point usually extends throughout two complete bars, making this place the most logical starting point for correct application of the two bar *breaks*. The next place to look for the possible insertion of a *break* is at the 7th and 8th bars, as the melody note sometimes extends throughout two bars. In short a *break* may be inserted anywhere throughout the chorus, though the most logical place is the 7th and 8th, – 15th and 16th, – 23rd and 24th bars. Too many *breaks* in a chorus has a tendency to obscure the original melody . . . For one measure *breaks* use the 1st measure of any *break* given.[88]

What is described above was, of course, intuitive to experienced musicians, particularly pianists who have always had to play notated or improvised fills. There is no clear evidence to suggest how much the breaks or fills used by the lead instruments (brass, reeds etc.) to jazz up choruses before 1923-4 resemble the so-called hot breaks that became fashionable in Australia after 1923. Writing about Australian jazz in the 1920s as a whole, Bruce Johnson suggests that:

> Because improvisation was not understood, it tended to be perceived as an arbitrary departure from melody. And because it was perceived as an arbitrary exercise, it is almost certain that for many musicians attempting to play jazz, it *was* conducted more or less arbitrarily. The charge that jazz was cacophonous was frequently, therefore, not just a deficiency in the listener's eductation, but an accurate perception of deficiencies in the performer's education.[89]

This is a cogent argument but it cannot be applied without qualification to the professional jazzing of dance music in the pre-1923 period. Lead instrumentalists who had the ability to fill-in probably often did so on the basis of simple, familiar diatonic or chromatic patterns, such as those in notated fills. It should also be recalled that jazzing methods such as *The Rag-Time Saxophonist* (published before 1920) which systematically illustrates how to 'fill in sustained notes' and 'play variations', had been available to Melbourne musicians from the beginning of the jazz era (Figure 5.1b above). Furthermore, by 1920 such systematised ragging and jazzing had gained a degree of legitimacy through the endorsement of white American band and orchestra musicians.

A comparison of individual instrumental parts in early Melbourne arrangements suggests how choruses may have been elaborated in a simple scalic or triadic way (compare Musical Ex. 5.12a-c). This filling-in is the type most likely to have been adopted by brass band or orchestral musicians unfamiliar with the jazz idiom. Musical Example 5.12c is also a reminder that it has always been the role of the flute to add excitement to arrangements by elaborating the lead. Obbligatos such as that shown in Musical Example 5.13 (upper system) could also have provided performers with an internalised array of stylish licks that could subsequently be used to fill-in rests and sustained notes in other choruses.

Influence of Imported Recordings

The early period of Australian jazz offers a classic example of the effect of cultural context and isolation on improvisatory performance practice. Before the arrival late in 1923 of the first band to provide a complete prototype for jazz (the 'real jazz' of the white American/British dance band, Ralton's Havana Band), local dance/jazz musicians were largely guided on what to play and how to play it by popular aesthetics and preferences in dance style, conservative American band and orchestra literature and the demands of Melbourne's equivalent of Tin Pan Alley marketing culture. They also saw merit in employing any 'effects' from successful theatrical jazz that could be incorporated without interfering with the music as 'foot food'. They were further guided in how to play by peer pressure from a local band and orchestra culture whose values derived from its past and ongoing struggles for congruency and musical standards. In this context, any chance exposure to more authentic jazz on record is unlikely to have had much influence on what was played or how it was played. These are all reasons why, in 1923, Australians were still playing in a way that was strikingly out-of-sync with African-American and even white American jazz development.

Musical Ex. 5.12a. Bars 1-12 of the chorus of 'Oh, Mother, I'm Wild' (1921; cornet part), arranged by Fred Hall. Compare with first violin and flute parts below.
Musical Ex. 5.12b. Bars 1-12 of the chorus of 'Oh, Mother, I'm Wild' (first violin part).
Musical Ex. 5.12c. Bars 1-12 of the chorus of 'Oh, Mother, I'm Wild' (flute part).

It is not clear exactly when the jazz practice of absorbing musical ideas and style directly from recordings, rather than learning from notated models, became important to these Australian orchestral musicians who played dance music. In this early period American journals such as the *Metronome Orchestra Monthly* often advertised orchestral arrangements of the latest hits along with advice to 'hear it' on a particular recording and/or piano roll. However, 1920s issues of *Australasian Band and Orchestra News* give no indication that listening to recordings was considered an important aspect of musical learning for dance musicians. In fact, the absence of such references suggests that learning from recordings was considered too unorthodox for professional practice.

Before 1923, when brass band and orchestra culture began to be subverted by an emerging jazz subculture, professional musicians were generally more concerned with learning how to play what was popular with the Australian public in the correct style

Musical Ex. 5.13. Bars 1-4 of the chorus of 'June', arranged by Maurice Guttridge, 1922.

than with listening to more 'exotic' jazz for its own sake. Leading dance bands featured the Tin Plan Alley hits currently promoted by music houses such as Allan's or Collin's this being part of the system of 'plugging' (Tin Pan Alley style promotion). Furthermore, Allan's and other music houses often released imported recordings of these hits. It follows that, if professional dance musicians were 'aurally retrieving' style characteristics (such as novelty embellishment) from recordings before 1923, they were most likely to have been of the type belonging to the prominently advertised recordings of the period, such as those regularly listed in the *Age* entertainment pages.

Retrospective Evidence from Recordings

Many examples of jazz recorded in Australia after 1925 have survived as primary evidence of performance practice. Without access to the specific arrangements used at the recording sessions, however, it is often impossible to distinguish performance based on the notated representation of improvisatory practice (e.g. one involving a written out break) from spontaneous inventiveness. Furthermore, few would agree on what degree of deviation from a written model makes a notated break classifiable as improvisatory. These problems must be borne in mind in relation to all subsequent discussion of recorded examples.

The first known Australian recording of a jazz band performance involving an Australian musician was made in or around May 1925. This is a Melbourne recording of the imported [Bert] Ralton's Havana Band, which at this time included Harry Mehden (formerly of the First Jazz Band) on trombone. While such early recordings say much about post-1923 influence, they offer very little information about pre-1923 Australian conceptions of jazzing. There are a number of recordings by Australian bands, however, which appear to have retained elements of the pre-1923 sound. One significant example is 'Home to Ballaarat' (Sydney 1927), played by the 2FC Studio Dance Orchestra. 'Home to Ballaarat' has a trombone solo (possibly by Dave Meredith) which is only slightly jazzed up with vaudeville-style vibrato, smears and curiously rigid rhythmic paraphrase.[90] While the densely textured piano ragging behind the vocalist contains some of the rhythmic elements of novelty style, it sounds like the accompaniment practice of a much earlier period. The very stiff, square, brass band-like ensemble work and the very minimal jazzing up of instrumental breaks and vocals on this track may be a prime example of the retention of a pre-1923 Australian sound.[91] 'You'll Miss Me When I'm Gone', recorded several days later, presumably by the same musicians, sounds similarly archaic and features a trombone solo with some oddly exaggerated dotted note ragging or jazzing.[92]

Another significant example is the well-known recording of 'Freshie' by Sydney Simpson and his Wentworth Cafe Orchestra (Sydney, 1926), which is often cited as the first recording by an Australian jazz band. This track features several solo breaks by Australian musicians which could reflect earlier practice. A rare, second track of 'Freshie', although bearing the same master and catalogue number, varies greatly from the well-known track in terms of tempo, routine and the degree to which breaks are embellished.[93] For the sake of clarity I will refer to these as track one and track two respectively. Musical Example 5.14a is the unembellished melody of 'Freshie'. Musical Example 5.14b shows Harry Larsen's trombone solo over the A section of track one while Musical Example 5.14c shows his solo over the same section of track two. Musical Example 5.14d is his solo over the B section of the latter track. There is no B section trombone solo on track one.

Harry White's piano breaks over the A section of 'Freshie' differ markedly between the two tracks. On track one, for example, the first and second solos over the A section are linked with a Zez Confrey style fill. This is absent from track two. In track one the second half of each solo is a simple syncopated paraphrase of the melody, whereas at this point on track two White substitutes three short, rhapsodic, two-handed runs which also paraphrase the melody, but in a non-syncopated way.

A number of features therefore characterise improvisatory practice in Australian jazz before 1923:

1. The influence of the stage jazz model (in the absence of others).
2. The drummer as the primary generator of jazz.
3. The formal simplicity of published dance music routines.
4. The absence of chord nomenclature and, especially, scored provision for improvisation in stock arrangements.
5. An emphasis on 'novelty' chromaticism.
6. Extreme decontextualisation from American jazz and especially African-American jazz.
7. The absence of a strong subculture of specialist professional dance musicians (which came later), making the oppositional influence of brass band playing and straight orchestral work particularly powerful in relation to improvisatory practice.
8. A rhythmic and harmonic perception of breaks and fills that was still strongly influenced by earlier common improvisatory practice and ragtime.

Jazzing between 1923 and the Australian Swing Era (1936)

'Hot' Music

An important feature that distinguishes the pre-1923 jazz period from that which followed was an emphasis upon the concept of 'hot' music – a notion that can be traced back to the cakewalk/coon song era in Australia. The term 'hot' is commonly found in 'break system' methods and it was used increasingly to distinguish the supposedly more authentic forms of jazzing, such as the interpolation of hot rhythm. Dance musicians routinely encountered this concept in the rhythmic transformations scored into the final chorus of dance arrangements. One 1920s white perception of hot rhythm is clearly illustrated in a dance band arranging book published in Australia under licence in the late 1920s (Musical Ex. 5.15).

Although the 1920s have been described as the 'Golden age of white jazz in Australia', the (albeit meagre) writings associated with the popularisation of the blues after 1923 indicate the beginning of an awareness that some elusive but important elements of jazz were intrinsically African-American. There was no Australian print forum for jazz enthusiasts during the 1920s. However, the first issues (in 1932) of the *Australian Dance Band News* (which became *Australian Music Maker and Dance Band News* in 1933) provide ample evidence of a grudging acknowledgment that the hottest jazzing was that of African-American jazz musicians. One Australian band leader writes, for example, that 'these coloured players can get a snap and rhythm into their music that the white musician can never equal. It seems part of them'.[94] One African-American band, Sonny Clay's Colored Idea, did reach Melbourne in 1928, but its short-lived visit was overshadowed by remarkably virulent local hostility and racism.[95] The apparent lack of enthusiasm for their music, therefore, could be attributed to these shameful non-musical reasons.

Fairly clear evidence is available of what African-American jazz recordings reached Australia during the 1920s, but the broad consensus is that these models exerted little direct influence upon local musicians until the end of the decade or later. As more recordings of black jazz became available, it also became obvious that the hottest jazz included very sophisticated forms of rhythmic, tonal and timbral ambiguity presented in a seemingly spontaneous and highly creative way. Yet the continued reluctance on the part of Australian commentators to acknowledge the ability of African-American musicians is apparent in a 1935 remark by Eric Sheldon, editor of *Australian Music Maker*, that, 'The coloured race, whose influence on dance music was only felt as late as 1928, is already on the wane. Brilliant technicians, yes; but only one in a million ever becomes really brilliant as a musician'.[96]

Forces Oppositional to Hot Style

There were various reasons why this exciting, 'spontaneous' and creative style of jazz improvisation did not immediately become the new model for up-to-date Australian dance music at the end of the twenties. The Depression brought a shift in Western popular musical taste towards a new, vocally-oriented, 'sweet' style of popular music – a style that was the antithesis of the seemingly ecstatic spontaneity and compelling incongruity of hot jazz. This shift corresponded with an alarmingly high level of unemployment, a resurgence of public interest in 'old time' dancing and the emergence

Opposite:
Musical Ex. 5.14a. 'Freshie': the unembellished melody.
Musical Ex. 5.14b. Transcription of Harry Larsen's trombone solo over the A section of the better known version of 'Freshie' ('track one').
Musical Ex. 5.14c. Transcription of Larsen's solo over the A section of the second version ('track two'). Compare with Musical Example 5.14a-b.

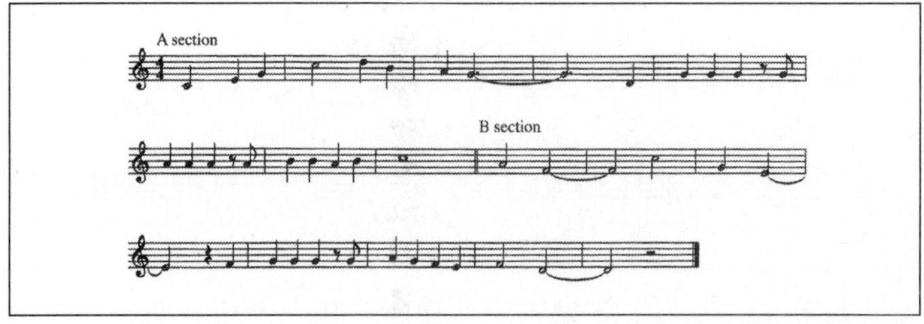
A section
B section

♩=120
Break/Fill
Fill
Fill
Last 8 bars of solo
Fill

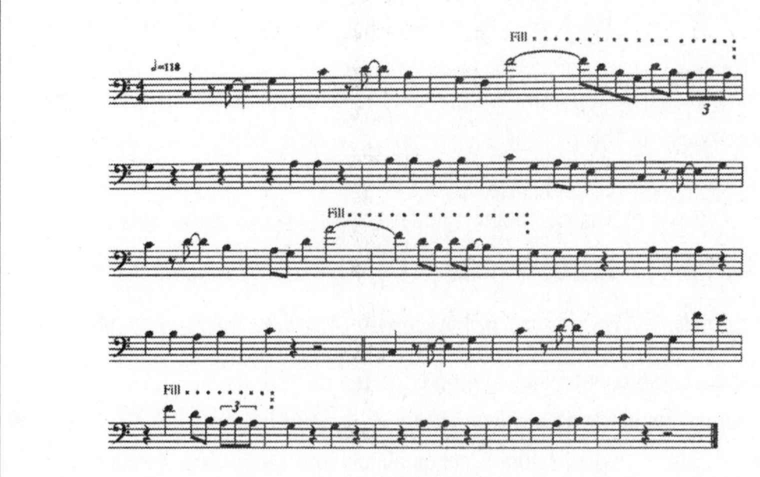
♩=118
Fill
3
Fill
Fill
3

Musical Ex. 5.14d. Transcription of Harry Larsen's trombone solo over the B section of the melody of track two. Compare with the B section of the model and note the dotted note ragging or jazzing.

of a relatively unified and codified dance music industry. In this context, the priority of the professional was not to seek self-expression and gratification through playing hot jazz but to build a reputation as a very competent, reliable 'modern stylist' (one who was broadly competent in all aspects of playing modern dance music). One 1933 editorial demands rhetorically, 'of what earthly use is it to play numbers in a style that the public has definitely decided it does not like?'.[97]

Conservative peer pressure, which was oppositional to musical spontaneity and self-expression, came from both the brass band movement and the 'legit' (art music) sector of the musical profession, which had long been scathing of popular music. Dance band leaders and highly-respected individual dance musicians also frequently espoused the importance of discipline, uniformity, deportment, poise and caution in the employment of jazz effects. In addition, Melbourne was reputed for its more conservative dance venues and was itself the heartland of the brass band movement. After 1930 Melbourne dance musicians no longer even had a local forum in *Australasian Band and Orchestra News*, which had reverted almost exclusively to brass band news (see Figure 5.10).

What remained most important to the professional dance musician at the beginning of the 1930s was not the type of ecstatic inventiveness, commonly associated with African-American jazz improvisation, but precise control over the formulae of imitation ecstatic improvisation. The competent modern stylist was required only to create a convincing imitation of the jazzing heard on popular American or British recordings.

1930s Australian Writing on Improvisatory Practice for Dance Musicians

Given Australia's traditional reliance upon imported musical models, it seems remarkable that during the 1930s *Australian Music Maker and Dance Band News* featured numerous articles on improvisatory practice almost entirely by local dance musicians.

These articles, together with frequent inquiries from subscribers about improvisatory aspects of jazzing, map out increasing interest in this topic as the decade proceeded. This literature must be treated with caution as it often seems directed at the less experienced dance musician. Nevertheless, the articles (and various answers to queries) represent, for the most part, sincere attempts to inform musicians about what was currently required of competent dance musicians and practical approaches towards meeting these requirements.

Although late 1920s Melbourne dance musicians were sometimes exhorted to 'get hot, blow hot, stay hot', by 1932 what had formerly been described as a 'jazz band' was now simply a dance band which dispensed 'modern rhythmic' or 'rhythm style' dance music.[98] The very phenomenon of a specialist dance music journal indicates an industry fully aware of its own autonomy and the importance of creating and maintaining congruous industry standards. Until around 1936 the most important aspect of jazzing from this industry's point of view was the systematised generation of dance

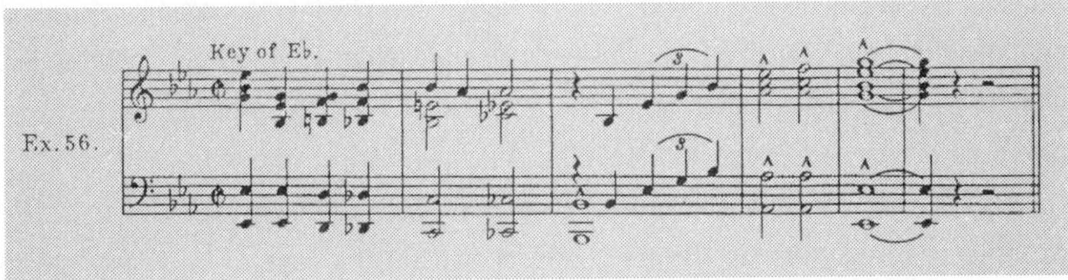

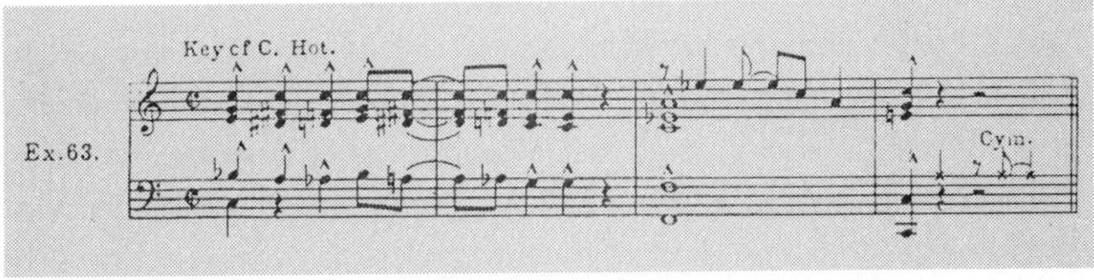

Musical Ex. 5.15. A comparison of straight, 'semi-hot' and 'hot' endings, from *Frank Skinner's Simplified Method for Modern Arranging.*

rhythm. And though 'rhythm' does not necessarily signify syncopation, it had long been understood that the hottest forms of rhythm assumed the inclusion of syncopation.

Hot Rhythmic Music

> Mix 8 ozs. 'flair for hot rhythmic music' with 1 pint 'knowledge of harmony,' 1/2 lb. 'passing notes' and 'a musical ear.' Add to this a good supply of both standardised and original phrasing. Mix well together, at the same time adding 'complete control of instrument.' Cook over a fire of 'experience', then sprinkle with a few 'smears and lip trills,' and serve hot.
>
> George Dobson, 'Recipe for Hot Style', 1934.[99]

Rhythm style can be conceptualised similarly to the commonly understood notion of textural activity in music. The basic generator of increased textural activity is temporal: the non-alignment of attack points reinforced by dynamic contrast. Contrast in other parameters (for example timbral or harmonic contrast, and even contrary pitch motion) also intensifies the sense of textural activity. A continuum of 'jazzing' lay between a 'straight' interpretation and the hot transformation of a given arrangement. Each level of transformation intensified textural activity and made it 'jazzier' or 'hotter'. The highest level of transformation or the 'hottest rhythm' was the so-called 'nigger style' (the style of jazz associated with reputed African-American jazz musicians such as Duke Ellington), characterised by its complex off-beat phrasing, call and response patterns, seemingly infinite timbral contrasts and (in the case of 'early jazz' style) contrapuntal lines.[100]

The higher levels of transformation or even the intermediate levels were not considered appropriate for the Australian dance music industry in 1932. By 1934, however, there is evidence of an increasing demand for knowledge of the higher levels of transformation, or hotter rhythm. Articles such as 'Hot or Not So Hot'(1934) indicate that hot rhythm, or at least hotter rhythm, was on the verge of becoming fashionable.[101] By 1936 hot rhythm had become the vogue, but under a term that had long been used in both popular and art music to describe good rhythmic style: 'swing'.

Bruce Johnson points out that there was general confusion about what the term 'swing' or 'Swing' as a style meant in Australia.[102] Here, I am only concerned with what the verb 'to swing' appears to have meant to Australian dance musicians of the period in relation to improvisation. In 'Swing It' (1934), George Dobson points out that this expression was an 'understood and regular expression amongst dance musicians'. He also makes clear that it was commonly understood to mean the intensification of the rhythm in various ways that were idiomatic to 'modern rhythm style'.[103]

The first and most crucial level of rhythm style transformation – what I still define as jazzing – included the playing of notes 'solidly right on the beat' plus the correct and idiomatic use of accented and shortened notes to give the music rhythmic 'bite' or 'punch' (Musical Ex. 5.16). In 'Straight or Dance Style' (1934), for example, Denis Collinson writes:

> For, after all, rhythmic playing is only a matter of accenting and stressing certain notes, which, combined with good phrasing, will give your interpretation of a number the necessary swing.[104]

Idiomatic accenting could be achieved through straight-forward dynamic stress on individual notes but it was also associated with the exaggeration of legato, staccato and 'timbral stress' through the use of hot effects such as the 'dinge', the 'flange' and so forth (Musical Ex. 5.17).

The next level of transformation was rhythmic paraphrase: the formulaic displacement of note 'attack points', or what was formerly known as ragging. In ensemble work this transformation might, of course, be only very slight and had to be initiated by the sectional leader to avoid the loss of overall rhythmic cohesion (Musical Ex. 5.18). These two levels of transformation were usually interrelated and involved those performance skills which distinguished the 'straight stylist' from those who could only play in brass band or 'legit' performance style.

The higher levels of transformation apply only to improvised breaks or solo choruses. These can be conceptualised as a gradient of practices falling between and inclusive of the following three levels:

1. A hot rhythmic paraphrase of the written break or chorus with various hot effects.
2. A hot rhythmic paraphrase with the interpolation of additional chords, passing and neighbour tones, and various hot effects.
3. The same as number two but with added 'heat' resulting from the interpolation of chromatic passing-tones, blues tonality and incongruous or 'dirty' timbre.

Musical Examples 5.19a-c illustrate each of the above.

These higher levels of transformation required varying degrees of inventiveness. As mentioned earlier, however, it was also common practice to interpolate hot breaks or choruses appropriated from recordings, jazz break methods or other notated sources (Musical Ex. 5.20). Segments from such memorised sources could also be recycled in the spontaneous construction of more personalised breaks or choruses. A system which some informants recall using was the British (Parlophone) 'Studies in Swing' series of recordings. These allowed the aspiring jazz soloist to play along with a

The Absent-Minded Ex-Jazz Merchant Who "Hotted Up" the Sacred Solo

Figure 5.10. Cartoon reflecting the brass band movement's attitude to jazz in the 1930s. Australasian Band and Orchestra News, 26 May 1936.

sequence of relatively rudimentary hot choruses by British performers such as Nat Gonella, backed by a small rhythm section.[105] Side B features only the rhythm section, so that once the student had memorised the choruses from side A he or she could play along with the rhythm section, thereby further internalising a set of useful 'licks'.

Jazzing Systems for Piano

The piano was the principal vehicle for improvisatory performance practice in Australia throughout all of the periods discussed so far, and after the mid-1920s the ability to jazz on piano became almost mandatory for professional and accomplished amateur performers of popular music. Imported jazz methods such as the various Shefte systems, and local systems such as the Jack Wood School of Syncopation for Piano, brought the 'jazzing of popular music' to countless Australians until the proliferation of new styles of popular music (e.g. rock 'n' roll) resulted in the natural decline of this approach. Most 'jazz piano' systems were basically recycled and updated versions of ragging instructors such as *Winn's How to Play Ragtime*. These codified and simplified

Right: Musical Ex. 5.16. An example of 'biting off' notes from George Dobson's 'Swing It'. *Australian Music Maker and Dance Band News,* 1 July 1934, p. 28.

Below: Musical Ex. 5.17. Examples of some stock jazz effects from Frank McLaughlin, 'Saxophone Interpretation of Orchestration'. *Australian Dance Band News,* 1 March 1933, p. 17.

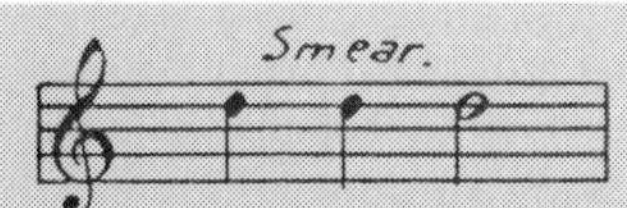

(In example 1, owing to an artist's error the word "smear" occurs over the second crochet in the bar instead of over the minim.—Ed.)

If written it would sound like this:

Next I will take the "Whip."

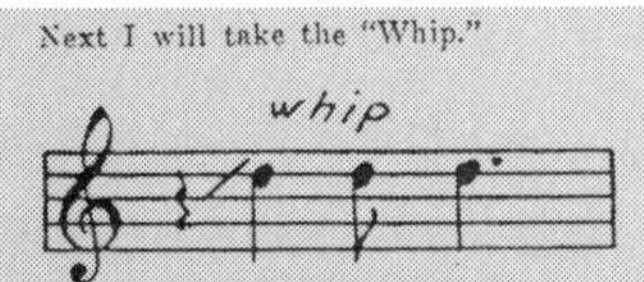

This is executed by playing a group of demi-semi-quavers preceding the D, and sounds thus:—

The glissando "Gliss," as I think we all know, is obtained by the gradual slackening of the lip going down and vice versa going up.

If the above examples are fingered by a quick choromatic run and lip-slurred at the same time it will sound much more finished, and if practised until thoroughly mastered the smear and whip effects will come more easily.

The "Dinge," I think, is the easiest and one of the most effective to articulate.

The usual way this is played is by using an exaggerated quick vibrate. The dinge is used in legimate music, but is called the "mordente" or "shake," thus:—

This is just a five-note trill, and I have noticed a number of recording bands using it in the legimate sense. I think both ways are effective.

the experience of many decades of professional improvisatory practice for a mass market of amateur and aspiring professional entertainers. For example, in one method produced in Australia, 'Jazz Made Easy' (1936), the reader is told that:

> [jazz] is syncopated music having (as far as the Piano is concerned) a specially arranged treble, and bass accompaniment. It is greatly enriched by much musical ornamentation

Musical Ex. 5.18. An example showing some of the more subtle nuances of 'straight stylist' interpretation. Compare the upper and lower staves of each system. Jack Moore, 'Style for Saxophonists', *Australian Music Maker and Dance Band News,* 1 July, 1933.

> and embellishment, technically known as 'breaks', 'fillings' etc., which fill up all gaps or 'rests' in the melody. In addition, it usually contains many ingenious novelties, 'trick effects' etc., all of which change a [dull] air . . . into the highly spectacular, irresistibly magnetic thing called Jazz.[106]

In relation to breaks or fills the method states 'they are generally quite stereotyped in form. Provided with a collection of them, one may interpolate them whenever occasion offers'.[107] Shefte's *Piano Improvising,* which was published in Australia the following year (1937), is based on the same principles as the Shefte methods published in the mid-1920s (see Figure 5.11).[108]

Such methods worked on the basis of the systematic rote learning of a set of models developed by professional pianists in the entertainment industry over many decades. Their key element is the reduction of a pool of common, professional, improvisatory piano techniques to the smallest possible range of standardised 'filling-in' and 'filling-out' devices. Their successful use lay in patience and both the ability to internalise the formulaic 'full bass' chord shapes in every key and to use the individual tones of each of these chords to construct treble breaks and fills. In this respect these systems were almost a natural extension of the rote learning of scales and arpeggios which is still an integral part of formal musical training. Of equal importance was the development of

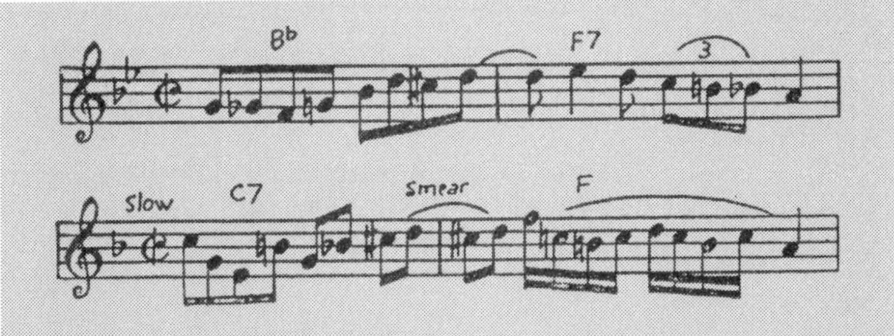

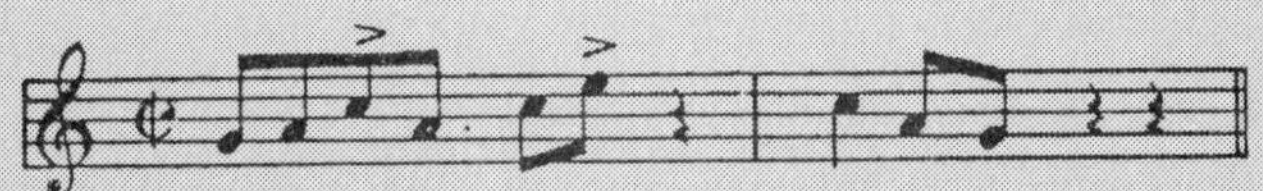

Now the whole idea is that instead of rigidly keeping to the actual notes and night after night playing the phrase "parrot fashion," we make use of our originality and invent a few different phrases, keeping in mind the actual notes of the first phrase.

How about something like this:

Musical Ex. 5.19a. Transforming or jazzing a chorus. Dudley Cantrell, 'Solo Playing', *Australian Music Maker and Dance Band News,* 1 October 1934, p. 27.
Musical Ex 5.19b. An example showing the use of passing notes in transforming a chorus. George Dobson, 'Recipe for Hot Style', *Australian Music Maker and Dance Band News,* 1 November 1934, p. 28.
Musical Ex. 5.19c. Transforming a chorus. George Dobson, 'Standardised and Original Phrasing', *Australian Music Maker and Dance Band News,* 1 December 1934, p. 29.

Musical Ex. 5.20. A 'special chorus': a type of notated or 'frozen' improvisation which a soloist could interpolate into the stock arrangement. Australian Dance Band News, 1 July 1932, p. 19.

the correct rhythmic feel or 'swing' in the application of memorised devices, although obtaining this feel was more than partly the result of very thorough internalisation of the patterns. After the 1930s the American *Shefte Rapid Course for Piano in Popular Music and Syncopation* more or less became the standard system taught throughout Australia, 'Shefte' itself becoming a household name.[109]

By placing so much emphasis on the common practice of Australian dance musicians in the first two decades of jazz in Australia, I may have inadvertently given the impression that all Australian dance musicians learnt to jazz from published jazz instructors or courses. As has always been the case in popular entertainments music, dance musicians in fact learnt mostly from experience: from the contingencies of the performance context, in which there was often no alternative but to 'have a go' at filling in. They also learnt by imitating visiting musicians, sound recordings, each other and, after the late 1920s, what they saw and heard at the cinema. In a letter describing the difficulties of learning about jazz improvisation in Melbourne in the 1930s, Fred Thomas concludes, 'we ad-libbed as best we could'.[110]

There were also many dance musicians in Australia before 1936 who were quite capable of extended jazz improvisation. The abilities of higher profile musicians such as Frank Coughlan, Ern Pettifer and Benny Featherstone are fairly well-known, but there are many lesser-known individuals who were once feted for their ability to 'take a chorus'. For example, George Dobson, who spoke to me with particular reserve and clarity about improvisation in the 1930s, described Australian saxophonist Harry Danslow as 'a master of extemporisation' and the 'greatest of them all', 'ad-libbing chorus after chorus after chorus in the most *original* style you've ever heard'.[111]

Figure 5.11. An Australian advertisement for some Shefte methods, from Art Shefte, *Jazz Breaks, Tricks, Blues, Endings*, Sydney n.d. (c. 1927).

Even in 1936, however, the beginning of the Australian Swing era, it is clear that the general approach of Australian dance musicians to improvisatory practice still embodied many concepts which originated well before the first local 'jazz bands'. The general concept of 'jazzing up', 'playing hot' or 'swinging' popular music shares similarities with the unscored surface transformations that made earlier 'show music' (e.g. circus music) sound excitingly different from more formal or legitimate music-making. Furthermore, just as blackface minstrel music included the characterisation of African-American performance practice, the jazzing of 1920s and 1930s palais musicians was, knowingly or otherwise, the highly stylised characterisation of this culture. Yet all of the levels of spontaneous caricature or characterisation involved in jazzing – even the application of 'hot' tone to a notated break – represented participation in improvisatory practice. Therefore, through 'modern' rhythmic dance music, a very broad base of Australian musicians was engaged at one level or another in improvisatory practice by the late 1930s.

It should also be recognised that even the earliest Australian jazz represented an imperceptible but important pointer towards the improvisatory 'experimental music' of Melbourne in the 1960s. The ragtime era brought a new style of music which gave local performers some freedom to transform and embellish the foreground detail of music as it unfolded. It also brought a new level of temporal and harmonic dissonance to popular music. With early jazz, however, the potential for musicians to shape music as it unfolded and explore 'weird effects' or dissonance increased almost exponentially, at least in relative terms. The conservative social and cultural context of professional music-making of the period reduced the potential for this musical exploration. Yet references to early Melbourne 'jazz' band performances suggest that, even by 1920, some local dance musicians were publicly exploiting a level of musical freedom that would have been unimaginable several years earlier, except on the stage.

6 Towards Experimentalism

Two early watershed periods of improvisatory practice in Australian jazz were the late 1930s 'Swing era', which generated enthusiasm for both the improvised jazz solo and collectively improvised jazz, and the late 1940s, which brought the radical new style of improvised jazz called bebop. The later period also saw the emergence of individual Melbourne musicians who ventured into the stylistic and cultural void that separated avant-garde jazz and experimental art music in Australia until the 1960s. Their activities reflect the fact that radical musical experimentalism before the 1960s was more often than not based on individual initiative.

Experimental (or exploratory) approaches to music-making have already been defined as exploration beyond the familiar: an approach commonly associated with the more progressive or avant-garde of any particular cultural grouping. In a sense most improvisatory musical practice allows for a degree of exploration or experimentation within the limitations of its specific musical situation. Furthermore, I have already mentioned numerous examples of earlier practice which embodied concepts recognised today as characteristic of 'experimental music'. These include the open-ended musical procedures found in theatrical entertainments accompaniment; the cumulation of musical structure through performance time intuitive group or director/group interaction; experimentation with unorthodox sounds and extended instrumental and vocal techniques; and also the recognition of environmental sound (and silence) as an element of the music being performed, most notably in circus and silent film accompaniment.

These practices were mostly utilised in the spirit of functionality, or 'problem solving', to embellish, amuse or support stage action. At times they were performed as enjoyable interactive musical clowning. Much less frequently they were executed as

26/7/21 *The Australasian Bandsman* 13

Playing Chords

E. H. ORMEROD The Man Who Does It

Years ago I read in the "British Bandsman" a sketch of the career of Mr. John Hartmann. The name will be familiar to bandsmen everywhere, for we all know the fine solos he wrote for the cornet, of which instrument he was a master. John Hartman died some years ago, but his solos will live while cornet playing is popular.

The article said "Mr. Hartmann can still do wonderful things on his cornet. He can play a four part melody, and he can play two scales at one time, one ascending and the other descending!"

Think of that, ye present day champions who display with pride a medal won at Ballarat or elsewhere for your cornet playing.

Some people will tell that this playing of four part melodies is a freak and that there is little or no utility in it. Perhaps not, but it will be noted that those who decy it are those who are not able to do it. It is the old story of the fox and the grapes. You know the story, how the fox saw the grapes hanging on the vine, and how he did his best to reach them. After repeated failures he gave it up with the remark: "They are sour, anyhow!" I like to hear of men who can do wonderful things, for I note that they belong to the class who can do ordinary things with ease. The Paris Chambers and the John Hartmann stamp made easy work of the "Old Kentucky Home" style of compositions, and all because they could do the more wonderful things.

Last month the Editor gave us a photo and a brief sketch of E. H. Ormerod, the solo euphonium player of the Newcastle Municipal Band. I would add to that by saying something of the wonderful things he can do in the way of range and duet and quartette playing. Here is his range:

It is not the range of a Paris Chambers, but it "is no' so bad," as a Scotchman would say. Perhaps after the Editor reproduces a few of the examples of Chamber's cadenzas, Mr. Ormerod will buck up and try till he can master them. Or perhaps you, reader, will show us how it is done. I am sure the Editor will give us your photo if you succeed.

Below is an example of Mr. Ormerod's quartette playing. He gave a Sydney audience a taste of it once, but believing too much excellence was a bad thing the Band Association officials refused to allow him to repeat the performance, which goes to prove how foolish the player is who tries to get too far out of the ruck.

Musical Ex. 6.1. A transcription of E.H. Ormerod's 'quartette playing' on euphonium. *Australasian Bandsman* 26 July 1921, p. 13.

creative exploration (or problem finding) – for the sake of pushing beyond and possibly even subverting established convention. The Australian brass band champion E.H. Ormerod's discovery of how to play four-part harmony on the euphonium is an example of what I mean by problem-finding experimentation (see Musical Ex. 6.1). The article which features this transcription reports that Band Association officials refused to allow him to perform, commenting that it 'goes to prove how foolish the player is who tries to get too far out of the ruck'.[1]

EARLY AUSTRALIAN MUSICAL EXPERIMENTALISTS

Even before jazz, Australia had produced some notable experimentalists, including some who demonstrated an interest in African-American influenced performance culture. The first of these was Isaac Nathan, who, as mentioned previously, performed 'extempore' for Port Phillip audiences in 1842. Among his musical explorations is one of the first musical caricatures of Australian Aboriginal music, including a bizarre, fully harmonised representation of the Aboriginal 'coo-ee' (a distinctive upward gliding bush call).[2] Nathan can perhaps be seen as a contemporary counterpart of early white American observers and imitators of African-American performance culture such as Rice, the 'inventor' of Jim Crow. Nathan was, in fact, interested in blackface minstrelsy and wrote relatively extensive newspaper reviews of many of the minstrel shows that reached Sydney.

The Melbourne composer and journalist Henry Tate is best known for his radical notion of an Australian musical language based on Aboriginal music, bush sounds and what he calls 'deflected' musical scales, derived from Australian bird calls. These ideas are discussed in his 1917 pamphlet, *Australian Musical Resources*, and his 1924 mono-

Musical Ex. 6.2. The last eight bars of 'Coo-ee' (1919) by Henry Tate in his own hand.

Musical Ex. 6.3. Bars 12-18 of 'In Dahomey: Cakewalk Smasher', by Percy Grainger in his own hand.

graph *Australian Musical Possibilities.*[3] In his previously mentioned cakewalk, 'Coo-ee' (which he calls an 'Australian foxtrot'), Tate creates the coo-ee effect on the piano with a glissando (see Musical Ex. 6.2).

By far the most significant of the early Australian musical experimentalists is Melbourne-born Percy Grainger. Grainger was both an improvising pianist and a significant theoriser on various aspects of improvisatory practice. He was also directly influenced by African-American performance culture. As early as 1903 he wrote his own piano version of the ragtime song, 'The "Rag"-Time Girl'.[4]

Although Grainger spent most of his life away from Australia he claims that the inspiration for his notion of 'free music' (music free of fixed pitch and temporal relationships) was generated during his early years in Melbourne. He writes 'My impression is that this world of tonal freedom was suggested to me by wave-movements in the sea that I first observed as a young child at Brighton, Victoria, and Albert Park, Melbourne'.[5] His continuing identification with Australia also substantially influenced his musical inventiveness, his 'democratic polyphony' being just one example. Grainger describes this as 'My Australian ideal of a many-voiced texture in which all, or most, of the tone-strands (voices, parts) enjoy an equality of prominence & importance'.[6] He also writes that 'In my early years (1889-1907) as a modernist I took it for granted that I *as an Australian*, would be ahead of my European tone-fellows in original inventivity [sic] & experimentalism'.[7]

Grainger's best known early experiment with controlled improvisation is 'Random Round' (1913), which greatly predates the work of experimentalists such as John Cage, Morton Feldman and others. 'In Dahomey: Cakewalk Smasher', which Grainger began in 1903 and more or less completed during a 1909 visit to Australia, combines hot rhythm with several indeterminate characteristics. The tempo, for example, is given as 'Any speed between M.M. = 96 and M.M. = 126'. The performer is instructed to leave out particular segments or interpolate others at will. An abundance of various types of glissando is suggestive of the gliding tones of Grainger's 'free music' concept. He also provides instructions such as 'clumsy and wildly' or 'like Brass Band explosive', presumably to generate a representation of what he perceived as the ecstatic improvisatory character of African-American stage performance. Grainger wrote on the cover page, 'Prompted by the Williams & Walkers Darkies Co performance of "In Dahomey"'. Grainger was also influenced by Walt Whitman's notions of individual freedom. Grainger writes of his 'Schwärmerei for Walt Whitmanism . . . [and his] huge wish for ever greater freedom in all possible ways'.[8]

Progressive Tendencies in Australian Jazz

A relationship between experimentalism and Australian jazz can be traced through progressive tendencies in jazz improvisation. It was mostly among the core community of progressive professional dance musicians (and those who aspired to join this community) that sufficient technical skill and theoretical knowledge was available for the exploration of the more technically advanced improvisational concepts. It is therefore not surprising that the improvisers discussed below were, with some important exceptions, associated with this core community or its periphery.

The aesthetics associated with progressive tendencies in jazz include recognition of the value of musical originality, this being almost a prerequisite for less utilitarian musical exploration (see Musical Ex. 6.4). Appreciation of 'originality in breaks', for

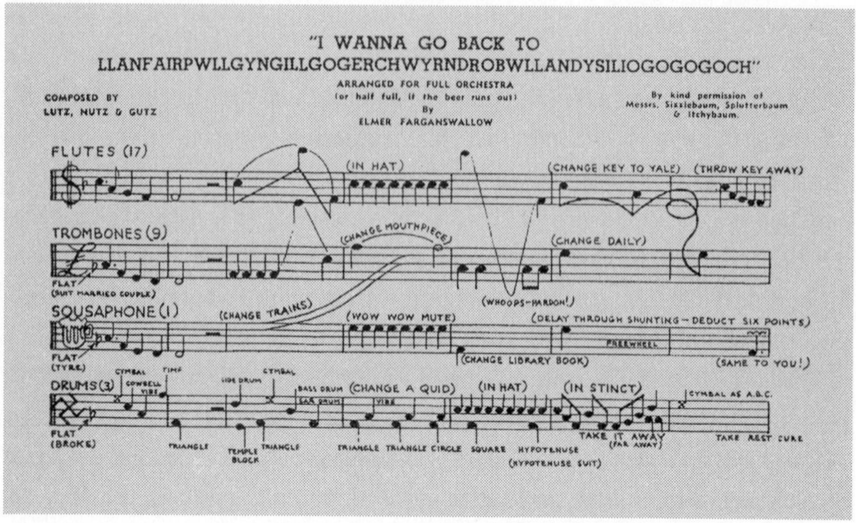

Musical Ex. 6.4. A humorous flash of originality and an unwitting gesture towards graphic scoring. 'A new style of orchestration' from the 'technical editor' of *Australian Music Maker and Dance Band News*, 1 September 1939, p. 42.

example, is present in the judge's comments for the first Australian Jazz Band Contest (1926) and some pre-Swing era Australian articles on jazz improvisation. Even published jazz methods sometimes refer to the importance of 'sounding original'.[9] Sounding original and being original, however, are not necessarily the same thing. George Dobson mentions (with some irony) that he gained a reputation for originality early in his career through his access to Armstrong recordings such as 'West End Blues'. After studying and memorising several of Armstrong's solos he began to sound very original to his colleagues, who were initially unable to grasp what he was doing.[10]

The late 1930s Swing era brought a marked change in Australian perceptions of African-American influenced improvisatory practice – a change that not even the powerful forces of Australian musical conservatism could reverse. This was the emergence of a broader enthusiasm for spontaneously improvised music: not just as the jazzing up of dance music but as jazz music, a unique vehicle for ecstatic expression and creativity. Published discussion of improvisation now referred more frequently to the notion of originality or individuality and, where earlier articles had focussed on simple embellishment or rhythmic paraphrase (jazzing), there were increasing indications of interest in how to construct entire choruses in performance time. One indication of this shift was a 1936–7 series of articles on creating extended or 'rhapsodic' embellishment

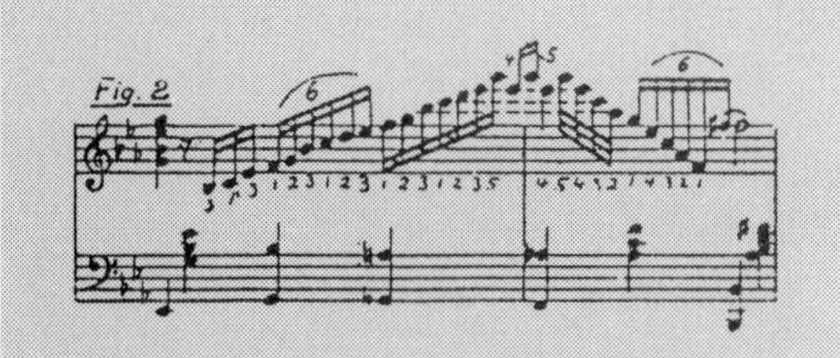

Musical Ex. 6.5. Examples of 'rhapsodic-style embellishment', from Jimmy Sampson's 'The Simplicity of Slow Swing Style Playing', Australian Music Maker and Dance Band News, February 1937, p. 51.

on the piano (Musical Ex. 6.5), an approach based not just on filling-in around basic chord tones but on the use of scales associated with the underlying harmony.

By 1938, however, there are references to a much more exploratory approach – that of composing entire choruses over standard chord sequences. Clarinetist Ern Pettifer writes that 'The freedom of playing cannot be believed . . . and it forms a basis for hot playing that reduces any tune to a series of chords that can be extemporised upon at the will of the player'.[11] He even suggests conceptualising the chorus as a graphic pitch profile (he provides an example) to develop a feel for overall structure, claiming that 'Boldness of design, boldness of outline, and boldness of movement will make your work full of vigour, and infect your listeners with the full swing of the music'.[12] Others refer specifically to personal creativity. Describing the difference between the 'straight' musician and the 'good dance man', trombonist Geoff ('Dutchy') Turner stipulates that in addition to 'legitimate' skills, the dance musician's 'accomplishments must include an ability to create, so that his individuality comes out in his playing'.[13] Turner's articles underline the almost schizophrenic state of mind required of Australian dance stylists who always had to span the gulf between 'legit' playing and some degree of musical creativity.

The Late 1930s: 'Early Modern Jazz'

The Jam Session

Older Melbourne musicians often express the opinion that 'modern jazz' in Australia began in the 'Fawkner Park jam sessions' of the late 1930s. The term 'modern' was applied to almost any contemporary form of jazz around this time. It is clear, however, that these musicians are referring to small ensemble playing in which relatively uninhibited improvisation was the key element, in contrast to the highly arranged and minimally jazzed music which palais musicians were required to play most of the time.

The Fawkner Park jam sessions were just one manifestation of a growing public enthusiasm for spontaneously improvised jazz fuelled by exposure to the new, mostly undefined array of genres which Australians described as Swing music. The term 'jam session' describes the coming together of musicians in a situation which allows them the freedom to improvise and extend themselves musically, as opposed to just playing to please paying patrons. These are usually held in private venues but also occur after hours at the band's regular venue. Similar situations have already been noted in the private social gatherings of variety artists during the ragtime era. It was only during the Swing era, however, that the term jam session came into wide use. The exciting spontaneity of jamming began to attract a relatively large following at various Swing venues, of which Fawkner Park, in the Melbourne suburb of South Yarra, seems to have been the most significant. One music journal even suggests that the Fawkner Park band was 'the first to introduce Swing music and Jam sessions to Australia'.[14]

The Fawkner Park Band

In the mid-1930s the Melbourne tenor saxophone player Bob Tough and several other musicians began offering Sunday afternoon entertainment for Swing fans at the Fawkner Park Kiosk. By 1939 the band had increased to around eight members under the leadership of his brother Ern Tough (guitar, string bass), although other ensembles and visiting and local artists were sometimes given a spot during the afternoon. Many outstanding improvising musicians played with this band before its demise around 1940, but the two musicians who left the deepest impression on my informants are Bob Tough and the remarkable multi-instrumentalist, Benny Featherstone, who may indeed have represented the 'cutting edge' of improvised jazz performance style at the time these sessions were started. As there are no known recordings of the Fawkner Park sessions, I discuss the music played there mostly on the basis of informants' recollections and examples recorded elsewhere which feature improvisation by Featherstone, Tough and other known members of the Fawkner Park band(s).

The band itself was in fact much more than an arbitrary meeting of variably skilled dance musicians for 'a jam'. The core members of the band remained relatively constant and were often cited in the trade journals as also working together in similar ensembles during the week. Individually, the Fawkner Park musicians were at, or close to, the top of their profession as dance musicians and many were noted for their ability to 'swing' (improvise in hot style). The models over which they improvised were mostly old standards such as 'Dinah', 'Margie', 'Nagasaki', 'I've Got Rhythm' or 'Avalon', which were well established in the jamming repertoire. The band therefore comprised notable improvising musicians who were familiar with each other's capabilities and who improvised over familiar forms, keys and chord patterns. In other words, it was an ideal situation for the development of a style based on a spontaneous, intuitive group response and extended jazz solo improvisations. In addition, this excitingly informal context brought these local jazz 'stars' of the period into close physical proximity with an ardent following of 'Swing buffs' – a context which undoubtedly encouraged spontaneity and musical risk-taking. Given this unique combination of factors, just how exploratory was the music played at Fawkner Park?

Figure 6.1. Advertisement featuring Bob Tough. *Australian Dance and Dance Band News*, 24 December 1937.

A typical Fawkner Park routine is recalled by drummer Don Reid. Playing without written arrangements, the chosen tune was first played

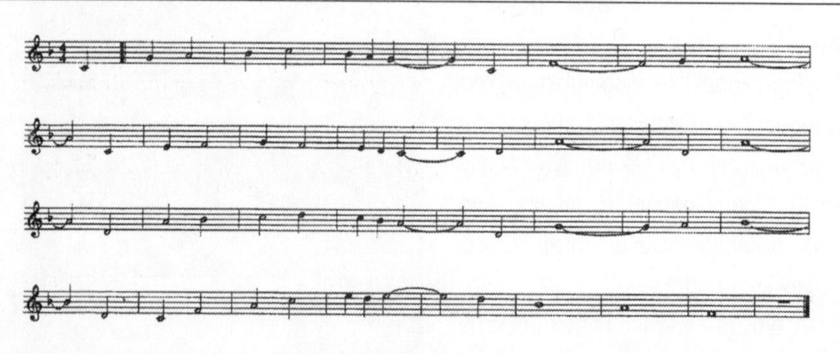

Musical Ex. 6.6a. Transcription of Bob Tough's tenor saxophone solo from 'Avalon', Orme Stewart's Group, Melbourne, c.1942. Compare with the tune of 'Avalon' below. Note also the tempo marking.
Musical Ex. 6.6b. Melodic model for 'Avalon'.

'straight' several times by one lead instrument or with various doublings of the lead line. This was supported by the rhythm section and improvised harmony on brass and reed instruments. Reid describes the rhythm section as:

> a fairly rigid four-in-the-bar swing type rhythm section, four in the bar chords on piano and the drummer not riding a ride cymbal – almost using his side drum more than even his high hat . . . Even the Jo Jones high hat [style] was not yet [being used] . . . The drummer was probably playing four in the bar on the bass drum . . . The bass was more slapped than a walking, progressive 'largo-type', Ray Brown type of bass.[15]

This was followed by a string of improvised solo choruses: usually two but sometimes many more if they felt inspired. At some stage during these choruses a brass or reed player might introduce a simple riff which would be picked up spontaneously by the others as a backing texture for the improvising soloist. This open-ended routine would often finish with what Reid describes as a Swing band equivalent of collective improvisation in early jazz style.[16]

Clearly, the music played by the Fawkner Park band was highly improvisatory in comparison to the type of dance music already discussed. Former Fawkner Park band

Musical Ex. 6.7. Transcription of Benny Featherstone's clarinet solo from 'Jazz Me Blues', Frank Coughlan's Band, Melbourne, 1942–3. This example is typical of Featherstone's clarinet work on record.

bass player Don (Pixie) McFarlane compared it to the music of the Benny Goodman Sextet, a progressive small group style based on the jam session format (model → string of improvised choruses based on model → model). Small group progressive Swing represented an important stage in the transition from fully arranged, large ensemble Swing to the radical 1940s small group style known as bebop, bop, or rebop. Among the local recordings which offer some insight into the Fawkner Park band's music are several which feature the type of spontaneous harmonisation, riffing and collective improvisation mentioned above.[17]

Bob Tough

Bob Tough is described as being able to command excellent cooperation onstage through his dignified demeanour and his notable reputation in both legitimate and jazz performance.[18] In this respect he was still a part of the culture of the great 'stylists' of the 1930s such as Pettifer, Dobson and Turner, whose professional roots went back to a time before 'orchestral' musicians began to define themselves as either 'legit', 'semi-legit' (e.g. popular theatre musicians) or dance stylists. Tough was possibly the most technically progressive improvising jazz soloist in Melbourne in the late 1930s. However, it can be assumed that his performance time exploration of the musical freedom provided by the open-ended Fawkner Park routines was always tempered by long-held notions of what was tasteful within stylistic boundaries. These boundaries are certain to have been determined largely by what appear to have been important models for his style (and many other Melbourne tenor players of the time): the rich vibrant (wide vibrato) tone and melodic and rhythmic characteristics of African-American tenor saxophonists, Chu Berry and Coleman Hawkins. Their influence is heard clearly in all the examples of Tough's playing that I have been able to obtain. Musical Example 6.6a gives an indication of his impressive facility. Note in particular the skilfully shaped melodic contour.

If Tough sometimes pushed beyond familiar stylistic boundaries, this was not perceived as a weird attempt to subvert popular style. Tough's improvisation was considered the acme of stylishness and he and other improvising stylists of his calibre were seen, not as musical iconoclasts, but as 'heroes' (see Figure 6.1).[19]

Benny Featherstone

Bruce Johnson describes Featherstone as 'one of the most fascinating and gifted musicians in the history of Australian jazz'. In the early 1930s he was described in a trade paper as:

> the most modern mind in Melbourne for dance rhythms. Unfortunately he is unable to demonstrate his astounding powers to the full, for our dancers are still stepping some years behind rhythmic progress.[20]

Featherstone told the Melbourne jazz discographer Ernst Grossmann that in the early 1930s his enthusiasm for the new, complex and ecstatic African-American styles earned him a reputation as a young radical within the dance music industry.[21] After allegedly learning from Armstrong during his 1933 visit to London, Featherstone seems to have set out to subvert the status quo of the early 1930s Melbourne dance band. The available evidence suggests that, unlike the minstrel delineators of African-American performance culture, he held a genuine admiration for the transcendent and spontaneous nature of African-American performance style which was clearly reflected in his own performances.

Unlike Tough, Featherstone's reputation was built substantially upon his ability to play an astonishing array of instruments which he exchanged in performance with equally astonishing spontaneity, sometimes to the alarm of the other players on stage:

> The Palais lights are turned down, the dancers crowd round the stand, and Ern Pettifer takes Ben's place at the drums. The band strikes up a fast tempo, and Ben emerges from the back playing a penny whistle. One chorus of this, and then follows an Armstrongish vocal. A jump takes him to the piano, and a four-handed chorus follows, Ben taking some marvellous hot chords up at the treble end. Not satisfied, he then takes up a trombone and shows how a Dorsey might do it. Another grab gives him a tenor sax, which is played à la Hawkins. Finally a trumpet is handed up, and a reversion to the great Louis continues for a couple of choruses. And then, even though it is his seventh chorus and all at a colossal speed, he is able to finish on a simply tremendous sustained high note.[22]

All this was before he even met Armstrong! Recordings featuring Featherstone on trumpet, trombone, drums and clarinet prove that he had sufficient technical freedom to produce convincing choruses and breaks on these instruments and demonstrate an intensity of expression in his playing (see Musical Ex. 6.7). However, they do not in themselves indicate that Featherstone's natural ability and spontaneity were manifest in a particularly exploratory approach to jazz improvisation.

Undoubtedly Featherstone possessed the intelligence, imagination and natural ability to become a markedly progressive and original Australian voice in improvised jazz. Yet his great respect for Armstrong and his desire to sound as much as possible like such current jazz idols (in conjunction with some serious personal problems) must have done much to preclude this possibility. George Dobson, however, maintains that 'he really was an individualist, he was never a copyist. If he played like Louis Armstrong it was also very like Benny Featherstone'.[23]

Fawkner Park and similar late 1930s venues, in which the relatively open-ended jam session routines allowed musicians such as Tough and Featherstone to play extended improvised solos, collectively represent the first major watershed of improvisatory performance practice in twentieth century Australia since the disappearance of the silent cinema pianist. In a sense the Fawkner Park sessions also represent the first comparatively large-scale acceptance of 'collectively improvised' jazz in Melbourne, by which I mean that, unlike arranged jazz, the music was improvisatory from the string bass part upward and the form was open-ended enough to leave considerable latitude

Musical Ex. 6.8. Transcription of Abe Romain's saxophone countermelody behind the vocalist Len Maurice, in 'Baby Your Mother Like She Babied You', Sydney, 1927. A number of non-legitimate voice leadings (e.g. the last two bars) suggest that this example was improvisatory. Note the dotted note jazzing.

for intuitive group response. Furthermore, the small improvising Swing band that Bob Tough brought to Fawkner Park in the mid-1930s provided a live model for the small 'progressive swing' ensembles which experimented with much more radical improvisatory concepts in Melbourne of the late 1940s.

More importantly, the extended improvisatory soloing that became possible through the increased popularity of jamming represented a significant bridge between jazz and art music. The transcription of Tough's solo in Musical Example 6.6a above is clearly more than just the jazzing of popular music. It shows that, by the time of this performance, jazz was at least marginally accepted in Australia as a vehicle for improvisation/composition. On the recording of 'Avalon', for example, Tough unexpectedly grasps the banal, grossly overused theme from an untidy scramble of weaving parts and shapes it into something vigorous and new.

Collectively Improvised Jazz

Another highly improvisatory form of music to emerge in Melbourne in the late 1930s was the collectively improvised and highly contrapuntal style of jazz which had reached its pinnacle or 'golden age' in America a decade earlier. The emergence of what subsequently came to be known as the Australian 'traditional jazz' movement is one of the most significant events in Australian jazz history. Its origins can be attributed substantially to the enthusiasm for collectively improvised jazz style generated by a small group of Melbourne-based musicians including the brothers, Graeme and Roger Bell. The 1937 formation of the Melbourne University Rhythm Club by Ade Monsborough and Sam Benwell was another landmark in its development. Much has been written about these origins, including a detailed chapter in Graeme Bell's autobiography. Discussion here is therefore confined mainly to collectively improvised jazz as a form of exploratory or experimental music.

The ability to harmonise spontaneously against a lead line had of course always been (and still is) a necessity for dance musicians in situations where arrangements were either absent or problematic. Musical Example 6.8, recorded in 1927, features the same type of obbligato work that is still played today by veteran Melbourne dance musicians such as Ron Richards. It will also be recalled that in the ragtime to jazz transition period trombonists had to learn to fill-out below the lead line as their role in dance music became more independent of the bass line. The very first jazz recordings cut in Australia (Ralton's Havana Band, Melbourne, mid-1925) feature some collectively improvised style jazz and recordings from the late 1920s similarly demonstrate that local musicians were familiar with this style.[25] A report of a 1933 Melbourne jam session attended by Dobson, Featherstone and Coughlan mentions that 'all harmonising was spontaneous! . . . Clever harmonies, hot phrases, and obbligatos crowded one after the other, all in the most modern style'.[26] It is also clear from recordings and numerous interviews that, at least until the mid-1940s, many of those who were most committed to technically progressive jazz also enjoyed playing in a collectively improvised style – although not necessarily one that resembled 'golden age' jazz.

Collective Improvisation as 'Modernist Music'

In culturally isolated Australia of the early 1940s, this 'early jazz' style was, ironically, perceived by some as a form of 'modern' or 'modernist' jazz. Moreover, whereas small group 'progressive swing' was regarded simply as a slightly obscure form of popular music, by the early 1940s collectively improvised jazz had become identified with radical left-wing politics through its association with the modernist art and literature movement, the Angry Penguins. According to Graeme Bell:

> We jazz musicians and the contemporary artists discovered that we were in the same camp. To be modern or anti-conservative during the prevailing climate was to be anti-fascist and therefore left-wing . . . The other cities, however, particularly Sydney, had nowhere near the rebellious vitality in art, jazz or literature that there was in Melbourne. Leading writers such as Max Harris saw jazz as part of a total art phenomenon.[27]

One colourful account of the rebel Contemporary Art Society's Melbourne exhibition of 1941 notes that 'jitterbugs shimmied to a weird new brand of swing music and lank-haired, collarless "modernists" argued about what-have-you at the Contemporary Art Society exhibition'.[28] The 'weird new brand of swing music' mentioned here was the collectively improvised jazz of 'Graeme Bell and his Jazz Gang'.

The program notes for the Contemporary Art Society's 'First Concert of Hot Jazz' emphasise in particular the fundamental importance of improvisation to jazz. They also provide some insight into why this intellectually progressive group of artists, writers and musicians should have adopted such a seemingly unsophisticated and out-dated form of jazz.[29] They hint, for example, at the left-wing ideological attraction of this music and present notions that correspond aesthetically with the 'primitivism' of the Melbourne modernists:

> [a] spontaneous musical expression of the life of its time [which] always springs from the less intellectual sections of the community, sections uninhibited by traditional culture, reacting to life in a purer, more elemental way.[30]

The program notes also assert that while Swing music is 'ideologically impure' (commercially adulterated) and 'classical' playing only requires the performer to interpret, in playing 'the real Jazz' (collectively improvised jazz) 'the musician himself creates the music, weaving extemporaneous patterns in the Jazz idiom around the melody or theme being played'.[31] According to the writer, this 'real' or 'pure' form of jazz is only heard 'where a group of musicians are free to get together and improvise on tunes in their own way'.[32] The program states that 'The band will improvise upon the following tunes', including the politicised title, 'The First on the Left and Second to the Right', composed for the exhibition by Roger Bell.[33] Here, therefore, was the promotion of a subversive new concept in Australian jazz: a non-commercial style dependent on spontaneous creativity and intuitive group response. Unlike Swing, this style was directly oppositional to orthodox practice. Graeme Bell states that:

> the sound of true jazz is entirely different. You can squeeze out notes like the cry of a strangled rat or you can nonchalantly drop them out like a brazen fart. You can slide up a note, you can slide down . . . And you can break all the rules of harmony and phrasing and place the accents where you like . . . The main ingredient in jazz, however – improvisation – is neither new nor exclusive.[34]

'Collective Improvisation'

Collectively improvised style does not always involve the type of improvisatory practice implied by the term. In fact traditional jazz 'purists' are often displeased when 'golden age jazz classics' are played differently from the original 1920s recordings. Australian approaches to playing in collectively improvised style include memorising written-out parts, working out parts around a given melody 'by ear' in rehearsal and, finally, spontaneous or seemingly spontaneous collective improvisation over a given theme – usually one belonging to a widely-known repertoire. The last approach is commonly used in jam sessions and similar contexts.

Most Australian performances of collectively improvised style jazz are based on some permutation of the last two approaches. Yet even where a performance is predetermined almost note for note, there is still scope within the style for a unique form of spontaneous exploration. Johnson describes it as follows:

> In the act of collective improvisation, it is necessary continuously to be making split second decisions wholly on the basis of what is being heard at any moment from (in the classic format) two other horns, not to mention the interweavings of [other] units in the rhythm section. Even playing over a basic triad with its underlying scale in mind, the ear has be ready to evaluate at any instant the sound of two other horns seeking purchase on the chord, complicated of course by deformations such as flattened thirds [and] fifths.[35]

There is also a certain non-linearity about the way in which Bell Band members and, for that matter, most later Australian exponents of this style developed the ability to play in this manner. Other forms of jazz improvisation such as the improvised break or chorus could be studied, to a substantial degree, from scores, recordings and 'jazz methods'. However, the most common method for learning collective improvisation was, and still is, personal exploration, trial and error and gradual performance time training of the ear to recognise what works and what does not in the type of ambiguous shifting musical context described above.

The early 1940s collectively improvised jazz of the Bell Band included performance characteristics that, to some extent, pointed much more in the direction of later 'free jazz' and non-jazz 'creative ensemble' music than other forms of jazz at the time. Even the approach to learning to play in this style was, by necessity, far more exploratory than in other styles. This music, moreover, was initially considered by some to be 'weird' or 'noise' (or both) as well as aesthetically and politically subversive. Yet ultimately 'traditional jazz' became far more influential musically than politically and had already begun to emerge as a reactionary force in Australian jazz by the mid-1940s.

Bebop and Musical Experimentation in the Late 1940s

Melbourne in the late 1940s was not only a watershed for progressive tendencies in Australian jazz; it also provided a context for the first strong impulse towards progressive tendencies in art music. But how exploratory were these progressive tendencies in jazz, and what was the relationship of jazz to progressive tendencies in art music during this period?

Following the emergence of small group progressive Swing and specialist collectively improvised style jazz bands, no markedly progressive development occurred until just after the Second World War. This was the time when local musicians first began to experiment with elements of the radical style of small group jazz most commonly known as bebop.[36] An early influence on this development was the visit late in 1943 of the Artie Shaw (U.S. Navy) Orchestra. The previous models for Swing band sound had mostly been radio broadcasts, recordings and musicals on film, or those models that were endlessly recycled within the 'closed circuit' of the local jazz performance community – models which lacked the precise attack (and release) and overall dimension of the Shaw band's sound. Moreover, the model for individual improvisation presented by Shaw must have seemed, for some, the antithesis of the collectively improvised jazz aesthetic:

> The man is a perfect artist, he has no crowd fetching mannerisms; he does not contort himself . . . he just stands and plays with hardly a movement. He seems to have an unlimited fund of ideas and the music just pours out in a never ending stream.[37]

Technically Progressive Jazz

The Shaw visit marked the beginning of a slow polarisation of the more ardent lovers of collectively improvised jazz and those attracted to the model of relatively orthodox technical brilliance provided by Shaw's band. Up-and-coming young Melbourne dance musicians such as pianist Don Banks, drummer Charlie Blott, bass player Lyn Challen and tenor saxophonist Splinter Reeves, who had previously identified with collectively improvised jazz, shifted their interest to what were now seen as the new progressive styles of jazz.[38] These were 1940s big band Swing and the progressive small group jazz of American (including African-American) leaders such as Benny Goodman, Count Basie and John Kirby. Soon after the War these influences also included the 'transitional bop' style of the Nat King Cole Trio and the progressive big band Swing of the Stan Kenton band, which was immediately identified with the term 'bop' in Australia. The style known as boogie-woogie, with its simple harmonic structure, also became identified with 'bop' in Australia but, if anything, its remarkably sustained popularity here served mainly to retard technically progressive style development.

The First Bebop

Information about authentic Parker/Gillespie-style bebop (early bebop) began to reach Australia during 1946, first in writings. In a guest editorial in *Music Maker*, 'They Call it "Be-bop": an Exciting New Style that will Replace Swing', for example, Wally Norman relates:

> [I came] across a pile of imported records made late last year by a practically unknown trumpet man, Dizzie Gillespie . . . The tempo is usually very fast, with four-beat bass predominating in the rhythm section, drums on open hi-hat all the way and piano playing short sustained chords every two bars or so. The first chorus is invariably an intricate unison phrase by the lead instruments with clever emphasis on the added notes in the chords. No set theme is used (as for instance 'Lady Be Good' or 'Dinah'); the composer of the first unison chorus selects his own chords, which usually bear little resemblance to the hackneyed line of progressions as we know them today . . . One typical phrase consists of a triple[t] starting a run of quavers, that goes on for eight bars or so, ending in two quavers that sound like the word 'Be-bop'. The last chorus is the same as the first, with a sudden, unexpected ending, or else fading out for no apparent reason in the middle of a phrase.[39]

This is a surprisingly accurate description of the most audible aspects of early bop and provides a critically important insight into one aspect of bop harmony: the notion of improvised lines based on higher chord extensions.

Some weeks after this article appeared, Dizzy Gillespie's 'Salt Peanuts' was played over ABC Radio's national network, drawing caustic comments from the Sydney jazz record reviewer, Ron Wills.[40] Such predictably negative responses to this transgressive new style notwithstanding, bebop had an impact on many young Melbourne musicians that is difficult to understand from a present-day perspective. One such musician, Bruce Clarke, recalls that 'someone announced a program of new releases and played four Dizzy Gillespie tracks in a row: '"Nite in Tunisia", "Anthropology", "52 Street Theme", and "Ol Man Rebop". I sat dumbfounded as the lid blew off my whole musical world'.[41]

The Modern Music Society

At almost the precise moment the traditional jazz movement became manifest in the first Australian Jazz Convention (December 1946) and Australia was poised to enter the 'jazz concert boom', young, technically advanced Melbourne players such as Banks and Blott adopted bebop as the emblem of their progressiveness. This style threatened to subvert both the increasingly popular traditional jazz style and mainstream Swing. In December 1947 Wally Norman reported that, in Sydney, '[bop] has taken a firm hold on the imagination of the younger players. In one of our large dance bands a bitter, personal struggle went on for weeks between the two opposing factions'.[42] Such was the enthusiasm generated by this new avant-garde jazz in Melbourne that in late 1947 a loose-knit cooperative of professional musicians, the Modern Music Society, was formed around the notion of performing 'non-commercial music'.[43] Several successful Modern Music Society concerts were held and Society members had set up their own record label, Jazz Art, through Bob Clemens' music shop.

Coinciding with the impact of bebop on Melbourne, a progressive Swing ensemble from Adelaide (initially called The Rockettes) led by vibraphone player Jack Brokensha had begun to provide both an influential model and focal point for the emerging culture of the 'bopper'. In addition to the band's special blend of youthful showmanship, fast tempo routines, orthodox technique and a relatively advanced harmonic and rhythmic approach, their programs combined classical music items by composers such as Chopin and Rimsky-Korsakov with what was perceived as ultra-modern jazz.

While the Modern Music Society used the New Theatre as a performance venue, there is no evidence that the Society had an overtly political agenda or sought other than to provide a forum for the performance of music. In fact, during 1948 the relationship between the Communist Party (who controlled the New Theatre) and the jazz community deteriorated. Nor do those most involved in the establishment of the

Society appear to have had significant associations with the other arts. Perhaps this partly reflects the lower socio-economic background of most professional dance musicians, a background that did not emphasise 'high' cultural pursuits. More importantly, the culture of professional dance band music in Australia incorporates a distinct irreverence for anything that smacks of artistic (or social) elitism or pretension. Saxophonist Eddie Oxley, states, for example, that he and his colleagues were simply too preoccupied with their work to be interested in that 'airy-fairy stuff'.[44]

Jazz Musicians and Contemporary Art Music

In addition to the emergence of this new jazz subculture of 'modernists' or 'progressives', the post-war period brought with it a change of direction for 'art music' in Melbourne which was, in certain ways, associated with jazz. Four figures are particularly significant to this jazz/contemporary music connection: Doug(las) Gamley, Keith Humble, Don Banks and Bruce Clarke. All were jazz musicians, but only Banks and Clarke became identified with bebop. Humble and Clarke did not really become significant as Australian experimentalists until after this period but all of them are significant from the point of view of mapping the emergence of 'improvisatory experimentalism' in jazz and contemporary music between the late 1940s and the 1960s.

In 1944 *Angry Penguins*, the principal publication of the Angry Penguins movement, published and favourably reviewed the 'Ern Malley poems'. These poems had been created by two conservative poets, James McAuley and Harold Stewart, from randomly selected text fragments with the purpose of exposing the shallowness of contemporary poetry. The poems' favourable reception succeeded in destroying the credibility of the Angry Penguins and created general suspicion towards aesthetic radicalism.[45] Music reactionaries had little to fear from the art music community of Melbourne, however, since local interest in even relatively recent music was minimal. One exception was the pianist and former child prodigy Douglas Gamley, who, around this time, began to interest young Melbourne jazz musicians, such as Banks, Humble, Blott and Ted Preston, in contemporary music developments.

Douglas Gamley

Though born in Melbourne, Gamley is best known in Australia as a London conductor, arranger and composer and is not mentioned in any Australian jazz literature after 1940. Nevertheless, he was the pianist for Frank Coughlan's Trocadero Orchestra for a brief period in the early 1940s and he was also associated with many of the young Melbourne progressives who championed bebop in the late 1940s. He was particularly

Figure 6.2. Doug Gamley c.1945. Photograph by Charlie Blott.

admired by progressive young jazz pianists for his keyboard improvisations, which incorporated elements of contemporary art music.

There is no doubt that Gamley's outstanding aural ability was an important aspect of his approach to improvising and the impact he had upon other musicians. In our interview he casually mentioned, for example, his early ability to transcribe from memory the music from film sound tracks. He also discussed his method of transposing accompaniments by reading the score, then simply playing the piece by ear in any key requested – a habit which affected his ability to transpose in the orthodox manner (by intervals). Gamley became widely known for his remarkable musical spontaneity through the popular 3XY radio program, *Musical Clue*. This program was a game in which Gamley was required to play on the spot any title suggested by the audience. If he failed, which was uncommon, the participant received the 'jackpot' prize. When a false title was given, Gamley would trick the cheat by spontaneously inventing a tune with characteristics that somehow matched the title. He was also a rehearsal accompanist for ballet students and was often asked to invent spontaneous accompaniments in the style of composers such as Chopin or Tchaikovsky.

Ironically, it was a jazz musician, Frank Coughlan, who was most influential in encouraging Gamley to begin a serious study of art music. Gamley recalls:

> it sounds incredible, but in the early 1940s Debussy was considered 'way out' modern – this is true – and the minute I heard on the radio the first piece of Debussy and the first piece of Stravinsky, I was hooked . . . So, instead of acquiring the kind of repertoire that [the Melbourne Conservatorium] would have liked me to acquire – which was a lot of Beethoven and Brahms . . . I learnt almost the entire output of Debussy for piano.[46]

It seems to have been Gamley's Debussy-influenced improvisations that most fascinated and inspired his following of young jazz musicians, although he personally believes his main influence was in getting these players to listen to Debussy, Ravel and other comparatively modern composers:

> Charlie [Blott] was one of my very first converts, I played him some records of Debussy and I played him some pieces by Debussy – and then he would go to the piano and find a fairly like-sounding chord – and then move it up a semitone. He was fascinated by this kind of progression.[47]

Gamley was both 'very excited' and 'fascinated' by bebop, but for various reasons he chose not to explore this style. It is also clear from our discussion that, unlike his Melbourne contemporaries Humble and Banks, his interest in the musical potential of improvisation did not develop much beyond what he had already experienced before leaving Australia at the end of the 1940s. He comments, for example, that he was totally unable to cope with the notion of aleatoric (chance-based) music.[48]

That this remarkable musician was more or less bypassed by both Australian jazz and art music history demonstrates the need such talented individuals felt in the 1940s to leave the artistic constraints of Melbourne. Indeed they were actively encouraged to do so by those who recognised their potential. In any event, Gamley's ability to improvise in contemporary art music style would not have been accepted in Melbourne for at least another decade. While local interest in whole-tone scales and emphasised tritones cannot be attributed solely to Gamley's influence, it is very likely that he provided musicians such as Banks with the first live model for the use of such elements in improvisation.[49]

Humble, Banks and Gamley: Similarities and Differences

Gamley, Humble and Banks were all born in the mid-1920s and became child prodigies on piano with a natural leaning towards improvisation and composition. Only Humble, however, went on to international success as a pianist. They all describe their frustration at the absence of living role models for composition in Australia. Therefore, jazz improvisation and arranging became an important channel for creative energy. The only one to become fully absorbed by the aesthetics of jazz and the jazz subculture, however, appears to have been Banks who, unlike Humble and Gamley, grew up among dance musicians and was associated musically and socially with the collectively improvised style of jazz until the mid-1940s (initially as a trombonist and soon after as a pianist). After this, he was drawn to the new ecstatic style of African-American oriented jazz, bebop.

Humble claims never to have been interested in the loose overall surface structure of collectively improvised jazz, much preferring very tightly arranged jazz which hems in and greatly accentuates the momentary freedom of the improvised jazz solo. This was also Gamley's position.[50] Humble speaks of his jazz improvisations of this period as having developed substantially from common (non-jazz) improvisatory practice. He mentions, for example, his daily practice 'drill' set by his teacher, Mrs Butcher, which included playing short musical models transposed into every key, and he cites specific published exercises that influenced this approach.[51] Around this time he also recorded some tracks in which he improvised in the style of Bach with a jazz rhythm section. Those who remember his jazz improvisations recall, not ecstatic jazz abandonment, but technical brilliance. Yet recorded evidence from the late 1940s demonstrates that he could bring an ecstatic quality to his classical playing as I have personally observed many times.[52]

Humble's concern for tightly-framed improvisational freedom increasingly became Banks' own trademark as he moved towards the notion of what is now called 'third stream music'. If third stream can be defined as the juxtaposition of jazz and art music, it can be argued that Humble and Gamley began from a position which was conceptually quite similar to that which Banks eventually adopted. It is also interesting to compare the respective attitudes of Gamley, Humble and Banks towards the relationship of improvisation to composition. Banks states that 'some people call composition "frozen improvisation" – this is quite wrong', while Gamley states that 'composition *is*, in a sense, improvisation – it has to be'.[53] Humble went very much further in perceiving his entire compositional output as 'frozen improvisation' or 'improvisation/composition' (see Chapter Seven).

In addition to leading various bands of his own, Humble became established as a respected jazz pianist in the 1940s through jamming and work in night clubs, palais, variety, stage and radio broadcasting. When he took over from one of Melbourne's most experienced pianists in the Tom Davidson Orchestra, *Music Maker* described him as 'a sensation'.[54] Given his later role in experimental music it may seem surprising that he was not at the forefront of local modern jazz development in the late 1940s, but at this time he was fully engaged in establishing what was already a most promising career as a concert artist. Nevertheless, he acknowledges that his 1940s jazz experience helped to imprint, albeit subliminally, certain important ideas relating to improvisation that would become very significant in his later work, although in much more complex forms.[55]

Bruce Clarke: Problem-Solving Experimentalist

The fact that Clarke, a former plumber's apprentice, was virtually self-taught contributed to his developing a remarkably individualistic and exploratory approach to music. Melbourne composer Helen Gifford describes him as 'the original inquiring mind: he doesn't take on received ideas at all, he makes his own judgment'.[56] His 'break' in modern jazz came when he was invited to join Banks' bop group in 1949. He was also introduced to contemporary music through concerts attended by Banks and his classical music colleagues. Clarke later became involved in experimental art music to the extent that he became president of the Melbourne branch of the International Society for Contemporary Music in the late 1960s.

The Melbourne Conservatorium: the 'Golden Years'

Humble and Banks followed Gamley's example and began formal studies at the Melbourne Conservatorium of Music shortly after the war. Jazz musicians Eddie Oxley (reeds) and Tommy Davidson (leader, clarinet) were also enrolled around this time and all of these musicians interacted professionally outside Conservatorium hours. Humble, for example, played in various palais bands with Oxley, including Davidson's. Similarly, Oxley played in Banks' bebop groups, while Humble and Banks often deputised for each other as jazz pianists.[57] Although improvisation was not a part of the Conservatorium syllabus, both Banks and Humble were particularly noted for this ability. In fact, Humble's ability to improvise short fugues helped him obtain a prestigious scholarship to study in London.

The post-war Conservatorium environment of which Banks and Humble were a part was not stifled by the same level of conservatism that Gamley had experienced there a few years earlier. Banks states, for example, that Gamley had been 'asked to leave the conservatorium because he played professionally at the Melbourne Town Hall accompanying a singer'.[58] In the post-war period, however, with the influx of ex-servicemen taking up their rehabilitation training option, the institution came alive with activity. These relatively mature and assertive individuals helped to create the more open egalitarian atmosphere of a period sometimes described as the Conservatorium's 'Golden Years', during which an impressive array of high achievers in Australian music emerged. Nevertheless, even in the late 1940s, 'new music' was still confined to composers such as Debussy and Ravel, and knowledge of more advanced concepts could only be gained through personal experimentation or relatively rare books such as Ernest Krenek's *Studies in Counterpoint* (1940). During this particular phase of the Conservatorium's history such extreme decontextualisation somehow served to generate an exciting climate of experimentation amongst students. Humble describes it as their 'looking and searching era', during which they began to discover the sparse and angular sound world of composers such as Schoenberg, and explored sound relationships beyond the tonal system.[59]

Exploration of 'Dissonance' In Jazz and Contemporary Music

Humble believes that Banks was particularly drawn to bebop because of its clipped, modern sound, a belief which the last recordings of Banks' Boptet, made in early 1950, appear to confirm.[60] There is also an important parallel between the exploration of 'dissonance' by the 'boppers' and the clandestine exploration of 'dissonance' at the Conservatorium. Banks recalls that he and his mentor at the Conservatorium, composer Dorian Le Gallienne, 'would argue about certain things, because I'm not sure whether Dorian accepted the level of dissonance that was appearing in my work at the time; but it was all very friendly'.[61]

Banks' explanation of the conventions of bebop harmony, published in an article in 1948, suggests the tentative way that he and others were individually exploring their way towards an understanding of the unfamiliar level of dissonance in this music:

> Firstly the harmony is now extensively chromatic, instead of a plain statement of diatonic chords. These have been embellished by added notes, and connected by the use of passing chords (such as the major 7th [he probably means minor 7th here]). There is a frequent use of richer chords, a favourite being the augmented 11th, and others more dissonant in character . . . the (at times) dissonant harmonic basis will mean that weaving of the melodic line on this, will include many notes, which to the un-initiated ear, will appear to be wrong ones.[62]

Here, the emphasis on the augmented eleventh suggests a preoccupation with what Banks seems to have interpreted as Debussy-like whole-tone relationships. In a 1949 article, Graeme Bell also claims that 'boppers' (referring specifically to Banks) use a whole-tone scale in which the intervals are altered, giving an entirely new sound similar to 'the works of such modern composers as Hindemith and Bartok'.[63] Fairly typical criticism of the boppers' perceived use of dissonance or atonalism can be found in a 1948 *Music Maker* editorial, 'How Dissonant Can You Get and Still Make Music'.[64]

Don Banks: from 'Bebop' to Incipient Third Stream Music

Banks' later experimentation with third stream music, open scoring and electronic music is far better acknowledged than his early involvement with jazz. It is possible that his former jazz colleagues sometimes retrospectively exaggerate the significance of his 1940s jazz profile in the light of his later achievements. However, numerous conversations and interviews (including a collective video interview of surviving boppers) all indicate that, in the 1940s, Banks was considered at the forefront of Australian attempts to come to grips with bebop – the new jazz of previously inconceivable tempos, harmonic and rhythmic complexity, melodic inventiveness and overall improvisatory freedom.[65]

To evaluate just how exploratory these attempts were, the activities of Banks and his colleagues must be related, not to cutting edge jazz development in America, but to the backdrop of the isolated post-war Melbourne musical environment. Challen, for example, describes a recording session in 1946 or 1947 when, to his great excitement, he and several colleagues spontaneously invented a style of jazz which they had not heard before, even on imported jazz recordings.[66]

> It was only because the front line phrased it like they did [that] it left gaps in the section, so I sort of decided to fill it in, and when it happened it sounded good . . . [The front line players] looked around as if to say 'that sounds good', and so I persevered with the thing right through the record.[67]

There is no drummer on this recorded track, 'Swanee River', and Challen carries the rhythm totally with a strong, sometimes embellished 'walking bass' (four notes per bar bass). The resulting open texture leaves the pianist (Bob Young) free to interject with chord patterns and runs in a very sparse, rhythmically relaxed way. This texture supports clipped unison phrasing on trumpet (Fred Thomas) and tenor sax (Bobby Limb), which provides a tight frame for rhythmically relaxed soloing and contrapuntal work on the latter instruments. It is easy to understand how this music would have sounded very stylish and sophisticated in the isolation of Melbourne in 1946–7, but it is difficult to think of it as 'experimental' music from a present-day musical perspective. Yet there is no doubt that Challen experienced being part of a ground-breaking improvisatory musical experiment at this time: it was experimental in relation to the cultural context in which it took place.

Although by early 1946 Banks, Blott, Challen and others had already heard Nat King Cole's 1944 transitional swing/bebop group on record, the period of most interest is that immediately following the Australian release of the first Gillespie recordings (April

1947), which gave them their first stark confrontation with the new style in its fully developed form.

As a style, bop was initially perceived as still at an experimental stage, or at least without fixed harmonic conventions. Banks is actually cited as describing bop as 'an experimental type of progressive jazz'.[68] This perception is quite understandable, first, because bebop came into being in America through experimental jam sessions, and second, because it confronted local musicians aurally with such practices as 'tritone substitution', the practice of exchanging a given dominant seventh chord for one a tritone away. This type of chromaticism is easily confused aurally with arbitrary, chromatic, semitone step movement or the arbitrary use of whole-tone relationships, principally because tritones within the exchanged chords remain aurally identical, although the note names change. Consider, for example, the exchange of A7 for the seventh chord a tritone away, E♭7. Here the A7 tritone is C♯-G and the E♭7 tritone is G-D♭. In fact, a comparable use of tonal ambiguity (notably the 'flattened second') had been common to dance arranging as a cadential form of jazzing up since late 1920s (see Musical Ex. 6.9).

By the end of the 1940s this 'experimental phase' had passed. In addition to the greater accessibility of bebop recordings, various technical articles by Australian musicians had been published and a 'method', George Evans' *Re-bop: How to Play It, How to Write It*, had become widely available.[69] This method includes a description of improvised lines based on high chord extensions and chromatic passing chords (without explaining tritone substitution) and, consistent with all the improvisation systems I have discussed, provides a system of transposed models for improvisatory interpolation. Not only had the initial shock of authentic 'early bebop' style lost much of its momentum in Australia by the end of the 1940s, but in America, more restrained or 'cool' styles of modern jazz were already superseding it – at least according to Australian jazz literature of the period.

The first recorded Melbourne experiment with 'bebop' (and possibly the first Australian bebop composition) was Banks' 'Feelin' Dizzy' (Musical Ex. 6.10). This track was recorded privately around the time of the first Gillespie releases in 1947, and provides a solitary aural 'snapshot' of the boppers' first musical response to bebop: another example of how decontextualisation can result in interesting style synthesis. In 'Feelin' Dizzy', Banks seems to have laid out a framework featuring what he considered the important elements of bebop. These include:

1. A rhythmically complex introduction.
2. An oddly proportioned unison 'head' (tenor saxophone and clarinet) in 'clipped'

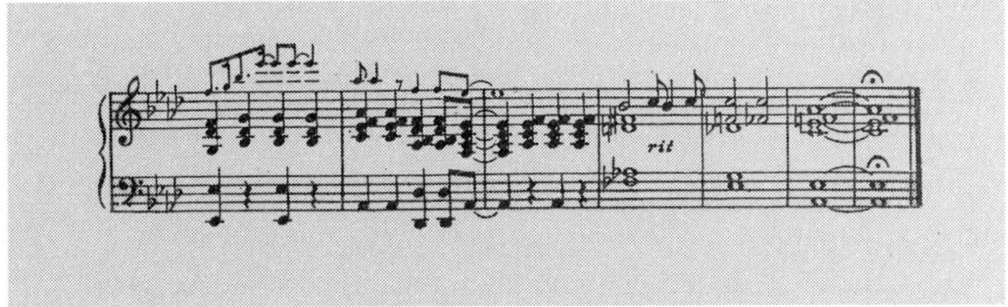

Musical Ex. 6.9. The last seven bars of 'What's the Use' (1930) by Isham Jones and Charles Newman, revised arrangement by F.E. Barry. Note that the fourth bar of this example can be heard as an altered and extended E7 chord: a tritone substitute for B♭7 in a II-V-I cadence.

paraphrase style with some unconventional chord progressions, including a clear reference to chromaticism (in the form of semitone step motion).

3. A suitably 'weird' ending which emphasises the bebop trademark, the flattened fifth.
4. The non-periodic syncopated interjection of piano chords.

Over this framework he simply lets each musician improvise in the most modern way available to them, this being the Benny Goodman small group style or the more rhythmically relaxed 'Kansas' style equivalent. Banks' own piano playing overlays this framework with sparse, non-periodic off-beat chordal interjections in the Kansas style. Aspects of this track, such as the late entry of some solos, suggest that the performers were not all entirely at ease with Banks' experiment.

Just how experimental 'Feelin' Dizzy' was in 1947 remains a subjective question; and here it should be noted that Banks was already familiar with the Kansas style, which this performance most resembles.[70] What seems most probable is that 'Feelin' Dizzy' was an experimental synthesis, a first attempt to graft elements of the radical new style onto what was already considered modernist at that time in Melbourne, the provision of an 'ultra-modern' setting for modern jazz improvisation. If there is any form of jazz which can be said to relate uniquely to isolated post-war Melbourne, it is the curiously dislocated style juxtaposition heard in this recording.

Other jazz recordings associated with Banks in the late 1940s indicate that he never imitated the authentic Parker/Gillespie 'early bop' style directly. On 'Maternity' (1948) one hears an Australian version of classic small group early bebop texture: solid walking bass, a continuous wash of sound from the large cymbal, sparse but loud syncopated interjections on bass drum (sometimes called 'dropping bombs') and fairly

Musical Ex. 6.10. A transcription of the composed theme or 'head' of 'Feelin' Dizzy', Charlie Blott's Band, Melbourne, c. April 1947.

typical bebop chordal interjections on piano. There is even a short quote from the famous bebop standard, 'Ornithology', by Charlie Parker. Apart from this, however, Banks' piano improvisation is presented in his own distinctive style: a fluent, delicate legato with a variety of interesting contours and a preference for lower chord extensions (e.g. major and minor ninths) and, in particular, recurring devices. One of these devices, the syncopated octave, is seen in Musical Examples 6.11, 6.12 and 6.13.

The reverse side of this record, 'Pennies from Heaven', bears no resemblance to early bebop style but is nevertheless an interesting attempt to produce an unusual 'modern jazz' sound. The track begins with a curious paraphrase of the melody on trumpet supported by a weirdly stilted piano accompaniment by Banks. This is later overlaid with a vibraphone set on slow vibrato to accentuate the eeriness of the texture. Banks' own solo includes harmonies that probably would have sounded very avant-garde for post-war Melbourne. For example, the last bar of Musical Example 6.12 from this solo features a very exposed tritone dissonance: instead of the expected dominant chord (E♭7), aural attention is drawn to a syncopated pattern of A natural notes (a tritone substitution for E♭). Needless to say, there was no apparent attempt to release 'Pennies from Heaven' commercially.

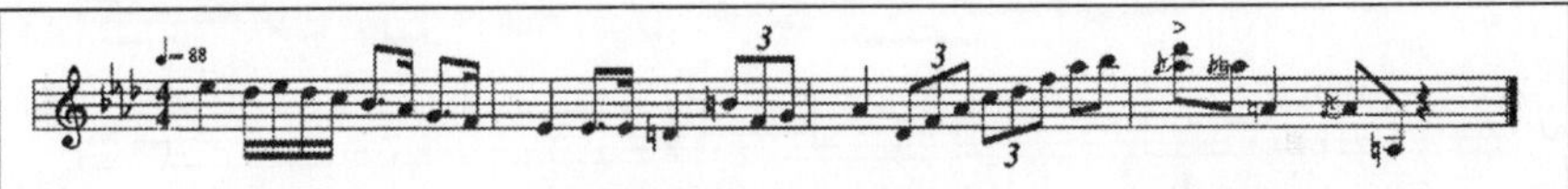

Musical Ex. 6.11. Transcription of Don Banks' piano solo from 'Maternity' (right hand only) beginning with a quote from 'Ornithology'. The central B section of the solo has been omitted.
Musical Ex. 6.12. Transcription of Don Banks' piano solo from 'Pennies from Heaven' (right hand only).

In later years Banks frequently discussed his theories on the fusion of jazz improvisation with art music – third stream music. He mentions, for example, the appropriation of the improvising performer's creative instinct as a compositional device, stating that 'the improvising ability of the musician adds an extra dimension, a kind of extension of variation technique'.[71] In referring to third stream music he also suggests that the ecstatic aspect of jazz improvisation can be appropriated to 'jazz up' art music. He comments that 'there is a genuine excitement generated by live improvisation of music, and this is something that has been lost to serious music for centuries'.[72]

Felix Werder states that he discussed the possibility of a synthesis of jazz and art music with Banks before he left Australia in 1950. The nature of Banks' last four 'bebop' recordings suggests that he had in fact already begun to explore this possibility. It may also be relevant that these recordings by Banks' Boptet (five piece) are released under the title 'Don Banks' Orchestra'.[73]

What is immediately noticeable in these tracks is the overall sophistication of the arranged sections of his routines, particularly in the vertical and horizontal juxtaposition of jazz ambiguity and 'straight' non-jazz musical characteristics, which creates remarkably varied tapestries of sound. 'I've Got my Love to Keep Me Warm', for example, begins (♩ = 60) with an 'impressionistic' texture in which the components are played with 'straight' or 'legitimate' phrasing. A rhythmically 'straight' but timbrally expressive trumpet presentation of a repeated A section of the melody passes through a variety of scored sound environments. These include imitation, oblique, parallel and contrary motion between instruments and short instrumental breaks which momentarily destabilise the texture with jazz ambiguity. The centre piece of the track is Banks' piano solo (see Musical Ex. 6.13) which, although actually very restrained in character, leaps out of the tightly orchestrated texture with great vitality, creating a stark

Musical Ex. 6.13. Transcription of Banks' piano solo in 'I've Got My Love to Keep Me Warm', Don Banks Orchestra, Melbourne, 1950. String bass part included.

juxtaposition between jazz and non-jazz. Banks had obviously already discovered the compositional potential of the simple dichotomy: fixed structure versus improvisatory freedom.

The solo itself is carefully contoured and while there are enough elements to classify it as a jazz solo, it could equally be described as a miniature performance time tonal composition incorporating a minimalist approach to jazz syncopation and idiomatic jazz effects. A more remarkable example of this approach is found in 'Can't Help Loving Dat Man' (recorded with the same musicians). This track features a characteristically restrained jazz solo by Banks, supported throughout by an even more restrained rhythm section. This is the most sophisticated and modern sounding jazz solo found on Banks' Melbourne recorded repertoire. It is only in the last twenty seconds of the track that a delicately orchestrated choral backing (brass and reeds) unexpectedly surfaces momentarily, disappears as if it never was, and then resurfaces on the last three chords of the final cadence. As this was Banks' last Melbourne recording session, 'Can't Help Loving Dat Man' conceivably represents a subliminal statement that his personal synthesis of jazz style was finally perfected. This was a style poised somewhere between jazz and contemporary art music, and one which Banks could take no further from a purely jazz perspective.

A 'New Melodic Form of Bop'

Banks' departure for England in 1950 more or less corresponds with the end of an era characterised by the excitement and technical challenges created by the sudden confrontation with bebop. Reviewing Australian jazz for the year 1949, Tom Sterne's comments on Sydney apply equally well to Melbourne:

> while some twelve months ago, Bop was a controversial subject in this country, it has now become an established fact, and while there are comparatively few musicians who play an out-and-out Bop style, the Bop influence may be noticed in the style of practically every modern musician in this town.[74]

The overall local response to bop seems to have been the syntheses of modern jazz styles, influenced by an ongoing Australian public preference for the simple, the unambiguous and the congruous. The influence of the pianist George Shearing and other overseas promoters of commercially viable bop (or 'bop for the people') also contributed to this stylistic trend. As early as 1947 the Melbourne boppers are described as playing a 'new Melodic form of Re-Bop', and by the early 1950s 'Bop for the People' had become the catchcry of the successful Melbourne jazz concert entrepreneur, Bob 'King of Bop' Crawford.[75] After 1950 the type of technical article on improvisation that had saturated Australian jazz literature in the late 1940s was now conspicuously absent, along with the previously numerous general references to bop. The slick commercial sound of Bruce Clarke's 1954 Jaguar label album (which was reviewed favourably in America) probably represents the end product of this process of refinement.[76] This clean commercial sound would, with certain exceptions, remain characteristic of mainstream small group modern jazz in Melbourne for at least another decade.

7 Beyond Jazz Improvisation

The 1960s are of far greater significance to the history of improvisatory experimental music in Australia than is generally understood. The widely-held impression that the emergence of experimentalism was a phenomenon of the 1970s is partly attributable to the various 'new music' cooperatives that were established over this period. In Melbourne these include the New Music Centre, NIAGRA (New Improvisors' Action Group for Gnostic and Rhythmic Awareness), the North Melbourne Commune (where experimental jazz synthesis took place) and later (in 1976) the Clifton Hill Community Music Centre. The 1970s saw the emergence of a whole new generation of post-1960s experimentalists as documented in John Jenkins' *22 Contemporary Australian Composers.* This is not to mention the 1970s advent of institution-based experimental art music and jazz courses, such as those established at La Trobe University; and also what Philip Brophy describes as post-punk avant-garde rock.[1] Yet in some respects, an accelerating progression towards style eclecticism and the use of open musical forms had already reached the point of revocation by 1970 or soon thereafter.

Two 1960s events particularly highlight the special nature of improvisatory experimental music of this period. The first of these, the emergence of the 'McKimm, Rooney and Clayton Trio' (Barry McKimm, Robert Rooney and Syd Clayton), involved a unique collaboration of Melbourne musicians who, by 1965, had made a remarkable transition from experimental jazz to experimental art music. The second, Keith Humble's return from Europe in the 1960s, is significant for the sheer breadth and depth of the concepts and philosophies of improvisatory musical practice he promoted in Melbourne at the time. In both cases there is a striking resemblance between their respective approaches and important tenets of modernist art.

Jazz musicians, because of their natural association with improvisatory practice, initially played a more significant role in 1960s Melbourne musical experimentation than is acknowledged by art music or jazz historians. Individuals such as Bruce Clarke and Brian Brown were not only significant experimentalists but also maintained their position in the local jazz hierarchy over decades of development and refinement as jazz improvisers. Humble and McKimm, Rooney and Clayton are, however, of special interest, because by the mid-1960s they were already fully aware of the binding nature of the jazz idiom – its inherent repetition of patterning – on freedom to explore radical new forms of improvisatory musical gesture.

Experimentalism in Art Music and Jazz: The Context

An Emerging New Music Movement

The late 1940s in Melbourne not only saw the emergence of some innovative Australian contemporary composers such as Felix Werder, Humble, Banks, Peter Sculthorpe and George Dreyfus but also produced an incipient new music movement in the form of the Society Of New Music. SONM was formed by the ABC broadcaster Kevin McBeath in 1949 and is described as the 'only organization in Australia to have been solely concerned with presenting 20th century music until the mid-1950s'.[2] It was not established as a forum for local musical experimentation; nor was there any specific connection between this incipient new music movement and radical experimentation in the other arts. In fact, far from being a focus for cultural dissidents, its meetings were 'very stylish gatherings' with a long waiting list for membership.[3] The satirist Barry Humphries recollects that 'When the New Music Society met, the small theatre was thronged with long-haired youths in suede shoes and corduroy trousers smoking Turkish cigarettes with the wrong fingers'.[4] 'New music' basically meant music new to culturally isolated Melbourne, although SONM programs occasionally featured recordings of music by experimentalists such as Varèse, Partch, and Cage.

The fall of the Australian Labor Party in 1949 and such events as the 1951 Communist Party Dissolution Bill had created a climate of increasing distrust of artistic or political subversion. There was still a left-wing intellectual movement in Melbourne, but nothing comparable to the coming together of new literature, visual art and 'new music' (the Bell band's collectively improvised jazz) around left-wing politics during the first half of the previous decade. There were isolated 'underground' events such as

Barry Humphries' introduction of neo-dadaism to Melbourne in his 1952 'Dada Exhibition' which 'opened to a medley from [the musical] "South Pacific" interspersed with records of insane, diabolical laughter'.[5] Shortly after, Humphries produced an improvisatory music-theatre work which one writer described as an:

> experiment in anti-theatre that must surely be unparalleled in our land. Vegetables and obscenities were hurled at the audience, blanks fired over their heads, whilst the orchestra consisting of combs, bottles and gongs beat out a relentless 4-bar score.[6]

This theatre work also incorporated Humphries' three movement 'Malouf Concerto' for piano, recorder, viola, organ, whistles, voice and, amongst other things, 'a sinister commercial for Lux soap' and an 'irritating ragtime' (cakewalk) theme repeated ad nauseam by Humphries on piano. Yet, although this music is created in the spirit of a peculiarly Australian brand of iconoclasm or 'larrikinism', some of the freely improvised musical textures reach a prophetic level of interest and complexity which, if it were not for Humphries' audible clumsiness at the keyboard, could be easily mistaken for 'creative music' of the 1970s or 1980s. The 'Malouf Concerto' and some of the 'subversive improvisations' of his Dada group can be heard on the CD *Barry Humphries – Dada Days and the Moonee Ponds Muse*, vol. 2 (Raven RVCD-34).

Apart from Humphries, the most radical form of exploration in the early 1950s was probably Clive Douglas' attempts to 'use the aboriginal idiom in Symphonic work'.[7] These explorations identify him with such earlier musical 'Jindyworobaks' as Tate and, in Sydney, John Antill, composer of the famous 1946 work 'Corroboree'.[8] Douglas does not appear to have been specifically concerned with improvisatory performance practice, but his approach to freezing into notation the ecstatic or 'hot' performance characteristics of black Australians is reminiscent of earlier white representations of African-American performance practice (even to the use of the primary cakewalk figure).[9]

By the late 1950s the SONM was defunct and the main impetus for an Australian 'new music' movement had shifted to Sydney, where an Australian branch of the International Society For Contemporary Music (ISCM) had been established through the efforts of the energetic Professor Donald Peart.

In 1956 Humble returned from Europe to take up a position at the Melbourne Conservatorium. However, despite his progressive zeal and new ideas, he was unable to make any headway against the musical conservatism he encountered. For him, the true measure of the reactionary nature of Melbourne's musical community was its lack of respect for the great Australian experimentalist, Percy Grainger, a frequent visitor to the Conservatorium at the time.

Towards the end of the decade new music in Melbourne seems to have been mostly represented by the Conservatorium-based Camerata Society for Contemporary Music, which revolved around a loose collective of local composers including Felix Werder. By 1961 this had been superseded by George Dreyfus' New Music Ensemble, which remained the main conduit for locally composed new works until the formation of a Melbourne branch of the ISCM in 1965. The first ISCM concerts included a number of indeterminate works by young local composers and what is claimed to be the first Australian performance of a Stockhausen work ('Kreuzspiel').[10] Up to this point, Richard Meale's 1963 ABC broadcasts of new music had been the most significant catalyst for local interest in Cage and similar experimentalists.

One form of experimental music that was more strongly established by 1965 was electronic music. In addition to such pioneer non-commercial experimentalists as Val Stephen and the bass player/electronics inventor Steve Dunstan, there was a group of problem-solving experimentalists who served the television and radio advertising industry. By far the most significant of these was Bruce Clarke who ran electronic music workshops for ISCM members during its first year. By the end of the 1960s Clarke, Humble and others had presented various electronic music workshops; an electronic music studio had been established at the Grainger Museum by Humble; and a number of Melbourne composers, including Werder, had begun to incorporate electronic sounds into their works.

Since the mid-1960s there had also been growing educational interest in 'creative music' (including electronic music) for children. In 1969 a local music teacher, Geoffrey D'Ombrain, published *Music Now*, which offered 'an exciting "creative" approach to learning music, in which the exploration of sounds leads the student to a greater appreciation of improvisation and experiments in composition'.[11] Two years earlier Humble had begun directing creative music workshops for children at the Grainger Museum.

The ISCM concerts remained an important focus for experimental art music throughout the late 1960s, although from 1966 their significance in this respect was rivalled by Humble's more radical Society for the Private Performance of New Music (SPPNM). Barry McKimm also hosted regular Sunday afternoon sessions at his home in South Yarra, bringing together symphonic, theatre, jazz, brass band and even lay musicians in a variety of improvisatory experiments. The establishment in 1967 of the experimental theatre, La Mama, also provided an important outlet for improvisatory music-theatre.

LIST OF WORKS PERFORMED AT ISCM CONCERTS 5/3/65 - 10/5/67

GILBERT AMY
Epigramme

DON BANKS
Trio

RICHARD RODNEY BENNETT
Winter Music

LUCIANO BERIO
Sequenza

IAN BONIGHTON
Mosaics

COLIN BRUMBY
Wind Quintet

NIGEL BUTTERLEY
Laudes

STUART CHALLENDER
Piano Piece No. 1

LUIGI DALLAPICCOLA
4 Lyrics

PETER MAXWELL DAVIES
Piano Pieces, Op.2; Ricercar & Doubles; Magnum Mysterium; 7 In Nomines

MAX DEACON
Deja vu

GEORGE DREYFUS
From Within Looking Out; The Seasons; Wind Quintet

GRAHAME DUDLEY
Two Pieces for Pianoforte

DARYL EDWARD
Trio

ROSS EDWARDS
Sextet; Wind Quintet

HELEN GIFFORD
Lyric; String Quartet; Red Autumn in Valvins

GRAHAM HAIR
5 Lyrics of Salvatore Quasimodo

HANS WERNER HENZE
Piano Sonata; Being Beauteous

PAUL HINDEMITH
Wind Quintet

[illegible]ITH HUMBLE
Piano Sonata

WLADIMIER KONTONSKI
Trio

BARRY McKIMM
One or Two Thunders

BRUNO MADERNA
2 Dimensions

RICHARD MEALE
Las Alboradas

OLIVIER MESSIAEN
20 Regards; Poemes Pour Mi

GEORGE MICHELL
Directions; Quintet; Interlude

LUIGI NONO
Polifonica; Monodia; Ritmica

J.V. PETERS
Wind Quintet

GOFFREDO PETRASSI
Sapho Poems

ARIBERT REIMANN
Ricercare y canzones

ROGER REYNOLDS
Mosaics

ROBERT ROONEY
End of October

PETER SCHONBACH
CanticumPsalmi Resurrectionis

ARNOLD SCHONBERG
Phantasie for Violin & Piano, Op. 47; Piano Pieces, Op. 33

GUNTHER SCHULLER
Quintet

PETER SCULTHORPE
Sonata for Viola and Percussion

KARLHEINZ STOCKHAUSEN
Zeitmasse; Kreuzspiel; Refrain

MARGARET SUTHERLAND
Oboe Trio

GEORGE TIBBITS
Zia; Quintet; 'silop; Sextet; Qashq

ANTON WEBERN
4 Pieces for Violin & Piano; 5 Canons, Op. 16; Op.2

FELIX WERDER
Piano Trio, Op. 56; Sonata for Wind Quintet (1965)

Figure 7.1. List of works performed at ISCM concerts, 1965-1967

THE JAZZ CONTEXT

From the mid-1950s various factors, including the advent of television, rock 'n' roll and the LP recording contributed to declining public interest in the live performance of modern jazz in Australia. Towards the end of the 1950s, however, there was a small modern jazz revival in Melbourne, most notably through the efforts of a younger generation of musicians surrounding the saxophonist Brian Brown at their principal venue, Jazz Centre 44. Brown and his associates were particularly influenced by the ecstatically aggressive 'hard bop' style of jazz associated primarily with black musicians such as the saxophonist Sonny Rollins.[12] The local adoption of hard bop was partly a counter-reaction to the slick, congruous (cool) sound which typified mainstream modern jazz in Melbourne at the time.

Important new influences such as 'free jazz', modal jazz and so-called Eastern music began filtering through to Melbourne jazz musicians in the early 1960s. By the mid-1960s these included experimental art music concepts, including the extended use of electronic sound. A 1967 ISCM performance at the Garden of Eden Jazz Lounge, for example (including the saxophonist Barry Duggan as leader and Dunstan), featured:

> a well modulated parade of natural and concrete sound . . . united with purely electronic noises to provide a sensory cavalcade at once ordered as all art must be and as natural as the noises one overhears while walking down the street . . . After some minutes the activity was changed and a great assortment of sound producing implements was handed to members of the audience and they, the band playing free-style and unscheduled and the electronic equipment, provided a wildly amusing and thoroughly engrossing interlude of genuine unplanned indeterminism . . . an arrangement of sound which John Cage himself might have enjoyed.[13]

Free Jazz

Free jazz is a generic term used to cover a spectrum of styles which abandoned functional harmony and the closed structure of bebop for means of articulation and cohesion that increasingly resembled those found in improvisatory art music (e.g. textural, timbral, motivic). Recordings by the African-American free jazz pioneer, Ornette Coleman, began to arrive in Melbourne around 1960 and soon became objects of interest, puzzlement or scorn to the different factions of the jazz community. In 1960 Clayton was apparently 'shouted down by unimaginative traditional modernists' at Jazz Centre 44 for playing the saxophone in an ecstatic stream-of-consciousness style.[14] Nevertheless, such early isolated local forays into free jazz improvisation represent the first explicit deviation from an otherwise relatively linear Melbourne modern jazz tradition.

One concept of free jazz that gained a small degree of acceptance among Melbourne musicians was derived from the 'early Coleman style'. Local inspiration for playing in this style also came from an ensemble style associated with the white American jazz performer and arranger, Gerry Mulligan. In this piano-less jazz ensemble style, a string bass and drum can provide the strong underlying rhythm section pulse of jazz, while the single line instruments (trumpet and saxophone) have wide latitude to construct imaginative melodic lines and establish contrapuntal relationships. This freedom requires remarkable stamina and powers of melodic invention.

Many Melbourne jazz musicians individually explored this concept of free jazz, albeit only briefly in most cases and they can be placed in several categories. Progressive professionals such as drummers Graham Morgan and Alan Turnbull played this music as part of the challenge of being at the top of their profession.[15] Others, such as the saxophonist Heinz Mendelson and trombonist Peter De Vissor, were interested in the juxtaposition of free improvisation against a framework of tightly arranged jazz.[16] There were also musicians such as bass player Brian Fraser who joined De Vissor and Mendelson out of mild curiosity, but with no idea how or what to contribute to the music.[17] Resolute devotees of the hard-bop style such as Duggan were undoubtedly drawn to the free jazz style by the ecstatically intense improvisations of black performers such as Coleman. However, there were others such as Clayton, McKimm and the bass player David Tolley who were clearly attracted to both the ecstatic intensity and the transgressive nature of the music.[18]

Modal Jazz

By the early 1960s Brown, McKimm and others had also begun to explore the so-called modal jazz system, often on the basis of George Russell's *The Lydian Concept of Tonal Organization for Improvisation.*[19] This style was demonstrated in the seminal 1959 American jazz recording, 'So What', which was publicised in the 1960 ABC television program, 'The Sound of Miles Davis'. Since each mode can be taken to have its own 'centre of gravity', structure and syntax (as in the ecclesiastical use of modes), the modal jazz performer is potentially liberated from the tonal hierarchy (and sound) of the major/minor key system and its harmonic syntax. This approach was in fact most commonly applied over conventional chord patterns as a 'freer' (and easier) approach to improvisatory melodic construction.[20] However, it was also used by local musicians as the basis or take-off point for more exploratory improvisation. Brian Brown, for example, used the term modal jazz synonymously with free jazz in relation to the music of his mid-1960s group.[21]

'Eastern' influences

The best known Australian synthesis of jazz and eclectic 'Eastern' influences can be found in Charlie Monro's album *Eastern Horizons* (Sydney, 1967).[22] The same year, at the previously cited Melbourne ISCM concert, Duggan played 'a reflective mood-piece based on an Indian Raga' backed by gongs and temple bells in a set which finished with Coleman's 'Forerunner' and Parker's 'Ornithology'.[23] However, the influence of 'Eastern' music had reached Melbourne much earlier than this. In 'Old Calcutta Rag' and 'Kama Sutra Feeling', recorded by a jazz ensemble (flute, tenor sax, guitar, bass and drums) led by Bruce Clarke in 1963, the invention of raga-like melodic lines takes place over additive rhythms (e.g. 3+3+3+2 = 11/12 time) unrestricted by the usual fixed framework of vertical jazz harmonies.[24] Setting aside the tongue-in-cheek titles, the effort to evoke a non-Western sound is unmistakable.

Broader Influences on Improvisatory Music

The 1960s

All the events I have described took place against the backdrop of increasing social, political and artistic upheaval that characterised the 1960s. By the early 1960s a groundswell of youthful rebellion against the restrictive aesthetics, morals, education, politics, philosophies and prejudices of the 1950s in Australia had already become discernible. Around the mid-1960s this social ferment rapidly intensified, particularly as a result of the debate over conscription to the Vietnam War and increasingly alarming headlines such as 'Diggers Fight Back 600 Viet Cong Toll'.[25] Although the emerging counterculture was most widely reflected at the level of youth fashion, hairstyles and the following of popular music trends such as the Beatles, it was also apparent in a broadening acceptance of unfamiliar, abstract and even 'alien' concepts. For example, improvisatory experimental music – that of McKimm and his associates – was given a relatively high profile as 'teenage music' during 1963–4 and was even chosen as soundtrack music for the 1964 ABC television production, *Dark Song*. This increasing acceptance of new concepts also became manifest in experimental literature, art, theatre and finally experimental rock.

Experimental Literature

Barry Humphries' early 1950s Dada group activities represent an isolated case of combined literary and musical experimentation. The changing cultural climate of the 1960s, however, made such associations much more possible. In discussing the 'Spon literature' which Robert Rooney began to produce shortly before the 1960s, Rosemary Adam writes:

> Most of us were avid Goon fans who would impersonate the main characters and re-enact scenes from the shows; this triggered off more spontaneous clowning and led to the evolution of a curious style of spoken and written language which crept into the Spon literature. Spon took from the Goons a dada sense of the absurd and iconoclastic, together with a spontaneity akin to Surrealist automatism, or the free association of words, images and thoughts. The innovative writing style of Gertrude Stein and Jack Kerouac's spontaneous prose and poetry also played an important role in the formation of Spon, as did jazz and rock 'n' roll.[26]

In 1960 Adrian Rawlins, who was similarly influenced by 'beat' poets such as Jack Kerouac, began to present at Jazz Centre 44 some of the first Australian experiments with poetry and jazz. A *Music Maker* article published around this time describes two approaches to this genre: either the poet read while the musicians improvised freely around the spoken text; or the musicians played while the poet responded spontaneously to the music.[27] The presence, and particularly the improvisatory presentation, of experimental literature tended to encourage a similarly 'free' approach to musical improvisation. Furthermore, it pointed in the direction of new forms of improvisatory sound gesture that challenged the traditional notion of an autonomous musical language.

Experimental Theatre

Angela Hillel notes in 'Against the Stream: Melbourne New Theatre 1936-1986', that in the 1960s:

> Street theatre, 'happenings' and improvisation were catch-words in a decade of experimentation. In Australia a response came to these overseas trends with the development of new funded theatres, and a host of 'experimental' groups, often developing within the universities and, in Melbourne, around Carlton.[28]

From 1935 until the early 1960s the most confrontational theatre productions in Melbourne were, not unexpectedly, those produced by the radical left-wing and strongly nationalistic New Theatre company. After the New Theatre movement began to lose its political momentum in the early 1960s, Emerald Hill Theatre became an important focus for alternative theatre until the opening, in 1967, of La Mama (modelled on New York's experimental space, Cafe La Mama). La Mama, a converted shirt factory holding no more than sixty people, was the turning point for experimental theatre in Melbourne. In addition to providing a context for improvisatory music-theatre, it broke with older Australian theatre tradition by bringing together performers and audience in close proximity to participate in an ecstatic creative experience:

> In a sense the medium was the message; the way that the thing was done was as powerful as what was done. Away with the greasepaint, dictatorial directors, high admission prices and furs in the foyer. It was the whole middle-class syndrome that was being rejected.[29]

Visual Arts

The major changes which took place in the visual arts during the 1960s were, as with experimental literature and theatre, largely precipitated by American innovations. By the 1960s local artists were influenced by American abstract expressionism or 'action painting', which in turn drew on notions of spontaneous creativity inherent in surrealism and the more recent influence of Eastern philosophies (such as Zen) and Japanese and Chinese art, especially gestural painting. The artist and jazz musician Ken White, for example, described how he began to look more directly to the 'East' for inspiration in the 1960s. Peter Upward, whose influences were Buddhism, beat poetry, jazz improvisation and calligraphy, had given two exhibitions of gestural abstraction before he left for Sydney in 1960.[30] The main momentum for experimental art, however, came around the mid-1960s through the influence of American pop art, and hard edge art, a school which was largely a reaction against abstract expressionism. The Field exhibition, held in Melbourne in 1968, represented the new experimentalism of artists such as Robert Rooney and Dale Hickey. Patrick McCaughey observed at the time that the exhibition aligned Australia not only with current American and international trends but, more importantly, with some of the tenets of modernism. In describing the paradigm shift demonstrated by the exhibition, he commented:

> Each work becomes an experiment, an attempt to solve a particular sculptural or pictorial problem. This problem solving attitude has caused the widest dismay and the deepest misunderstanding in response to the Field. The shift from the referential qualities of a work to its conceptual properties comes particularly hard in Australia . . . [31]

Melbourne composers such as Helen Gifford and Humble commented on the lack of exchange between artists and contemporary composers which characterised the 1960s.[32] Melbourne figures such as Dunstan, White, Rooney and Tolley, however, did span both experimental music and experimental art and there was also a small but unified subculture of artists and art students who supported experimental music (particularly that of McKimm and his colleagues).

Experimental Pop: the 'New Music'

The years 1967–8 represent a pivotal point in Melbourne's – and indeed Australia's – cultural history: the beginning of what some describe as the early or 'hot period' of social, cultural and artistic experimentation.[33] 'Hot' refers not so much to the quantity or type of experimentation as to the particular intensity of the turbulence produced by the sudden yielding of the old order.

It was electric pop music, however, not experimental poetry, theatre, painting, jazz or art music, which finally swept past the forces of musical conservatism and opened the way to an anarchic orgy of eclectic style synthesis. Around 1967–8 the artistic 'revolution' was appropriated by the new 'progressive' or 'psychedelic' rock as the musical emblem of burgeoning youth counterculture. The most significant early manifestation of psychedelic rock to reach Australia was the Beatles' *Sergeant Pepper's Lonely Hearts Club Band* album, with its confronting collage or 'cut-up' of genres (including raga), textures, sound masses and single effects. A 1967 article in *Farrago* (the Melbourne University student newspaper), 'The New Music' by Terry Counihan, gives a brief background to the emergence of this album and genre and also its relationship to youth politics, drug taking, Marshall McLuhan's theories on media and mass culture and its American musical counterpart, Californian 'psychedelic rock'. Counihan also notes that the 'New Music' heralded a new era in popular music by introducing complex forms previously associated with art music.[34] One Australian response to the *Sergeant Pepper* album was the Twilights' 1968 album, *Once Upon a Twilight* (Columbia 05X7870).

The band Nutwood Rug, a musical representative of the San Francisco hippie movement and Californian psychedelic rock, arrived in Sydney soon afterwards. Their musical and socio-cultural message of 'do your own thing' was reinforced (at least in Sydney) by the formation of the psychedelic rock ensemble Tully and the staging of the rock musical *Hair*, in which Tully (augmented for the show) sometimes presented free-for-all improvisation in conjunction with dramatic light effects. An Australian jazz reviewer of the period, John Clare, tentatively compares Tully's free improvisations with a mix of King Crimson, Albert Ayler, Pharaoh Sanders and Pink Floyd.[35] Other Australian groups that were influenced substantially by psychedelic or progressive rock include James Taylor Move, Taman Shud, Sons of the Vegetal Mother and Spectrum. This avant-garde form of rock was an important factor in the introduction of the notion of extended, individualistic instrumental improvisation into Australian rock, something that was formerly the province of jazz.

Even by August 1967 the Twilights' guitarist, Terry Britten, had introduced raga-based rock improvisations to Melbourne audiences 'following the trend popularised by the Beatles that made Indian music – and its best known exponent, Ravi Shankar – icons of "progressive" pop music'.[36] This new avant-garde did not have to resist the aesthetics and orthodoxy of a long established music tradition, as in the case of musically adventurous Australian jazz musicians. Instead, they were more or less free to present any potpourri of Eastern mysticism, psychedelia, folk music, visual or

Figure 7.2. A cartoon by Terry Counihan from 'The New Music' (1967), which reflects the uncertainty surrounding the more extreme cultural changes that were taking place in Australia (Courtesy of Terry Counihan).

sound effects, art music, jazz or whatever, as an artistic gesture or simply as an invitation to 'freak out'.[37] Nevertheless, progressive rock bands were able to incorporate the improvisational talents of jazz musicians. Conversely, Bruce Clarke, Brian Brown, John Sangster (in Sydney) and other jazz musicians incorporated elements of rock into their own jazz.

Contemporary art music composers such as Humble and Peter Sculthorpe also produced work that featured rock elements. Sculthorpe, a colleague of Humble and Banks from the 'golden years' of the Melbourne Conservatorium, helped to further promote psychedelic rock in Melbourne through the 1970 performance of his work 'Love 200' which incorporated Tully. At the time he spoke of the expediency of using such a widely promoted rock group and the important role 'pop music' was currently playing in subverting nineteenth-century notions of music and its presentation.[38] Philip Brophy points to two possible interpretations of this:

> The first is to see the avant-garde of rock as a pitiful bastardisation of the original thrust of twentieth century avant-garde art, a cooption of the polemic intensity that motivated the radical nature of its ideas and pursuits. The second is to acknowledge its nature as mutation, as an artistic activity born of visions that arise more from a developed social environment than from a studied historical lineage.[39]

In *Sound Effects: Youth, Leisure, and the Politics of Rock 'n' Roll*, Simon Frith describes how rock musicians effortlessly gained the creative freedom that had been denied to generations of frustrated jazz/commercial musicians.[40] In a sense, this was a repetition of what had already happened many decades earlier through the importation of ragtime and jazz. Musically transgressive elements (such as improvisatory practice and novelty 'dissonance') had entered the mainstream of musical practice as new popular culture, thereby outstripping or overshadowing progressive developments in art music (at least in Australia). The musical 'breaking out' of the late 1960s was also, to a large extent, a mutation born of a broader social development. One can imagine that around 1970 individuals, such as Humble and McKimm, who had been involved in improvisatory musical experimentation before the universal invitation to 'do your own thing', may have felt that the 'polemic intensity' which had motivated their own improvisatory experimentation had somehow been 'coopted' and would never be as valid again.

Experimentalists

Bruce Clarke and Frank Smith

Bruce Clarke and many of his talented jazz associates can be heard on Clarke's compilation of 1960s recording sessions on the album, *Looking Back*. Of Clarke's associates, those generally cited as specifically associated with experimentation are the expatriate American Dick Healey (reeds, bass) and Frank Smith, who was widely recognised as the most talented jazz saxophonist in Melbourne at this time and noted for the originality of his sound and general approach to improvisation.

By the early 1960s Clarke, Healey and Smith were engaged in providing, among other things, commercial musical backings for the television industry. Clarke was also providing studio work for many of the jazz musicians he admired, including many of the 'pre-Brown' generation of modernists or boppers. The experience and remuneration yielded by this utilitarian form of musical experimentation enabled Clarke to establish his highly successful Jingle Workshop. More importantly, it enabled him and his colleagues to indulge collectively in some private experimentation with avant-garde improvisational concepts, such as those heard on *Looking Back*.

Besides the continuous refinement of his jazz musicianship and teaching methods, Clarke's career has comprised an ongoing, individualistic search for musical possibilities and solutions to musical problems. His 1960s experimental activities extended far beyond those already mentioned in passing and include his 1968 direction of a controversial music-theatre production, David Reck's 'Blues and Screamer', which 'stimulated local creative artists to develop their approach to theatre music'.[41] He also produced two 'Electronic Rock Spectacular' concerts featuring Tully and his own Moog synthesiser which, 'prompted by his jazz background he quickly learned to use as an improvising instrument'.[42] In the late 1960s he became a recognised avant-garde composer, president of the Melbourne branch of the ISCM and an acknowledged local expert on electronic music technology. He also initiated and directed orchestral performances of improvisatory works, such as Stockhausen's 'Plus and Minus'.

What distinguishes Clarke's experimentalism in particular is its orientation towards practical, commercial applications and problem-solving experimentation. His scepticism towards the notion of 'art for art's sake' is undoubtedly based on the egalitarian, though pragmatic, philosophy which has always been central to the strongly union-based culture of the fully professional Melbourne dance/jazz musician, the tradition from which Clarke emerged. In 1956, for example, he taught himself to apply Joseph Schillinger's 'automatic principals of composition' to commercial composition, arranging and jazz improvisation.[43] Similarly, most of his later experimentation with acoustically and electrically produced sound found applications in commercial recording, jingles and teaching enterprises. In a paper presented to a 1971 Melbourne seminar on electronic music, Clarke unequivocally stated that musical experimentalists could only successfully overcome the stifling Australian artistic climate by promoting and presenting their work as a 'saleable commodity'.[44]

Musical Ex. 7.1 From a transcription of Frank Smith's solo in 'I've Just Seen Her'. GTV9 Studio Band, Melbourne c 1967, (see Discography). Transcribed by Ralph Whiteoak.

This ethos manifests itself audibly in some of Clarke's music. On recordings such as 'Scratch Sheet' (1965) or 'Colour Me Jazz' (1967) there is a slick overall congruity which almost parodies the moments of less inhibited playing. Yet in the earlier 'Kama Sutra Feeling' and 'Old Calcutta Rag' recordings (1963) – in which Clarke, Smith, Healey and Billy Hyde (drums) make gestures towards an 'alien' form of non-jazz music – they seem to have been conceptually freed to transgress the jazz idiom and its inevitable repetition of patterning. The sparse texture woven around Smith's solo in 'Kama Sutra Feeling', in which Clarke interpolates unorthodox scratching sounds, and the free-floating collective improvisation in the last section of 'Old Calcutta Rag' are among the most progressive examples of improvisatory music recorded in Melbourne to that date.

Frank Smith had adopted Hindemith's hierarchical system, which organises all possible intervals within the chromatic scale, and developed it for use in his own jazz improvisation – something which many of his colleagues frowned upon as too unorthodox. Clarke and others also speak of Smith as being remarkably experimental in his approach to the use of sound in a much broader sense. The pianist, Bob Sedergreen recalls:

> [Smith] presented me with a challenge at the time when I was representing the American model; he'd make me do things like, 'Play an Aborigine jumping out from behind a bush', and he could do that because he played from inside himself.[45]

Ken White, who worked with Smith on film animation in the mid-1960s, has described some of Smith's inventive solutions to various sound production problems. He mentioned, for example, that Smith 'took delight' in using conventional and invented acoustic instruments to create the type of sound structures normally associated with electronic music technology. These acoustically produced sounds were recorded onto magnetic tape which hung in long strips around his workshop labelled by pitch (C, C#, D, D#, etc) awaiting use as raw sound material for musical 'backing' to advertisements.[46] Many hours of Smith's improvisatory experiments with unorthodox sounds and invented instruments survive on privately-held studio tapes.

Brian Brown

Following his hard bop activities at Jazz Centre 44 in the late 1950s, Brian Brown became widely recognised as central to 'innovative jazz' in Melbourne. His persistent belief in the importance, above all, of seeking one's personal voice influenced his approach to jazz education in a way that has provided many of his students at the Victorian College of the Arts with an opportunity to explore and evolve personal forms of improvisatory musical gesture.[47]

Although Brown vigorously rejects the label 'nationalist musician', in the late 1950s he became concerned by the extent of American hegemony of Australian jazz development. This concern led him to develop in the early 1960s an unorthodox control process for improvisation based around the parameter of 'musical tension', a concept which has continued to shape his music up to the present day.

Through his association with hard bop, Brown became interested in the peaks of musical and ecstatic intensity (e.g. dynamics, textural density and activity) which occurred at certain points during his band's performance of this relatively aggressive and rhythmically complex style of jazz. He also noted that these 'peaks' could produce momentary loops of intense ecstatic response between ensemble and audience – momentary 'real life' or 'theatre of life' experiences – and he began to draw up graphs representing a profile of rising and falling tension. By the time his mid-1960s band (with Tony Gould (piano), Barry Buckley (bass) and Ted Vining (drums)) had been formed, he had evolved a system whereby this 'drama profile' represented not only the main referential point for moment-to-moment improvisatory interaction but also the formal design of the improvised work as a whole (Musical Ex. 7.2). In practice, this relatively open-ended form of improvisation (mostly utilising the modal jazz system) became a series of performer-controlled dramatic episodes, each shaped by the ensemble's effort to produce a peak of intense musical tension or 'drama'. At a higher level, the performers were concerned with the overall design or 'architecture' of the entire work being generated through collective improvisatory interaction. The importance of the holistic or Gestalt perspective of improvised performance undoubtedly related to Brown's interest and professional training in architecture.[48]

Throughout the late 1960s Brown continued to seek original ways of shaping improvised music. These include what he claims to have been the first use of electric bass and electronic sound effects (provided by Stephen Dunstan) in Melbourne jazz, graphic scoring and a type of psychodrama technique in which 'story telling' of evocative text was used to initiate and intensify the 'drama' aspect of the band's improvisations. He also experimented with an alternative form of 'big band' in which the brass

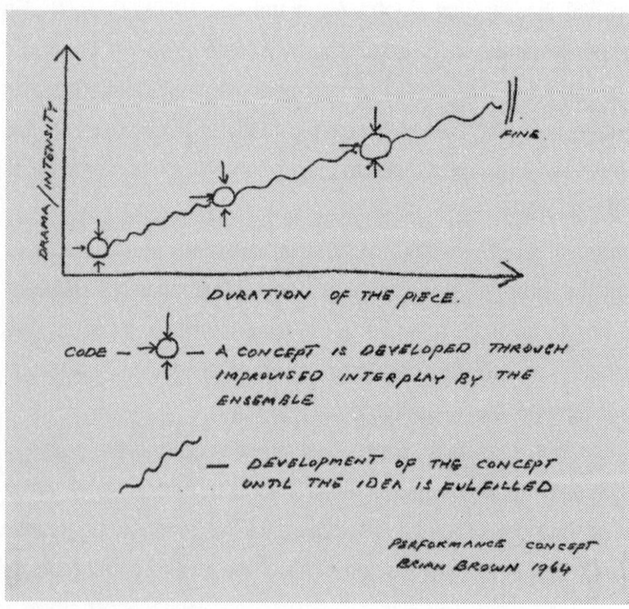

Musical Ex. 7.2. Diagram of Brian Brown's musical 'drama'/intensity concept.

and rhythm section was augmented to provide sophisticated backing for the much more open-ended playing of his own quartet. Between 1968 and 1970 he was involved in jazz/rock synthesis with a group which sometimes included the vocalist Linda George and the guitarist Billy Green, musicians already experienced in this crossover genre. There were several local jazz/rock fusion groups which Brown admired:

> I liked that power, and saw how it could be a huge pad for some of the things I wanted to do. I was also very interested in the textures and colours of electric sound.[49]

This notion of jazz/rock power underlines an important difference between the 1960s experiments of Brown and those of McKimm, Rooney and Clayton. Brown was always concerned with the basic element of most African-American derived genres: the notion of a driving pulse as a solid lineal 'pad' or foundation over which improvisatory interplay took place. McKimm, Rooney and Clayton, on the other hand, sometimes actively sought to negate this sense of propulsion. Brown later extended this passacaglia-like unifying principle into a system of what he described as 'time capsules'. These are durationally open-ended units of multi-metric ostinato played by the rhythm section which provide both a drone pitch reference for the improvising soloist and a complex rhythmic loop, which the soloist is free to engage with or play against.[50]

Brown's most active period of experimentation was undoubtedly in the 1970s during the time of his creative collaboration with David Tolley and the percussionist Dure Dara. It is significant, however, that some of his most important concepts to do with the shaping of improvisation and 'improvisation as communication' evolved in parallel with other important events of the 1960s described below.

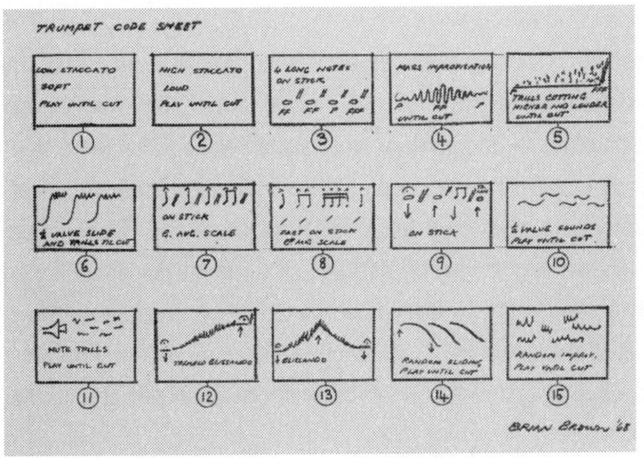

Musical Ex. 7.3 A code sheet developed by Brown for his band in the late 1960s.

McKimm, Rooney and Clayton

> SPON is spon taneous re spon sible re spon dence res pon spon dentia re spon sless re spon der re spon er spon sions re spon sive re spon sory spon ger spon dee spon dulicks spon dyl spon y louse spon diac spon ger spon goid spon o is spon sal spon salia spon toon spon sing spon dilitus as gertrude stein says: spon is spon is spon.
>
> Robert Rooney, 'Spondee Review', 1961[51]

The improvised music of the McKimm, Rooney and Clayton Trio was partly the result of serendipity: the fortuitous coming together of three contrasting artistic personalities, each with a strongly individual approach to improvising, the use of controlling processes and the scoring of these processes. Rooney had a formal background in graphic design and this manifested itself in a particularly visually-oriented approach to music. His interest in the symmetrical formation of the black and white keyboard, for example, is reflected in the symmetry of some of his musical themes, compositions and improvisations. His approach was very cerebral, emphasising structure at all levels, whereas McKimm's creativity in scoring and improvising tended to be intuitive, the result of his immediate reaction to the musical problem at hand. Unlike Rooney, McKimm expressed his creativity through 'lyrical melodic line' and was far more absorbed by the African-American jazz aesthetic (or what he describes as the 'emotion' or the 'passion' in this music).[52] Clayton's creative tendency was intuitively to move away from what he considered to be conventional.

To some degree, the music of Rooney, McKimm and Clayton was a reaction to the relatively bland and conservative Melbourne jazz environment of the late 1950s and early 1960s. By the 1960s modern jazz had become a long established cultural tradition with its own social milieu, modes of speech and dress and orthodox performance practice. McKimm, Rooney and Clayton all objected to and reacted against this notion of a rigid jazz performance orthodoxy.

The visual arts, theatre and to a lesser extent literature were a significant part of the artistic and social context from which the improvised music of McKimm, Rooney and Clayton emerged. Non-western cultural traditions were also influential. Rooney's Neo-Dadaist writing has already been mentioned and all three musicians cited stream-of-consciousness 'beat' poetry as a significant influence.[53] McKimm and Clayton were closely associated with theatre and to varying degrees all three musicians identified with the visual arts and its community. In fact there is a definite correlation between the way McKimm, Rooney and Clayton each approached visual art and improvisatory performance. Their respective approaches can be loosely characterised as intuitive, cerebral and aleatoric.

Barry McKimm and the McKimm/Mendelson Quartet

In 1963 McKimm was co-leader of the McKimm/[Heinz] Mendelson Quartet (MMQ), a free jazz group and Melbourne's first specialist experimental jazz ensemble. It is probably a measure of the expanding openness to new concepts during this period that they received excellent publicity in the mainstream press and were able to pack their venue, The Fat Black Pussy Cat, nightly with 'arty-type' young people.[54] The ensemble (tenor sax, trumpet, string bass and drums) was based upon the so-called free jazz model, which allowed for relatively unrestricted development of horizontal lines and contrapuntal relationships. What distinguishes the MMQ from other Melbourne ensembles of the period was the emphasis upon experimentation for its own sake over the need to sound like Coleman or other American free jazz exponents. Ken White, who keenly observed (and sketched) this group, mentions for example the quirky gesture towards pop art in the piece 'Neddy Nod'. The theme is a musical imitation of the peculiar jerking movement made by a strange little plastic toy, Neddy Nod, which came free in a popular local brand of breakfast cereal.

The music played by the McKimm/Mendelson Quartet was based upon a variety of systems, but the most common basis for the development of a new piece was a short, original written theme – typically a melody line without chord indications. This theme was developed spontaneously and the overall structure of the piece (order of solos, contrapuntal sections and other special features) would gradually become defined in the minds of the ensemble members through repeated improvisations. In this way they soon built up a large repertoire of pieces which their fans could recognise and request by name. The idea that intuitive group response to a simple theme could eventually, through repeated improvisations, bring random elements together to form a complex, living musical structure was an important discovery for McKimm – one which would strongly influence his subsequent approach to improvisation. It was also an important step in the direction of non-jazz indeterminacy. Two studio recording tracks by this band survive (see Discography), but they convey little of the excitingly exploratory unfolding of their music as described by those who heard them at the Fat Black Pussy Cat.[55]

Among the followers who regularly visited the Fat Black Pussy Cat during 1963 was the young jazz pianist and visual artist, Robert Rooney. Shortly before McKimm left the 'Cat', Rooney began to improvise informally with McKimm and Clayton and these three musicians were to become the creative core of various rehearsal and working line-ups during late 1963 and 1964.

Robert Rooney

Rooney had been experimenting with the notion of combining jazz with elements of contemporary music since the late 1950s, albeit in a fairly basic or naive way. Early explorations included the use of tone rows and fragments from Bartok's 'Microcosmos' as vehicles for jazz improvisation. He also used what he calls 'synthetic chords': chords constructed from the melodic intervals of the theme itself (a device also employed by Bartok).[56] Some important influences on his jazz piano playing were the angular, sparse and highly structured improvisations of the African-American pianist Thelonious Monk, the extended melodic lines of Lennie Tristano and later the forceful, percussive, 'almost jerky' piano style of another African-American, Cecil Taylor. Rooney was only convinced of the validity of his own attempts to synthesise a mix of contemporary music and jazz after hearing Taylor's explicit references to contemporary art music idioms on the album *Looking Forward*.[57]

Syd Clayton

By late 1963 Syd Clayton's jazz experience included both traditional and modern jazz on drums, saxophone and finally string bass. However, an extremely unorthodox musical background and belated formal training had left him with some severe technical shortcomings, particularly in timekeeping and jazz harmony. These shortcomings, coupled with his idiosyncratic personality, eventually led him to develop a very individual style of improvisation. He compiled a chart which catalogued every sound that he could produce on the bass; and this collection of sounds became, in effect, a personal timbral language replacing, to some extent, the conventional tonal language which was somewhat problematic for him. McKimm comments:

> It was Syd's nature to avoid conventionality, it just drove him mad. He couldn't stand doing things that were clichés. He actually experimented with various techniques and developed all sorts of unusual ways of playing the bass [which were] very much suited to free improvisation.[58]

The 1963–4 Barry McKimm Quintet

The 1963–4 quintet which formed around McKimm, Rooney and Clayton generally included Peter Webster (reeds) and Barry Quinn (drums). Available recordings feature extended improvisations which explore countless varieties of textures. Ensemble and solo playing characteristic of modern jazz of the period are combined or juxtaposed abruptly with melodic lines, rhythms and textures which relate directly to contemporary art music. The listener soon notices certain recurrent musical elements that are idiomatic of each performer or the group as a whole. One characteristic that often infuriated colleagues was Rooney and Clayton's tendency deliberately to avoid the propulsive, accented, 'swing feel' characteristic of jazz in favour of what Rooney describes as a 'pushing and pulling' at the regular accent. This was intended to create what he calls a 'timeless' or 'floating' effect – a concept which he partially attributes to the influence of Japanese visual art.[59] The improvisation heard on these recordings is sometimes based on tone-rows, unsupported single line themes or two part symmetrical structures (Musical Ex. 7.4a-b). The influence of Rooney's earlier experimentation with Bartok fragments is apparent in the symmetry of pieces such as Musical Example 7.4b. In one example collective improvisation develops spontaneously from a single stack of intervals presented by the piano.[60] Musical references to George Russell's modal theory and relatively conventional modern jazz harmony are sometimes present.

By early 1964 this new group was gaining recognition on the Melbourne jazz scene and on 13 July the Quintet was broadcast nationally on the ABC's Jazz Club program. Many regular listeners were probably unable to believe their ears when they heard the strange strands of sound that incrementally overpowered the voice of the commentator

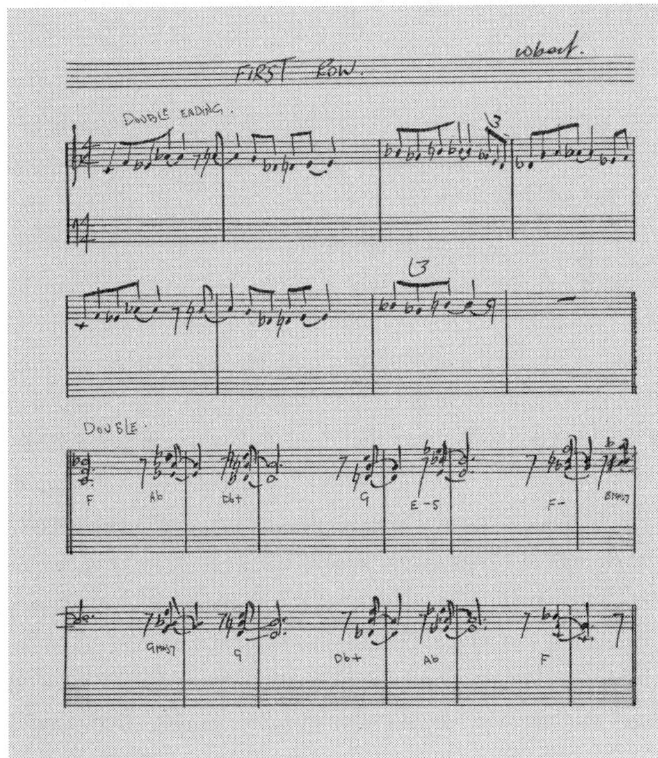

Musical Ex. 7.4a. Theme for 'First Row' (piano part) by Robert Rooney (a twelve-tone row: prime form-retrograde-prime and harmonisation are all derived from the row).

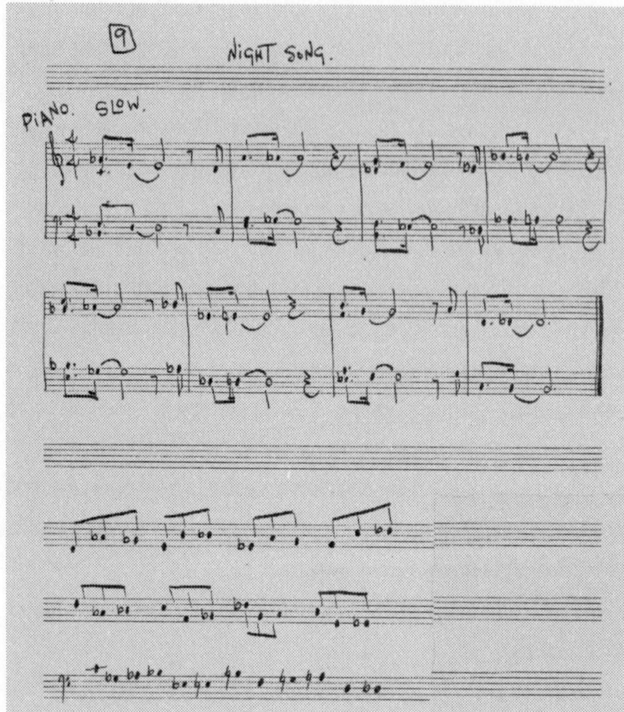

Musical Ex. 7.4b. Theme for 'Night Song' (piano part) by Robert Rooney. Note the sparse symmetrical structure and the level of dissonance.

introducing the Quintet. Some may have thought they had tuned into a science fiction drama by mistake. The rest of the program was for the most part less confronting and the broadcast received several good reviews.

Ironically for McKimm, Rooney and Clayton, this event marked what was almost the end of their serious interest in jazz playing. Although they had a strong following, particularly among young art students, they were never really accepted by the core of the local jazz-playing community. This was principally because their approach was too progressive or unorthodox, but there were also other reasons. They were prepared to take musical risks in live performances – risks that did not always work out. Furthermore, on occasions they deliberately subverted what they perceived as jazz dogma. McKimm mentioned, for example, that when he sat in with other groups he sometimes found himself introducing radically contrasting musical ideas just to express his impatience with the timid conservatism of the other performers.[61] While McKimm, Rooney and Clayton would all reject the label neo-dadaist, this influence, which had earlier been particularly important for Rooney, seems occasionally to have become manifest at public performances. Their bohemian social environment, comprising aficionados of the avant-garde visual arts, theatre and literature, also tended to make them outsiders in the Melbourne jazz community.

Even from their own standpoint the concept of the quintet had not been entirely successful. Improvisation with five instruments often resulted in textures which lacked the space necessary for individual expression or spontaneous, skilfully-shaped changes of musical direction. After McKimm recovered from a serious illness late in 1964, the group functioned principally as the McKimm, Rooney and Clayton Trio.

The McKimm, Rooney and Clayton Trio

In 1965 the three musicians became involved in the newly formed Melbourne branch of the ISCM. However they had already begun to formulate their approaches to improvised art music before this. Rooney had independently developed an interest in contemporary music (e.g. Satie, Stravinsky, Berg, Schoenberg) during the 1950s via recordings and radio broadcasts. In the early 1960s he discovered the music of John Cage, Morton Feldman, Earle Brown and other exponents of indeterminacy (controlled improvisation) and aleatoric (chance-based) music; and subsequently interested McKimm and Clayton in this music. By late 1964 he had written his first graphic score, 'Synops', which anticipates his later approach to scoring for improvising musicians: scoring that allowed for freedom of interpretation within tightly structured systems (see Musical Ex. 7.5).

Figure 7.3. The McKimm, Rooney and Clayton Trio, c.1965. Photo by Bill Sykes.

The Trio performed McKimm's first indeterminate work, 'One or Two Thunders', at the ISCM's July 1965 concert (see Musical Ex. 7.6a-b). This performance still featured very explicit jazz elements and the incongruous mix of jazz and contemporary music received considerable criticism from

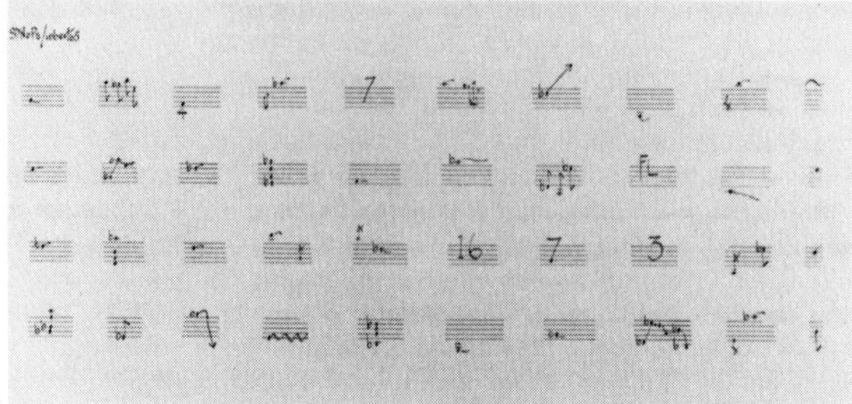

Musical Ex. 7.5. Graphic score for 'Synops', Robert Rooney, 1964 (1965 redraft).

Musical Ex. 7.6a (below). Graphic score for 'One or Two Thunders' (piano part), Barry McKimm, 1965.

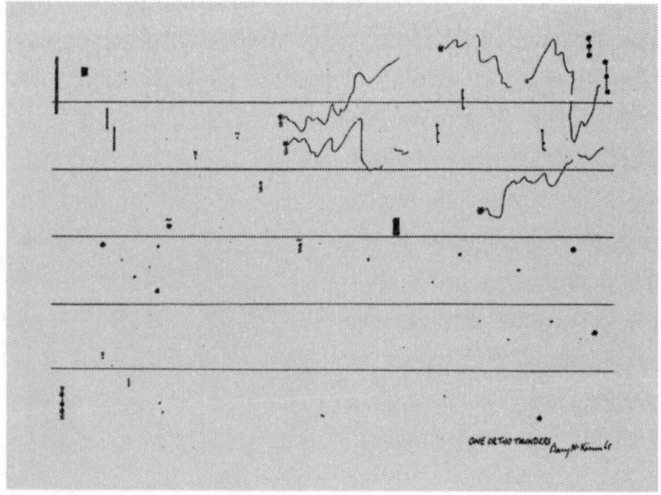

some prominent members of the new music movement. This initial discouragement was partly why the Trio remained on the periphery of the community that considered itself the champion of new music in Melbourne.

Duo 1 2 3

Robert Rooney's 'Duo 1 2 3' was recorded for the ABC Jazz Club in August 1965 but was apparently rejected before going to air as too progressive for the program. The score for this work was based upon a system of 'exits and entries'. The work itself is divided into three sections or 'Duos', each one scored on a separate page (Musical

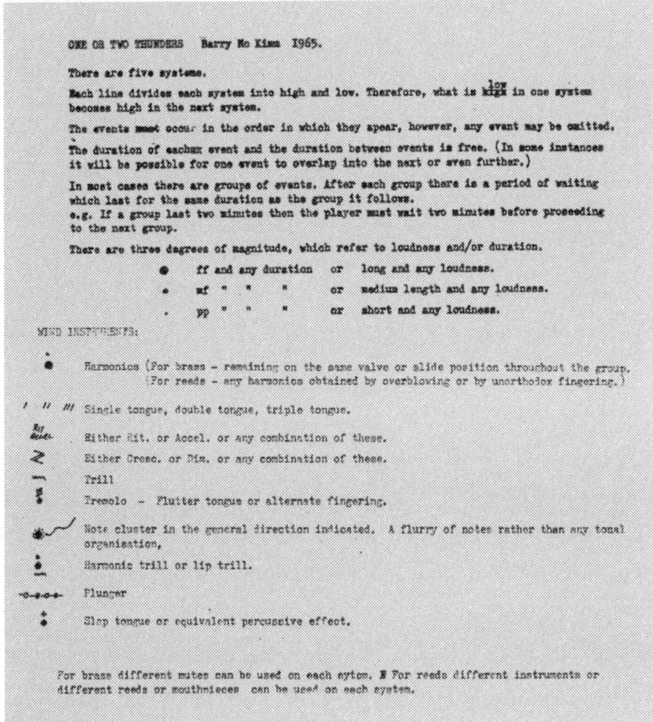

ONE OR TWO THUNDERS Barry Mc Kimm 1965.

There are five systems.

Each line divides each system into high and low. Therefore, what is low in one system becomes high in the next system.

The events must occur in the order in which they apear, however, any event may be omitted.

The duration of each event and the duration between events is free. (In some instances it will be possible for one event to overlap into the next or even further.)

In most cases there are groups of events. After each group there is a period of waiting which last for the same duration as the group it follows.
e.g. If a group last two minutes then the player must wait two minites before proseeding to the next group.

There are three degrees of magnitude, which refer to loudness and/or duration.

●	ff and any duration	or	long and any loudness.
•	mf " " "	or	medium length and any loudness.
.	pp " " "	or	short and any loudness.

WIND INSTRUMENTS:

Harmonics (For brass – remaining on the same valve or slide position throughout the group.
(For reeds – any harmonics obtained by overblowing or by unorthodox fingering.)

/ // /// Single tongue, double tongue, triple tongue.

Either Rit. or Accel. or any combination of these.

Either Cresc. or Dim. or any combination of these.

Trill

Tremolo – Flutter tongue or alternate fingering.

Note cluster in the general direction indicated. A flurry of notes rather than any tonal organisation,

Harmonic trill or lip trill.

Plunger

Slap tongue or equivalent percussive effect.

For brass different mutes can be used on each sytem. For reeds different instruments or different reeds or mouthpieces can be used on each system.

Musical Ex. 7.6b.. Key to symbols in 'One or Two Thunders'.

Ex. 7.7a-b). It begins with two performers interpreting the first 'Duo' score, while a third improvises, not to the score but to the musical material evolving from its interpretation by the other two players. The second and third 'Duos' are read the same way except that there is a rotation of players: in each 'Duo' a different performer takes the role of 'feeding' off the reading players' interpretation of the score.

The recording of 'Duo 1 2 3' provides a good example of how the contrasting creative approaches of McKimm, Rooney and Clayton could combine in a complementary way.[62] In the 'Duo 3' section, Rooney's sparse angular piano style is in clear contrast to McKimm's barely contained compulsion to create lyrical lines. Over this, Clayton's excitingly intense and imaginative responses to the other performers' interpretation of the score can be heard – responses that, from a purely diatonic viewpoint, often seem based on a quite arbitrary choice of notes. Idiomatic jazz rhythm and harmony are absent. The piece is shaped and unified by a language which owes its internal logic to both the reworking of elements on the score and more importantly hundreds of hours of intuitive musical interaction. Wide contrasts in pitch space,

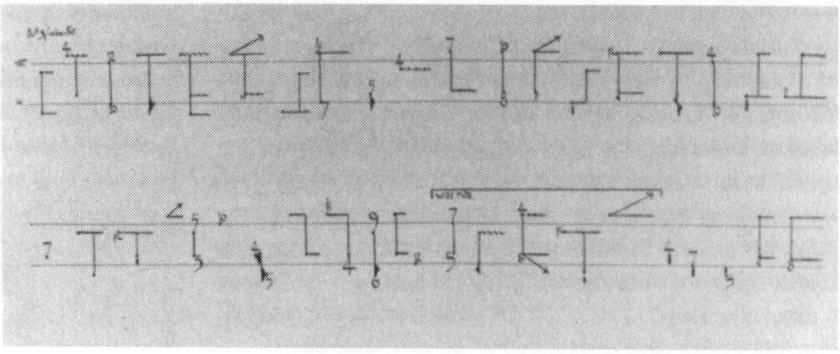

Musical Ex. 7.7a. Graphic score for 'Duo 3' from 'Duo 1 2 3' by Robert Rooney, 1965.

dynamics, timbral variety, textural activity and density are the main elements in this language. Coherence is also achieved through the chain of 'call and response' type interaction which runs throughout the performance of each 'Duo' and the recurrence of distinctive personal devices. While there is repetition of patterning, the patterns are mostly those synthesised by the Trio.

In performance, each of the 'Duos' (notably Duos 2 and 3) is heard as a sequence of short, mostly detached episodes, with the close of each 'Duo' articulated by what can be described as a 'dramatic final episode' of maximum textural complexity and density. 'Duo 1 2 3' is played in the sparse angular language of contemporary art music, but using a hot or abandoned style characteristic not of European art music but of jazz. This music is probably as genuinely ecstatic as any form of jazz, African-American or otherwise. At the same time, it would not sound notably out-of-date at a Melbourne new music concert today, more than thirty years after it was recorded.

The scores produced by members of the Trio up to this time often employ devices derived or synthesised from imported scores that they were able to examine. However, as McKimm points out, these were intended neither as musical monuments to their compositional skill nor as a means of identifying with the various philosophies associated with Cage and other experimentalists. They were simply take-off points for improvisation: a means of obtaining new levels of improvisational freedom. The level of freedom they achieved can be observed by comparing the dense complexity of the last few seconds of 'Duo 3' on the recording with the relatively sparse notation of the corresponding section of the score.

Duo 1.2.3 Robert Rooney 1965:

Trumpet:

5 phrase. 3··· repeated notes ~~~ tremolo

~~~ trill ½··· ½ valve glide FL. flutter tongue

X percussive sound or noise.

Piano:

H note P pluck string chord cluster S across strings

~~~ trill ~~~ tremolo.

Bass: cl col legno P pizzicato o-o harmonic

~~~ trill ~~~ tremolo X percussive sound or noise.

Overview: Through flow, second time first, we are to play them as trios with the third instrument improvising on material being played by other two.

Stein: for voice and instruments 1976. Robert Rooney

Musical Ex. 7.7b. Key to symbols to 'Duo 1 2 3', in Rooney's hand.

Diverging Artistic Directions

Late in 1966 McKimm, Rooney and Clayton became intensely involved in Humble's newly formed Society for the Private Performance of New Music, where they performed the works of others and had their own works performed. By this time, however, the diversity of their approaches was leading them in quite separate artistic directions and during the late 1960s they gradually ceased to function as a performing trio.

By the end of the 1960s McKimm had explored a variety of controlling processes for improvisation and had also produced a series of quite enigmatic scores for interpretation by improvising musicians (see Musical Ex. 7.8). Several were performed by a large group of jazz and non-jazz musicians, directed by Humble's colleague, Jean-Charles François, at La Mama in 1970. McKimm saw such methods as a means of avoiding the repetition of patterning that is fundamental to jazz improvisation and of getting classical musicians involved in improvisation. Eventually, however, he began to tire of what he perceived as the unavoidable musical 'blemishes' inherent improvised music. His collaboration with large groups of improvising performers during this period marks the final working-out of his ideas on intuitive group response which had preoccupied him since his experiences in 1963 with the McKimm/Mendelson Quartet.
~~~

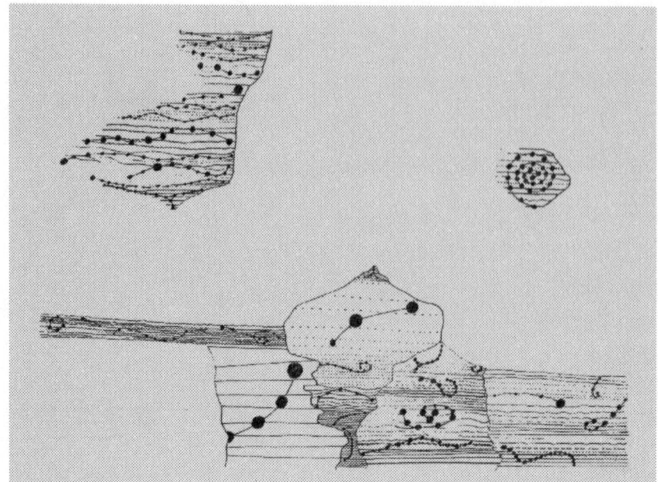

Musical Ex. 7.8. One of a series of untitled graphic scores for interpretation by improvising musicians, by Barry McKimm (late 1960s)

At the same time Clayton was developing both his own style of chance-based music and a style of music-theatre broadly comparable with the 'gesture school' of Giuseppi Chiari. 'Snakes and Ladders' (1966), for example, is based upon the throwing of dice, while 'Yehudi' (1968) uses processes determined by a miniature roulette wheel. Clayton's involvement with the visual arts in the 1960s, particularly in his assemblage of found objects, became manifest in collage-based graphic scores such as 'Snakes and Ladders' and to some extent the nature of the improvisation they prescribed. The works that were performed at La Mama juxtaposed and combined music and theatre improvisation in a way that even Clayton's peers have difficulty in defining. The Melbourne poet and critic Kris Hemensley observed:

> His music was living theatre which dramatised all too clearly the fumblings at drama by the majority of La Mama playwrights . . . Syd made music. The others cut and chiselled 'workable' plays. [Syd] created an extra dimension. Perhaps ritual was the basis of his music. Maybe it was humour. Or silence. Whatever the basis the effect was magic.[63]

The direction sheets for these works give a superficial idea of how they might have sounded. For example, the basic musical performance elements in 'Yehudi', (for brass and string duo) comprise clapping, double stopping, 'sing[ing] with instrument', 'extremely soft' playing, 'slow uneven vibrato', 'rhythm patterns' and 'noise'; and also call for sounds beyond the normal range of the instruments.[64] In addition, performers are required to speak, act, sing and perform 'magical gestures'. Hemensley gives an intriguing first-hand description of various theatrical aspects of Clayton's approach and it is easy to see why he grasps upon the word 'magic' in the above quotation: 'conjuring' might be a more appropriate term.[65] A performance of 'Yehudi' recorded at

La Mama in May 1968 demonstrates that suspense, generated through extended, non-periodic silences and a very minimalist approach to sound, was a very important element of these early works and their effect upon audiences.

Rooney's work moved in yet another direction. In 1968 Patrick McCaughey described his paintings as 'a lunatic type of visual syncopation, deliberately disjointed and disconcerting', a description that could be applied equally to his piano improvisations.[66] McKimm and others identified a distinct correlation between Rooney's visual art and his music but stopped short of attempting to define this. However, specific aspects of Rooney's personal philosophy were strongly influencing the direction of both his visual art and his music by the late 1960s. For example, he was fascinated by the concept of repeated action or routine and was equally intrigued by banal, mass-produced objects from his immediate suburban environment. In particular, he was interested in variation, (albeit minute) between seemingly identical repeated actions or mass produced objects.

Artistically, this fascination with repetition led to an interest in the complex relationships that can be perceived when repeated visual patterns are grouped symmetrically, but with each pattern slightly realigned and therefore recontextualised or recycled within the overall image. This is comparable to phase shifting in music in which identical lines of sound move out of vertical alignment to create increasingly complex relationships. This concept is manifest, for example, in his 1967 Slippery Seal series, in which the three sections of the profile of a seal balanced on a ball resting on some sort of base or rock, are recycled (Figure 7.4). The recycling results in a visual work in which an infinite variety of internal relationships can be discovered as the eye moves over the canvas. The seal image was originally appropriated from a Kellogg's cereal packet, a quirky reference to Rooney's own daily routine and banal mass production.

Phasing in Rooney's music is most audible in some of his later, fully scored musical works such as 'Piece for Gertrude Stein'. In 'Second Landscape' (1968), however, the use of the seal shape in a graphic score creates an (abstract) link between his controlled improvisation and his visual art (see Musical Ex. 7.9a).

In the 1968 recording of 'Second Landscape' performed at La Mama there is an intriguingly clear correlation between the graphic score (a visual art work in its own right) and the improvised music.[67] The score was written for interpretation by an improvising orchestra and the musicians have to follow the horizontal duration lines and find ways of realising the contour of the objects they encounter (see Musical Ex. 7.9a). In the process they create an audible 'landscape'. It is probably a manifestation of Rooney's notoriously quirky artistic humour that the nature of the score virtually precludes any possibility of banal repetition.[68] Rather, the recorded realisation of 'Second Landscape' gives a sense of a very unfamiliar sonic landscape, full of variety and aural surprises. The use of unusually long silences also creates an effect analogous to the object/ space/object design often found in hard edge painting.

McKimm, Rooney and Clayton's collaboration as improvising performers only lasted a few years: a very short part of their respective careers. During the time their collaboration formed part of the local jazz scene their work often met with misunderstanding and distrust from other jazz musicians. Yet, from the perspective of early experimental jazz in Australia, they represent the cutting edge in a jazz environment which, up to that time, had all too often comprised direct and unashamed style imitation. Furthermore, there is no doubt of the historical significance of their collaboration as an improvising chamber ensemble devoted to experimentation. There were others who by 1965 had tried out similar improvisational concepts but none, to my knowledge, who became so closely identified with live performance based on comparable concepts. Even by 1967 they were recognised by Roger Covell as pioneering the use of graphic scoring in Australia.[69] Without the benefit of overseas experience, institutional training, grants or even the basic moral support of the contemporary music

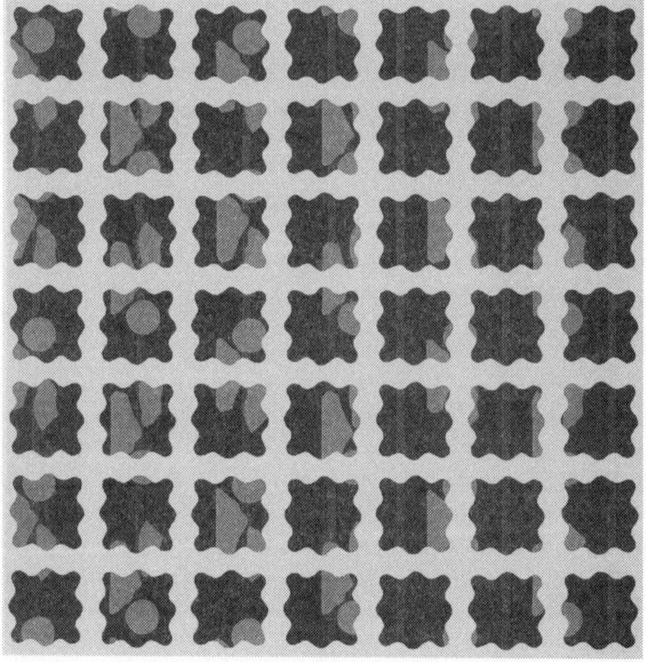

Figure 7.4. Robert Rooney's Variations Slippery Seals III 1967 (acrylic on canvas 106.7 x 106.7), Monash University Collection.

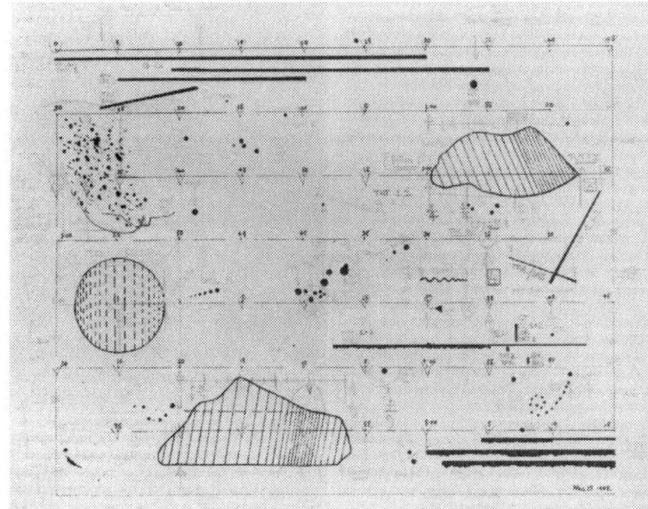

Musical Ex. 7.9a. Robert Rooney's graphic score for 'Second Landscape' (photocopy with performer's annotations), 1968. Performers follow the numbered duration lines.

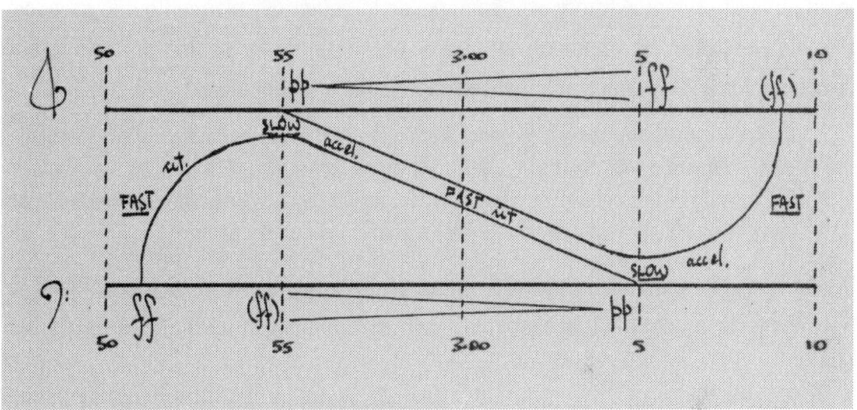

Musical Ex. 7.9b. 'Second Landscape': a diagram showing the ensemble's solution to the problem of negotiating the ball shape.

establishment, they experimented and exhaustively worked through their individual philosophies and approaches to improvisation. In the process they created a small but important legacy of recordings and scores for improvisers.

Humble observes of McKimm, Rooney and Clayton that 'they seemed to me a little bit – not "off the planet" – but not quite aware of what had been accomplished – as if they'd read the book but not heard the music, which is probably true; but the product was really . . . very refreshing'.[70] In contrast, Humble's own approach to experimentalism was substantially based on direct personal contact with European and American avant-garde traditions.

Keith Humble

> the spectacle of one composer producing music for thousands of musical drones (totally uncreative themselves, and hence comparatively out of touch with the whole phenomenon of artistic creation) will no longer seem normal or desirable, and then the present gulf between the mentality of composers and performers will be bridged.
>
> Percy Aldridge Grainger, 1915[71]

The exploratory approach to music-making in which Keith Humble was engaged at the time of his return to Australia in 1966 provides an important illustration of the complexity of the relationship between the terms 'improvisatory', 'experimental' and 'exploratory', and further, between improvising and composing. Humble sometimes made the provocative claim that he considered all of his compositions 'frozen improvisations'. By this he meant they were the end product of a particular approach to the assembly of musical material.[72] In this approach, the musical material is assembled in an intuitive or improvisatory way, as opposed to being fully planned out in advance. Humble describes his approach as based, not on arbitrary choice or chance but intuition informed by deeply internalised experience and technique:

> If I know what I am doing in advance I am just dealing with a product. It's rather like a cook – I'm not a cook but I can read a recipe, and I'm very good at cooking from recipes, but a cook, or the equivalent as a musician, would be someone who 'throws the book away' – and 'makes up' something. That's what it's about you know.[73]

It was Humble's particular interest in 'process' – the action of making up music, as opposed to its 'product' – that shaped his work and influenced others in the 1960s and later.

Humble recognised a number of improvisatory processes as influential in the approach he had developed by 1966. These can be loosely placed in two main categories:

1. The intuitive organisation of material within 'closed' systems:
    a. The spontaneous realisation of internalised formulae: 'performance-time' jazz or concert hall keyboard improvisations which can also be fixed or frozen into notation (this type of process ceased to be of particular interest to Humble after the late 1940s).
    b. The spontaneous organisation of internalised paradigms: the notion that a fixed system (e.g. serialism) can be internalised to the degree that composing on paper becomes virtually the transcription of sound relationships as they unfold conceptually, albeit out of performance time. Humble cites Schoenberg as having worked in this manner.[74]

2. More exploratory or 'open' processes:
   a. Creative interaction: the process by which a work is created or modified by a director/group or collective performance-time creative interaction.
   b. The intuitive juxtaposition or layering of sound complexes (textures, masses, genres, media, etc.). By 'intuitive juxtaposition' I mean juxtaposition that is based, not on arbitrary placement, but a highly developed personal system.

The end-products of such processes, scored or otherwise, are what Humble described as frozen improvisation or, alternatively, 'improvisation/composition'. It was, however, his use of open processes and in particular the personal philosophy behind their use, which had the greatest impact on Melbourne in the late 1960s and later.

Humble acknowledged that his 1940s jazz experience helped to imprint – if subliminally – certain important ideas relating to improvisation that would become very significant in his later work.[75] Through jazz arranging he had worked with the concept of notated (fixed or frozen) improvisation and had discovered the musical potential of the binary relationship between musical structure and freedom. He had become aware that musical structure could emerge and 'gel' through interactive workshopping or intuitive group response to repeated improvisations (notions that are inherent in the so-called head arranging tradition in jazz). He had also experienced the relatively democratic social dynamics of the small jazz rehearsal or jam session ensemble in which individual members often make a significant creative contribution (as opposed to the relative anonymity of the 'legit' orchestral musician).

Having worked as a vaudeville pianist Humble was also aware that, at a basic level, a live jazz band performance was a form of improvisatory music-theatre. Unlike the conventional staging of a play, a jazz performance is a non-representational form of theatre – it is itself. (This is of course putting aside white representation of African-American performance culture.) This notion of an improvisatory performance art that 'comes out of itself' became very important to Humble in the 1960s.

A more direct influence came out of his unsuccessful return to Australia in 1956 to take up a position at the Melbourne Conservatorium. His failure to come to terms with the reactionary attitudes to music and education he encountered led him to devise a particular concept of decentralised musical activity. This was the establishment of regional cultural centres throughout Australia which would provide a performance environment in which performance-time creative interaction and exchange of ideas could take place.

By 1960 this idea had been realised not in Australia but in Paris at the Centre de

Musique (CDM). This was a unique collective of creative talent, directed by Humble and seen to rival Pierre Boulez' famous but less exploratory Domaine Musicale.[76] At the core of Humble's conception was the 'process' of music-making and particularly creative participation.

The Society for the Private Performance of New Music

Humble visited Melbourne briefly late in 1964 and took the opportunity to promote vigorously his workshop concept to an incipient new music community – and at least one incredulous music critic, Kenneth Hince, who seems to have been unable to cope with Humble's proposals.[77] When Humble returned in 1966 the new music movement was already manifest in a Melbourne branch of the ISCM. Yet even the ISCM contained reactionary elements who preferred to distance themselves from the work of radical young experimentalists such as McKimm, Rooney, Clayton, and Clive O'Connell. Consequently, Humble's Society for the Private Performance of New Music (SPPNM) which he established at the Grainger Museum the same year, became an important outlet for these experimentalists and others who wished to perform new music. From his 1956 experience in Melbourne he had concluded that the conservatism of Australian musical education could only be subverted by clandestine means. The SPPNM was, in a sense, a manifestation of this.

In 1956 Humble had witnessed the social and artistic rejection of Grainger and, by implication, all he symbolised as an Australian-born experimentalist. It is therefore no coincidence that his earliest efforts on returning to Australia involved (with the help of Jill Humble, Ian Bonighton, Robert Hyner, Meta Overman and others) the more or less clandestine revival of the neglected Grainger Museum as a (historically 'charged') context for the SPPNM's experimental music activities. Moreover, his establishment of an electronic music studio at the Museum represented, at least in a philosophical sense, a continuation of Grainger's quest for a 'free music'. Similar effort went into the promotion and performance of Grainger's neglected works, including more radical examples such as 'The Warriors' and 'Random Round'.

During 1966 and early 1967 the SPPNM comprised a pool of around twenty musicians. Society members apparently made arrangements among themselves for the basic preparation of works and then came together at the Grainger Museum for a monthly 'concert'. These were performance workshops, directed by Humble or the composer of the work. The SPPNM basically involved the recontextualisation of the experiences and concepts that had come out of Humble's Paris-based Centre de Musique. Unlike the virtually autonomous CDM, however, the SPPNM's activities

S.P.P.N.M. Grainger Museum

S.P.P.N.M. :- 1. 24th June, 1966. 3 p.m.

Programme

1. SNAKES AND LADDERS .... SYD CLAYTON
2. TRIO (for Clarinet, Flute and Bassoon) ...... ROBERT ROONEY
3. CHAURASPANCHASIKA .... CLIVE O'CONNELL

Graham Abbott - Flute, Indian Flute

Stuart Challender - Clarinet, Piano

Gerard Lester - Bassoon

Barry McKimm - Trumpet

Judy Golder - Violin

Syd Clayton - Double Bass

Clive O'Connell - Conductor, Percussion

Robert Rooney - Piano

Figure 7.5. Program for the first SPPNM concert (Courtesy of Jill Humble).

functioned within and in spite of the deeply ingrained conservatism of the Melbourne Conservatorium (with which the Museum was associated); and whereas the CDM comprised a pool of musicians who had expertise, understanding and total commitment to experimental music, the resources of the SPPNM lay much more in interest, enthusiasm and emerging talent. In Australia, Humble found himself working with a quite incongruous array of performance skills.

Programs of the SPPNM concerts show that the first year of this organisation represented a watershed of intense creative interaction, giving members the opportunity to explore their own ideas and confront what had already been explored overseas (see Figure 7.5 and Appendix). Many of the pieces workshopped at the Grainger museum were improvisatory but Humble did not promote a free-for-all approach to ensemble improvisation, partly because of what he saw as the technical limitations of players. He hoped instead 'to encourage people to discover that if they wanted to fulfil their musical ideas they had to be free from technical limitations and they had to know and understand lots of music'.[78]

There was however, a more complex reason for his lack of enthusiasm for free-for-all collective improvisation. As noted previously, Humble's jazz aesthetic favoured improvisation that was hemmed or boxed in by controlling processes or principles.

Moreover, he was fascinated by sounds (e.g. individual sounds, textures or sound complexes), not only as building material for musical structures but as sound 'objects' to be 'displayed' (sounded correctly) and admired for their inherent beauty or interest. This was immediately apparent in his approach to producing sounds on the piano. He believed that even improvised sounds, textures or sound complexes had to be played or 'sounded' with a certain level of precision, or within precise parameters. This presents a paradox that appears to undermine the notion of Humble as someone committed to intuitive musical exploration, just as it sits uneasily with some of the discussion which follows. Yet one must accept that this paradox was integral to Humble's creativity in order to understand works such as *Trois Poèmes à Crier et à Danser* (1968), in which gestures of remarkable poignancy are created through almost total composer/director control over 'windows' of ecstatic improvisatory expression by choristers singing while wielding musical toys.

The Conceptual Basis of Humble's Improvisatory Works

An important aspect of Humble's approach to 'process' in the creation of his own works involved various levels of assemblage: the intuitive bringing-together or juxtaposition of related or unrelated materials. This creative process unfolded – as I will explain – both in and out of performance time. Assemblage was used in late 1960s works such as 'Music for Monuments' (version for bassoon, Melbourne, 1967); 'Nunique III' (Melbourne, 1968); 'Arcade 1' (Melbourne, 1969); and 'Nunique IV' (Melbourne, 1969).

'Music for Monuments' and 'Arcade 1' illustrate the use of a relatively straightforward form of horizontal juxtaposition or layering. The 1968 Melbourne performance of 'Music for Monuments', for example, comprised

> a Prepared Tape consist[ing] of a collage of orchestral sounds, randomly produced percussion sounds, choral sounds, and the sounds of a children's class in contemporary music. [79]

Overlaying these prepared tape sounds, one of Humble's SPPNM protégés, Gerald Lester, played a bassoon part 'from which the player selects at random to play against the recorded sections [and] other new areas discovered by Gerald Lester himself'.[80] Similarly, 'Arcade 1' comprises a prepared tape which, although unfolding in a more organic and abstract way than the 'Music For Monuments' tape, provides both the overall formal structure and the musical referent for (previously outlined) improvisation by Douglas Lawrence (pipe organ) and Jean-Charles François (percussion). The use of a prepared tape in this piece also represents one of Humble's solutions to the absence of a pool of experienced and committed improvising musicians such as he had in Paris. 'Arcade 1' is, incidentally, also of historic interest in that it represents a nexus between the unbroken tradition of improvisatory organ playing and the more recently emerged tradition of improvisatory experimental art music.

The 'Nunique' works, which one program describes as 'improvisatory music-theatre pieces', illustrate some much more complex and explicit forms of juxtaposition and layering.[81] Contemporaneous criticism suggests a local perception of the 'Nuniques' as little more than an arbitrary and bizarre cobbling together of events to create yet another form of late 1960s 'happening' or Neo-Dadaist celebration of nonsense, with little purpose beyond entertainment and the ridicule of musical conservatism. However, these were serious experimental works which serve to demonstrate many of the key concepts behind Humble's musical approach and that of his CDM colleague, Jean-Charles François, with whom he frequently collaborated in Australia.

The program notes for 'Nunique VI' (1971) state that 'All the *Nuniques* are collages of gestures, visuals and diverse musical styles. On the musical side, they are concerned with certain aspects of sound such as the progression of textures and spatial direction'.[82] The notes also point out that 'Humble's concept of theatre, stemming from the theatre of the early twentieth century French playwright, Pierre Albert-Birot, is

Figure 7.6. A photograph of Keith Humble's creative music workshop for children at the Grainger Museum, c.1967.

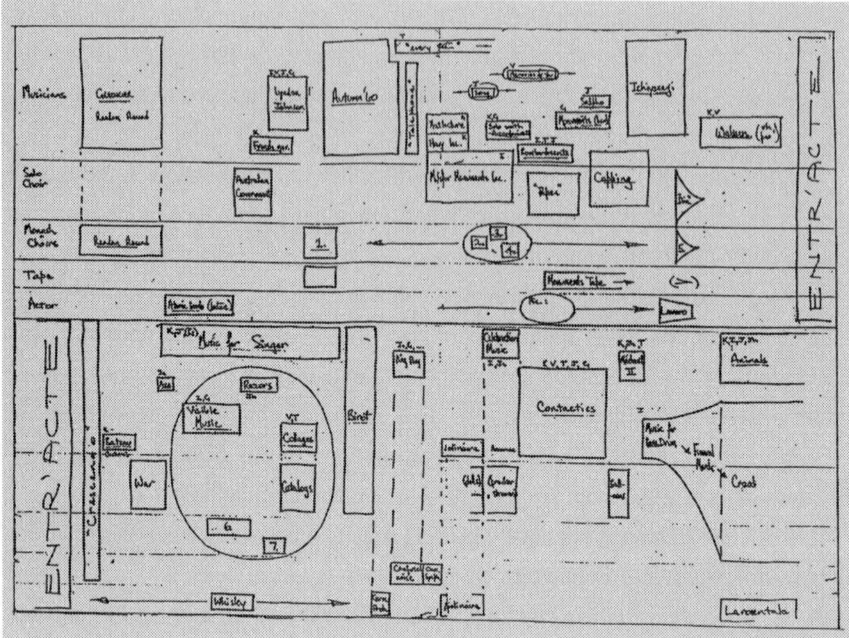

Musical Ex. 7.10. Director's 'score' for 'Nunique IV' (1969). Read upper and then lower system (divided by the thick horizontal line) from left to right.

specially designed to effect various unusual reactions from the audience'.[83] While all these comments are accurate, they do not adequately explain the basis of the works.

The 'Nuniques': Structure

As theatre, the structure of the 'Nuniques' is superficially comparable to the blackface minstrel or Pierrot show or revue. As in these earlier forms, they contain certain fixed core elements around which contrasting improvisatory or fully determined events can unfold in variety show style, overlap or (as was very common in the Nuniques) occur simultaneously. Just as the minstrel/variety show was characterised by the 'minstrel overture', the 'stump speech', the 'walk-around' and the riotous finale, the important structural elements of the 'Nuniques' were the 'monument' (the performance of a renowned musical work), a 'statement' (a type of performance/lecture-demonstration), and 'Larountala' (a riotous finale with several functions) (see Musical Ex. 7.10). Unlike the minstrel show and similar theatrical forms, however, these structural elements (and all other aspects of these works) present important statements about 'participation', 'anecdote', 'gesture' and 'ecstatic experience' in relation to performance and sound.

Participation: Making 'Noise'

In explaining the importance of participation in the process of music-making, Humble pointed to certain similarities between the radical ideas found in Jacques Attali's controversial book, *Noise: the Political Economy of Music* (1977) and those he had begun proposing many years earlier.[84]

In *Noise,* Attali outlined an exciting new paradigm for analysing the significance of music and its relationship to society. His premise is that 'noise is violence': to express the social condition (e.g. dissatisfaction) through social/cultural information encoded in noise (confronting sound) represents a form of violence against order. Therefore, the suppression and control of sound enables dominant power structures to 'silence' this 'violence' and prevent destabilising change.[85] He suggests further that the mass of Western society has been progressively disenfranchised from the expression of its condition through noise (i.e. 'silenced') via an historical sequence of subversively oppressive political/economic processes which he terms 'ritual', 'representation' and 'repeating':

Ritual: Ceremonial-type performance (which was nevertheless still part of a multi-dimensional, real life participatory experience for performers and observers alike).

Representation: Concert hall-type performance, in which music has become a commercially viable product and takes the form of a spatially isolated representation (imitation/ substitute) of real life experience, observed by obediently silent and detached bourgeois auditors. In this imitation ritual, the social/cultural 'messages' encoded in the music and its potential to subvert (change/replace) the existing order are further degraded.

Repeating: The mass production of recorded music, dispensed through mass marketing and mass media. 'Repeating' results in the further disenfranchisement of society from the process of individual expression. 'Messages' of the human condition encoded in sound (noise) are rendered meaningless (silenced).

Attali predicts a coming era in which 'musical power' (control of the production and distribution of music) will be decentralised and 'repeating' will be superseded by 'composing'. By composing, Attali means a return, not to the nineteenth century notion of the 'hero composer', but to the literal meaning of the word, 'putting together'. In this new era:

> Music is no longer made to be represented or stockpiled, but for participation in collective play, in an ongoing quest for new, immediate communication, without ritual and always unstable. It becomes non-reproducible, irreversible.[86]

Shortly after the Melbourne performance of 'Nunique III' (1968), Humble himself explained that, for the 'hero composer',

> a hundred piece orchestra . . . will do my works in order that this work can be projected out to 5,000 people who have to sit down and admire my particular work. I find this a rather Fascist way of doing things.[87]

Several years earlier Humble had stated that the environment in which music was created should be, instead, *'un lieu de conflit'* (a place of conflict).[88] During his brief visit to Melbourne in 1964 he reportedly proposed new performance environments in which:

> physical and conventional barriers between audience and performers disappear. There is an emphasis on the practical, the immediate, on music being made (even composed) for [the audience], here and now, on the spot.[89]

The nature of Humble's musical output in fact corresponds uncannily with Attali's prophecy for the music of the future – music that is unstable, seeking, irreversible and participatory.

An important function of the 'Nuniques' was, therefore, to elicit unusual responses from the audience: to create situations in which the audience experienced spontaneous participation in the performance by, for example, having to listen actively, move around the performance area and make gestures in sound and movement. Active listening was induced by such means as the simultaneous presentation of contrasting events and the fading in, fading out and redirection of sound through a speaker system subversively controlled by Humble. The most explicit inducement to audience participation, however, was in the last structural section, 'Larountala', which represents Albert-Birot's poignant character, Larountala, the messenger who died through being misunderstood. (Albert-Birot's exploratory work was similarly misunderstood and ignored).[90] In this section the audience is asked, without explanation, to protest against, attack and (verbally) destroy a messenger trying to deliver a message about the future which they are incapable of understanding. Incidentally, this allegory curiously anticipates Attali's 1977 statement that '*noise is violence*: it disturbs. To make noise is to interrupt a transmission, to disconnect, to kill. It is a simulacrum of murder'.[91]

In the process of angrily 'destroying' Larountala and his message the audience also contributes to the performance a specific type of improvisatory gesture in sound and movement. As part of this process they unwittingly end up on stage in an ecstatic finale, which transforms seamlessly into a real onstage party with food and alcohol. The traditional perceptual and physical partition between performance and spectator has, at this point, been totally removed.

Participation: Listening

In *Noise*, Attali also points to the link between public disenfranchisement from participation in 'noise making' and the loss of 'aural literacy': a dangerous atrophy of the ability to discern the environment through sound (a phenomenon described by Marshall McLuhan in his famous *The Medium is the Message*, 1967).[92] Attali states, 'Listening to music is listening to all noise, realizing that its appropriation and control is a reflection of power, that it is essentially political'.[93] He also observes that while society has been made 'silent' and aurally illiterate, the dominant groups have increased their powers of listening through such means as electronic surveillance.[94] There is evidence that Humble and François had developed similar concerns by the late 1960s and probably earlier. A 'statement' proclaimed in 'Nunique IV' begins:

> The work of Art is Language and necessary sense; to exist it must achieve communication. The notion of communication is well placed in the cultural industry which reckons upon relationships of cause and effect and finally in application of the market study which seeks to determine what should be the intellectual products likely to find buyers.[95]

The 'Nuniques' themselves were directly concerned with conveying a message about aural literacy. The statement above continues, 'It is a question of eliminating everything which prevents the ears from opening, of suppressing any screen between the work and its auditor.'[96]

The 'Nuniques' and Anecdote

The notion of aural literacy is also directly associated with another important idea conveyed in the 'Nuniques', described as 'the phenomenon of anecdotic characteristics of sounds' (the interest inherent in detached sound events or 'objects').[97] What is signified below is that individual sounds have a 'history' which the creative musician is free to follow or ignore:

> Don't use cluster[s] on [the] piano because you'll play immediately the Klavierstück X of Stockhausen. Don't use this chord because it's Tristan. Don't use this scale because it's Debussy. Don't use this chord because its Webern. Something new please! New sounds! *Un Puzzle ou un th[éâ]tre?*[98]

Gesture

At one level the 'Nuniques' were themselves a gesture of defiance against the 'message' encoded in concert hall performance and Australian musical conservatism in general. But besides this, they demonstrated individual, often improvisatory forms of musical gesture unfamiliar to the Australian public and oppositional to the notion of

Event No.	Description	Suggested Duration
1.	Lo. cluster (Ah) → gliss up; on cue → clap clap X cue	20 sec
2.	All speak; ff > pp	15 sec
3.	Mmmm —— (cluster) shuffle feet (pp)	45 sec
4.	Stand quickly together / Sit slowly / snap fingers WHILE RUBBING HANDS TOGETHER (unison)	40 sec.
5.	Choir A; cheek pop clapping with gloves on ff > ppp Choir B; clicking frogs dim. as above clapping Diminuendo may be achieved by systematically reducing the number of clappers (choir A) /clickers (choir B.)	10 sec.
6.	"Imaginary Landscape" Score will be provided Each performer will need a transistor radio	2 min.
7.	Choir A: Clink, blow into, pass bottles Choir B; Crumble paper, quietly and slowly	3-4 mins
8.	"Funeral March" → "Larountala" Choirs descend on to stage area while singing cluster (on various vowels). Priest-like procession. The funeral march and "Larountala" which follow, involve some movement and crowd-like reactions only.	
Props;	Clicking Frogs (5) Will be provide Transistor Radios (6) Choir members to bring Bottles (7) Will be provided Paper (7) Will be provided Gloves (5) Choir members to bring	

Musical Ex. 7.11. Typed event sheet for 'Nunique IV'.

music as a pure, autonomous language. For example, in place of precise musical gestures, such as the deceptive cadence of tonal music, the musical gestures in the 'Nuniques' were performed mostly on the basis of written, spoken or graphic instructions and generally produced broad improvisatory brush-strokes of sound (see Musical Exs. 7.10, 7.11). Furthermore, these musical gestures comprised an amalgam of improvisatory physical actions, visuals, lighting and other effects. Most confronting of all, however, was the fact that these gestures were made by two professional improvising musicians of international standing with a level of musical ability that was never questioned, even by their most vitriolic critics.

The 'Nuniques' and Ecstatic Improvisation

Humble was careful to point out at the time that the 'Nuniques' were 'not meant to be spontaneous and should not develop into an happening'.[99] Although individual

Musical Ex. 7.12. Part of a handwritten cue sheet for 'Nunique IV'.

elements of the performance (such as the music of the Barry McKimm Quartet) were improvisatory, staging plans and other documents show that the 'Nuniques' were very precisely planned (see Musical Ex. 7.12). Improvisation was always controlled and contained within each separate unit of the performance. The music critic Andrew McIntyre noted at the time that:

> Humble knows what to expect from each group, so that he can vary the recourses by cutting in and out with microphones, adjusting volume controls, and is able to thus control directly the final product.[100]

In other words, provision was made for improvisational freedom within a tight framework of instructions and Humble, as stage director, was able intuitively and clandestinely to manipulate certain parameters of the work as it unfolded.

Considering what has already been said in this book about imitation ecstatic and ecstatic improvisatory practice, it is interesting that a primary aim of the 'Nuniques' (Nun is Greek for now) was to create a 'large simultaneous whole, containing all the means and emotions whereby an intense and ecstatic existence can be communicated to the spectator'.[101] This statement indicates that, while improvisatory practice in the 'Nuniques' was controlled, it was not intended as a representation or imitation of spontaneity but, rather, a genuinely ecstatic activity within fixed boundaries. One method of avoiding 'representation' in the Nuniques was through subversion – by withholding the overall intent of the work and blocking the passage of information between the various self-contained performance units. In this way the work unfolded with a sense of authentic spontaneity.

The Large-scale Assemblage and Layering of Materials

> His compositions were a performer's, written in an eruptive notation that demands a flow of spontaneous gestures. In performance he was a composer: his charged piano playing pointed to compositional processes; his fluid conducting infected a contemporary score with a sense of being an *event*. By extension, his projects in education, both inside and outside institutions, had the character of composition in action. He believed that musical learning thrived in the contradictions between new ideas.
>
> John McCaughey, 'A Stimulus and Agent for Change', *Age*, 15 June 1995, p.16.

Humble's concept of 'frozen improvisation' underlines the difficulty of proposing a clear distinction between certain compositional processes and improvisatory music practice. Just as some improvisatory musical practices can be seen as composing in performance time, working with an open-ended compositional process can be thought of as a type of improvisatory musical practice – even when this process does not unfold in performance time. An obvious example of the latter is the 'improvise and transcribe' approach to composing, which has always had some application for the professional pianist/composer.

A comparable 'out of performance time' improvisatory process was used in the production of each 'Nunique'. Through a process of intuitive assemblage over a period of perhaps several months, Humble brought together contrasting musical genres, concepts, idiosyncratically talented people (e.g. Jean-Charles François, Barry McKimm and John McCaughey), staging and lighting devices, live and pre-recorded electronic sounds, choral and instrumental ensembles, visual props and political and didactic statements as well as acting, audience participation and so forth. The resulting product was a carefully planned but also improvisatory one-off event – a frozen improvisation.

This same process of intuitive juxtaposition and layering can also be seen operating on a greatly expanded scale when viewed in the context of Humble's entire creative output. At this macro level, a complex, ongoing, large-scale process of recycling and recontextualisation of 'materials' (concepts, systems, instrument designs, individual performance talent, recorded sound, technology, music or texts by others, etc.) is apparent. His creative efforts from the 1960s were a continuously unfolding exploration of musical and educational possibilities in which separate experimental projects superseded each other, overlapped and unfolded concurrently. Each project and work-in-progress generated raw materials (as defined above) which were recycled for use in the extension of that project or a concurrent project or as the basis of, or material for, an entirely new project. For example, 'Music for Monuments' (bassoon version, 1968) and 'Arcade 1' (1968) both featured the juxtaposition of materials from other projects, while the mixed-media work, *'La Légende'* (1971), created in collaboration with the Melbourne artist Noel Counihan, was a watershed of diverse 'materials' which had been accumulating since or even before Humble's first improvisatory music-theatre project (Paris 1963).

European Influences on Humble's Approach

Some significant aspects of Humble's approach involved the extension and recontextualisation of concepts and philosophies already present in the European avant-garde tradition. Humble's years at the Centre de Musique exposed him to a wide variety of approaches in improvisatory music-making, particularly after 1962. His Paris milieu was one in which intense creative and philosophical exchange between musicians and those involved in other branches of the arts was already a long tradition. Many of the concepts mentioned in relation to the 'Nuniques', such as 'nowism', everyday sounds as art, audience confrontation and so forth, can be linked broadly to the French Futurist movement of a much earlier era. He also had strong associations with expatriate American culture through the American Student and Artist Centre in Paris, which hosted CDM activities.

An important influence was Humble's collaboration with the French playwright/director, Marc 'O, in experimental theatre productions which, in 1964, were described as:

> creat[ing] entirely new theatrical works, *'théâtre total'*, which are a blend of the arts of music, painting, drama and dance, and which make what they believe to be the most complete theatrical experience possible'.[102]

Through Marc 'O, Humble discovered a mode of performance which projected a genuinely ecstatic immediacy and demonstrated beyond doubt the artistic potential of intuitively assembled material. Using highly-trained actors and psychodrama techniques, Marc 'O developed a form of experimental theatre that was based not on a script but a process, in which the detail was defined, layer by layer, through repeated improvisations on suggested real life situations. Humble adopted a similar cumulative approach to incorporating music into the plays which, in some cases, required the invention of new instruments.

The controversial writings and experiments of the British stage designer and theorist, Edward Gordon Craig, are also reflected in Humble's approach and philosophy. Best known for his radical ideas on stage design, Craig was also particularly concerned about the inadequacy of conventional representation as a means of conveying the essence of a work. He pointed to the role of informed intuition in the creative process and argued that the 'spirit and essence' of a work could only be communicated effectively through the 'broad brush-stroke' of the abstract gesture.[103] He rejected the notion of 'pure' autonomous languages in art and promoted the concept of the mastermind stage manager who creates, organises and subversively controls all parameters of a theatrical production: plot, lighting, staging, music and dance. He was also concerned with action and immediacy, considering that the theatre should emphasise the direct experience of sound, movement, light and colour:

> the Art of the Theatre is neither acting nor the play, it is not scene or dance, but it consists of all the elements of which these things are composed: action, which is the very spirit of acting; words, which are the body of the play; line and colour, which are the very heart of the scene; rhythm, which is the very essence of dance.[104]

Laughton Harris points out, however, that:

> perhaps the strongest influence on Humble during his involvement with music theatre in Paris, came from a literary quarter, a *drame comique la femme pliante,* by Pierre Albert-Birot (1876–1967) in which Humble recognised a valid literary counterpart to many of the techniques he had been seeking in music.[105]

Albert-Birot's anonymity seems to have been, in some way, deeply symbolic to Humble and the influence of his radical theories and writings pervades Humble's work of the 1960s and after. He provided Humble with a powerful set of symbols (Larountala, for example) and his dada poetry further revealed the communicative power of abstract gesture. His development as a playwright, beginning in the late 1910s, was characterised by a continuous exploration of futuristic concepts, including very radical stage design which provided for simultaneous events and audience confrontation. It was in fact Albert-Birot who called for a form of theatre that was a 'large simultaneous whole, containing all the means and emotions whereby an intense and ecstatic existence [could] be communicated to the spectator'.[106] Like Craig and, in later years, Marc 'O, Albert-Birot was preoccupied with the notion that theatre should be a living interpretation of itself – not a representation of something else – a notion that is conceptually inseparable from improvisatory activity.

If Humble's approach was indebted to his experience in the artistic milieu of Paris in the early 1960s, it is equally the product of his Australian background, in which the common solution in the absence of musical models was to invent, improvise or adapt. His earlier Melbourne jazz experience was clearly also very important. Indeed it is very difficult to imagine any composer who would not have been substantially influenced by the experience of working in the exciting jazz environment that Melbourne provided in the 1940s. Yet, notwithstanding his use of the jazz idiom in, for example, *'Le Printemps'* and 'Nunique IV', for various reasons he made a conscious decision not to dabble with the third stream concept. It is nevertheless significant that a musician with a jazz influenced background introduced to Melbourne forms of improvisatory music that were considered radical even in Paris and did so at a critical turning point in Melbourne cultural history. Even more importantly, he brought a message about the need to be involved in the process of 'composing', in the broadest sense of the term, instead of just being 'a composer'.

The Humble example is especially important in that it closes the narrative of *Playing Ad Lib* with a discussion centred more on improvisatory process and philosophy than individual improvisatory practices. This is a suitable vantage point from which to speculate briefly on the relevance of improvisatory music, as interpreted in this book, to a broader understanding of music in Australia.

The decades since the 1960s have seen the ascendancy of digital music technology which allows for the creation of exciting, functional and highly imaginative (and totally reproducible) soundscapes: music without performance. Digital technology, furthermore, permits meanings to be easily encoded into music during studio post-production – that is, *after* it has been performed. Yet this period has also produced numerous fascinating forms of integration between improvisatory performance and technology, both in experimental art music and in popular forms such as hip hop. Even the process of arranging performed and sampled elements to produce a hip hop track in the recording studio is described by Steve Petridis of Illegal Substance as entirely 'improvisational'.[107]

Australia is poised geographically, culturally and socially to become one of the most complex and interesting places for improvisatory music. There is a vigorous jazz, experimental, contemporary rock and 'world music' scene. Our emerging musical identity includes the new improvisatory soundscapes produced by ensembles such The Catholics, Intersect, That, the Australian Art Orchestra, The Necks, Jouissance and Dome. Acceptance of the notion of a multicultural Australia has begun to reveal an astonishingly rich tapestry of transplanted oral musical traditions. Moreover, our geographical position within the Asia-Pacific region ensures that Australia will become the locus for as yet unimaginable musical syntheses based on presently little-known improvisatory practices and processes, such as the expanding and contracting melody concept of Javanese gamelan music.

The notion of improvisatory music can provide a unique alternative perspective on the historical, social, cultural, musicological and political aspects of music in specific sites such as Australia. Yet Keith Humble's music points to the most fascinating, important and least understood aspect of improvisatory music. This is also the aspect that is most relevant to understanding the mosaic of indigenous, long-established and recently-transplanted improvisatory performance cultures that make up Australian musical life at the end of this century. I am referring to the importance not only of knowing what types of macro or micro improvisatory gestures musicians make in terms of performance practice and sound, but also of understanding their true intent, meaning and cultural significance. This is the challenge for future writing on improvisatory music.

In a recent replay of an ABC interview between the commentator Andrew Ford and the Australian guitarist John Williams, broadcast from the Grainger Museum, Williams commented on some Grainger piano roll performances that had been played earlier. His words aptly express what is most important to me, personally, about improvisatory music and provide a fitting close to this book:

> I immediately thought of [David] Helfgott, I thought of that totally free approach of interpretation. Not simply to follow slavishly our nineteenth century narrow-minded view of interpretation – that it has to be done in this rationally taught-way – but to play – it's almost like short circuiting the heart and the mind's ideas – straight through to what you want to do.[108]

Appendix

Concert Programmes: The Society for the Private Performance of New Music

<u>24/6/1966</u>	
Snakes and Ladders	Syd Clayton
Trio (for Clarinet, Flute and Bassoon)	Robert Rooney
Chauraspanchasika	Clive O'Connell
<u>10/7/1966</u>	
Concerto for Flute and Percussion	Lou Harrison
Duo 1,2,3	Robert Rooney
Responses 1 and 2	Daryl Edwards
<u>24/7/1966</u>	
End of October	Robert Rooney
Random Music 1757	C.P.E. Bach
Intermission 5,6a	Morton Feldman
Autumn '60 for Orchestra	Cornelius Cardew
<u>7/8/1966</u>	
Variations on a Theme of Max Reger for Flute	Ian Bonighton
Envoys	Stuart Challender
Duet for Clarinet and Bassoon	Ludwig van Beethoven
Room-Music Tit-Bits, No.3 Walking Tune for Wind-Five some	Percy Grainger
<u>12/9/1966</u>	
Autumn '60 for Orchestra (first Australian performance)	Cornelius Cardew
Fantasie for Violin and Piano Accompaniment, Op. 49	Arnold Schoenberg
Four Pieces for Violin and Piano, Op. 7	Anton Webern
Contrasts	Bela Bartok

Two Worlds (first Australian performance)	George Cacioppo
Music for Albion Moonlight	David Bedford
<u>2/10/1966</u>	
Intermission 6a	Morton Feldman
Intermission 5	Morton Feldman
Seven Early Songs	Alban Berg
Interview with Stockhausen	
Six Little Pieces for Piano, Op. 19	Arnold Schoenberg
Monotony for 8 Trumpets	Barry McKimm
<u>20/11/1966</u>	
Mobile for Bells	Stuart Challender
Dream	John Cage
Waiting	John Cage
Piano Piece 1963	Morton Feldman
Three Pieces for One Quintet or More	Barry McKimm
<u>21/5/1967</u>	
Hora Decima	Johann Pezel
Vertical Thought III	Morton Feldman
Random Round (first performance)	Percy Grainger
Divertimento K.188	Mozart
Density 21.5	Edgar Varese
Spoon River	Percy Grainger
<u>6/8/1967</u>	
Cassation in G Major KV 63	Mozart
Pieces for Prepared Piano and Strings	Toshiro Mayuzmi
Concerto for String Orchestra	Margaret Sutherland
Sinfonia IX	Mendelssohn

Notes

Introduction

1. *Musical Quarterly,* July 1915. Reprinted in Teresa Balough (ed.), *The Musical Genius From Australia: Selected Writings by and about Percy Grainger,* University of Western Australia, 1982, p. 72.
2. Charles Keil, 'Participatory Discrepancies and the Power of Music' in Charles Keil and Steven Feld, *Music Grooves: Essays and Dialogues,* Chicago: University of Chicago Press, 1994, p. 104. See also a special issue of *Ethnomusicology* on participatory discrepancies, vol. 39 (1) Winter 1995. In Australia, Jeff Pressing has been engaged in computer technology-based analysis of what he calls the 'micro- and macrostructural design of improvised music' since the mid-1980s.
3. Bruno Nettl, 'Thoughts on Improvisation: A Comparative Approach', *Musical Quarterly,* 60 (1) January 1974, p.6.
4. 'Modernism' in Rodger Fowler (ed.) *A Dictionary Of Modern Critical Terms,* New York: Routledge and Kegan, 1973, p. 117.
5. Richard Middleton, *Studying Popular Music,* Buckingham: Open University Press, 1990, p. 13.
6. Conversation: Whiteoak/Barry Duggan.
7. David Cahill, 'David Tolley – Iconoclast', *Sounds Australian,* 17, Autumn 1988, p.16.

Chapter 1

1. *Port Phillip Patriot and Melbourne Advertiser,* 18 February 1841, p. 3
2. *Sydney Gazette,* 1 March 1836, p. 3.
3. *Sydney Gazette,* 7 June 1836, p. 4.
4. *Sydney Herald,* 21 March 1836, p. 2.
5. *Sydney Gazette,* 7 June 36, p. 4.
6. Colin Roderick and Hugh Anderson (eds), *Miska Hauser's Letters from Australia 1854-1858,* translated by C. Roderick, Maryborough, Victoria: Red Rooster Press, 1988, pp. 9, 49.
7. Carl Czerny, *A Systematic Introduction to Improvisation on the Pianoforte (Systematische Anleitung zum Fantasieren auf dem Pianoforte)* Op. 200, translated and edited by Alice Mitchell, New York: Longman, 1983, p. 108.
8. Robin Stowell, *Violin Technique and Performance Practice in the Late Eighteenth and Early Nineteenth Centuries,* Cambridge: Cambridge University Press, 1985, p. 342.
9. *Argus,* 29 December 1854, p. 5.
10. *Empire,* 11 February 1863, p. 5.
11. *Bell's Life in Victoria,* 30 May 1857, p. 2.
12. *Sydney Gazette,* 16 February 1836, p. 3.
13. *Argus,* 22 February 1851, p. 2. *Argus,* 19 February 1851, p. 4. *Argus,* 18 December 1854, p. 5.
14. Colin Roderick and Hugh Anderson (eds), *op. cit.,* p. 32.
15. Carl Czerny, *op. cit.,* p. 86.
16. Colin Roderick and Hugh Anderson (eds), *op. cit.,* p. 65.
17. Carl Czerny, *op. cit.,* p. 5.
18. Emily S. Patton, *Harmony Simplified for Popular Use: an Original Method of Applying the First Principles of Harmony to the Object of Accompanying the Voice on the Pianoforte,* p. 148. Allan & Co. (Wilkie's), Melbourne, and Novello, Ewer & Co, London, are listed as publishers, Allan's having arranged publication through Novello on Patton's behalf (see preface). Patton's preface is dated Christmas 1877.
19. *ibid.*
20. 'The Accompanist', *Musical Australian,* August 1914, p. 18.
21. Robert Donington, *The Interpretation of Early Music,* 2nd rev. ed., London: Faber & Faber, 1979, p. 181.
22. 'The Use of Musical Signs' (part one), *Illustrated Australian News and Musical* Times, 2 September 1889, p. 10.
23. Colin Roderick and Hugh Anderson (eds), *op. cit.,* p. 22.
24. *Illustrated Australian News and Musical Times,* 2 September 1889, p. 14.
25. 'To Be or Not To Be' (a translated excerpt from Hector Berlioz, *À Travers Chants*), *Illustrated Australian News and Musical Times,* 1 June 1889, p. 15.
26. Colin Roderick and Hugh Anderson, (eds), *op. cit.,* p. 55.
27. 'Mr Wilkie's Concert', *Argus,* 6 December 1850, p. 2.
28. *Illustrated Sydney News,* 14 April 1855, p. 174.
29. Harold Love, *The Golden Age of Australian Opera: W.S. Lyster and his Companies 1861-1880,* Sydney: Currency Press, 1981, pp. 104-5.
30. *ibid.,* p. 62; p. 164.
31. Will Crutchfield, 'Vocal Ornamentation in Verdi: the Phonographic Evidence', *Nineteenth Century Music,* 7 (1), Summer 1983, pp. 3-55.
32. Comment on local musical taste is found in 'Music in Victoria: the Popular Taste' (by W.T.C.), *Musical Monthly,* 1 December 1905, p. 4.
33. Robert Donington, *The Interpretation of Early Music,* 2nd rev. ed., London: Faber & Faber, 1979, p. 289.
34. *ibid.,* pp. 289-190.
35. This comprised a series of thirty lectures which were given in 1844 at Sydney College. The first three were published by Nathan in 1847 as *Theory and Practice of Music.* See pp. 7, 12, 13, 24, 33, 41, 45.
36. Emily Patton, *op. cit.,* 'Introductory Remarks'.
37. Emily Patton, *op. cit.,* p. 57.

38. *ibid*, p. 54; 'Introductory Remarks'.
39. *ibid.*, p. 124.
40. Oscar Comettant, *In the Land of Kangaroos and Gold Mines,* translated by Judith Armstrong, Adelaide: Rigby, 1980, p. 178. (First published as *Au Pays des Kangourous et des Mines,* Paris, 1890).
41. R.E.N. Twopenny, *Town Life in Australia* (London 1883): facsimile by Sydney University Press, 1973, p. 218.
42. Mary Francis De Lacy, *De Lacy's Book on Vamping for the Piano,* Melbourne: Allan & Co; *Mrs Russell's Vamping Method* (this may not be the actual title), undated; *W. M. Perrier's Harmonizer or, Instructions in the Art of Vamping or, Extemporizing on the Piano or Organ,* Melbourne: Spectator Publishing, 1890.
43. Perrier, *op. cit.*, p. 15.
44. *ibid.*, p. 24.
45. *ibid.*, p. 10; p. 11.
46. *ibid.*, p. 9; see also Emily Patton, *op. cit.*, 'Introductory Remarks'.
47. *Extemporization* was one of the cheap and popular Novello's Music Primers and Educational Series, (no. 33, London: Novello, undated (1890s)). Allan's was the Melbourne agent for Novello. W.H. Webbe, *The Pianist's ABC Primer and Guide*, 2nd ed., London: Forsyth Brothers, undated (copyright W.H. Webbe, New Zealand, 1900).
48. Edwin Evans, *How to Accompany at the Piano,* London: William Reeves, 1917.
49. Claude Kingston, *It Don't Seem a Day Too Much,* Melbourne: Rigby, 1971, p. 28.
50. W. Carne, *A Century of Harmony, the Official History of the Royal Melbourne Philharmonic Society,* Melbourne: Royal Melbourne Philharmonic Society, 1954, p. 52.
51. Rev. John O'Reilly, 'Gregorian Chant', a paper read at the Australasian Catholic Congress, Sydney, 1904 (original held at the State Library of Victoria), p. 13.
52. These connections and aspects of Floyd's early contact with improvisatory practice are discussed in William Chappell, 'A.E. Floyd', *Australian Journal of Music Education,* 13 October 1973, pp. 15-19. Kaye discusses his association with Floyd on a cassette of the ABC 'Encounter' program: 'God Has Perfect Pitch', 28 August 1988.
53. 'God Has Perfect Pitch', *op. cit.*
54. *ibid.*
55. Phil Kerr, *Music in Evangelism and Stories of Famous Christian Songs.* California: Gospel Music Publishers, 1944, p. 186.
56. Rev. Dr Keith Cole, *Robert Harkness: the Bendigo Hymnwriter,* Bendigo: Keith Cole Publications, 1988, p. 45.
57. *ibid.* p. 18. This and many other quotations in this source are not referenced. In our conversation Dr Cole stated that this quotation was from an issue of *Sacred Musician: a Sacred Music Magazine,* 1932, founded and edited by Harkness. He could not provide exact details. Other writings by Harkness are discussed in *ibid.*, pp. 33-37.
58. *ibid.*, p. 33. *Evangelistic Hymn Playing,* 2nd ed., has the copyright date of 1930.
59. Cited in Keith Cole, *op. cit.*, pp. 52-3.
60. Cited in *ibid.*, p. 25.
61. *ibid.*, p. 53.
62. *Conservatorium Magazine*, Sydney, December 1916, p. 16.
63. For example, a late 1830s vocal performance by Wallace's sister (Mrs Bushelle) was described on different occasions as 'full of ad captandum meretricious ornament[s]', and several years later as in a 'chaste classic style . . . her avoidance of every extraneous embellishment proved the correctness of her taste'. Cited and referenced in E.J. Lea-Scarlett, 'Music Making in Early Sydney', *Miscellanea Musicologica* 5, 1970, p. 43. Although famous for his fantasias and pot-pourris, pianist Edward (Eduard) Boulanger is described as having 'none of that meretricious style that solo performers are so apt to assume to astonish the vulgar'. 'Eduard Boulanger's Concert', *Illustrated Sydney News*, 17 March 1855, p. 118.
64. Emily Patton, *op. cit.*, 'Introductory Remarks'.
65. 'The Man at the Piano', *Conservatorium Magazine,* December 1917, p. 12 (reprinted from *Musical Opinion*).
66. Oscar Comettant, *op. cit.* p. 149.
67. Mr Hamilton, 'The Orchestra', *Illustrated Australian News and Musical Times,* 1 September 1889, p. 10.
68. Don Fairweather, *Your Friend Alberto Zelman*, Melbourne: Zelman Memorial Orchestra, 1984, pp. 27-8.
69. Interview: Whiteoak/Esther Rofe.

Chapter 2

1. Melbourne: La Trobe University Press, 1994, p. 19. Melbourne musician and linguist, Kim Bastin, advised me that the Bob Short language was a colonial adaptation of the language style of Charles Dickens' character, Jingle, in *The Posthumous Papers of the Pickwick Club,* London: Chapman & Hall, 1836-37.
2. Edmund Finn ('Garryowen'), *The Chronicles of Early Melbourne, 1835-1852: Historical, Anecdotal and Personal,* Melbourne: Heritage Publications, undated (facsimile ed. of Melbourne, Fergusson & Mitchell, 1888), p. 487.
3. See for example *Port Phillip Patriot and Melbourne Advertiser,* 27 March 1839, p. 4; music for balls: *Port Phillip Gazette,* 7 August 1839, p. 1; dancing lessons: *Port Phillip Patriot and Melbourne Advertiser,* 4 June 1840, p. 4.
4. *Port Phillip Gazette,* 22 April 1841, p. 3.
5. These dances are mentioned in Edmund Finn, *op. cit.*: Yankee Breakdown (1843), p. 457; Tarantella (1845), p. 471; Polka (1846), p. 477.

6. See for example Harold Love, 'Drama and Music in Colonial Victoria', in A.G.L. Shaw (ed.), *Victoria's Heritage*, Sydney: Allen & Unwin, pp. 179-200.
7. See Margaret Williams, *Australia on the Popular Stage 1829-1929: An Historical Entertainment in Six Acts*, Melbourne: Oxford University Press, 1983, Ch. 1 and p. 100.
8. Edmund Finn, *op. cit.*, p. 452.
9. *ibid.*, p.460.
10. Alex Bagot, *Coppin the Great*, Melbourne: Melbourne University Press, 1965, p. 88.
11. *ibid.*, 105.
12. Edmund Finn., *op. cit.*, p. 479.
13. Michael Booth, *Victorian Spectacular Theatre, 1850-1910*, London: Routledge & Kegan Paul, 1981, p. 9.
14. Harold Markham, *The Amateur Theatrical Handbook: a Guide to the Amateur Production of Plays*, London (and Melbourne): Isaac Pitman & Sons, 1927, p. 15.
15. Edmund Finn, *op. cit.*, p. 481.
16. Review of an 1851 Geelong pantomime, 'Harlequin Separation' in *Geelong Advertiser*, 3 January 1851, p. 3.
17. Edmund Finn, *op. cit.*, p. 454.
18. Program for *Rob Roy* and the *Widow's Victim*, *Port Phillip Patriot and Melbourne Advertiser*, 24 February 1842, p. 3.
19. Alex Bagot, *op. cit.*, pp. 94, 90. The cornet-à-piston (cornopean) superseded the keyed bugle but preceded the saxhorn. See Wally Horwood, *Adolfe Sax 1814-1894*, Hampshire, UK: Bramley Books, 1979, p. 28.
20. Edmund Finn, *op. cit.*, p. 489. An abortive performance by this band is mentioned in a review of the 'Bachelor's Ball', *Port Phillip Patriot and Melbourne Advertiser*, 14 January 1840, p. 4.
21. Vic and Sheila Gammon, 'From 'Repeat and Twiddle' to Precision and Snap: the Musical Revolution of the Mid-Nineteenth Century' in Trevor Herbert, *Bands: the Brass Band Movement in the 19th and 20th Centuries*, Milton Keynes: Open University Press, 1991, p. 125.
22. F. Lancelott, *Australia As It Is: Its Settlements, Farms and Gold Fields*, vol 2, London: Colburn & Co., 1852, p. 112.
23. Alex Bagot, *op. cit.*, p. 189.
24. This was a common playbill heading of the period; see Alex Bagot, *op. cit.*, p. 163.
25. Gerald Taylor (ed.), *Magical Nights at the Theatre: A Chronicle by Charles Waller*, Melbourne: Gerald Taylor, 1980.
26. For example Jim Crow: *Port Phillip Patriot and Melbourne Advertiser*, 2 June 1842, p. 3; Billy Waters: *Argus*, 7 July 1849, p. 2; Congo Minstrel: *Argus*, 24 April 1849, p. 3. See also the advertisement for the 'Congo Minstrel', *Argus*, 24 April, 1849.
27. Oscar Comettant, *In the Land of Kangaroos and Gold Mines*, Adelaide: Rigby, 1980 (translated from the French, first published Paris, 1890) p. 147.
28. Henry Mayhew, *London Labour and the London Poor*, vol. 3, London: Frank Cass, 1967 (from original ed. 1851, 1861-2), pp. 158-203.
29. *ibid.*, pp. 158-190. For playing by ear see for example p. 183.
30. Edmund Finn, *op. cit.*, p. 490.
31. J.S. Noble's Olympic Circus programs: *Argus*, 26 April 1852, p. 5; 6 May 1852, p. 5; 7 May 1852, p. 3; 26 May 1852, last page. See Alfred Dressler (ed.), *California's Pioneer Circus* (Memoirs of Joseph Andrew Rowe), San Francisco: 1926. See also the index entry in Mark St Leon, *Spangles and Sawdust: the Circus in Australia*, Melbourne: Greenhouse Publications, 1983, p. 86.
32. Ballroom music: e.g. *Argus*, 27 December 1849, p. 2; promenade concerts: e.g. *Argus*, 11 March 1851, p. 2; formal concerts: e.g. *Argus*, 5 March 1850, p. 3; predecessor of silent film: see 'Theatre Music' in Part Two of this chapter; string band: *Argus*, 18 May 1852, p. 8.
33. See for example the advertisement placed by the conductor George Chapman, *Argus*, 26 January 1853, p. 7.
34. For example, the Queens Theatre orchestra is mentioned as featuring 'a variety of New Overtures, Polkas, Quadrilles, Waltzes, just received from England', *Argus*, 17 October 1850, p. 3.
35. Arthur R. Taylor, *Labour & Love*, London: Elm Tree Books, 1983, p. 6.
36. J. Orde Hume, *Chats on Amateur Bands*, Book 2, London: R. Smith & Co., 1902, p. 7.
37. 'Mannerisms in Music', *Australian Band News*, 26 April 1918, p. 15 (probably by the editor T.L. Hellings).
38. For example, Harry Larsen, Dave Meredith, Harry Mehden, Frank Coughlan and Harold Barlow all feature as soloists on the very early jazz recordings discussed in Chapter Six.
39. See Waterhouse's comments regarding the 'continuity of a [working] class tradition of audience participation' in Richard Waterhouse, *From Minstrel Show to Vaudeville: the Australian Popular Stage, 1788-1914*, Sydney: University of New South Wales Press, 1990, p. 127.
40. For example, in 1861 a Melbourne critic complained of a particular actor who 'overstepped the modesty of nature by indulging in the old melodramatic action of bygone days'. 'Theatricals and Music', *Bell's Life in Victoria*, 10 August 1861. p. 2.
41. For discussion of Australian 'realist' melodrama see Margaret Williams, *op. cit.*, pp. 100-262.
42. Celestine McDermott, 'National Vaudeville' in Harold Love (ed.), *The Australian Stage: A Documentary History*, University of New South Wales Press, 1984, pp. 135-43. For a more general history of Australian vaudeville see Richard Waterhouse, *op. cit.*, pp. 116-138; Charles Norman, *When Vaudeville was King*, Melbourne: Spectrum

Publications, 1984; Katrina Bard, 'The History of Vaudeville in Australia from 1900 to 1930', B.Lett. thesis, University of New England, 1983.
43. Charles Norman, *op. cit.*, p. 9.
44. Richard Waterhouse, *op. cit.*, p. 138.
45. See Charles Norman, *op. cit.*, p. 61.
46. Rev. C. Stuart Rose, 'Two American Types That Left their Stamp on Victorian History', *Victorian Historical Magazine,* 7(3), July 1919, p. 126.
47. Daniel and Annette Potts, *Young America and Australian Gold: America and the Gold Rush of the 1850s*, St Lucia: University of Queensland Press, 1974. See the chapter, 'Trans-Pacific Thespians' pp. 123-153.
48. See Harold Love, *The Golden Age of Australian Opera: W.S. Lyster and His Companies, 1861-1880*, Sydney: Currency Press, 1981. Regarding J.C. Williamson see for example Viola Tait, *A Family of Brothers, the Taits and J.C. Williamson: a Theatre History*, Melbourne: William Heinemann, 1971.
49. Mark St Leon, *op. cit.*, p. 73.
50. Karl King, 'Barnum and Bailey's Favorite', Oskaloosa USA: C.L. Barnhouse Company, 1913. Recorded on, for example, Crest Records: 4096.
51. Richard Waterhouse, *op. cit.*, pp. 40-43.
52. *ibid.*, p. 43.
53. *Argus,* 10 June 1878, p. 8.
54. See, for example, *Australian Variety and Show World* (title changes), 1(1), 15 October 1913 to mid-1914.
55. Shirley Andrews, *Take Your Partners: Traditional Dancing in Australia,* 2nd ed., Melbourne: Hyland House, 1976, p. 78.
56. Shirley Andrews describes local hostility to ragtime in *ibid.*, p. 79. I also discussed the political dimension of this hostility with Andrews' informant, political historian Les Barnes whose recollections go back to 1913.
57. See for example the *Age,* 6 July 1918, p. 6. See also Shirley Andrews, *ibid.*, pp. 79-80.
58. *Footlight Star,* June 1919, p. 16; 'Dancers and Dancing', *Footlight Star,* December 1919, p. 20.
59. *Photo-Play* (Sydney) 20 April 1912, p. 22.
60. For an account of this event see Graham Shirley and Brian Adams, *Australian Cinema: the First Eighty Years,* Sydney: Angus & Robertson and Currency Press, 1983, pp. 5-6. Rev. edition Currency Press, 1989.
61. Rita Sheehan, 'The Talkies Ended Smithy, Lollyboys and the Picture Show Draggers', *Sydney Morning Herald,* 19 February 1983, p. 35.
62. *Musical Monthly,* 1 August 1906, p. 8 (part 4 of a series).
63. 'On the job' conversations with Teddy Ellis in the late 1960s.
64. 'Some Random Ramblings: Boy in a Dance Band' (by T.B.), *Australasian Band and Orchestra News,* 27 April 1936, p. 9.
65. Mary Fortune, 'Arrival in Melbourne', in Lucy Sussex (ed.), *The Fortunes of Mary Fortune,* Ringwood, Victoria: Penguin, 1989, p. 8 (see comments on p. xvi regarding the reliability of this account).
66. Shirley Andrews, *op. cit.* Andrews provides an anthology of published eyewitness accounts of mostly rural dancing and dance music for the period 1803-1951, pp. 47-66. She comments elsewhere about how so many played by ear, p. 191.
67. See J. Meredith, R. Covell and P. Brown, *Folk Songs of Australia and the Men and Women Who Sang Them*, vol. 2, New South Wales University Press, 1987, preface.
68. Melbourne: George Robertson, pp. 21-6.
69. J. Meredith, R. Covell and P. Brown, *op. cit.*, p. 11.
70. *ibid.*, p. 12.
71. "The Bachelors' Ball', *Port Phillip Patriot and Melbourne Advertiser,* 16 January 1840, p. 4.
72. Some are listed in Ken Snell, *Australian Popular Music: Composer Index*, 2nd ed., Bentleigh, Victoria: Quick Trick Press, 1991, p. 23. Other examples of colonial dance music composition are published and/or discussed in Nell Challingsworth, *Dancing Down the Years: the Romantic Century in Australia.* Melbourne: Craftsman Press, 1978.
73. W.M. Perrier, *W.M. Perrier's Harmonizer or, Instructions in the Art of Vamping or, Extemporizing on the Piano or Organ*, Melbourne: Spectator Publishing, 1890, pp. 28-9 (addenda).
74. Fred Lyster is credited as the composer but I suspect that, while he may have written the melody, Alfred Plumpton (composer of the remainder of the music for this play) probably harmonised it and wrote the variations.
75. St John Caws, 'Experiences of a New Chum in Victoria in the Early Sixties: a True Story' (part two), *Musical Monthly,* 1 June 1906, p. 16.
76. *ibid.*, p. 18.
77. *ibid.* p. 17.
78. Fred H. Gooch, 'Dancing and its Music – 1890: Retrospect', *Australian Music Maker and Dance Band News,* 1 January 1935, p. 37.
79. Andrew Bisset, *Black Roots White Flowers: A History of Jazz in Australia*, Sydney: Golden Press, 1979, p. 5. This part of Bisset's interview with Pearse was also broadcast on program one (14 July 1987) of the ABC radio series, 'Jazz Transplant', prepared by Bisset and Mike Sutcliffe.
80. William Kelly, *Life in Victoria: or Victoria in 1852, and Victoria in 1858,* Kilmore, Victoria: Lowden Publishing Co., 1977, Historical Reprint Series no. 6, p. 62.
81. F. Lancelott, *op. cit.*, pp. 113-114.
82. Here I am citing Eric Irvin, who examined the texts of melodramas produced at Levey's Theatre Royal (Sydney, 1830s) and the Royal Victoria (Sydney). Eric Irvin, *Dictionary of the Australian Theatre 1788-1914*, Sydney: Hale & Iremonger,

1985, p. 205.
83. Henry Mayhew, *London Labour and the London Poor* (vol. 3), London, Frank Cass (facsimile of 1851 and 1861-2 editions), p. 123.
84. Frank Rahill, *The World of Melodrama*, Pennsylvania State University Press, 1967, p. 121.
85. Valantyne Napier, *Act as Known: Australian Speciality Artists on the World Variety Circuits from 1900 to 1960*, Brunswick, Victoria: Globe Press, 1986, p. 132.
86. Axel Christensen, *Instruction Books for Vaudeville Piano Playing, Book Five: Vaudeville Cue Music*, Chicago: Axel W. Christensen, copyright 1912, n.p.
87. *Australian Variety*, 27 May 1914, p. 10.
88. *Melbourne Daily News and Port Phillip Patriot*, 27 October 1848, p. 2.
89. *ibid*, 15 November 1848, p. 2.
90. *Sydney Gazette*, 17 September 1836, p. 2.
91. *Argus*, 14 June 1853, p. 9.
92. Gerald Taylor (ed.), *op. cit.*, p. 50.
93. Kohler appears on an 1855 Theatre Royal program as 'Solo-Flagolet (first time in the Colony)', *Age*, 9 November 1855, p. 8. During 1858 he toured Victoria with the American blackface minstrel troupe, the San Francisco Minstrels, featuring 'all kinds of music'. *Bell's Life in Victoria*, 18 September 1858, p. 2. In 1859 he performed at Beechworth as 'Professor Kohler', styling himself as the 'Wizard of The North' [a send-up of the famous magician] assisted by 'Madame Flora'. *Bell's Life in Victoria*, 22 January 1859, p. 2. A few months later 'Kohler's celebrated band' was reported as engaged for a newly opened dancing venue, the Argyle Rooms, Bourke St, Melbourne. *Bell's Life in Victoria*, 28 May 1859, p. 2. Some other aspects of Kohler's career and work are discussed and referenced in Harold Love, *The Golden Age of Australian Opera*, *op. cit.*, pp. 57, 95, 227.
94. *Argus*, 5 September 1904, p. 6.
95. *Age*, 1 July 1912, p. 8.
96. *Argus*, 7 December 1850, p. 2.
97. *South Australian Advertiser*, 12 June 1862, p. 2. Cited in Ann Wentzel, 'The First Hundred Years of Music in Australia, 1788-1888', M.A. thesis, University of Sydney, 1963, p. 153. In Melbourne they produced a piece describing the death of explorers, Burke and Wills. See *ibid.*, pp. 152-4.
98. Cited in Chris Long, 'The Thomas Rome Recordings' in *International Association of Sound Archives: Australian Branch Newsletter*, 19 January 1985, p.10.
99. *Argus*, 19 September 1850 (one page supplement).
100. *Argus*, 19 February 1851, p. 2.
101. *Argus*, 27 February 1851, p. 3.
102. Quoted in Chris Long, *op. cit.*, pp. 10-11.
103. *Photo-Play* (Sydney) 20 April 1912, p. 22.
104. Interview: Whiteoak/Bill Witnish (former silent film projectionist).
105. See also Diane Collins, *Hollywood Down Under: Australians at the Movies, 1896 to the Present Day*, North Ryde, NSW: Angus and Robertson, 1987, pp. 77-107.
106. Interview: Whiteoak/Ron Richards.
107. Interview: Whiteoak/Esther Rofe.
108. Interview: Whiteoak/Ron Richards.
109. *Age*, 10 April 1920, p. 20.
110. Edith Lang and George West, *Musical Accompaniment of Moving Pictures*, Boston: Arno Press & *New York Times*, 1970 (reprint of 1920 ed.).
111. *ibid.*, p. 8.
112. *ibid.*, pp. 8-13.
113. *ibid.*, p. 5.
114. *ibid.*, pp. 13-21.
115. *ibid.*, p. 26.
116. Rita Sheehan, *op. cit.*
117. Interview: Whiteoak/Carmen Naylor.
118. This video is a clip from the Channel 10 (Sydney) television program 'Good Morning Australia', 25 April 1986.
119. Interview: Whiteoak/Carmen Naylor.
120. An Australian-composed and published example is Herbert de Pinna, *Album of Cinema Music*, Sydney: W.H. Paling, c. 1916.
121. Interview: Whiteoak/Esther Rofe.
122. Rita Sheehan, *op. cit.*
123. My personal experience includes playing brass band music in circumstances in which it was often necessary to fake parts or make fairly drastic spontaneous modifications on the basis of visual or verbal signals. This was in the 1960s when I played for the Melbourne Metropolitan Fire Brigade's Friday Circus, a weekly public demonstration of firefighting skills, acrobatics, clowning and feats of daring at great heights. Circus act accompaniment, as such, similarly required a high degree of spontaneous musical reaction.
124. 'Band Life in Early Australian Days', *Australasian Bandsman*, 26 October 1923, pp. 13, 15.
125. William Kelly, *op. cit.*, pp. 275-6.
126. Oscar Comettant, *op. cit.*, p. 147.
127. T. L. Hellings, 'Reminiscences of Band Life', *Australian Band News*, 26 January 1917, p. 12.
128. 'Hallas' Band: an Old Bendigo Body', *Australasian Band and Orchestra News*, 26 January 1927, p. 35.
129. From an anonymous poem published in the *Australasian Bandsman*, 26 March 1920, p. 19.
130. 'A Famous Cornetist', *Australasian Bandsman*, 26 April 1920, pp. 6-7.
131. June 1893. Playbills and Programs, Mitchell Library, Sydney.
132. Letter from George F. Howes published in the *Australasian Bandsman*, 26 May 1920, p. 3.
133. 'A Famous Cornetist', *Australasian Bandsman*, *loc. cit.*

134. George Wirth, *Round the World with a Circus.* Melbourne: Troedel Cooper, 1925.
135. *ibid.*, p. 17.
136. John Clare, 'Harry Larsen', *Music Maker,* 19 December 1970, p. 5. See also 'Philip Wirth was an Instrumentalist', *Australasian Dance and Brass Band News,* 27 September 1937, p. 7; A.E. Mason, 'Philip Wirth Stars in Band!', *Australasian Dance and Brass Band News,* 27 March 1939, pp. 19, 27.
137. Sid Baker, 'Circus Bands of Yesteryear', *Outdoor Showman,* September 1961, p. 25.
138. See Mark St Leon, *op. cit.*, pp. 10-11 and index: Aboriginals.
139. For a graphic description of the hardship of a small Australian outback family circus see Fred Lord, *Little Big Top,* Adelaide: Rigby, 1965.
140. *ibid.*, p. 146. The author Fred Lord is paraphrasing Winn Seymour's account, as he does throughout the book. See *ibid.*, 'Author's Note'.
141. See Peggy Joseph interview in Mark St Leon, 'Australian Circus Reminiscences', Ultimo, NSW (unpublished manuscript): pp. 294-5. See also Mark St Leon (ed.), *The Silver Road: the Life of Mervyn King, Circus Man,* Springwood, NSW: Butterfly Books, 1990, pp. 54-5.
142. Interview Whiteoak/Mervyn King.
143. Interviews: Whiteoak/Ron Shand, Australian actor from a circus family, and Whiteoak/Mervyn King.
144. Mervyn King discusses circus musicians playing 'clarinet parts on cornet' and 'melodies as solos on $B^{\flat}$ bass' in Mark St Leon, 'Australian Circus Reminiscences', *op. cit.*, p. 180.
145. Sid Baker, *op. cit.*, p. 25.
146. George Wirth, 'The Romance of a Great Circus', *Theatre Magazine,* 1 April 1920, p. 6.
147. For example, a full standard brass band arrangement might comprise 1 soprano cornet ($E^{\flat}$), 4 solo cornets ($B^{\flat}$), 1 repiano cornet ($B^{\flat}$), 2 second cornets ($B^{\flat}$), 2 third cornets ($B^{\flat}$), 1 solo horn ($E^{\flat}$), 1 first horn ($E^{\flat}$), 1 second horn ($E^{\flat}$), 1 first baritone ($B^{\flat}$), 1 second baritone ($B^{\flat}$), 1 first trombone ($B^{\flat}$), 1 second trombone ($B^{\flat}$), 1 bass trombone (G), 2 euphoniums ($B^{\flat}$), 2 bass ($E^{\flat}$), 2 bass ($B^{\flat}$), 1 drum.
148. For example, Von Der Mehden 'rarely used music other than his own arrangement[s]'. 'An Appreciation by an Old Member of his Band', *Australasian Bandsman,* 26 February 1920, p. 5.
149. One reference to Fitzgerald's 1904 circus band arrangements describes them as 'serviceable', possibly meaning that they were suitable for a constantly changing band structure. *Australasian Bandsman,* 15 December 1904, p. 9.
150. Sid Baker lists the names of notable circus musicians in, amongst other writings, 'Under the Big Top', *Australian Music Maker,* 1 November 1948, p. 40.
151. This was mentioned in a discussion about learning to play in collectively improvised jazz style with trombone section members of the Melbourne Musicians' Club Workshop Band who had been brass band musicians. Ron Richards also mentioned that his ability to play counter-melody on soprano saxophone was partly a legacy of playing violin obbligato as a silent cinema musician. From one of many discussions with the 1920s dance and cinema musician, Ron Richards.
152. For a very comprehensive annotated compilation of the technical devices which formed the basis of the competent brass player's technique, see one of the various translated editions of J.B. Arban, *Complete Method of Instruction for the Cornet-à-Pistons and Saxhorn,* Paris, 1864. This method has been adapted for other members of the brass family and became known in Australia as the 'bandsman's bible'.
153. Mervyn King mentions the introduction of the 'laughing saxophone' effect into local circus bands, probably in the early 1920s. Interview: Whiteoak/Mervyn King.
154. Reference is made to Chambers' remarkable range in the *Australasian Bandsman,* 15 December 1904, p. 9. See also Glen Bridges, *Pioneers in Brass,* Detroit, U.S.A.: Sherwood Publications, 1965, pp. 19-20.
155. Colonel Percival Dale, 'Mudgee The Marvel' (part one), an undated cutting in the Arthur Stirling Collection about the remarkable abilities of Tom Robertson (b.1800s) from Mudgee, NSW. This cutting is cited as a reprint from the Salvation Army journal, *Local Officer and Bandsman,* 1947.
156. Interview: Whiteoak/Mervyn King.
157. Sid Baker states that the band was sometimes taken out on a lorry to play a few tunes from memory. Sid Baker, 'Circus Music' (part three), *Bandsman,* 12 October 1956, p. 11. Ron Shand (cited above) states that performer/musician members of small family circus bands were often ear players. Interview: Whiteoak/Ron Shand.
158. This was mentioned in one of my many extensive discussions with Arthur Stirling about Australian band music. However, Stirling conceded that he had never heard a leading professional circus band such as Wirth's.
159. Interview: Whiteoak/Arthur Withers.
160. *ibid.*
161. *ibid.*

Chapter 3

1. A version of this chapter is published as 'From Jim Crow to Jazz: Imitation African-American Improvisatory Musical Practice in Pre-Jazz Australia' in *Perfect Beat* 1 (3), July 1993, pp.50-74.
2. A field holler is a highly expressive, often melismatic African-American solo work-song or cry.
3. For further discussion see John Hasse, 'Ragtime: From The Top' in John Hasse (ed.), *Ragtime: Its History, Composers and Music,* London:

Macmillan Press, 1985. p. 20. In regard to ragtime composers, see the chart of 'Most Prolific Composers of Instrumental Rags', pp. 18-19 of the above source.

4. See the extensive discussion and musical examples published in Hans Nathan, *Dan Emmett and the Rise of Negro Minstrelsy*, Oklahoma: Oklahoma University Press, 1962, pp. 160-188.

5. Lynne Fauley Emery, *Black Dance from 1619 to Today*, 2nd rev. ed., Princeton, New Jersey: Princeton Book Company, 1988, pp. 181-185.

6. *ibid.*, p. 185.

7. Quoted from a minstrel program, cited in Robert Toll, *Blacking Up: the Minstrel Show in Nineteenth Century America*, New York: Oxford University Press, 1974, p. 30.

8. *ibid.*, p. 52.

9. *Clipper* (New York), 16 December 1865, cited in *ibid*, p. 202.

10. Richard Waterhouse, *From Minstrel Show to Vaudeville: the Australian Popular Stage, 1788-1914*, Sydney: New South Wales University Press, 1990, p. 102. Waterhouse cites Peter Bourke's *Popular Culture in Early Modern Europe*, London: 1978, p. 100.

11. Robert Toll, *op. cit.*, p. 68.

12. Described in Hans Nathan, *op. cit.*, p. 52. Musical accenting for the jump is noted in 'Jim Crow', *Weippert's Selection of Country Dances*, London: G. Weippert, n.d. (after 1850), p. 9.

13. *Border Post*, 28 March 1957, p. 3.

14. A description of mid-nineteenth century London blackface minstrel performance practice suggests that instrumental skill was sometimes the last thing to be learnt by minstrels. For example: 'As soon as I could get in to vamp the tunes on the banjo a little, I went at it, too . . . We finished up with the 'Railway Overture', and it was more like the railway than music, for it was all thumping and whistling, for nobody knowed how to play the banjo then'. Henry Mayhew, *London Labour and the London Poor*, vol. 3, London, Frank Cass, 1967 (original eds, 1851 and 161-2), p. 191.

15. Harry Reynolds, *Minstrel Memories: the Story of Burnt Cork Minstrelsy in Great Britain from 1836 to 1927*, London: Alston Rivers, 1928, p. 163.

16. W.C. Handy, *Father of the Blues*, Arna Bontemps (ed.), New York: Collier Books, 1971, p. 80.

17. *Age*, 4 December 1855, p. 5.

18. *Empire* (Sydney), 30 March 1863, p. 4.

19. *ibid.* This is also mentioned in a review in the *Age*, 3 February 1863, p.5.

20. *Argus*, 1 January 1853, (back page).

21. Hans Nathan, *Dan Emmett and the Rise of Early Negro Minstrelsy*, Oklahoma University Press, 1962, p. 129. Nathan cites William Francis Allen, *Slave Songs of The United States*, (1867) New York, n. p., republished 1951, pp. vi, xx.

22. Flautina solo with variations, *Argus*, 24 September 1853. Flautina solo 'Away With Melancholy' with variations, *Argus* 15 February 1854. Fantasia for flautina, *Argus*, 21 April 1854, p. 5. Fantasia on concertina with pianoforte accompaniment, *Argus*, 1 June 1854, p. 8.

23. Hans Nathan, *op. cit.*, p. 403.

24. *ibid.*, p. 128.

25. *ibid.*, p.128.

26. *ibid.*, p. 147.

27. *Ovens and Murray Valley Advertiser*, 12 May 1855, p.1 and the *Argus*, 15 October 1853, last page.

28. Robert Winans, 'Early Minstrel Show Music: 1843-1852' in Glenn Loney (ed.), *Musical Theater in America: Papers and Proceedings of the Conference on the Musical Theater in America*, Westport: Greenwood Press, 1984, pp. 78-9.

29. See for example the *Age*, 21 April 1854, p. 5; *Illustrated Sydney News*, 29 October 1853, p. 30; *Empire*, 25 February 1863, p. 4.

30. Nathan, *op. cit.*, p. 149.

31. *ibid.*, p. 151.

32. See, for example, *Argus*, 24 April 1849, 16 July 1849.

33. Winans, *op. cit.*, p. 73.

34. *ibid.*, p. 79. 'Sleigh ride', *Argus*, 2 March 1863, p. 8; 'Horse race imitations', *Argus*, 17 November 1853, *Age*, 4 December 55, p. 5.

35. Harry Reynolds, *op. cit.*, p. 99. *Argus*, 1 April 1854, p. 5.

36. *ibid.*

37. From a blackface minstrel program reprinted in Paul Magriel (ed.), *Chronicles of The American Dance from the Shakers to Martha Graham*, New York: Da Capo Press, 1948, pp. 44-5. Winans suggests that the minstrel tambourine, being larger than the modern tambourine and having fewer rattles, was more a drum than a rattle. Robert Winans, *op. cit.*, p. 73.

38. Henry Mayhew, *op. cit.*, p. 191.

39. Describing the attributes of the British minstrel show in broad terms, Reynolds speaks of 'smart and spectacular performance with bones and tambourine' by the corner men. Harry Reynolds, *op. cit.*, p.71. A faint residue of this practice is probably seen in the occasional contemporary performance of the 'spoons' (rhythmic variations in the form of accompaniment to music or a rhythmic paraphrase of a well known tune on a pair of hand-held spoons). I personally recall that this practice was very common amongst London street buskers about thirty years ago and was also a common 'party trick' in Australia even earlier.

40. *Bell's Life In Victoria*, 18 September 1858, p. 2.

41. John Allen Wyeth, *With Sabre and Scalpel*, New York: Harper Bros., 1914, p. 59. Cited in Lynne Fauley Emery, *Black Dance: From 1619 to Today*, Princeton: Princeton Book Company, 1988, p. 97.

42. Charles Sherlock, 'From Breakdown To Ragtime, *Cosmopolitan*, (U.S.A) October, 1901,

p. 635.
43. *Age,* 3 February 1863, p. 5.
44. In the statement 'Percussive rhythms were emphasised from the early forties on, when clogs began to be used occasionally', Nathan is citing 'Amusement Annals', *New York Clipper* 14 July 1887, n.p. Hans Nathan, *op. cit.* p. 75.
45. Some dances mentioned on Melbourne minstrel programs are 'Virginny Breakdown': *Geelong Advertiser,* 24 July 1840, p. 3; Dance of Lucy Long: *Argus,* 17 September 1853, last page; Plantation Jig: *Argus,* 20 September 1853, n. p.; Plantation Breakdown: *Argus,* 6 May 1854, p. 8; A Clog Hornpipe 'more extravagant than anything we have ever witnessed': *Bell's Life in Victoria,* 18 September 1858, p. 2; New Plantation Walk Around: *Age,* 2 August 1873, p. 8; 'The champion dancer of Australia in [the] wonderful Rattlesnake Jig': *Argus,* 3 November 1862, p. 8; Challenge Dance: *Argus,* 19 February 1863, p. 8; Silver Belt Jig: *Argus,* 6 December 1863, p. 8. In relation to the Rattlesnake Jig cited above, Hans Nathan states 'How much variety was possible in minstrel dances is shown in John Diamond's 'Rattle Snake Jig'. It consisted of as many as 120 steps'. Hans Nathan, *op. cit.,* p. 83.
46. From an undated (pre-1850) handbill for the production, *Old Kentucky Nigger.* Cited in Robyn Annear, *Bearbrass: Imagining Early Melbourne,* Melbourne: Mandarin, 1995, p. 274.
47. Marian Hannah Winter, 'Juba and American Minstrelsy', in Paul Magriel (ed.), *op. cit.,* p. 46. In jazz terminology 'lick' usually also implies a stock jazz phrase or personal cliché.
48. *ibid.,* pp. 60-61.
49. Isaac Goldberg, *Tin Pan Alley: A Chronicle of American Popular Music,* New York: Frederick Ungar, 1961, p. 141.
50. For discussion of the Western concept of divisive rhythm see for example Mantle Hood, *Ethnomusicologist,* New York: McGraw Hill Book Company, 1971, pp. 35-6.
51. Douglas Gilbert, *Lost Chords,* Garden City, New York: Doubleday, 1942, pp. 13-14, cited in Lynne Fauley Emery, *op. cit.,* p. 192.
52. Nathan, *op. cit.,* p. 233.
53. Marshall and Jean Stearns, *Jazz Dance: the Story of American Vernacular Dance,* New York: Macmillan, 1968, p. 50. Here they are citing a white dancer, James McIntyre: 'a pioneer, who prided himself on introducing a syncopated buck-and-wing on the New York Stage around 1880 (it did not become popular until later)'.
54. *Empire,* 30 March 1863, p. 4. See discussion of the 'double shuffle' in Hans Nathan *op. cit.,* pp. 83-5. William Kelly mentions doing this at a Melbourne dance in the 1850s. William Kelly, *Life in Victoria* (1852-58), Kilmore, Victoria: Lowden Publishing Co., 1977, pp. 132-6.
55. Brander Mathews, 'The Rise and Fall of Early Negro Minstrelsy', *Scribner's Magazine,* June 1915, p. 755, cited in Lynne Fauley Emery, *op. cit.,* p. 194.
56. Hans Nathan, *op. cit.,* p. 71.
57. *ibid.,* p. 213.
58. Robert Winans, *op. cit.,* pp. 71, 73.
59. Hans Nathan, *op. cit.,* p. 209.
60. *ibid.,* pp. 209-213.
61. *ibid.,* p. 128.
62. *ibid.,* p. 209, citing *Ben Harney's Rag-Time Instructor,* Chicago: Sol Bloom, 1897.
63. Nathan mentions that 'Genuine Negro Jig', 'Negro Jig', and 'Dr. Hertog's Jig' (which are included in Nathan's book) 'may well be the originals or close to them', *ibid.,* p. 208.
64. Robert Winans, *op. cit.,* pp. 78-9.
65. Lowell Schreyer, 'The Banjo In Ragtime' in John Hasse (ed.), *Ragtime: Its History, Composers and Music,* London: Macmillan, 1985, p. 56.
66. *ibid.*
67. *ibid.*
68. Robert Winans, 'The Folk, The Stage, and the Five-String Banjo in the Nineteenth Century', in *Journal of American Folklore,* no. 34, 1976, pp. 407-37.
69. *Argus,* 21 April 1854, p. 5.
70. The following references will provide entry points to finding programs and reviews of these troupes. Waterland and Readings: *Argus,* 15 July 1850; Howard's Serenaders: *Argus,* 15 August 1850, p. 2; American Black Serenaders: *Argus,* 6 August 1851, p. 3; Rainer's Original Ethiopian Serenaders: *Argus,* 4 December 1851 p. 1; Barlow's Sable Minstrels: Argus, 18 July 1854; Totten's Harmoneons: *Argus,* 1 June 1854, p. 8; Backus Minstrels: *Age,* 4 December 1855, p. 5.
71. *Geelong Advertiser,* 10 July 1850, p. 2.
72. *Argus,* 15 July 1850, p. 2.
73. *Geelong Advertiser* 23 July 1850, p. 2.
74. 1. *Argus,* 26 May 1853, (back page). 2. *Argus,* 1 January 1853, (back page); 3-5. 27 May 1853, (back page); 6. 15 February 1854.
75. Robert Winans, 'Early Minstrel Show Music, 1843-52, *op. cit.,* p. 78.
76. Nathan, *op. cit.,* p. 183.
77. Emerson's Californian Minstrels, *Age,* 4 August 1873, p. 2.
78. *The Ovens and Murray Valley Advertiser,* 10 August, 1878, p. 5.
79. Garry Shearston, 'Bessy Campbell, Australia's Queen of Banjo' in *Tradition,* 3(3), October 1966, p. 3.
80. *Ellis's Thorough School for the Five Stringed Banjo,* London: John Alvey Turner, 1886, p. 48.
81. Because of its percussiveness the banjo was the ideal instrument for early acoustic recording and it is principally by this medium that banjo embellishment technique of the ragtime era can be studied. Numerous banjo solos by Van Eps, Ossman and Brooks, including cakewalks, 'coon

song' and 'Rag Time' are catalogued under 'Banjo Solos' in Allen Koenigsberg, *Edison Cylinder Records. 1889-12*, New York: Stellar Production, 1969.
82. From a Tivoli Theatre Program for 9 April 1904 reproduced, along with the catalogue containing the reference to 'Dreams Of Darkie Land', in Mike Tucker, 'The Federal and Australian Cylinder Record Company: A History' *Australian Record and Music Review*, 5 April, 1990, p. 7.

Chapter 4

1. *Australian Musical News*, 7 (10), 1 April 1918, p. 260.
2. Joe Laurie Jnr, *Vaudeville: From the Honky-Tonks to the Palace*, New York: Henry Holt, 1953, p. 62.
3. *Ben Harney's Rag Time Instructor* (arranged by Theodore H. Northrup), Chicago: Sol Bloom, 1897.
4. See the chapter 'Cake Walk in the Sky' in Rudi Blesh and Harriet Janis, *They All Played Ragtime: The True Story of an American Music*, rev. ed., New York: Oak Publications, 1966; Isaac Goldberg, *Tin Pan Alley: A Chronicle of American Popular Music*, New York: Fredrick Ungar, 1961, pp. 147-9; Edward Berlin, *Reflections and Research on Ragtime*, New York: Institute for Studies in American Music, 1987, pp. 31-34; Russell Sanjek, *American Popular Music and its Business: The First Four Hundred Years*, vol. 2, New York: Oxford University Press, 1988, pp. 291-2; William Schafer and Johannes Riedel, *The Art of Ragtime: Form and Meaning of an Original Black Art*, New York: Da Capo Press, pp. 15-16.
5. Berlin claims in *Ragtime: A Musical and Cultural History*, (Berkeley: University of California Press, 1980, p. 24) that Harney was black, but later in *Reflections and Research on Ragtime* (*op. cit.*, p.84) he provides evidence that more or less counters his original claim. William Schafer and Johannes Riedel (*op. cit.*, p. 27), Ian Whitcomb (*Irving Berlin and Ragtime America*, London: Century Hutchinson, 1987, p. 112), and William Tallmadge ('Harney, Ben(jamin), R(obertson)' in *The New Grove Dictionary of American Music*, vol. 2, London: Macmillan Press, 1986, p. 327), all state that Harney was white.
6. Ian Whitcomb, *ibid.*, p. 114.
7. Maxwell Marcuse, *Tin Pan Alley in Gaslight*, New York: Century House, 1959, p. 200, cited in Edward Berlin, *Reflections and Research on Ragtime*, *op. cit.*, p. 32.
8. Ben Harney, *op. cit.*; Chicago: Axel W. Christensen; New York: Winn's School of Popular Music.
9. From an illustrated advertisement in *Ragtime Review*, 1916 (undated), p. 25.
10. See for example an advertisement for the *Ragtime Review* in *Etude*, April 1915, p. 313 (originally purchased in Melbourne but published in Philadelphia).
11. Ian Whitcomb, *op. cit.*, p. 100.
12. By Charles Trevathan, New York: White-Smith Music Publishing Co., 1896. Reproduced in Stanley Appelbaum (ed.), *Show Songs from 'The Black Crook' to 'The Red Mill'*, New York: Dover Publications, 1974, pp. 78-81.
13. Isaac Goldberg, *op. cit.*, p. 150.
14. Isidore Witmark and Isaac Goldberg, *The Story of the House of Witmark: From Ragtime to Swingtime*, New York: Lee Furman, 1939, p. 153.
15. Edward Berlin, *Ragtime: A Musical and Cultural History*, *op. cit.*, pp. 64-66.
16. Edward Berlin, 'Ragtime Song' in John Hasse (ed.), *Ragtime: Its History, Composers and Music*, London: Macmillan Press, 1985, p. 77.
17. Similarly, in the modern day Barn Dance I have noted that the lead player will greatly exaggerate the dotted note/triplet rhythm to create a bright, bouncy beat.
18. New York: Ted Snyder, 1911.
19. Witmark & Sons, 1897.
20. Rupert Hughes, 'A Eulogy of Rag-Time', *Musical Record and Review* (Boston) 447, 1 April 1899, pp. 158-9.
21. 'Rag-Time', *The Times*, 8 February 1913, p.11.
22. 'At the Piano and Elsewhere', *Footlight Star*, February 1919, p. 6.
23. Rupert Hughes, *op. cit.*, p. 159.
24. Rupert Hughes, *op. cit.*, p. 158. Edward R. Winn, 'Ragtime Piano Playing' (lesson 15), *Melody* 2(1), January 1918, p. 26.
25. See Editorial in *Conservatorium Magazine*, Sydney: August 1917, p. 4. See also Henry Tate, 'Modern Musical Tendencies', *Australian Musical News* 7 (10), 1 April 1918, p. 260.
26. From a review of Orpheus McAdoo's Georgia Minstrels and Alabama Cake Walkers in the *Sydney Mail*, 24 June 1899, p. 1456.
27. Henry Sampson, *Blacks in Blackface: A Source Book on Early Black Musical Shows*, Metuchen, NJ: The Scarecrow Press, 1980, p. 2.
28. Bruce Johnson, *The Oxford Companion to Australian Jazz*, Melbourne: Oxford University Press, 1987, p. 4.
29. *Sydney Morning Herald*, 17 June 1899, p. 12.
30. Criterion Theatre program, *Sydney Morning Herald*, 11 July 1899, p. 2.
31. *Argus*, 5 August 1899, p. 12.
32. *Sydney Mail*, 24 June 1899, p. 1456.
33. Review of the McAdoo troupe, *Sydney Mail*, 15 July 1899, p. 152.
34. *Sydney Mail*, 24 June 1899, p. 1456.
35. *Australasian*, 12 August 1899, p. 371.
36. *Sydney Morning Herald*, 19 June 1899, p. 2; *Argus*, 31 July 1899, p. 6.
37. *Sydney Morning Herald*, 10 June 1899, p. 12.
38. *Sydney Morning Herald*, 19 June 1899, p. 8. This quotation is allegedly McAdoo's description of the dance's origins.

39. *Argus,* 7 August 1899, p. 6.
40. *Sydney Mail,* 24 June 1899, p. 1456.
41. *ibid.*
42. *Sydney Morning Herald,* 3 July 1899, p. 4.
43. Rupert Hughes, *op. cit.*, p. 159.
44. *Sydney Mail,* 24 June 1899, p. 1456.
45. *Albury Daily News,* 20 July, 1899, p. 3.
46. *Geelong Advertiser,* 24 July 1899, p. 4.
47. Joseph Howard and Ida Emerson, 'Hello Ma Baby', New York: T. B. Harms & Co, 1899; Will Marion Cook, 'Who Dat Say Chicken in This Crowd', New York: M. Witmark & Sons, 1899.
48. For discussion of coon songs on the Australian stage before 1899 see Richard Waterhouse, *From Minstrel Show to Vaudeville: the Australian Popular Stage, 1788-1914*, Sydney: New South Wales University Press, 1990, pp. 89-90, 97.
49. *Theatre Magazine,* 1 November 1911, p. 35.
50. *Argus,* 23 September 1912, p. 15.
51. 'Ragtime and Broken Time: Clever Gene Greene', *Theatre Magazine,* 1 November 1913, p. 12.
52. T.A. Ricketts, 'Ragtime in Australia', *ABC Weekly,* 16 July 1949, p. 2.
53. *Allan's How to Dance,* Melbourne: Allan & Co., n.d.
54. An excellent example from the latter category is 'Hopscotch' (described as a 'Cakewalk and Two-Step'), by F. Larkin, *The Tivoli Album* no. 23, Sydney, Joe Slater, 1904 (1899).
55. 'Heads in the Old Flour Bag: Some Collingwood Memories', *Australasian Band and Orchestra News,* 26 September 1936, p. 12.
56. T.E. Bulch: 'The Coon's Festival', 'Sambo's Birthday' and 'All Coon's Day'. These are listed in 'Sutton's Brass Band Journal Subscribers' List' for 1906. 'The Coon's Patrol' is listed in an advertisement for Sutton's in *Australasian Bandsman,* 15 August 1905, p. 14. I hold most of what remains of Bulch's collection as part of the Arthur Stirling Collection.
57. 'The Coons Patrol', 'King of the Coons' and 'Sambo's Birthday' are by Bulch. 'Sutton's Brass Band Journal Subscribers' List' for 1905 and 1906.
58. *ibid.*
59. 'Half-Naked Women for Obscene Observation: Carnal Cake Walk', *Truth,* 16 January 1904, p. 5.
60. 'Music with Humour: Mr Charles E. Lawrence' (a biographical article), *Star,* January/February 1921, p. 16.
61. *Albert's American Annual* no. 4, 1907, pp. 30-3.
62. *Theatre Magazine,* 1 February 1911, pp. 9-11.
63. Suttons Proprietary Limited, Melbourne.
64. See for example the *Argus,* 15 July 1899, p. 12, and 2 April 1904, p. 4; *Argus,* 5 December 1903, p. 20.
65. Jack Davis, 'Twenty-Five Years of Popular Songs: The Silver Jubilee of Ragtime in Australia', *Australian Music Maker and Dance Band News,* June 1937, p. 13.
66. *Argus,* 7 December 1912, p. 20.
67. *Age,* 23 December 1912, p. 10.
68. A review of the newly arrived American Ragtime Octette in the *Daily Sketch,* London, (c.25 September 1912), cited in Ian Whitcomb, *op. cit.*, p. 159.
69. 'What is Ragtime?', *Lone Hand,* 1 August 1913, pp. 26-8.
70. 'Rag-Time', *The Times,* 8 February 1913, p. 11.
71. *ibid.*
72. *ibid.*
73. *ibid.*
74. 'Grace and Beauty' by James Scott, *Allan's 14th Dance Album,* c.1913; 'Quality' by James Scott, and 'Maple Leaf Rag' by Scott Joplin, *Allan's 18th Dance Album,* c.1916. Melbourne: Allan & Co.
75. See Ronald Riddle, 'Novelty Piano Music', in John Hasse (ed.), *Ragtime, op. cit.*, pp. 285-94.
76. For these titles see Mike Sutcliffe, *op. cit.*, or Kenneth Snell, *Australian Popular Music: Title Index*, Bentleigh, Victoria: Quick Trick Press, 1991. 'Golden Wattle Rag' by the Australian Lee-Aldous Trio is mentioned in *Australian Variety,* 26 November 1913, p. 12. For 'Coo-ee!, an Australian Fox Trot', see endnote 78 below.
77. See Ross Laird, *A Discography of Popular Music Recorded in Australia or by Australians Overseas 1924-1950*, 5th rev. ed., Canberra: Discographical Researchers, 1997, p. 124.
78. 'Coo-ee! An Australian Fox Trot' in an unpublished, undated manuscript in Henry Tate's own hand, held in the Henry Tate Collection at the Grainger Museum, Melbourne.
79. See Peter Game, *The Music Sellers*, Melbourne: Hawthorn Press, 1976, pp. 141-4.
80. Interview: Whiteoak/Les Barnes.
81. Information on ragtime recording from Australian discographer, Peter Burgis.
82. Michael Montgomery, Trebor Jay Tichenor and John Hasse, 'Ragtime on Piano Rolls', in John Hasse (ed.), *Ragtime, op. cit.*, p. 97.
83. Interview: Whiteoak/Barclay Wright.
84. *ibid.*
85. *Argus,* 2 March 1914, p. 9.
86. 'Half-Naked Women for Obscene Observation: Carnal Cake Walk', *op. cit.*
87. From a letter from H.O. Allen, Secretary of the St Kilda Foreshore Committee, published in the *Argus,* 19 December 1913, p. 17.
88. *Argus,* 29 December 1913, p. 6.
89. *Age,* 31 March 1914, p. 16.
90. George Salinger, *How to do the Turkey Trot, Hesitation Waltz & Tango*, Sydney, Albert's Music Stores, 1914, p. 3.
91. *ibid*, p. 31.
92. *ibid*, p. 6.
93. *Robert's Manual of Fashionable Dancing or How and What to Dance,* Sydney: J Albert & Son, 1912, pp. 61-2.
94. George Salinger, *op. cit.*, p. 6.
95. *ibid*, p. 30.

96. *Age,* 28 October 1912, p. 7.
97. *Australian Variety,* 24 June 1914, p. 8.
98. *Australian Variety*: (1) 22 October 1913, p. 12; (2) 26 November 1913, p. 12; (3) 11 February 1914, p. 5; (4) 25 March 1914, p. 7; (5) 1 April 1914, p. 6; (6) 28 January 1914, p. 5. (7) 10 December 1913, p. 12; (8) 12 August 1914, p. 5; (9) 30 September 1914, p. 6; (10) Carr: 1 July 1914, p. 3; Leonard: 9 September 1914, p. 3; Carney: 9 September 1914, p. 6.
99. *Australian Variety*: (11) 14 January 1914, p. 7; (12) 22 October 1913, p. 9; (13) 11 February 1914, p. 2; (14) 'At the Theatre', *Australian Musical News* 3(9), 2 March 1914, p. 283; (15) 26 August 1914, p. 5; (16) *Argus,* 15 December 1913, p. 6; (17) *Theatre Magazine,* 1 January 1914, p. 30.
100. New York: Winn's School of Popular Music, 1923.
101. Ian Whitcomb, *op. cit.,* p. 162.
102. Recollection of Guy Grenville, cited in *ibid,* p. 157.
103. *Argus,* 10 November 1913, p. 13.
104. *Age,* 10 November 1913, p. 10.
105. *Argus,* 17 November 1913, p. 11.
106. *Argus,* 15 December 1913, p. 11.
107. *Australian Variety,* 4 February 1914, p. 3.
108. *Argus,* 29 December 1913, p. 6.
109. 'A Gifted Serenader: Operatic Soprano and Ragtime Artist, Miss Edith Huxam', *Footlight Star* (Melbourne), March 1919, pp. 16-17.
110. Ian Whitcomb, *op. cit.,* p. 174.
111. Correspondence dated 31 August 1991.
112. *Australian Variety,* 1 April 1914, p. 3.
113. See Discography: George Sorlie, 'Down on Bull Frog's Isle', c. February 1929; 'Ragging the Baby to Sleep' and 'Ida Sweet as Apple Cider', c. September 1929.
114. For example, see the reference to Charles Pope and Irving Sayles in *Australian Variety,* 25 February 1914, p. 7, and to Billy Brown in *Australian Variety,* 25 March 1914, p. 3.
115. *Argus,* 29 June 1914.
116. Thornton Hagert, 'Band and Orchestral Ragtime' in John Hasse (ed.), *Ragtime, op. cit.,* p. 277.
117. *ibid,* p. 283 (note 12); second quote: *ibid.,* p. 282.
118. *Australian Variety,* 30 September 1914, p. 6.
119. Regarding Bernard's vaudeville ragging see Joe Laurie Jnr, *op. cit.,* p. 61.
120. Book 4: 'Playing from Bass Parts – Transposing – Modulating, etc.', Chicago: Axel W. Christensen, 1912, p. 12.
121. *ibid,* p. 13.

Chapter 5

1. (1) *Australian Musical News* 7(12), 1 June 1918, p. 319; (2) 'The Jazz Band: the New American Craze', *Australian Musical News,* 1 July 1918, p. 12; (3) William Deane (an untitled discussion of the Jazz Band and jazz bands in general), *Australian Variety and Show World,* 5 July 1918, p. 7; (4) Andrew McCunn, 'Music or Noise', *Theatre Magazine,* 2 December 1918, p. 7.
2. Frank Coughlan, 'A Short History of Jazz in Australia' (part one), *Australian Music Maker and Dance Band News,* December 1936, p. 7.
3. 'Jazz Band at the National', undated cutting, Billy Romaine file, MS. 4140, National Library of Australia.
4. *Sydney Morning Herald,* 27 April 1918, p. 2.
5. Jim Godbolt, *A History of Jazz in Britain 1919-50,* London: Paladin Grafton Books, 1986, p. 2.
6. William Deane notes that jazz bands functioned to provide syncopation for rag-shouters. *Australian Variety and Show World,* 5 July 1918, p. 7.
7. Morgan is cited as working in America in *Australian Variety,* 20 January 1915, p. 12. Andrew Bisset mentions that Morgan worked in *Hullo Ragtime,* but gives no source. *Black Roots White Flowers,* Sydney: Golden Press, 1979, p. 9.
8. *Conservatorium Magazine,* June 1918, p. 22.
9. Deane, *op. cit.,* p. 7.
10. For example, at one point in his description Deane writes in brackets, '(such as the one at the National)'. Towards the end of the article he rambles off into a seemingly unrelated discussion which reads like a description of jazz dancing taken from American literature.
11. *Herald,* 22 July 1918, p. 9.
12. *Advertiser,* 19 August 1918, p. 7.
13. *Table Talk,* 25 July 1918, p. 15.
14. See for example *Australian Variety* over the period 1914-15.
15. *Age,* 29 July 1918, p. 7. *Table Talk,* 25 July 1918, p. 13.
16. *Age,* 29 July 1918, p. 7.
17. *Age,* 5 August 1918, p. 5.
18. Undated review cutting: Romaine file MS. 4140 National Library of Australia.
19. *Register,* 27 August 1918, p. 17.
20. *Age,* 22 July 1918, p. 8.
21. *Age,* 5 August 1918, p. 7.
22. *Table Talk,* 25 July 1918, p. 16.
23. Eric Sheldon, 'Where Will It All End? Dance Music in Retrospect from Jazz to . . . ?', *Australian Music Maker and Dance Band News,* 1 December 1933, p. 38.
24. *Australian Musical News* (Melbourne), 1 July 1918, p. 12.
25. Jim Godbolt, *op. cit.,* p. 3.
26. (1) *Australian Variety and Show World,* 12 July 1918, p. 9; (2) Eric Sheldon, *op. cit.,* p. 38; (3) *Graphic of Australia,* 8 August 1918, p. 26; (4) *Graphic of Australia,* 1 August 1918, p. 26; (5) *Graphic of Australia,* 26 July 1918, p. 26; (6) Undated (Sydney) cutting, Billy Romaine file, MS. 4140 NLA.
27. Charles Norman, *When Vaudeville was King: a Soft Shoe Stroll Down Forget-me-not Lane,*

Melbourne: Spectrum Publications, 1984, p. 82.
28. Valantyne Napier, *Act as Known: Australian Speciality Acts on the World Vaudeville/Variety Circuits from 1900 to 1960*, Brunswick, Victoria: Globe Press, 1986, p. 133.
29. Eric Sheldon, 'Modern Music is an Expression of Modern Thought', *Australian Dance Band News*, 1 December 1932, p. 6.
30. James Blades, *Percussion Instruments and their History*, London: Faber & Faber, 1971, p. 459.
31. Jim Godbolt, *op. cit.*, Ch. 1.
32. *Age*, 10 October 1918, p. 6.
33. *Age*, 12 January 1920, p. 8.
34. 'The Sons of Jazz: Musicians Who Set the World Dancing Mad', *Graphic of Australia*, 29 July 1920, p. 14.
35. 'Stage Lights', *Graphic of Australia*, 2 August 1923, n.p.
36. *Graphic of Australia*, 26 July 1923, p. 15.
37. 'Mocking the Classics', Mastertouch LP366, and 'Operafox', Mastertouch D1805.
38. Interview: Andrew Bisset/Dave Meredith (early 1970s), which was broadcast on program two of the ABC Series 'Jazz Transplant' (ten weekly programs beginning 14 July 1987), prepared by Bisset and Mike Sutcliffe and produced by Ted Hutchison for ABC Adult Education Radio.
39. Interview: Andrew Bisset/Frank Coughlan (early 1970s), broadcast on program two of 'Jazz Transplant', *ibid.*
40. *ibid.*
41. *Fuller News*, 14 March 1925, p. 2. This promotional photograph and caption are reproduced in Andrew Bisset, *op. cit.*, p. 16.
42. *Fuller News*, 22 September 1923, p. 14. Like Billy Romaine of the 1918 Jazz Band, Curnick was a dancing violinist.
43. *Fuller News*, 20 October 1923, p. 3.
44. Conversation with Bruce Johnson.
45. 'Musicians Under the Microscope: Roger Smith', *Australian Music Maker and Dance Band News*, 1 October 1939, p. 34.
46. Interview: Whiteoak/Ron Richards.
47. 'The Craze of the Dance: Going Mad to Music', *Age*, 10 April 1920, p. 20.
48. 'The Gentle Art of Jazzing: Famous Exponents at the Tivoli Describe the Latest Dancing Craze', *Graphic of Australia*, 12 August 1919, p. 8.
49. 'McEwan's Jazz Band', *Footlight Star*, November/December 1919, p. 26.
50. *Graphic of Australia*, 18 March 1920, p. 12.
51. See for example 10 June 1920, pp. 10, 20.
52. 'The Craze of the Dance: Going Mad to Music', *Age*, 10 April 1920, p. 20.
53. 'The Gentle Art of Jazzing', *Graphic of Australia*, 12 August 1919, p. 8.
54. 'Hallam's Orchestra', *Australian Band and Orchestra News*, 26 August 1926, p. 23.
55. Vol. 35, October/November, 1919, p. 34.
56. *ibid.*
57. *ibid.*
58. *ibid.*
59. *ibid.*
60. I purchased this collection of early Australian arrangements from Ken Snell. Ian Hellings, leader of the 1920s-style dance/jazz band, the Radio Rhythm Orchestra, also provided various examples, some of which had belonged to the Allietti dance band.
61. (1) Composed by Johnson, Pease and Nelson, Melbourne: Allan & Co. (copyright N.Y., Leo Feist); (2) by Jack Marley and Harry Grunden, Melbourne: Collins; (3) by Neil McBeath and Maurice Guttridge, Melbourne: Allan & Co.; (4) by Jack O'Hagan, Melbourne: Allan & Co.; (5) by Jack O'Hagan, Melbourne: Allan & Co.
62. Published Melbourne: Allan & Co.
63. 'Drum Beats: their Musical Function', *Australasian Band and Orchestra News*, 26 March 1927, pp. 39-40.
64. Percy Baker, 'Percy Baker Takes a Chorus on The Xylophone', *Australian Dance Band News*, 1 August 1932, p. 15.
65. *ibid.*
66. H. Kling, *Kling's Modern Orchestration and Instrumentation*, (rev. and trans. Gustav Saenger), New York: Carl Fischer, 1905, p. 191.
67. 'Bright and agreeable' is the term used in the entry on the glockenspiel in Percy Scholes, *The Oxford Companion to Music*, 10th ed., London: Oxford University Press, 1970, p. 775.
68. *Greenhide* by Charles Chauvel.
69. Published Melbourne: Loebel & Co, c. 1920. This date is calculated from Kenneth R. Snell, *Australian Popular Music: Composer Index*, Bentleigh, Victoria: Quick Trick Press, 1991, p. 145.
70. *Graphic of Australia*, 2 August 1923, p. 28.
71. 'Chicago' (Fox-Trot) by Fred Fisher, Mastertouch S9121, a re-issue of Duo Roll 227. Played by Laurel Pardey and James P. Taylor (this is probably a tongue-in-cheek reference to Edith Pardey as co-performer).
72. 'Jazz-O-Mine Waltz', Sydney: Nash; 'Jazz Band Rag', Sydney: J. Harris & Co. 'Mischievous Tom March' is a hand-written manuscript courtesy of Pat Ward, granddaughter of Lithgow (it is also arranged for brass band). The others are all published by Allan's except for 'Jazzin' the Blues' and ''Deva' Jazz', which are published by Loebel & Co., Melbourne. The dates for 'Jazz-O-Mine Waltz', 'Deva Jazz', and 'Jazzin' the Blues' were calculated by Ken Snell. See Kenneth R. Snell, *op. cit.*, p. 145.
73. *Book 2, Winn's School of Popular Music*, 1923, p. 2.
74. Interview: Whiteoak/Meryvn Simpson.
75. Edward R. Winn, ''Ragging' the Popular Song Hits', *Melody* 2(3), March 1918, p. 21.
76. New York: Jack Mills, 1923; New York: *Winn's School of Popular Music*, 1923. Confusingly, books 1-3 of the latter method also bear the title *Winn's*

How To Play Ragtime on the cover.
77. In 'Jazz: What is It?', 'The Music World' section of the *Graphic of Australia*, 23 March 1922, p. 11.
78. Edward R. Winn, ''Ragging' the Popular Song Hits', *Melody* 2(6), June 1918, p. 2.
79. 'The Chinese Blues', Ciro's Club Coon Orchestra, 1917, Columbia 2812; 'Livery Stable Blues', 26 February 1917, Victor 8255.
80. *Graphic of Australia*, 17 April 1924, p. 18.
81. *Graphic of Australia*, 17 April 1924, p. 19.
82. *Graphic of Australia*, 17 January 1924, p. 10.
83. Composed by Al H. Maneson, arranged M. Guttridge, Melbourne: L.F. Collins & Co, 1923 or 1924.
84. Donald Williams, 'Confessions of a "Cat" ' (part 1), *Australian Music Maker and Dance Band News*, 1 February 1939, p. 26.
85. Frank Coughlan, 'The Confessions of a Swing Addict', *Jam* (annual), 1938, p. 27.
86. Advertised on the trombone part for 'I'm Going to Plant a Rose in California' (by Tom Swift and Al Sparks), Melbourne: Allan & Co., 1927.
87. Joe Tarto, *Bass Noodles: 100 Modulations Breaks and Hot Choruses for Tuba, Trombone, Mellophone, String bass and Baritone*, New York: Alfred & Co., 1929.
88. Art Shefte, *Jazz Breaks, Tricks, Blues, Endings*, Sydney: Albert & Son, undated (c. 1927; original copyright: Art Shefte, 1925), instruction page.
89. Bruce Johnson, *The Oxford Companion to Australian Jazz*, Melbourne: Oxford University Press, 1997, p. 10.
90. 'Home to Ballaarat', 2FC Studio Dance Orchestra, Sydney: 14 January 1927, Columbia 0564.
91. Also discussed as such by Australian recorded sound and film historian, Chris Long on the 3CR Radio (Melbourne) program, 'Steam Radio', 9 January 1992.
92. See Discography: 2FC Studio Orchestra, Sydney: 17 January 1927.
93. 'Freshie', Sydney Simpson and his Wentworth Cafe Orchestra, Sydney: July 1926. Both versions have the same master number, R-1, and catalogue number, Columbia 0514. Rare version provided by Chris Long.
94. Ted Henkel, 'The USA as Seen by Ted Henkel', *Australian Dance Band News*, 1 June 1932, p. 11.
95. See, for example, 'Federal Cabinet to Ban Entry of All Colored Artists', *Truth*, 31 March 1928, p.14; or Mike Sutcliffe, 'Sonny Clay and the Colored Idea' in *Australian Record and Music Review*, 35, October 1997, pp. 3-13.
96. 'Trend of Modern Music: Dance Band Leaders Give their Opinions', *Australian Music Maker and Dance Band News*, 1 January 1935, p. 39.
97. 'Three Minute Talks', *Australian Music Maker and Dance Band News*, 1 April 1933, p. 34.
98. See Bruce Johnson, *op. cit.*, pp. 14-16.
99. *Australian Music Maker and Dance Band News* 1 November 1934, p. 29.
100. See George Dobson, 'Brass Interpretation', *Australian Music Maker and Dance Band News*, 1 April 1934, p. 30.
101. *Australian Music Maker and Dance Band News*, 1 February 1934, pp. 14-15. This article is allegedly written the by British bandleader, Jack Hylton.
102 Bruce Johnson, *op. cit.*, pp. 23-25.
103. George Dobson, 'Swing It', *Australian Music Maker and Dance Band News*, 1 July 1934, p. 28.
104. *Australian Music Maker and Dance Band News*, 1 October 1934, p. 29.
105. 'Studies in Swing' series 1-4 is advertised in *Australian Music Maker and Dance Band News*, August 1936, p. 23.
106. Bert Guy, 'The 'Jazz-Made-Easy' Method of Piano Playing', unpublished manuscript, Sydney: 1936, p. 2 (Mitchell Library).
107. *ibid.*, p. 3.
108. Art Shefte, *Piano Improvising*, 2 vols, Sydney: Albert & Son, 1937.
109. Books 1-3, Sydney: Albert & Son, 1928 (original copyright: Chicago: Forster Music, 1927).
110. Letter from Fred Thomas, dated 5 March 1985.
111. Interview: Whiteoak/George Dobson.

Chapter 6

1. 'Playing Chords', *Australian Bandsman*, 26 July 1921, p. 13.
2. Part of this composition, 'Koorinda-braia', is reproduced in Roger Covell, *Australia's Music: Themes of a New Society*, Melbourne: Sun Books, 1967, pp. 68-70.
3. Melbourne: Edward Vidler, 1924.
4. This piece, which is saturated with the basic cakewalk figure, is published in the *Grainger Journal* 3(1), August 1980, pp. 14-15.
5. Document dated 6 December 1938 on display at the Grainger Museum and reprinted in John Bird, *Percy Grainger*, Melbourne: Macmillan, 1977, pp. 283-4; revised edition forthcoming: Sydney: Currency Press, 1999.
6. From a five page typescript dated September 1949, published in Teresa Balough, (ed.), *The Musical Genius from Australia: Selected Writing by and about Percy Grainger*, University of Western Australia, 1982, p. 86. He also attributes his experimentation with 'wide-tone' scales to his 'Australian standpoint'. *ibid.*, p. 83.
7. From Percy Aldridge Grainger, 'English-Speaking Leadership in Tone-Art', dated 21 September 1944 and published in Thomas C. Slattery, *Percy Grainger: the Inveterate Innovator*, Evanston, Illinois: The Instrumentalist Company, 1974, p. 271.
8. Letter to Karen Holton, 12 February 1908, published in Kay Dreyfus (ed.), *The Farthest North of Humanness: Letters of Percy Grainger, 1904-14*, Melbourne: Macmillan, 1985, p. 184.
9. 'Jazz Band Test', *Australian Band and Orchestra*

News, 26 October 1926, pp. 35-6.
10. Interview: Whiteoak/George Dobson.
11. Ern Pettifer, 'Getting Acquainted with the Clarinet' (part 3), *Australian Music Maker and Dance Band News,* 1 February 1938, p. 31.
12. Ern Pettifer, 'Getting Acquainted with the Clarinet' (part 4), *Australian Music Maker and Dance Band News,* 1 March 1938, p. 54.
13. Dutchy Turner, 'Talking of Trombones' (part one), *Australian Music Maker and Dance Band News,* 1 April 1938, p. 28.
14. Part of the caption to a photograph of Benny Featherstone in *Tempo,* June/July 1940, n.p. (a cutting from the Benny Featherstone scrapbook).
15. Interview: Whiteoak/Don Reid (late 1930s Fawkner Park Kiosk patron and respected commentator on jazz in Australia).
16. Interview: Whiteoak/Don Reid.
17. Originals or copies held by the author.
18. Interview: Whiteoak/Don McFarlane.
19. Interview: Whiteoak/Don Reid.
20. Bruce Johnson, *The Oxford Companion to Australian Jazz,* Melbourne: Oxford University Press, p. 154. Second quotation: 'Reaching for Rhythm with Both Hands', *Victorian Dance News,* 24 November 1934, p.16.
21. Interview: Whiteoak/Ernst Grossmann.
22. 'Melbourne's Own Louis Armstrong', *Australian Dance Band News,* 1 December 1932, p. 4.
23. 'Obituary' (interview with George Dobson), *Jazzline,* June 1977, p. 43.
24. *Graeme Bell, Australian Jazzman: his Autobiography,* French's Forest, NSW: Child & Associates, 1988.
25. For example, Ralton's Havana Band, Melbourne: c. May 1925 (Austral Duplex): 'Doo Wacka Doo', (1/7), 'Blue Evening Blues' (3/8), 'Sob Sister Sadie' (11/26), 'Copenhagen' (6/) and 'Big Bad Bill' (2/4).
26. 'Melbourne – a Stronghold of Amateurs', *Australian Dance Band News,* 1 March 1933, p.16.
27. Graeme Bell, *op. cit.,* p. 44.
28. *Truth,* 1 November 41, p. 6.
29. 'The Contemporary Art Society's First Concert of Hot Jazz', 28 October 1941.
30. *ibid.,* p. 4. This quotation seems to be borrowed from American jazz literature.
31. *ibid.,* p. 6.
32. *ibid.*
33. *ibid.,* p. 5.
34. Graeme Bell, *op. cit.,* p. 29.
35. Bruce Johnson, 'Orality and Jazz Education', *NMA (New Music Articles)* 10, 1992, p. 43.
36. Bebop is the style of small group jazz which first became defined in the early 1940s around the playing of African-Americans Dizzy Gillespie, Charlie Parker and associates. By the end of the 1940s in America this genre had begun to divide into two main streams: a more restrained and congruous 'cool' style and the more ecstatic and rhythmically complex 'hard' style. The latter became much more strongly identified with African-American musicians and culture.
37. From a Sydney review of the band by Ron Wills, *Tempo,* July/August 1943, cited in Harold Kaye, 'Artie Shaw in Australia – 1943', *Australian Record and Music Review,* April 1991, p. 7.
38. Interviews: Whiteoak/Lyn Challen, Keith Humble, Splinter Reeves, Charlie Blott and others.
39. *Music Maker,* 20 August 1946, p. 1.
40. 'Hot Records', *Tempo,* November 1946, p. 11.
41. Bruce Clarke, 'Guitar Workshop', *Jamm: Journal of Australian Music* (Melbourne) 38, February 1981, p. 46.
42. 'Well I'll be Be-bopped', *Music Maker,* 20 December 1947, p. 9.
43. 'Modern Music Society Hopes to Play at Princess Theatre,' *Tempo,* September 1948, p. 84.
44. Interview: Whiteoak/Eddie Oxley.
45. A detailed analysis of this episode is found in Michael Heyward, *The Ern Malley Affair,* University of Queensland Press, 1993.
46. Interview: Whiteoak/Doug Gamley.
47. *ibid.*
48. *ibid.*
49. Interview: Whiteoak/Keith Humble.
50. Interview 1: Whiteoak/Keith Humble; interview: Whiteoak/Doug Gamley.
51. Interview 1: Whiteoak/Keith Humble.
52. This is very apparent in an extant recording of Keith Humble with the Victorian Symphony Orchestra, Melbourne Town Hall, 18 May 1949: 'Piano Concerto (D♭)' by Khatchaturian, 2nd and 3rd movements.
53. From the transcript of an interview with Banks, 12 August 1972, De Berg series tape 626, National Library, p. 4. Interview: Whiteoak/Doug Gamley.
54. 'Keith Humble 'A Sensation'', *Music Maker,* 20 February 1947, p. 28.
55. Interview 2: Whiteoak and Tim Dargaville/Keith Humble.
56. Interview: Whiteoak/Helen Gifford.
57. Interview 1: Whiteoak/Keith Humble; interview: Whiteoak/Eddie Oxley.
58. Interview with Banks, De Berg series tape 626, *op. cit.,* p. 7.
59. Interview 1: Whiteoak/Keith Humble.
60. Stated in the 1987 video documentary about Banks, *The Melbourne Jazz Days 1938-50,* by Simon Banks (with research assistance from the author). Copy held at NFSA.
61. Interview with Banks, De Berg Tape 626, *op. cit.,* p. 8.
62. Don Banks, 'Be-Bop', *Tempo,* November 1948, p. 9.
63. 'Jazz Then-And Re-Bop', *Woman,* 4 July 1949, p. 30.
64. Jim Bradley, 20 August 1948, p. 1.
65. This collective interview was conducted by the author for the video documentary, *The Melbourne*

Jazz Days 1938-50, *op. cit.*
66. See Discography: Lyn Challen Group, 'Swanee River', Melbourne, c.1946.
67. Interview: Whiteoak/Lyn Challen.
68. 'Don Banks Explains Be-bop', *Tempo*, September 1948, p. 10.
69. London, Cosmo Music Co., 1947.
70. Banks mentions 'the Count Basie influence, before the bop influence' in Mike Williams, *The Jazz Explosion*, London: Angus and Robertson, 1981, p. 48.
71. Here Banks is cited by Di Gaston in 'Expanding the World of Sound', *Soundblast* (previously *Music Maker*), May 1973, p. 17.
72. Don Banks, 'Jazz in our Musical World', p. 1. This is the typescript of a lecture annotated by hand: 'script for BBC 3 1971' (no other details).
73. See Discography: Don Banks' Orchestra, Melbourne: 16 January 1950.
74. 'Rhythm in Retrospect', *Music Maker*, 2 February 1950, p. 9.
75. Jack White, 'Melbourne Notes', *Tempo*, September 1947, p. 9.
76. See Discography: The Splintette, 'Olympia a la Bop', Melbourne: 2 February 1952.

Chapter 7

1. Philip Brophy, 'Avant Garde Rock: History in the Making?' in Marcus Breen (ed.), *Missing in Action: Australian Popular Music in Perspective*, Melbourne: Verbal Graphics, 1967, pp. 127-144.
2. Helen Gifford, 'Subliminal Co-ordinates . . . Drawing Threads', *NMA* 7, 1989, p. 6.
3. Interview: Whiteoak/Helen Gifford.
4. Barry Humphries, *More Please*, London: Viking (Penguin Books), 1992, pp. 104-5.
5. Graeme Hughes, 'A Memoir of Barry Humphries', *Melbourne University Magazine* (MUM), Spring 1961, p. 42-3.
6. *ibid.*
7. See Clive Douglas, 'Folk Song and the Brown Man: Means to an Australian Expression in Symphonic Music', *The Canon* 10(3), October 1956, pp. 81-5.
8. Artists and writers in this period who sought inspiration from Aboriginal culture became known collectively as 'Jindyworobaks'.
9. For example, in outlining his explorations with this musical medium he mentions that 'The rhythms used are basically simple with a subtle displacement of the rhythm to heighten the effect'. Douglas also writes of Aboriginal music as unmusical, monotonous, crude and primitive, a notion similar to the old minstrelsy concept of 'grotesque' performance culture. Clive Douglas, *op. cit.*, p. 81. For his use of the cakewalk figure see also Examples 3-4, *ibid.*, pp. 83-5. See also Gregg W. Howard, 'Clive Douglas, 1903-77' in Frank Callaway and David Tunley (eds), *Australian Composition in the Twentieth Century*, Melbourne: Oxford University Press, 1978.
10. The July 1965 ISCM concert included 'Directions' for piano, vibraphone, viola and cello by architecture student George Mitchell, based on 'a completely new method of composition' (controlled improvisation based on graphic notation and live direction) and Barry McKimm's 'One or Two Thunders', also based on graphic scoring. See 'Messiaen Outstanding in Contemporary Concert', *Farrago*, 26 July 1965, p. 12. The May 1965 ISCM concert included Wladimier Kontonski's Trio for Flute, Guitar and Percussion, which is scored without barlines.
11. Geoffrey D'Ombrain, *Music Now: a Discovery Course for Children*, Melbourne: Cassell Australia, 1969, back cover notes.
12. For recorded examples of early Melbourne hard bop see 'Brian Brown' in Jack Mitchell, *Australian Jazz on Record 1925-80*, Canberra: Australian Government Publishing Service, 1988, p. 54.
13. 'Adrian Rawlins Looks at the Garden of Eden', *Music Maker*, December 1967, pp. 11, 13.
14. Adrian Rawlins, 'Caught in the Act', *Music Maker*, November 1962, p. 21. Also mentioned in interview: Whiteoak/Syd Clayton and interview: Whiteoak/Adrian Rawlins.
15. Interview: Whiteoak/Alan Turnbull; conversations: Whiteoak/Graham Morgan.
16. Interview: Whiteoak/Barry Quinn; interview: Whiteoak/Brian Fraser.
17. Interview: Whiteoak/Brian Fraser.
18. Interview: Whiteoak/Barry McKimm; interview: Whiteoak/Syd Clayton; conversation: Whiteoak/David Tolley.
19. New York: Concept Publishing, 1959.
20. This more utilitarian use of modes is described by Geoff Ayling in 'The Modal Approach to Improvisation' *Music Maker*, July 1966, pp.10-11, 13.
21. Interview: Whiteoak/Brian Brown.
22. See 'Abstractions', *Music Maker*, January 1964, p. 3 and Trevor Graham, 'Charlie Munro's *Eastern Horizons*', *Music Maker*, November 1967, p. 3. See Discography: Charlie Munro, *Eastern Horizons*, Sydney, 1967.
23. 'Adrian Rawlins Looks at the Garden of Eden', *op. cit.*, p. 11.
24. See Discography: Bruce Clarke, 'Kama Sutra Feeling', 'That Old Calcutta Rag', Melbourne: 14 September 1963.
25. *Herald*, 20 August 1966, p. 1.
26. Rosemary Adam, 'Spons I Have Seen', in Jenepher Duncan (ed.), *From the Homefront: Robert Rooney Works 1953-1988*, Melbourne: Monash University Gallery, 1990, p.41.
27. J. Romer, 'Jazz and Poetry', *Music Maker*, August 1960. p. 9.
28. In Angela Hillel and Dot Thompson, *50 Years of New Theatre, Melbourne N.T. 1936-86*, Melbourne: New Theatre, 1986, pp. 34-5.
29. Barry Oakley's statement in Liz Jones and Betty

Burstall, *La Mama: the Story of a Theatre*, Melbourne: McPhee Gribble, 1988, p. 24.
30. Jennifer Phipps, *I Had a Dream: Australian Art in the 1960s*, National Gallery of Victoria, 1997, p. 37.
31. Patrick McCaughey, 'The Significance of the Field', *Art and Australia* 6(3), 6 March 1968, p. 235.
32. Interview: Whiteoak/Helen Gifford. Andrew McIntyre, 'An Interview with Keith Humble', *Lot's Wife*, 1 October 1968, p. 18.
33. A term apparently coined by the playwright Jack Hibberd for the period 1967-72. See Andrew Bovell, 'La Mama – Coming of Age or Just Old Age', *New Theatre Australia* 5, May/June 1988, p. 10.
34. Terry Counihan, 'The New Music', *Farrago*, 8 September 1967, p. 7.
35. John Clare, *Bodgie Dada and the Cult of Cool*, Sydney: University of New South Wales, 1995, p. 121.
36. From a 1967 review cited in Lawrence Zion, 'The Pop Music Scene in Australia in the 1960s', PhD thesis, Monash University, 1989, p. 302.
37. Some idea of what was permissible by the end of the 1960s can be gained from a review of the 1970 Melbourne 'Let It Be' concert, *Music Maker*, November, 1970, p. 5.
38. John Clare, 'Peter Sculthorpe', *Music Maker*, 19 December 1970, pp. 6-7.
39. Philip Brophy, *op. cit.*, p. 129. Brophy's article is about the post-Punk (post late 1970s) avant-garde, but his statement is equally applicable to the late 1960s.
40. London: Constable & Co, 1983, p. 74.
41. James Murdoch, *Australia's Contemporary Composers*, Melbourne: Macmillan, 1972, pp. 59-60.
42. *ibid.*, p. 61.
43. See Joseph Schillinger, *The Schillinger Method of Musical Composition*, 2 vols., New York: Carl Fischer, 1948.
44. Bruce Clarke, 'Random Discussions on the Composer's Source of Income Pre-World War II and Post-World War II', *The State of the Art of Electronic Music in Australia* (proceedings of a seminar held at the University of Melbourne: 913/1971), p. 47.
45. Quoted in Adrian Jackson, 'Bob Sedergreen Talks to Adrian Jackson', *Jazz* 1(6), December 1981, p. 22.
46. Interview: Whiteoak/Ken White and discussion with Monty Maizels who recorded some of Smith's improvisatory experiments.
47. This section is based largely on detailed discussion with Brown.
48. John Clare, 'Focus on Brian Brown', *Jazz Down Under* 1(3) January/February 1975, p.13.
49. *ibid.*
50. See detailed discussion of this concept in Matthew Cunliffe, 'Brian Brown – the Winged Messenger', *Sounds Australian* 17, Autumn 1988, pp. 16-18.
51. 'Spondee Review', Melbourne, The Robert, December to March 1961[sic] (an arts review issued by Rooney). Reproduced in Rosemary Adam, 'Spons I Have Met', in Jenepher Duncan (ed.) *From the Homefront: Robert Rooney Works 1953-1988, op. cit.* p. 12.
52. Interview: Whiteoak/Barry McKimm.
53. See Rosemary Adam, *op. cit.*, pp. 11-14.
54. Interview: Whiteoak/Barry Quinn.
55. These are 'Inta Something Else' (McKimm) and 'Neddy Nod' (Mendelson), recorded in a private studio, May 1963. See Discography: McKimm/Mendelson Quartet, 1963.
56. Interview: Whiteoak/Robert Rooney.
57. Cecil Taylor, *Looking Forward*, 9 June 1958, Contemporary, M3562.
58. Interview: Whiteoak/Barry McKimm.
59. Interview: Whiteoak/Robert Rooney.
60. 'Improvisation', McKimm/Rooney/Clayton Trio, Melbourne: 9 August 1964.
61. Conversation: Whiteoak/Barry McKimm.
62. See Discography: 'Duo 1 2 3', The McKimm/Rooney/Clayton Trio, Melbourne: August 1965.
63. Kris Hemensley, 'Syd Clayton's Farewell to Melbourne: Kris Hemensley Reports on the Passing of a Musician', *Theatre* 4, Winter 1983, p. 294.
64. The working scores for 'Flags or Dreams That Money Can't Buy ' (1968), 'Yehudi' (1969), 'How to Write a Chinese Poem' (1969) and 'Weena Does Not Know' (1970) are published in Kris Hemensley *op. cit.*, pp. 296-299.
65. Kris Hemensley, *ibid.*
66. Patrick McCaughey, 'Mainstream and Province', *Age*, 24 April 1968; cited by Charles Green in 'Robert Rooney', Jenepher Duncan (ed.), p. 9.
67. See Discography: Robert Rooney, 'Second Landscape', Melbourne: 1968.
68. It was noted in 1968 that 'Rooney's wit has a subversive effect on his "system-building and serializing".' Patrick McCaughey, *op. cit.* Noted by Jenepher Duncan, 'Robert Rooney: Biography' in Jenepher Duncan (ed.), p. 37.
69. Roger Covell, *Australia's Music: Themes of a New Society*, Melbourne: Sun Books, 1967, p.234.
70. John Whiteoak, 'Interview with Keith Humble', *NMA* 7, 1989, p. 24.
71. From 'The Impress of Personality in Unwritten Music', *Musical Quarterly*, July 1915; reprinted in Teresa Balough, comp. *A Musical Genius from Australia: Selected Writings by and about Percy Grainger*, University of Western Australia, 1982, p. 74.
72. John Whiteoak, 'Interview with Keith Humble', *op. cit.*, p. 25.
73. John Whiteoak, 'Interview with Keith Humble' *op. cit.*, p. 25.
74. For Humble, this approach developed partly through his rigorous composition studies under

René Leibowitz in the 1950s. Interview: Whiteoak/Keith Humble. The Humble Collection includes a typescript copy of Heinrich Jalowetz, 'On the Spontaneity of Schoenberg's Music', *Musical Quarterly*, October 1944.
75. Interview: Whiteoak/Keith Humble.
76. This comparison is made in Heinz-Klaus Metzger, 'Schnebel's Glossolalie in Paris: Official and Unofficial Musical Life', *Die Weltwoche* (Zurich), 18 November 1966. From a typed English translation in the Humble collection.
77. Kenneth Hince, 'Concert in the Round', *Australian*, 24 October 1964, p. 15.
78. John Whiteoak, 'Interview with Keith Humble', *op. cit.*, p. 25.
79. Program notes for the ISCM concert, 4 March 1968.
80. *ibid.*
81. Program notes for 'Nunique VI', ISCM concert, University of Sydney, 3 June 1971.
82. *ibid.*
83. *ibid.*
84. Attali, *Noise: The Political Economy of Music.* Manchester University Press, 1985 (trans. of 1977 French edition). Humble pointed to the importance of this analogy in a long conversation which preceded the interview published in *NMA* 7, *op. cit.*
85. *ibid.*, p. 26.
86. *ibid.*, p. 141.
87. Andrew McIntyre, 'An Interview with Keith Humble', *Lot's Wife,* October 1968, p. 18.
88. *'Un Lieu de Conflit', Nouvel Observateur,* 2 February 1966, p. 35.
89. Kenneth Hince, 'Concert in the Round', *Australian*, 4 October 1964, p. 15.
90. *'Du Surhumain Larountala Qui Meurt de N'être pas Compris'*, Jean-Marie Dunover, *'D'étonnantes Théories: Un Théâtre Antiréaliste', Le Monde*, supplement 7208, 16 March 1968, p. 3 (a tribute to Pierre Albert-Birot's theatre works).
91. Jacques Attali, *op. cit.*, p. 26.
92. Marshall McLuhan and Quentin Fiore, New York, Random House, 1967. pp. 113-117.
93. Jacques Attali, *op. cit.*, p. 6.
94. *ibid.* p. 7.
95. From the typed text of the statement 'Extensions/Gestures/Anecdotes', read/performed by Jean-Charles François as part of 'Nunique IV', p. 1 (Humble Collection).
96. *ibid.*
97. *ibid.*
98. *ibid.*, p. 3.
99. *ibid.*
100. Andrew McIntyre, 'Humble and Nunique IV', *Lot's Wife*, 24 July 1969, p. 15.
101. This statement is attributed to Pierre Albert-Birot on the program for 'Nunique IV', Monash University, 9 June 1969.
102. David M. Davis, 'Music Workshops: American Showcase in Paris', *Music Journal* (U.S.A.), March 1964, p. 72.
103. Edward Gordon Craig, *On the Art of the Theatre*, London: Heinemann, 1968 (1st ed., 1911), pp. 155-8.
104. *ibid*, p. 138.
105. Laughton Harris, 'Keith Humble' in Frank Callaway and David Tunley (eds) *Australian Composition in the Twentieth Century*, Melbourne: Oxford University Press, 1978, p. 120.
106. Jean-Marie Dunover, *op. cit.*
107. Ian Maxwell, 'How to Make a Rap Recording', *Sounds Australian* 15 (50), 1997, pp. 22-23.
108. 'The Music Show', Radio National, 18 April 1998.

Select Bibliography

Balough, Teresa (ed.). *The Musical Genius from Australia: Selected Writings by and about Percy Grainger.* University of Western Australia, 1982.

Bell, Graeme. *Australian Jazzman: His Biography.* French's Forest, NSW: Child and Associates, 1988.

Berlin, Edward. *Ragtime: a Musical and Cultural History.* Berkeley: University of California Press, 1980.

Bisset, Andrew. *Black Roots White Flowers: a History of Jazz in Australia.* Sydney: Golden Press, 1979.

Brisbane, Katharine (ed.). *Entertaining Australia: an Illustrated History.* Sydney: Currency Press, 1991.

Burt, Warren. 'Some Musical and Sociological Aspects of Australian Experimental Music, 1963 1993'. *Sounds Australian* 37, Autumn 1993, pp. 38 51.

Clare, John. *Bodgie Dada and the Cult of the Cool.* University of New South Wales, 1995.

Dreyfus, Kay, *Sweethearts of Rhythm: The story of Australia's all-girl bands and orchestras to the end of the Second World War.* Sydney: Currency Press, 1999

Ethnomusicology 39(1), Winter 1995, Special issue on Participatory Discrepancies.

Finn, Edmund (Garryowen). *The Chronicles of Early Melbourne, 1835 to 1852.* Melbourne: Heritage Publications, undated (facsimile of, Melbourne: Fergusson & Mitchell, 1888).

Ferand, Ernest T. *Improvisation in Nine Centuries of Western Music: an Anthology with a Historical Introduction.* Cologne: Arno Volk Verlag, 1938.

Jenkins, John. 22 *Australian Contemporary Australian Composers.* Melbourne: NMA Publications, 1998.

Johnson, Bruce. *The Oxford Companion to Australian Jazz.* Melbourne: Oxford University Press, 1987.

Johnson, Bruce. *The Inaudible Music: Jazz and Australian Modernity.* Sydney: Currency Press, forthcoming 1999.

Keil, Charles and Steven Feld. *Music Grooves.* University of Chicago Press, 1994.

Nathan, Hans. *Dan Emmett and the Rise of Early Negro Minstrelsy.* Oklahoma University Press, 1962.

Nettl, Bruno. 'Thoughts on Improvisation a Comparative Approach'. *Musical Quarterly* 60(1), Jan. 1974, pp. 1 19.

Nettl, Bruno with Melinda Russell (eds.). *In the Course of Performance: Studies in the World of Musical Improvisation.* University of Chicago Press. 1998.

Pressing, Jeff (ed.). *Compositions for Improvisers: an Australian Perspective.* Melbourne: La Trobe University Press, 1994.

Waterhouse, Richard. *From Minstrel Show to Vaudeville: the Australian Popular Stage, 1788-1914.* New South Wales University Press, 1990.

Wentzel, Ann. 'The First Hundred Years of Music in Australia, 1788-1888'. M.A. thesis, University of Sydney, 1963.

Whiteoak, John and Aline Scott-Maxwell (eds.). *Companion to Music and Dance Australia.* Sydney: Currency Press, forthcoming 1999.

JOURNALS

Australasian Bandsman, 1894-1926.

Australian Band News, 1909-

26/9/1925 became: *Australian Band and Orchestra News*

26/9/1926 became: *Australasian Band and Orchestra News*

26/1/1937 became: *Australasian Dance and Brass Band News*

30/4/1940 became: *Music Maker*, with which is incorporated *Australasian Dance and Brass Band News.*

Australian Dance Band News, 1/6/1932-

1/4/1933 became: *Australian Music Maker and Dance Band News*

30/4/1940 became: *Music Maker* with which is incorporated *Australasian Dance and Brass Band News.*

Australian Musical Monthly, 1903-1909.

Australian Musical News, 1909-1923.

Australian Variety, 1913-15.

Australian Variety and Show World, 1918-1919.

Graphic of Australia, 1917-1925.

Perfect Beat: the Pacific Journal of Research into Contemporary Music and Popular Culture, 1992-.

Sounds Australian: special issues on (mostly post-1960s) improvisatory music in Australia:

Special Jazz Issue, 17, Autumn 1988

Eleven Views of Music Improvisation, 32, Summer 1991 2

The Improvisatory Process, 14(48), 1996.

Tempo, 1937-1950.

Theatre Magazine, 1905-1922.

Discography

ABBREVIATIONS

as	alto saxophone	rds	reeds
bj	banjo	sax	saxophone
c	cornet	sb	string bass
cl	clarinet	ss	soprano saxophone
d	drums	t	trumpet
f	flute	tb	trombone
g	guitar	ts	tenor saxophone
ldr	leader	tu	tuba
mar	maracas	vc	violoncello
p	piano	vn	violin
pac	piano accordion	vcl	vocals
perc	percussion	vib	vibraphone

The following items are listed in alphabetical order by improvising performer or ensemble leader. The discography format is as close as practical to that of Jack Mitchell's *Australian Jazz on Record 1925-80*. Canberra: Australian Government Publishing Service, 1988. Details of commercially released recordings are from record labels, catalogues, record album cover notes, *Australian Jazz on Record 1925-80* or Ross Laird's *Popular Music Recorded by Australian Artists in Australia and by Australians in Britain 1925-1945: a Draft Discography*, 2nd rev. ed. Melbourne: Esoteric Publications, 1983; and his *A Discography of Popular Music Recorded in Australia or by Australians Overseas, 1925-1945*, 5th rev. ed. Canberra: Discographical Researchers, 1997. Other recording details have been supplied by the author, by researchers such as Jack Mitchell, Chris Long and Ernst Grossmann, or by the performers themselves.

The numbers and/or letters seen at the left of some composition titles are the means of identifying a specific recorded performance. This information is essential, as the same tune might be recorded several times during one recording session with a different musical outcome each time. Words, letters and numbers to the right of a composition title (following a dash) denote the catalogue details of the record company that issued, or reissued, a particular recorded performance.

BANKS, DON (see transcription: Musical Example 6.10)
Charlie Blott's Band (also listed as Don Banks' Group)
Ivan Halsall cl, Errol Buddle ts, Don Banks p, Joe Washington g, Charlie Blott d, Ken Lester? sb
Melbourne, c. April 1947
Feelin' Dizzy: theme by Banks
(disc held by Blott family)

BANKS, DON (see transcription: Musical Example 6.11-12)
Blott's Boppers
Don Banks p, Jack Brockensha vib, Charlie Blott d (others unknown)
Melbourne, 1948

Pennies from Heaven
Maternity
(disc held by author)

BANKS, DON (see transcription: Musical Example 6.13)
Don Banks' Orchestra
Ken Brentnall t, Eddie Oxley as, Bruce Clarke g, Don Banks p, Ken Lester sb Charlie Blott d
Melbourne, 16/1/1950
AWM-830B I've Got My Love To Keep Me Warm - Jazz Art JA-48
AWM-832A Can't Help Lovin' Dat Man - Jazz Art JA-49

BANKS, DON (performance of Bank's first third stream work)
Centre de Musique, Paris, 9/10/1965
Equation, for chamber group of twelve players: by Banks, 1964
(reel to reel tape in Keith Humble collection)

BELL, ROGER (early 1940s collectively improvised jazz involving 'progressives' Banks, Reeves, Blott, and Challen)
Roger Bell's Jazz Gang/Don Roberts' Wolf Gang Max Kaminsky t, Roger Bell c, Don Roberts cl ts, Don 'Splinter' Reeves ts, Ade Monsborough vtb, Don Banks p, Norm Baker bj g, Lyn Challen sb, Laurie Howells or Charlie Blott d
Melbourne, 19/9/1943
At the Jazz Band Ball: not released from this session
Ja Da: no cornet; Blott replaces Howell - Ampersand 1; Tempo A-4

BROWN, BRIAN (1950s Melbourne hard bop)
The Brian Brown Quintet
Keith Hounslow t, Brian Brown ts, David Martin p, Barry Buckley sb, Stewart Speer d
Melbourne, Nov. 1958
Diggers Rest: by Brown - Score 6357 715

CHALLEN, LYN (Lyn Challen's jazz 'experiment')
Lyn Challen's Recording session group
Fred Thomas t, Bobby Limb ts, Bob Young p, Lyn Challen sb
Melbourne, c. 1946
Swanee
(disc held by Challen family)

CLARKE, BRUCE (1950s commercial bop or 'bop for the people')
The Bruce Clarke Quintet
Fred Thomas t, Ted Preston p, Bruce Clarke g, Ken Lester b, Billy Hyde d
Melbourne, 1954
Lisa - Jaguar JP-803
Brazil
Strike Up the Band
Our Love is Here to Stay
Blue Skies
Tea for Two
Robbin's Nest
Kangaroo Boogie

CLARKE, BRUCE ('Eastern' influenced jazz)
Dick Healey f, Frank Smith ts, Bruce Clarke g, Ron Terry sb, Billy Hyde d
Melbourne, 14/9/1963
Kama Sutra Feeling - Cumquat CQR R12-02
That Old Calcutta Rag

CLAYTON, SYD (improvisatory music-theatre)
Barry McKimm t, Syd Clayton sb
Melbourne (La Mama), May 1968
Yehudi: Syd Clayton
(reel to reel tape in private collection)

COUGHLAN, FRANK (track includes 1930s rhapsodic-style jazz improvisation: see Musical Example 6.3)
Frank Coughlan and his Cheddar Five
Frank Coughlan t tb, Keith Atkinson cl ts, Stan Bourne p pac, Charlie Lees g, Norm Goldie sb
Sydney, 1936
Skip It - Macquarie Broadcasting Service MBS J-8

COUGHLAN, FRANK (see transcription: Musical Example 6.7)
Frank Coughlan's Band
Frank Coughlan t tb, Benny Featherstone cl, Bob Tough ts (some uncertainty regarding others)
Melbourne, 1942/3
Jazz Me Blues (disc held by Ernst Grossmann)
Basin Street Blues (disc held by author)

GAMLEY, DOUG (tracks feature Gamley as a jazz pianist)
Splinter Reeves cl ts, Doug Gamley p, C. Blott d
Melbourne, c.1942

China Boy
Sugar
(disc held by author)

HUMBLE, KEITH (recording features an example of Humble's ecstatic or 'explosive' approach to piano playing)
Keith Humble with the Victorian Symphony Orchestra
Melbourne Town Hall, 18/5/1949
Piano Concerto (Db) by Khatchaturian, 2nd and 3rd movements
(three 12" discs in the Keith Humble Collection)

HUMBLE, KEITH (improvisatory music-theatre: see Musical Examples 7-12)
Melbourne (Monash University), 9/6/1969
Nunique IV
(reel to reel tape in the Keith Humble Collection)

HUMBLE, KEITH (experimental theatre music with jazz elements)
Centre de Musique, Paris, 2/9/1963
Le Printemps
(reel to reel tape in the Keith Humble collection).

JONES, RUSSELL (an early example of Melbourne Swing band boogie-woogie)
Russell Jones and his Power House Band
Keith Malcolm t, John Weston as, [?] ts, Keith Chenu p, Geoff Wescott g, Ted Laing sb, Russell Jones d
Melbourne, 1938
Honky Tonk Train: arranged by Chenu
(disc held by Russell Jones)

LIMB, BOBBY (early Melbourne bebop)
Bobby Limb and His Orchestra
Ken Brentnall t, Bobby Limb ts, Don Banks p, Jack Brokensha vib, Joe Washington g, Ken Lester sb, Charlie Blott d
Melbourne, late 1947
Lady Be Good
Undecided
(disc held by Roger Beilby)

McKIMM, BARRY (free jazz)
The McKimm/Mendelson Quartet
Barry McKimm t, Heinz Mendelson ts, Brian Fagan, sb, Barry Woods d
Melbourne, May 1963
Neddy Nod: by Mendelson
Inta Something Else: by McKimm
(reel to reel tape in private collection)

McKIMM, BARRY (jazz and contemporary art music fusion; see Musical Example 7.4b)
The Barry McKimm Quintet
Barry McKimm t, Barry Webster rds, Robert Rooney p, Syd Clayton sb, Barry Quinn d
Melbourne, 13/7/1964 (ABC Jazz Club recording)
Night Song: by Rooney
Moloko: by Rooney
Melbourne, August 1964
Improvisation on Tone Row
(reel to reel tape in private collection)

McKIMM, BARRY (experimental music ensemble; see Musical Example 7.7)
McKimm, Rooney and Clayton Trio
Barry McKimm t, Robert Rooney p, Syd Clayton sb
Melbourne, June 1965
Duo 1 2 3: recorded for ABC Jazz Club but never broadcast
(reel to reel tape in private collection)

MUNRO, CHARLIE (late 1960s 'Eastern' influenced jazz)
The Charlie Munro Quartet
Charlie Munro ss as ts f vc bcl, Bob Mclvor tb, Neville Whitehead sb, Mark Bowden d vib mar
Islamic Suite - Philips JS-020; 44 6457 703
Malahari Raga
Japanese Love Song
[and five other titles]

PEARSE, ERIC (track reflects pre-1923 Australian performance style)
2FC Studio Dance Orchestra
Bert Heath, Dick Porter t, Dave Meredith? tb, Arthur Bennett/Arthur Ashe or Les Pogson/Stan Ashe or Dan Pogson rds, Eric Pearse p, Percy Watson bj,
Dooley Ward tu, Lisle Pearse d, Len Maurice vcl
Sydney, 14/1/1927
R-237 Home To Ballaarat - Columbia 0564 (two issued takes reported)
Sydney, 14/1/1927
R-238 You'll Miss Me When I'm Gone - Columbia 0564 (two issued takes reported)

RALTON, BERT (from the earliest known Melbourne jazz recording; features Harry Mehden of Australia's 'first jazz band' on trombone)
Ralton's Havana Band
probably George Eskdale t, Harry Mehden tb, Bert Ralton, Sam Babicci, another rds, unknown p, bj, sb, Whitey Higley d
Melbourne, c. May 1925
O.T.3 Doo Wacka Doo - Austral 7
O.T.6 Blue Evening Blues - Austral 3

RAWLINS, ADRIAN (poetry and jazz)
Adrian Rawlins with traditional jazz band led by Nick Polites
Melbourne, 1961
(cassette version only)

REEVES, DON (Reeves' hot tenor playing on this track demonstrates that 1950s 'bop for the people' was not always restrained)
Splinter Reeves' Splintette
'Boof' Thompson t, Don Reeves ts, Jack Gay g, Ken Lester sb, Charlie Blott d, Terry Mehan vcl
Melbourne, 2/2/1952 (Wirth Olympia, Bop for the People style Concert)
Olympia À, Bop Armstrong: Australian Jazz (unnumbered)
(disc held by author)

ROMAIN, ABE (transcription: see Musical Example 6.8)
Abe Romain as, Len Maurice vcl, (and others)
Sydney, 8/12/1927
WT-465 Baby Your Mother - Columbia 0879

ROONEY, ROBERT (experimental music based on visual art concepts: see Musical Example 7.9a-b)
Improvising orchestra led by Gerald Lester
Melbourne (La Mama), May 1968
Second Landscape for Instruments: by Rooney
(reel to reel tape in private collection)

SCHOOT, (Herr) 'Drum Demon' (vivid musical depiction of a Warnambool district train crash with drums and percussion effects)
Warnambool, Victoria 1897
(wax cylinder recording in Thomas Rome Collection, Performing Arts Museum; available from PAM on cassette)

SIMPSON, SYDNEY (transcription: see Musical Example 5.15b-c)
Sydney Simpson and His Wentworth Cafe Orchestra
probably Harold Barlow c, Harry Larsen tb, Sydney Simpson, Sam Babicci rds, Harry White p, Percy Baker bj, Sammy Cope d, unknown vcl
Sydney, July 1926
R-1 Freshie - Columbia 0514
R-1 Freshie - Columbia 0514, Lyric 3304

SMITH, FRANK (see transcription: Musical Example 7.1)
Frank Smith with the GTV-9 Television Studio Band
I've Just Seen Her (recorded from a television set with a hand-held microphone, mid-1960s)
(cassette version only)

SORLIE, GEORGE (see transcription: Musical Example 21a-b)
George Sorlie vcl, Beryl Newell p
Sydney, c. February 1929
A-337 Down on Bull Frog's Isle - Parlophone A-2624
George Sorlie vcl, Beryl Newell p, unknown t
Sydney, c. November 1929
A-464 Ragging the Baby To Sleep - Parlophone A-2869
A-465 Ida, Sweet [as] Apple Cider Parlophone A-2869

TOUGH, BOB (see transcription: Musical Example 6.6b)
Orme Stewart's group
Bob Tough ts, Frank Coughlan, t tb, Orme Stewart tb, Lyn Challen sb, Charlie Blott d (other personnel uncertain)
Melbourne, c.1942
Avalon: private session
(disc held by Orme Stewart and Challen family)

Index

ABC (Australian Broadcasting Commission) 226, 268, 271, 272, 285, 288 312
ABC Jazz Club 285, 288
Aboriginal music (use of) 233, 234, 267, 312
aesthetics: of black jazz xxi, 282; classical aesthetic 24, 60, 86-7; of jazz xix, 207, 211, 235-6, 242, 246-7, 248, 253; of ragtime 119, 121, 152; taste refinement 107; white aesthetic 112, 144, 156, 214. *See also* dissonance; noise
African-American music: jazz xxi, 83, 111, 222; influence of xii, 28, 41-3, 46, 83, 89, 134, 155, 209-10, 233-5, 243, 270, 281, 282; performance characteristics xiv, 4, 21, 156, 160, 218; representation of 117, 137, 152, 174, 177, 211, 229, 267. *See also* black musical theatre; influential non-visiting musicians; minstrelsy
African music, West 83, 98, 102, 115
aleatoric (chance-based) music 253, 282, 292, 296, 287
Ali-Ben-Sou-Alle 58
Allan's (Allan & Co.) 17, 24, 63, 116, 131, 134, 140, 145
Allietti's Orchestra 152, 184, 187
American Boys, The 181
American Ragtime Orchestra 165
Angry Penguins 246, 251
Anonymous genres, definition of xvi-xix
Antill, John 267
Approved genres, definition of xvi, xix
Armstrong, Louis 236, 243
Atkinson, Harry 58
audience-performer interaction xviii; in circus 80-3, 88; in colonial performance 2, 4, 6, 31, 40; in experimental jazz 280; in experimental music-theatre 304-5; in silent cinema 68-9. *See also* dance music: dance-music interaction
avant-garde xv, xxi, 231, 260, 309. *See also* experimentation; progressive musical tendencies
Ayler, Albert 275

Baker, Sid 76
ballet rehearsal accompaniment 25, 252
bands. *See* brass bands; dance: dance bands; German musicians; military bands; town bands
banjo 84-5, 90, 91, 92, 93, 100-10, 119, 122, 181, 194, 31n14; banjo imitations 126, 149, 158; classic-style 107-8
Banks, Don 249, 251, 253-4, 261, 262
Bargey, Roy 147
Barlow, Harold 72, 77, 317n38
Barnes, Les 147
baroque style 1, 11, 14
Bartok, Bela 256, 284, 285
Beatles, The 272, 274-5
bebop xx, 231, 242, 248-64, 269, 271, 277, 279
Bell Band, The 247-8
Bell, Graeme 245-7, 256
Bell, Roger 245, 247
Benwell, Sam 245
Berlin, Edward 118
Berlin, Irving 43, 118, 137, 147, 153, 157, 178
Bernard, Mike 113, 166
blackface minstrelsy. *See* minstrelsy
black musical theatre 116, 117, 121, 122, 235. *See also* ragtime
Blott, Charlie 249, 250, 251, 253, 260
blues 68, 83, 119, 181, 197, 206, 209-11, 217, 223; the blues (dance) 210
Bonighton, Ian 298
boogie-woogie 249
Boughen, Robert 21
Boulanger, Edward 1, 5, 316n63
brass bands xvi, xix; and cakewalk repertoire 126, 132-3; and circus 69-70, 74, 76, 78, 79-80, 82; and dance music 46, 47; early brass bands 33-4; experimentalists 232, 268; influence on jazz 204, 216, 217, 220, 223, 224; movement 37-8, 39, 45, 112; musical style 125
break 10, 47; in jazz 179, 180, 182, 202, 204, 205, 208, 211-3, 216, 217, 223, 226, 229, 235, 243; in minstrelsy 95-6, 97-100; in ragtime 126, 149. *See also* fills
Brenan, Jennie 151
Brewer, Mel 154
Briggs, Tom 101-2, 106
Britten, Terry 275
Brokensha, Jack 250
Brophy, Philip 265, 276
Brown, Billy 160
Brown, Brian 266, 269, 270, 271, 276, 277, 279-81
Buckley, Barry 280
Bulch, Thomas E. 9, 77, 132, 133, 134
burlesque (as comic distortion) xix, 35, 40, 88, 89, 90, 107, 110, 118, 124, 125-6, 154, 167, 174, 175, 180, 182, 183; definition 32; opera burlesque 89, 90, 140, 154, 173
Bushelle, Mrs. (Eliza) 316 n63
buskers (street musicians) 35-7, 70
busking (playing without notation). *See* improvisatory practices: faking

cadenza. *See* improvisatory practices: cadenza
Cage, John 181, 266, 268, 270, 287, 290
cakewalk dance and music 116, 119; Australian composition 132-3, 144, 234; as banjo repertoire 108; in black minstrelsy 86, 98, 100, 117, 121-4; in experimental music-theatre 267; as improvisatory music 133-4; as musical accompaniment 125-7, 128-9; 1903 craze 43, 131-4; and representation of Aboriginal music 267; as silent cinema music 67, 162; as social rebellion 150-2. *See also* ragtime
Camerata Society for Contemporary Music 268
Campbell, Bessie 108
Cantrell, Dudley 227
Carney, Denis 154
Carr, Russell 154
Caws, St John 58
Centre de Musique (CDM), Paris 297-8, 298
Challen, Lyn 249, 257
Christensen, Axel 57, 113, 116, 143, 144, 166, 167
church music. *See* organ music
cinema music. *See* silent cinema
circus music xviii, 35, 69-82, 231; American circus 42; as Anonymous genre xviii, xviii; and cakewalks 132; circus bands xvii, xviii, 38, 39, 69-82; clown bands 78; early circus 37; individual circuses xvii, 69, 72, 74, 75-6, 79, 132. *See also* improvisatory practices: trombone smears
Clarke, Bruce 250, 251, 255, 264, 266, 268, 275, 276-9
Clark, Leah 131
Clark, W. 199
Claus, Jenny 1
Clayton, Syd xx, xxi, 265-6, 270, 271, 281, 282-95, 298
Clementi, Muzio 3
Clifton Hill Community Music Centre 1
Cole, Nat King 249, 257
Coleman, Ornette 270, 271, 283
collectively improvised jazz (traditional jazz) xx, 16, 231, 245-9, 250; and 'Australia's first jazz band' 170-3, 180; and cakewalks 133; compared with minstrelsy 98
Collins, Arthur 145
Collinson, Denis 223
Commetant, Oscar 14, 25
Conduit, Owen 136
Confrey, Zez 141, 206-7, 209, 211, 217
conservatism in Australian music xx, 23, 236, 248, 255, 267, 274, 298, 299, 305; and Approved genres xvii; in brass band movement 38-40, 217, 220; in jazz 282, 286
contemporary (classical) music 266-8, 285-311; influence on jazz 251-63, 279, 284-5
coon song: accompaniment of 127; as banjo repertoire 108; coon shouters 117, 131, 170; definition of 117; introduction to Australia 43, 86, 121-5; 1903 craze 131-3, 137, 145-7; relationship to jazz 217. *See also* ragtime: ragtime song
Coppin, George 31, 33, 35, 56, 60, 97
Corona 154, 166
Corrick Lionel 192
Coughlan, Frank 170, 182, 212, 228, 241, 246, 252, 317 n38
Counihan, Terry 274-5
Courtney, Vince 145
Cowen, Bailey and Davis Trio 181
Cramer, J.B. 1, 7
Crawford Bob (King of Bop) 264
creative freedom 197, 230, 234-5, 42, 266, 270-1, 273, 275-6, 287. *See also* improvisatory freedom
creative interaction 283, 297-8, 299, 304, 307-8
cultural isolation. *See* decontextualisation
cultural politics xix, xx, 28, 33-4, 38-40, 69-70, 267; and jazz 180, 196-7, 246, 248-9, 251, 256, 270; and minstrelsy 84, 86; and 1960s experimentalism 274-6, 286-7, 297-8, 303-5; and ragtime 121, 140-1, 150-2
Curnick, Arthur 182
Czerny, Carl 3, 4, 6, 7, 8

Dada and Neo-dadaism 267, 272, 282, 286, 300, 310
dance music and dancing xvii, 12, 29-30, 33, 44, 49, 51, 52, 178, 238, 258; bands and orchestras 33, 34, 37, 38, 39, 44, 53, 110, 131, 150, 152, 183, 224, 238, 245, 251, 254, 255; dance-music interaction 44, 53, 54-5, 111, 115, 126, 150, 176-7, 186; dancing schools 29, 99, 151; music performance 12, 36, 46-55, 56, 133, 135, 150, 178, 183, 228, 236, 237-8, 323 n17; venues 5, 37, 44, 53, 55, 150, 186, 210, 220, 243. *See also* blues; cakewalk; jazz: jazz dancing; minstrelsy: minstrel dance; ragtime: ragtime dancing
Danslow, Harry 228
Dara, Dure 281
Davidson, Tom (Tommy) 254, 255
Davis, Josephine 152, 154
Deane family 2
Debussy, Claude 253, 256, 305
decontextualisation xiii, xiv, 107, 115, 124, 144, 168, 174, 180, 211, 213, 217, 246, 256, 257, 258, 259
De Gilio's Orchestra 44, 184
De Lacy, Mary Frances 16
Dennett, Fred 120, 175
De Vissor, Peter 270
dissonance: in early jazz 173, 186-7, 207, 209, 230, 276; in modern jazz 256, 260; in ragtime 120-1. *See also* noise
Dobson, George 222, 225, 227, 228, 236, 243, 246
D'Ombrain, Geoffrey 268
Douay, M. 59
Douglas, Clive 267
Dreyfus, George 266, 268
drumming and percussion: in circus music 78-9; in early jazz 170, 171, 177-80, 182, 183-4, 187-90, 192-4, 195, 196, 217; in goldfields dance halls 55; in minstrelsy 84, 85, 89 92, 94-6, 99, 104, 105, 106, 110, 179; in modern jazz 241, 43, 257; theatre drummers 41, 177-9, 183-4; as variety act 58, 60, 179-80
Duggan, Barry xx-xxi, 270, 271

Dunstan, Steve 268, 270, 274, 280
Durand, Rosalie 11
Durante, Jimmy 113

ear playing (playing by ear) 12, 16, 34, 37, 47-9, 51, 53, 63, 75-6, 79, 88-90, 95, 100, 108, 190, 247, 252. *See also* improvisatory practices: faking
Eastern influences 269, 271, 273-4, 275, 285
Easton, Hosea 108
ecstatic performance behaviour: represented in classical composition 235-6, 267; definition of xiv; in experimental music-theatre 290, 300, 302, 304, 307-8, 309; in experimental theatre 273, 311; in jazz xx-xxi, 218, 235, 236, 243, 270, 271, 279-80; in minstrelsy 110, 125; in third stream music 261; in variety 159. *See also* imitation ecstatic performance behaviour
effects, novelty musical xix, 4, 23; in circus 78-9; in jazz 172, 173, 175, 177-89, 192-4, 203, 206, 209, 214, 217, 223, 226, 230; in melodrama 67-8 in silent cinema 64. *See also* improvisatory practices: trombone smears
electronic music 268, 270, 277, 279, 280, 298, 300, 309, 311
Ellington, Duke 222
Ellis, Teddy 47
embellishment xii, xviii, 23, 24, 55, 72, 231; in jazz 170, 175, 176, 178, 181, 182, 19, 194, 208, 216, 226, 230, 236; in minstrelsy 84, 90, 92, 100, 103, 105, 108, 110; ornamentation 4, 8-11, 26, 50, 65, 67-9, 76; in ragtime 108, 109, 110, 112, 126, 127, 133, 135, 141, 148, 158, 159. *See also* breaks; fills; improvisatory practices: ragging, trombone smears
experimental music. *See* experimentation
experimentation xi, xv-xvi, xix, xx, xxi, 120, 231; in contemporary (classical) music xiv, xx, 182, 230, 231, 255, 265, 266-8, 274, 276, 277, 287-311; early experimentalists 144, 233-5; experimental literature 251, 272, 282, 310; experimental rock and pop 265, 272, 274-6; inventiveness 21-4, 89, 257; in jazz 190, 236-7, 239, 243-5, 247-8, 248-63, 266, 270, 271, 276-84; problem-finding xv, 232; problem-solving xv, xviii, 231, 255, 268, 277; in ragtime 144. *See also* theatre: experimental theatre
exploration, musical. *See* experimentation

faking. *See* improvisatory practices: faking
Fat Black Pussy Cat, The 283
Fawkner, John Pascoe 1, 27-8
Fawkner Park Band 238-45
Featherstone, Benny 228, 238, 241, 242-44
fills 10, 26, 41, 47, 51, 76-7, 79; in jazz 179, 180, 193, 194, 196, 201, 202, 208, 213, 217, 226, 228, 237; in minstrelsy 103 in ragtime 113-4, 126, 148, 165. *See also* breaks
Finn, Edmund (Garryowen) 28, 31, 33, 37, 51, 97
Floyd, Dr A.E. 20-1, 22
folk music 48-50, 275
François, Jean-Charles 291, 300, 305, 308
Fraser, Brian 271
Fraser, Jim 157
freedom, musical. *See* creative freedom; improvisatory freedom
free improvisation 267, 274, 299
Fuller, Ben 41, 153, 170
Futurist movement 309, 310

Gamley, Doug(las) 251-4
Gardner, John 137
Garryowen (Edmund Finn) 31, 33, 37, 51, 97
Gassman, Josephine 160
Gautrot family 2, 32, 57
Geelong 34, 45, 104, 105
Gellor, Billy 154
George Arnold's Band 198
George, Linda 281
German musicians 3, 69, 70-1; German bands 37, 38, 70-1
gesture, music as xix-xx, 180, 266, 273, 278, 279, 301, 302, 304, 305-6, 308, 310, 312; 'gesture school' 292, 312
Gifford, Helen 255, 274
Gillespie, Dizzy 249, 250, 257, 258, 259
Goddard, Arabella 1
goldfields and gold rush 5, 6, 34-5, 36, 37, 46, 53, 55, 96, 97
Gooch, Fred H.
Goodman, Benny 242, 249, 259
gospel piano 21-24
Gould, Tony 28
Grainger, Percy Aldridge xi, xii, xiii, xxi, 233, 234-5, 267, 296, 298, 312; free music 23-5
Grainger Museum xiii, 268, 298-9, 312
Green, Billy 281
Greene, Gene 119, 127, 147, 153, 154, 155, 156-8, 159, 176, 177, 201
Greenhorn, Davey 80
Grossmann, Ernst 24
grotesque, notion of xix, 85, 86, 88, 89, 93, 94, 99, 104, 105, 107, 108, 110, 122, 123, 124, 133, 174, 176, 180, 194, 197
Guttridge, Maurice 191, 196, 198, 210, 211, 215

Hair (the musical) 275
Hall, Fred 134, 137, 191, 192, 199, 214
Hall, R. 108
Hallam, Ken 187
Handy, W.C. 86, 89, 97
happenings xx, 273, 301, 306
Harkness, Robert 21-4
Harney, Ben 101, 102, 112, 113, 117, 119, 131, 137
Harris, Laughton 310
Harris, S.H. 146, 199, 201
Hart, Harry 154
Haselmayer, Louis 58
Hauser, Miska xix, 1, 6, 10, 34, 90
Hawkins, Coleman 242, 243
Healey, Dick 277, 278
Helfgott, David 312

Hemensley, Kris 292
Hemy, Henry 6, 60
Henlere, Herschel 181, 182
Herwyn, Mr. 6
Hindemith, Paul 256, 279
hip hop 311
Hogan, Ernest 117, 118, 121, 122, 125, 127, 145
Hore's Saxe Horn Band 33, 37, 38, 59, 60, 69
Horsley, Charles 20
Horton, George 149
hot (as a musical concept) 93, 94, 96, 100, 115, 118, 139, 143, 165, 198, 204, 213, 217, 224, 229, 235, 237, 239, 246; hot final chorus 117-8, 126, 127, 201
Hoyt and McKee Theatre Company 123, 125
Hughes, Rupert 120, 125
Humble, Keith xx, 251, 253-6, 265, 267, 268, 276, 291, 296-311; and Pierre Albert-Birot 301, 304, 310-1; and Jacques Attali 303-5; and Edward Gordon Craig 310; and Marc 'O 309-10; Nuniques 301-8
Humphries, Barry 267, 272
Huxam, Edith 157
Hyde, Billy 278
Hyde, Miriam 26
Hyner, Robert 298

iconoclasm (subversion of traditional practice) xix, xxi, 57, 111, 121, 180, 232, 242, 243, 247, 267, 269, 271, 272, 274, 276, 278, 284, 286, 305. *See also* unorthodox musical practice
imitation ecstatic performance behaviour xiv, 2, 100, 176-7, 180, 195-7, 307. *See also* ecstatic performance behaviour; improvisatory practices: jazzing, ragging
improvisatory freedom xi, xiii, xvii, xxi, xxii, 24, 72, 111, 120, 150-2, 237, 242, 254, 257, 263, 266, 270, 271, 273, 287, 290, 297, 307.
improvisatory practices: assemblage 292, 300, 308-9; cadenza 8-9, 10, 67, 78, 90; chance-based (aleatoric) music 253, 282, 292, 296, 287; collective improvisation 241-2, 244, 278, 285, 299 (*see also* collectively-improvised jazz); controlled improvisation 235,287, 307-8; controlling processes 279-80, 282, 288-9, 291, 293-4, 299, 307-8; creative music 268, 301; division 26, 50, 97; faking (playing without notation) xviii, 41, 46, 47, 48, 57, 70, 71-2, 76, 79, 89, 125, 165, 169, 172, 178, 180, 182, 183, 319 n23; fantasia xii, 2, 6, 24, 58, 67, 91, 94, 106; flexible scoring 76, 81-2; frozen improvisation xii, 111, 120 , 224, 228, 254, 296, 297, 308; gagging (impromptu spoken lines) 31, 39; graphic scoring 236, 237, 279-80, 287, 288-9, 290, 291-2, 293-4, 294, 295, 306; head arranging xviii, 88, 175, 183, 297; improvisatory processes 183, 296-7, 301, 304, 307-10; indeterminacy xii, xviii, 81-2, 88, 183, 235, 268, 270, 283, 287; intuitive group response xviii, 80-2, 89, 90, 231, 239, 245, 283, 289, 291, 297; jam session 98, 23, 153, 241-2, 25, 246, 247, 297; jazzing 51, 55, 78, 134, 168-230, 236, 238, 246, 258, 261; lead sheets 166-7; lick 97, 100, 206, 212; postlude 8, 20; pot-pourri 5-6, 24, 25; prelude 7-8, 9, 12, 20, 23, 26, 53, 66; ragging 46, 78, 84, 88, 97, 100, 101, 103-4, 109, 111-67, 168, 176, 178, 180, 190, 216, 221, 223, 224; relationship to composition xii, 245, 254, 296-311; thorough bass 8, 11-12; transposition 12, 13, 16, 17, 25, 26, 47, 48, 66, 165, 252, 254, 258; trombone smears 78, 119, 126, 134, 165, 169, 175, 182, 219-20; vamping 16-9, 47, 51, 53, 64. *See also* breaks; ear playing; embellishment; fills; variation
influential non-visiting musicians: experimentalists 266, 268, 287, 290; jazz 212, 222, 224, 242-3, 249-50, 257-60, 263, 270, 271, 284; ragtime 108, 113, 117, 118, 119, 147, 149, 166, 170
instructional books xiv; jazz 203, 206-7, 209, 212-3, 217, 220, 223-8, 248, 258; minstrel music 92, 94, 101-3, 106, 107, 108, 109; ragtime 101, 103, 113, 114, 115-6, 143-4, 155, 166; ragtime dance 131, 151-2; silent cinema music 46, 65-6; vamping 7, 12-18; vaudeville music 57
International Society for Contemporary Music (ISCM) 255, 267-8, 269, 271, 277, 287, 298
Irwin, May 117, 139, 170,

James Taylor Move 275
jazz: as Anonymous genre xvii, xviii; antecedents of Australian jazz 83-4, 86, 111, 119, 131, 133, 141, 150; 'Australia's first jazz band' 24, 70, 12, 170-80, 183; and circus 70, 72, 80, 81; compared with early colonial improvisation 2, 3; compared with vamping 17; and contemporary (classical) music 283-87, 290, 297, 311; and dance music 46, and decontextualisation xiii-xiv; as gesture xix-xx; jazz dancing and the jazz 150, 168, 177, 183-6, 187; Melbourne jazz context 1950-70: 269, 271; and rock 276. *See also* bebop; collectively improvised jazz; experimentation: in jazz; improvisatory practices: jazzing; jazz/rock; minstrelsy: compared with jazz; modern jazz; poetry and jazz; ragtime: ragtime to jazz transition; Swing, third stream music
Jazz Centre 44: 269, 270, 272
jazz/rock 276, 281
Johnson, Bruce 122, 183, 213, 222, 242, 247
Johnson, Duke 127
Jones, Blutch 125, 137
Jones, Ray 102
Joplin, Scott 111, 112, 115, 135, 138
jubilee singers 112, 121

Kaye, Norman 21
Kearns, Jack 154
Keil, Charles xii
Ketten, Henri 1
King, Mervyn 75, 79
Kingston, Claude 19
Klein, Mat 9
Knight, Troy 104, 105
Kohler, Richard 58, 96

La Mama Theatre 268, 273, 291-2
La Trobe University 265
Larsen, Harry 70, 74, 77, 216, 219-20, 317 n38
Lawrence, Douglas 300
Le Gallienne, Dorian 256
Leonard, Tom 154
Lester, Gerald 300
Limb, Bobby 257
Linn Smith's Royal Jazz Band 181-2
Lithgow, Alex 64, 73
Love, Harold 10, 58
Luscombe, Len 149
Lyster, William 42

McCaughey, John 308, 309
McClain, Billy 125, 127
McCoy sisters 124
McEwan, Nellie 184, 186
McFarlane, Don (Pixie) 241-2
McIntosh, George 134
McKimm, Barry xx, xxi, 265-6, 271, 272, 274, 276, 281, 282-4, 286-9, 291-5, 298, 307
McKimm/Mendelson Quartet 283, 291
McKimm Quartet 301
McKimm Quintet 284-7
McKimm, Rooney and Clayton Trio 281, 287-90
McLaughlin, Frank 225
McLuhan, Marshall 275, 305
McMahon, Hughie 77
Marion, Sam 124
Mastertouch Piano-Roll Company 149, 181, 198
Mayhew, Henry 36-7, 95-6
Meale, Richard 268
Mehden, Carl 165
Mehden, Harry 70, 165, 171, 216, 317 n38. *See also* jazz: 'Australia's first jazz band'
Mehden, (Herr) Henry Von Der xvii, 70, 71-2, 75, 78, 79, 320 n148
Melba, Nellie 10, 11
Melbourne Conservatorium 253, 255-6, 267-8, 297, 299
melodrama. *See* theatre
memorisation 8, 16, 17, 23, 25, 47, 56, 65, 69, 72, 80, 89, 175, 178, 213, 226, 228, 236, 247, 252. *See also* improvisatory practices: ear playing; faking
Mendelson, Heinz 270, 283
Meridith, Dave 182, 183, 216, 317 n38
military bands 33, 132
military influence 33, 38
Miller, Lynn 228
Milton, Katie 127
minimalism 263, 293
minstrelsy: African-American (black) minstrelsy 43, 85, 86, 89, 110, 121-31; African-American plantation culture 36, 88, 98, 108; as Anonymous genre xvii; blackface acts 36; blackface (white) minstrelsy xvii, 43-4, 83-110, 233, 243; blackface troupes 43, 85, 86, 90, 91, 93, 94, 96, 104-6, 107, 112; compared with jazz 88, 92, 95-6, 97-8, 104, 107, 172, 173, 174, 179, 207, 230; compared with contemporary music-theatre, 302; Jim Crow 28, 31, 36, 85, 86, 88; minstrel dance 84-5, 88, 96-100, 107, 110, 122, 126; minstrel song 55, 90-1, 100, 110; opera in minstrelsy 11, 90; orchestra and instruments 84, 89, 91, 92-6, 103, 105, 106, 110, 179; as vaudeville 41. *See also* banjo; black musical theatre; cakewalk; coon song
modern jazz 238, 246, 250, 254, 255, 259-60, 263-4, 269-70, 277; early modern jazz 238-46; free jazz xx, 248, 269-71, 283; Kansas-style 259; modal jazz 269, 270-1, 280; progressive Swing 242, 245, 246, 248, 249, 250, 257-8
Modern Music Society xx, 250-1
modernism xv, xx, xxi, 235, 246-7, 251, 259, 265, 274. *See also* progressive musical tendencies
Mole, Miff 212
Monk, Thelonius 284
Monsborough, Ade 245
Moore, Jack 48
moral transgression xvi, 133, 150-2
Morgan, Graham 270
Morgan, Mabel 170, 176, 177, 180. *See also* jazz: 'Australia's first jazz band'
McFarlane, Don 242
Mudgee the Marvel (Tom Robertson) 79
Mulligan, Gerry 270
Munro, Charlie 71
Murray, Billy 120, 147
music hall. *See* theatre
music houses (publishers) 17, 24, 63, 115-6, 131, 133, 134, 140, 145, 212, 215.
music-theatre. *See* theatre

Napier, Valentyne 57, 178
Nathan, Hans 91, 92-3, 96, 100, 101, 103, 106, 107
Nathan, Isaac 1, 10, 12, 28, 233-4
Navarro, Siren 125
Naylor, Carmen 66-7
Nellie McEwan's Jazz Orchestra 184, 186
Nettl, Bruno xii
New Improvisors Action Group for Gnostic and Rhythmic Awareness 265
Newman, 'Cocka' 80, 81
New Music Ensemble 268
new music movement xix, 265, 266-8, 287-8, 298
New Theatre 250, 273
noise: Attali's concept of 303-5; in music-theatre 292; in ragtime and jazz 122, 172, 173, 177, 179, 186-90, 206, 248, 292. *See also* dissonance; effects, novelty musical
Norman, Charles 41, 178
Norman, Wally 250
North Melbourne Commune 265
Nutwood Rug 275

O'Connell, Clive 298
O'Hagan, Jack 203
O'Neil, Eileen 181
opera xvi, 10-11, 40, 42, 86; opera burlesque 89, 90, 140, 154, 173; ragtime opera 122, 140, 154, 173

organ music and organists 1, 17, 19-22, 24, 25, 26, 63, 66, 300
Original Dixieland Jazz Band (ODJB) 170-3, 175, 210
originality, musical xx, 235-6, 243, 277, 280 *See also* experimentation
Ormerod, E.H. 232
ornamentation. *See* embellishment
orthodoxy: in musical practice xvii-xviii, 43, 55, 72, 196-7, 211, 247, 249, 250, 252, 275, 282; in musical training 16, 26, 204. *See also* unorthodox musical practice
Ossman, Vess 108
Overman, Meta 298
Oxley, Eddie 251, 255

pantomime. *See* theatre
Pardey, Laurel and Edith 149, 181, 198, 200-1, 205, 206, 208, 209
Parker, Charlie xx, 249, 259-60, 271
participatory discrepancies xii
Patton, Emily 7, 8, 9, 12-16, 24, 50, 167
Pearce, Eric 54
Peart, Donald 267
Peck, Mr. 5
Pendletons, The (Mr & Mrs) 96
percussion. *See* drumming and percussion
periodicals (contemporaneous) 115-6, 143, 153, 154, 168, 175, 179, 190, 193, 206, 208, 215, 218, 220, 224
Perrier, W.M. 16, 17, 53
Perry, Jimmy 76
Pettifer, Ern 228, 237, 243
Phillips, Nat 41
piano roll music 67, 112, 141, 148-50, 181, 198, 200, 204, 206, 209, 312
poetry and jazz 272-3
politics, left wing 235, 246-7, 248, 266, 271, 273; and collectively improvised jazz xx, 246-7, 250
Pope, Charles 41, 127
Poussard, Horace 59
Pressing, Jeff vii, 315 n2
Preston, Ted 251
Primrose Four 132
Prince, Jack 154
progressive musical tendencies xx-xxi, 111, 118, 120-1, 135, 141, 220-1, 231-64, 265, 274-6, 279, 286, 287, 288
Purnell, L.P. 135, 138

Quinn, Barry 284

racism 84, 86, 88, 117, 122, 124, 133, 150, 160-2, 207-8, 217
radio 170, 248, 254, 266, 268, 285
ragtime 111-167: in banjo playing 108-9; classic (piano) ragtime 43-4, 111, 112, 115, 119, 126, 141, 162, 178; compared to contemporary (classical) music 276; definition of 43-4; instrumental techniques 112-5, 120-1, 143-4, 148-9, 154; as jazz antecedent 111, 119, 141, 170, 174-7, 217; novelty-style piano 141, 149, 205, 206-9, 216, 217; orchestral ragtime 162-6; ragtime dancing 44, 61, 111, 141, 150-2, 154, 177, 203; ragtime era 107, 110, 230, 238; ragtime opera 122, 140, 154, 173; ragtime song 43, 116-21, 124-5, 127, 131, 155-62, 173, 174, 176, 234; ragtime stage accompaniment 125-7, 153-5; ragtime to jazz transition 118-9, 143, 167, 168, 183-217, 245; ragtime variety acts 153-5; in silent cinema 46; vaudeville (Tin Pan Alley) piano ragtime 112-6, 117, 134-7, 145, 160, 166-7; white ragtime tradition xix, 84. *See also* cakewalk; coon song; improvisatory practice: ragging
Ralton's Havana Band 213, 216, 245
rational recreation xvi, xvii, 38, 87
Rawlins, Adrian 272-3
Ready, Thelma 108
Reck, David 277
recordings 269; Australian banjo-playing 108; as evidence of musical practice 91, 108, 119, 125, 158-9, 170, 194, 204, 215-7, 245, 258, 276-7, 278-9, 283, 289-90, 293; as imported performance models xiv, 140, 141, 144-8, 158, 172, 204, 213-5, 218, 221, 228, 236, 247, 250, 257-8, 271, 274-5, 284, 287. *See also* piano roll music
Rees, Tom 181
Reeves, Don (Splinter) 249
Reid, Don 241
Reményi, Eduard 1
Rene, Roy 41
repetition of patterning xxi, 266, 278, 290, 291
Rhodes, T. 128-9
Rice, Thomas D. 85, 233
Richards, Ron 63, 165, 184, 245, 320 n151
Rickards, Harry 40-1
Ricketts, T.A. 131
Ringwood, Alfred 108
Rockettes, The 250
rock music 90, 265, 272, 274-6, 311; compared with minstrel music 90, 96; influences of overseas groups 275; rock 'n' roll xx, 151, 155, 156, 224, 269
Rofe, Esther 25, 63, 68-9
Rolfe, J. 199, 200
Rollins, Sonny 269
Roma, Rosa 154
Romain, Abe 183, 244
Romaine, Billy 171. *See also* jazz: 'Australia's first jazz band'
Rooney, Robert xx-xxi, 265-6, 272, 274, 281, 282-94, 298
Rosenthal's Orchestra 44, 184
Royal, Don 171. *See also* jazz: 'Australia's first jazz band'
Russell, Mrs. 16
Russell, George 270, 285
Ryder, C. 199, 202

St Leon, Mark 42
St Leon, Reginald 75
Salinger, George 151, 152
Salvador, Dom Rosendo 1

Sampson, Jimmy 237
Sangster, John 276
Sayles, Irving 41, 127
Schoenberg, Arnold 256, 287, 296
Schoot, Herr (the 'drum demon') 60, 61
Sculthorpe, Peter 266, 276
Sedergreen, Bob 279
serialism 256, 285, 296
Seymour, Madge, Lulu and Win 75
Shaw, Artie 248-9
Shefte methods 226-8, 229
Sheldon, Eric 178, 218
Short, Thomas Volver 77
silent cinema and cinema accompaniment xvii, 19, 25, 38, 39, 40, 41, 44-6, 57, 60, 61-9, 196, 231; cinema pianists 65, 66-9, 141, 167, 244; cue sheets 45; orchestras 45, 46, 62-3, 66, 68; organists 62, 63; percussionists 63, 178
Simpson, Mervyn 204
Smith, Linn 181-3
Smith, Frank 276-9
Smith, Wally 171
social context (influence on music) xvi-xviii, 16, 28-9, 33, 38-40; colonial concerts 3, 5, 6; and jazz 220, 238-9, 251; and 1960s experimentalism 272, 273, 283, 286, 287-8; and popular entertainment 31, 34-5, 46-7, 48, 49, 53-5, 57-9, 62, 68-9, 74-5, 75-6, 81, 82, 86; and ragtime 111, 150-2
Society for the Private Performance of New Music (SPPNM) 268, 291, 298-9, 313-4
Society of New Music (SONM) 266, 267
Sonny Clay's Colored Idea 218
Sons of the Vegetal Mothers 275
Sorlie, George 158-9, 160, 161
Sousa, Philip 119
Spectrum 275
Squires, Will 108
standardisation xvi, xviii, 33, 34, 38, 151-2, 162-164
Stanley, Stan 154
Statics, The 170
Stein, Gertrude 272, 293
Stender, Arthur 77
Sterne, Tom 263
Steven, Val 268
Stewart, Orme 240
Stirling, Arthur 79
Stockhausen, Karlheinz 268, 277, 305
Stone, Harry 154
Stoneham, Reginald (Reg) 143, 197, 199, 201, 208, 210
Straight, Charlie 113, 147, 153, 155, 156
street entertainers. *See* buskers
swing (as performance practice) 98, 178, 190, 204, 222-4, 229, 239, 285. *See also* 'hot'
Swing (as jazz band style) 168, 229, 231, 236, 238-45, 246, 248, 249, 250 *See also* modern jazz: progressive Swing
Sydney Simpson and His Wentworth Cafe Orchestra 216
Sylvia, Belle 170, 176, 177, 180

Tamun Shud 275
Tate, Henry 111, 144, 234, 235
Tatro, Al 165, 166
Taylor, Cecil 284
television 268, 271, 272, 277
Testar, Mrs. 10
theatre and theatre music xvii, xviii, 29, 30-3, 35, 36, 38, 39, 40-1, 56-61, 84, 112, 116, 156, 183, 282, 302; Barlow, Billy 31, 36; experimental theatre 273, 309-10; melodrama xix, 30, 40, 56-7, 60, 61, 65, 67; music hall 32, 36, 40; music-theatre 32-3, 90, 266, 268, 273, 293, 297, 301-11; orchestras 32-3, 34, 56-7, 58, 132, 153, 162; pantomime xix, 32, 37, 40, 60, 139-40, 145, 173; revue 41, 174, 302; theatres 30-1, 35, 40-1, 43, 63, 104, 108, 126, 131, 155, 157, 166, 264-5, 170, 181, 183, 268, 272, 273, 291, 292. *See also* black musical theatre; burlesque; circus; minstrelsy; variety
third stream music 254, 257-63
Thomas, Fred 257
Thompson, Jock 171. *See also* jazz: 'Australia's first jazz band'
Tin Pan Alley 25, 43, 84, 112-3, 117, 134, 141, 143, 145, 147, 148, 152, 155-6, 160, 168, 174, 175, 176, 199, 215
Tolley, David xxi, 271, 274, 281
Tom Davidson Orchestra 254
Tough, Bob 238-9, 242, 243, 244-5
town bands 29, 32-3, 34, 37, 46, 71
traditional jazz. *See* collectively-improvised jazz
Tristano, Lennie 284
tritones: use of 253; tritone substitution 258, 260
Tully 275, 276
Turnbull, Alan 270
Turner, Geoff (Dutchy) 237, 242
Twilights, The 275
2FC Dance Orchestra 54, 216

unorthodox musical practice xviii, 16, 17; circus music 82; colonial concerts 29; dance music 50; in minstrelsy 88, 89; as musical experimentation 231, 279, 282; popular stage 35, 58, 59, 60; in ragtime 111, 119; in stage jazz 173, 176. *See also* experimentation; iconoclasm
Upward, Peter 274

rhythmic vamp 115, 119, 120, 126-7, 135, 145, 199, 211
variation(s), musical xvii; silent cinema music 65, 68; circus music 77, 78; classical music 2-5, 9, 26, 59; dance music 50; in jazz 169-70, 192, 194, 197-8; in minstrelsy 88, 90, 91, 93, 94, 105, 106, 107, 109; in ragtime 120, 127, 154
variety and vaudeville 40-2, 45, 61, 86, 91, 100, 117, 134, 144, 238, 254, 302; musical accompaniment 31, 39, 41, 57, 164-7; musical variety acts xiv, xvii, xix, 25, 31, 35-6, 57-60, 72, 141, 153-62, 170-83, 184, 195, 297. *See also* ragtime; jazz
vaudeville. *See* variety
Victorian College of the Arts 279

Vining Ted 280
visual art 267; and jazz 246; and McKimm, Rooney & Clayton 283, 292-4; in mixed media theatre 309; 1960s experimentalism 273-4
Vitali, Ida 11
vocal techniques 58, 85, 90-1, 110, 117, 119, 127, 157, 176, 231. *See also* ragtime: ragging

Wallace, Charles 133
Wallace, Vincent 1, 2, 5, 6, 57
Waller, Mrs. 9
Waller, Charles 35
Waterhouse, Richard 86
Webbe, W.H. 18
Webern, Anton 305
Webster, Peter 284
Werder, Felix xx, 261, 266, 268
Weston, Frank 43
Whelan, Albert 147
White, Ken 273, 279, 283
White, Harry 216
whole-tone scales 253, 258
Williams, Billy 147
Williamson, J.C. (James Cassius) 42, 139
Winans, Robert 93, 10 1, 103, 106
Winn, Edward 113, 114, 121, 143-4, 155, 203, 206, 207, 208, 224
Wirth, George 74, 76
Wirth, John 71, 74
Wirth, Philip 71, 72, 74, 80
Withers, Arthur 80-2, 182
women 25-6, 57; banjo-players 108; in circus 75; and colonial dance music 48, 50; colonial instrumentalists and vocalists 1, 2, 10; in dance band jazz 184, 186; and dancing 55; in experimental jazz 281; and the Grainger Museum 298; in jazz-rock 281; piano-roll performers 149, 181, 198, 200, 204, 206, 209; ragtime performers 84, 117, 122, 124, 125, 127, 131, 152, 154, 157, 160-2; silent cinema accompanists 45-6, 66-9; in stage jazz 170, 176, 177, 180, 181, 184; and vamping systems 7, 12-16, 17, 19, 167
Wood, Jack 224
World Entertainers 131
Wright, Barclay 149

Young, Bob 257
youth culture xxi, 44, 155-7, 272, 274-5

Zelman, Alberto 68